Metaethical Issues in Contemporary Legal Philosophy

This volume explores the importance of constitutivism for legal studies. Constitutivism is the view that the normative force, or authority, of practical reasons is grounded in principles, capacities, aims, or functions that are essential to, and thus constitutive of, agency. While the implications that the constitutivist approach has on the fundamental metaethical disputes and central ethical debates have been extensively explored, the literature on the relations between constitutivism and law remains scarce, unsystematic, and sporadic. This collection brings together world-renowned practical philosophers and legal theorists to fill a noticeable gap in the literature. The authors systematically and innovatively address key dimensions of the relationships between constitutivism and the theoretical study of law, as well as programmatically offering novel insights into the conceptual connections between constitutivist claims, fundamental legal concepts and practices, legal issues, and, ultimately, the law as a distinctive concept. The book will be of interest to academics and researchers working in the areas of Legal Philosophy, Legal Theory, Jurisprudence, Moral Philosophy and Metaethics.

Stefano Bertea is Associate Professor at the Law Department of the University of Messina. The output of Stefano's research work has taken the form of monographs published by leading academic publishers and he serves as a journal referee for leading academic journals.

Jorge Silva Sampaio is Guest Assistant Professor at the University of Lisbon, School of Law. He is also an Effective Integrated Researcher of Lisbon Public Law, a co-coordinator and a member of Lisbon Legal Theory (LLT), and an associate of the Institute of Legal-Political Sciences.

Routledge Research in Legal Philosophy

Constitutional Imaginaries
A Theory of European Societal Constitutionalism
Jiří Přibáň

Human Dignity and the Law
A Personalist Theory
Michał Rupniewski

Legal Ethics for Lawyers
A New Model
Barbara Mescher

Moral Pluralism and the Complexity of Punishment
The Penal Philosophy of H.L.A. Hart
Nicolas Nayfeld

Sport, Law and Philosophy
The Jurisprudence of Sport
Miroslav Imbrisevic

Cosmopolitanism, State Sovereignty and International Law and Politics
A Theory
Jorge E. Núñez

Human Dignity, Judicial Reasoning, and the Law
Comparative Perspectives on a Key Constitutional Concept
Edited by Brett G. Scharffs, Andrea Pin, and Dmytro Vovk

Act and Omission in Criminal Law
Autonomy, Morality and Applications to Euthanasia
Roni Rosenberg

Metaethical Issues in Contemporary Legal Philosophy
A Constitutivist Approach
Edited by Stefano Bertea and Jorge Silva Sampaio

For more information about this series, please visit: https://www.routledge.com/Routledge-Research-in-Legal-Philosophy/book-series/RRLP

Metaethical Issues in Contemporary Legal Philosophy

A Constitutivist Approach

Edited by Stefano Bertea and Jorge Silva Sampaio

Routledge
Taylor & Francis Group
LONDON AND NEW YORK

First published 2025
by Routledge
4 Park Square, Milton Park, Abingdon, Oxon OX14 4RN

and by Routledge
605 Third Avenue, New York, NY 10158

Routledge is an imprint of the Taylor & Francis Group, an informa business

British Library Cataloguing-in-Publication Data
A catalogue record for this book is available from the British Library

Library of Congress Cataloging-in-Publication Data
Names: Bertea, Stefano, 1970- editor. | Sampaio, Jorge Silva, editor.
Title: Metaethical issues in contemporary legal philosophy: a constitutivist approach / edited by Stefano Bertea and Jorge Silva Sampaio.
Description: Abingdon, Oxon [UK]; New York, NY: Routledge, 2025. | Series: Routledge research in legal philosophy | Includes bibliographical references and index. |
Identifiers: LCCN 2024041282 (print) | LCCN 2024041283 (ebook) | ISBN 9781032665948 (hardback) | ISBN 9781032670539 (paperback) | ISBN 9781032670553 (ebook)
Subjects: LCSH: Law–Philosophy. | Jurisprudence. | Semantics (Law) | Metaethics.
Classification: LCC K235 .M47 2025 (print) | LCC K235 (ebook) | DDC 174/.3–dc23/eng/20240905
LC record available at https://lccn.loc.gov/2024041282
LC ebook record available at https://lccn.loc.gov/2024041283

ISBN: 978-1-032-66594-8 (hbk)
ISBN: 978-1-032-67053-9 (pbk)
ISBN: 978-1-032-67055-3 (ebk)

DOI: 10.4324/9781032670553

The Open Access version of Chapter 2 was funded by University of Modena and Reggio Emillia.

Contents

Contributors

María Beatriz Arriagada (Orcid: 0000-0002-0809-4510) is Professor and researcher in General Theory of Law at Diego Portales University (Chile). She teaches postgraduate courses at several Chilean universities, at the Chilean Judicial Academy, and in the Master in Global Rule of Law and Constitutional Democracy at the University of Genoa and the University of Girona.

Carla Bagnoli (Orcid Id: 0000-0003-2795-3795) is a Professor of Theoretical Philosophy at the University of Modena and Reggio Emilia, and Professorial Fellow at the Center for Ethics and Philosophy in Practice at the Ludwig-Maximilians-University Munich. From November 2023 until November 2026, she will be on secondment at the National Academy of Lincei and affiliated with the Interdisciplinary Center Beniamino Segre.

Stefano Bertea (*Orcid:* 0000-0002-6013-2326) is Associate Professor at the Law Department of the University of Messina. The output of Stefano's research work has taken the form of monographs published by leading academic publishers and he serves as a journal referee for leading academic journals.

Triantafyllos Gkouvasis (ORCID ID: 0000-0003-1686-7461) is Postdoctoral Researcher, Department of International Law, Ecclesiastical Law and Philosophy of Law, Charles III University of Madrid.

Jaap Hage (ORCID: 0000-0002-7643-5372) is a Professor Emeritus of Maastricht University, where he held the chair of jurisprudence.

Pablo A. Rapetti (Orcid: 0000-0001-5991-6353) is Associate Professor at the Instituto Tecnológico Autónomo de México (ITAM) a member of the Chair of Legal Culture at the University of Girona and a researcher at Conacyt (SNI – Level I).

Veronica Rodriguez-Blanco (ORCID: 0000-0002-1795-4463) is Professor of Legal and Political Philosophy (Jurisprudence) at the University of Surrey Centre for Law and Philosophy.

Jorge L. Rodríguez (Orcid: 0000-0002-1992-0101) is a professor of General Theory of Law and a researcher at the National University of Mar del Plata, Argentina.

Sebastián Figueroa Rubio (ORCID: 0000-0001-8181-4812) is a Ramon y Cajal Reseacher at the Universidad Autónoma de Madrid, Spain. He is also a member of the Centre for Law and Society at the Universidad Adolfo Ibáñez and the Chair of Legal Culture at the Universitat de Girona.

Jorge Silva Sampaio (ORCID: 0000-0002-8687-6622) is Guest Assistant Professor at the University of Lisbon, School of Law. He is also an Effective Integrated Researcher of Lisbon Public Law, a co-coordinator and a member of Lisbon Legal Theory (LLT), and an associate of the Institute of Legal-Political Sciences.

Torben Spaak (Orcid: 0000-0001-9725-117x) is Professor of Jurisprudence in the Department of Law and former Vice-Dean for Education at the Faculty of Law, Stockholm University.

Introduction

Stefano Bertea and Jorge Silva Sampaio

Constitutivism is the view that the normative force, or authority, of practical reasons is grounded in principles, capacities, aims, or functions that are essential to, or constitutive of, agency. Over the recent years, this view has been extensively debated. As a result, today constitutivism is a consolidated approach to practical philosophy that makes original meta-normative and normative claims. While the implications that the constitutivist approach has on fundamental metaethical disputes and central ethical debates have been explored to a great extent, the literature on the relations between constitutivism, on the one hand, and legal issues, theories, and practices, on the other, remains scarce, unsystematic, and sporadic. This gap in the literature is surprising and regrettable for at least two reasons.

To begin with, it would be reasonable to expect that philosophical accounts of practical reasons, such as constitutivism, should attract the attention of legal theorists in consideration of the fact that, especially since Joseph Raz's seminal work, an influential strand of contemporary jurisprudence regards practical reasons as fundamental units of the legal fabric. Indeed, nowadays advocates of positivism and non-positivism alike agree that our understanding of legal standards (be they rules, principles, policies, rulings, or other) and, relatedly, of legal systems, qua arrangements of legal standards of different kinds, would be merely partial, considerably incomplete, or even altogether distorted, in the absence of some reference to the idea of a practical reason. In fact, the legal significance of practical reasons has been argued to extend to the very concept of law. For, ever since H.L.A. Hart's powerful criticism of the 'gunman model' of law—the conception of law as a set of commands supported by the threat of harm—it has become increasingly standard in mainstream legal theory to accept that essential to law and its normative dimension is the capacity to issue reasons for action. On this approach (call it 'the conception of law as practical reason'), law is best conceived as a normative system purporting to provide practical guidance by specifically supplying legal subjects with reasons for or against certain courses of conduct. Accordingly, legal directives are claimed to figure in a fundamental way into our deliberation about how we ought to behave. This is why the law is to be conceived as a practice conceptually inseparable from practical reasons and reasoning. These claims make the

DOI: 10.4324/9781032670553-1

significance of constitutivism for the study of law apparent and direct. Insofar as (a) constitutivism is a general theory of reasons for action and (b) law is understood as a distinctive normative practice that is ultimately explainable in terms of reasons for action, there is an at least prima facie justification for taking constitutivism seriously when theorizing about law, since a general theory of reasons can legitimately be expected to possess the resources to conceptualize all forms of reasons for action, inclusive of the reasons for action generated by the law. Thus, its ability to contribute to one of the main inquiries regarding the nature of law—its alleged normativity—would be sufficient to justify this volume.

The importance of constitutivism for legal studies emerges from another set of considerations too. *Constitutivism* is a philosophical approach that distinctively puts action front and centre in its explanation of normative reasons, since it claims that the authority of practical reasons is grounded in the essential properties of agency, namely, in our status of *action*-performers. Likewise central is the place of action in the study of law: the directives of *law* are generally understood as standards governing the courses of *action* that are carried out in a given setting—the legal world. Even when they are not directly aimed at governing human action, they serve, for example, to constitute new institutional actions. There is, then, a material overlapping between constitutivism, qua a philosophical approach distinctively and programmatically associated with some theory of action, and the conceptualization of law, which deals with a practice largely aimed at governing action, as action is carried out in a specific context. This convergence is due to the fact that action lies at the centre of both constitutivist accounts of practical reasons and legal theory (as well as legal practice). This is why constitutivism, within which the conception of action figures prominently, should be expected to bear on our understanding of law, qua an institutional mechanism for the governance of action.

What precedes indicates that this collection of original essays, which systematically explore the implications of embracing constitutivism for our treatment of legal issues, fills a noticeable and hardly-justifiable gap in the literature. The proposed exploration of constitutivism, as it bears on legal matters, begins with Jaap Hage's characterization of constitutivism as an ambitious attempt to offer a non-subjectivist account of the practical sphere—the sphere to which law belongs—especially in its normative dimension. In this reading, constitutivism is claimed to be best understood as a stance that is alternative to two, radically different, approaches to the world we inhabit: the phenomenological view and the realist view. The phenomenological view reduces the external reality to a network of concepts and features generated by the human mind. The realist view, instead, conceptualizes the world as largely mind-independent. Conversely, it also asserts that normativity, qua a mind-dependent domain, does not exist objectively. In contrast to both those views, constitutivism conceives of normativity as a human creation with an objective foundation and, thus, as a component of human existence that commands universal recognition despite its being mind-dependent. The success of constitutivism, however, should not be taken for granted and, ultimately, depends on the existence of what Hage calls 'constructivist facts', namely, social facts the nature of which is not purely conventional.

In Chapter 2, Sebastián Figueroa Rubio discusses the conceptual relations between constitutivism and ascriptivism, a view that, at least in H.L.A. Hart's, J.L. Austin's, and Joel Feinberg's versions, not unlike constitutivism, connects the ascription of an action to the attribution of the responsibility for such an action and, thus, establishes a conceptual link between agency and normativity. In the theoretical framework defended by Figueroa, constitutivism invites us to programmatically reflect on how agency and personhood secure the foundations of our normative concepts and judgements. Accordingly, especially as it is championed by Philippa Foot and Michael Thompson, constitutivism can be argued to have the potential to support ascriptivism by providing the latter with a broader conceptual framework that can be appealed to make sense of the main theses underpinning ascriptivism. In this context, Figueroa further claims that, albeit philosophically solid, by itself alone constitutivism is insufficient to grant the truth of ascriptivism. In sum, for Figueroa the tenability of constitutivism is a necessary and yet insufficient condition of the possibility of ascriptivism.

The conceptual relations between constitutivism and the ascription of responsibility for one's actions is also central to the argument deployed in Veronica Rodriguez-Blanco's contribution, which is specifically concerned with the idea of responsibility for negligent action. After rejecting two influential candidates for explaining the problem of responsibility for negligence—the so-called 'reasonable expectations view' and 'responsibility as answerability conception'—Rodriguez-Blanco theorizes a variant of Aristotelian constitutivism that can successfully account for that problem. Key to Rodriguez-Blanco's Aristotelian constitutivism is the claim that there is a two-way relation between intelligent thinking and desires, each of which has the potential to impact on, and even transform, the other. Building on this claim, Rodriguez-Blanco argues that there is a conceptual space between attributionist explanations and voluntarist accounts of responsibility for negligence. This conceptual space, in turn, allows us to appreciate the role that the first-person perspective and the processes of practical reasoning undertaken by a socially situated agent—the agent qua a subject necessarily belonging to a specific group—plays in our discourses about responsibility for negligence.

Chapter 4, where Triantafyllos Gkouvas sets out to explain the normativity of conventional requirements, brings law into the picture even more explicitly than the previous contributions. In his explanation, Gkouvas takes constitutivism to be a promising contender for the normativity of social practices only insofar as the idea of a reason is deemed to be a suitable concept for making sense of (social) normativity. However, Gkouvas claims, this can be shown to be hardly the case, since, on the one hand, the notion of a reason is not a normatively primitive concept—that is, normativity is not exhausted by the concept of a reason—and, on the other hand, the normativity of social practices is more akin to the normativity of formal rationality than to the normativity of practical reasons. On this basis, Gkouvas concludes that the normativity of law cannot be accounted in terms of the reason (legal) subjects have to act as legal requirements demand.

The explanation of legal normativity is central to Jorge Silva Sampaio's contribution too. Sampaio embraces a kind of goal-oriented constitutivism and builds on evolutionary considerations in order to defend the thesis that legal normativity should be recognized as a robust kind of normativity. Law, in other terms, has the resources to create genuine (as opposed to merely formal) reasons for action, the quality of which is instrumental. Sampaio's argument to this effect is premised on three propositions: firstly, the claim that human beings are necessarily driven towards the goal of surviving; secondly, the assertion that law is an essential means to enabling cooperation; thirdly, the thesis that cooperation is necessary to our survival. On this basis, Sampaio concludes that complying with the statements of law, by thus acknowledging them as statements that have a non-optional, or universal, normative quality, is dictated by our constitutive drive towards survival.

In the next two chapters, the focus of the discussion shifts towards the norms inhabiting the legal realm. In Chapter 6, María Beatriz Arriagada and Jorge L. Rodríguez reflect on the conception of law as a system of norms organized in a hierarchical structure. This understanding of law is traditionally taken by lawyers to entail that in a legal system there must be an enacted legal norm prohibiting lower ranked authorities from performing normative actions that have not been expressly permitted by higher ranked authorities. Arriagada and Rodríguez challenge this view and defend the twofold thesis that (a) the norms conferring public powers have constitutive character and (b) the systems incorporating constitutive norms, including legal systems, are closed for logical (as distinct of legal) reasons. The discussion of this feature of legal systems also leads Arriagada and Rodríguez to theorize a constitutive approach to practical normativity.

In Chapter 7, Stefano Bertea discusses the implications that accepting constitutivism has for the conceptualization of a legal norm. After claiming that two fundamental families of constitutivism (function-constitutivism and capacity-constitutivism) can be distinguished, Bertea argues that those two variants of constitutivism should be associated to mutually irreducible accounts of practical reasons, practical authority, and action. From this statement, then he moves to the conclusion that function-constitutivism and capacity-constitutivism are coherent with different conceptions of a legal norm. The idea of a legal norm conceptually akin to function-constitutivism is broad, generic, less-than-discriminatory, and instrumentalist in quality: on this view, legal norms refer to standards, issued by an appropriate authority in accordance with certain procedures, that are instrumental to directing the courses of conduct of a social group towards certain collective objectives, ends, or goals. By contrast, from the perspective of capacity-constitutivism, legal norms are to be conceived as rationally defensible social standards, namely, as directives oriented to, and constrained by, rationally justifiable considerations. The account of legal norms resulting from the acceptance of capacity-constitutivism, thus, is far more discriminatory and demanding in its scope than the one associated with function-constitutivism.

In Chapter 8, Carla Bagnoli relies on a conceptual framework shaped by Kantian constitutivism to deal with the so-called 'sanctioner's dilemma', which is key to fundamental debates ongoing in the field of international law and politics. This dilemma arises when the cost of sanctioning a state for the violation of international law exceeds the benefits of punishing the law-breaker. It is Bagnoli's view that the traditional treatment of the sanctioner's dilemma, which is shaped by an instrumentalist logic, does not explain all the dimensions involved in that dilemma. Accordingly, Bagnoli argues that we should resort to Kantian constitutivism, which can not only offer a more accurate picture of the power and authority dynamics inherent in the sanctioner's dilemma, but also help us understand better the structure of international law, relations, and politics.

In the remaining two chapters of the volume constitutivism is used as a hermeneutic tool that can shed new light on the influential legal theories championed by H.L.A. Hart and Robert Alexy respectively. In Chapter 9, Pablo A. Rapetti develops a conceptual framework for the study of the relation between law and coercion that is deeply rooted in Hart's legal theory. In this process, he puts forward an original revisitation of Hart's considerations on this matter: whereas the received view is that for Hart there is no conceptual connection between law and coercion, in Rapetti's reinterpretation Hart should be taken to be committed to a threefold link between the two terms. More specifically, Rapetti claims, in Hart's theoretical framework law and coercion are interlinked at the (i) empirical, (ii) natural, and (iii) conceptual levels. This means that the connection between law and coercion is deep and necessary, vis-à-vis merely accidental and contingent. Rapetti attempts to further develop what the 'natural' connection is about -elaborating it in terms of rationality- and concludes his argument by eliciting the similarities between Hart's account of the connection between law and coercion, as he reinterprets it, and the argumentative strategies underpinning constitutivism in metaethics and the philosophy of action.

Finally, in the conclusive chapter, Torben Spaak discusses a possible legal counterpart of metaethical constitutivism—what he calls 'legal constitutivism'. In accordance with legal constitutivism, legal actions have some constitutive aim or, at least, involve a constitutive principle. It is this aim or principle that sets legal action apart from action *simpliciter*. After justifying the claim that Alexy's legal approach is best understood as a version of legal constitutivism, Spaak explains why legal constitutivism is untenable. On this basis, Spaak further suggests not only that the legal relevance of constitutivism may be limited but also that the prospects of constitutivism as a general metaethical view do not look good, since not just in law but *a fortiori* within the practical domain one can hardly identify aims and principles that are constitutive of action and thus yield normative practical standards.

1 Constitutivism and social reality

Jaap Hage

1.1 Introduction

According to Michael Smith (2015):

> Constitutivism is the view that we can derive a substantive account of normative reasons for action [...] from abstract premises about the nature of action and agency.

Millgram (2020) gives a similar description:

> A wave of recent philosophical work on practical rationality is organized by the following implicit argument: Practical reasoning is figuring out what to do; to do is to act; so the forms of practical inference can be derived from the structure or features of action.

This chapter aims to do four things. First, in Section 1.2, it will be explained why there seems to be a problem that constitutivism purports to solve. Second, in Section 1.3, it will be explained how this problem can be, and actually was, rendered as a logical problem about the possibility to derive Ought from Is. This second explanation at the same time indicates the direction of where the solution to the problem can be found. This solution was, not very explicitly, adopted by constitutivism. Third, by means of an account of social reality and the crucial role in it of rules, the question is addressed in Section 1.4 to what extent this possible solution is desirable. The relevance of this all for law is briefly discussed in Section 1.5, at the end of the chapter.[1]

1 This chapter could not have been written without the support and the sometimes critical comments of Stefano Bertea. Most likely, he still does not agree with all of its content, but that is less important. Thank you, Stefano!

DOI: 10.4324/9781032670553-2

1.2 Constitutivism and its background

1.2.1 Some conceptual background

Human beings form a mental representation of the world they live in. A large part of this representation is unconscious (Bargh 2017), but a small part of it is conscious. Let us call this conscious part the image a person has of the world. Typically, the image a person has of the world can be expressed by means of language. Humans often communicate with other human beings, first and foremost with persons who live in their own social group, but increasingly also on a global level. The image that persons form of the world is, as a result, very much the result of social interaction (Richerson and Boyd 2006). Moreover, this image evolves in the course of time, influenced by the results of science, which is itself a relatively recent kind of social interaction.

Because the image of the world that humans have is to a large extent the result of social interaction, the individual images of individual human beings have a substantial overlap. Moreover, they 'see' elements of the world as good or bad, beautiful or ugly, just or unjust. They do so, even if they disagree about what is good or bad, ... etc. Humans also use deontic words such as 'ought', 'duty', 'obligation', and 'being obligated' to denote normative positions, even though different persons or groups of persons may disagree about what precisely ought to be done, or ought to be the case.

An interesting aspect of this shared conceptual framework is that the applicability of many concepts is seen as dependent on the applicability of other concepts. Philosophers have a technical term for this phenomenon. They say that some characteristics *supervene* on other characteristics (McLaughlin and Bennett 2021), that these latter characteristics 'ground' the former (Bliss and Trogdon 2021), or that the conditions for applicability of some concepts include the applicability of other concepts (Carnap 1947). Notice, in this connection, the close interrelation between the existence of characteristics and the applicability of concepts. This interrelation is no coincidence, but a consequence of the fact that we are talking about two sides of the same coin: the ontological side, which deals with the presence of characteristics, and the conceptual side, which deals with the applicability of concepts. We might even identify a third 'side', namely the inferential one. From the presence of some characteristics, we can 'derive' the presence of other characteristics. For example, from the fact that something is a vehicle with four wheels that is propelled by a motor, we can derive that it is a car. From the applicability of the concepts 'vehicle', 'four-wheeled', and 'motor-propelled' we can derive the applicability of the concept of 'car'. In general, ontology, concepts, and derivation are closely connected to one another.

Especially in connection to value judgments (judgments about what is good or bad, beautiful or ugly) and deontic judgments (judgments about what an agent ought, or ought not, to do), the phenomenon of grounding is important. If something is good or bad, there must be reasons why this is so (Hare 1952, Section 1.5.2). Something similar holds for deontic judgments and facts: if somebody ought to do something, there must be a reason for it. This reason is a reason for action.

1.2.2 Some historical background

Humans form an image of the world around them and in the first instance they must have assumed that the world corresponds to this image. In modern terminology, we would say that the world was originally assumed to exist objectively and that the image people formed of this world was assumed to be objective as well. The objectivity of the world, ontological objectivity, means in modern philosophical terminology that the objective world is mind-independent. The objective world exists independent of the existence of minds and if there are mental images of it, the world does not depend for its existence on these images. The objectivity of the image that humans have of the world is epistemic objectivity. It is objectivity of knowledge about the world rather than objectivity of the world itself. An image of the world is objective to the extent that it reflects the world as it 'really' or objectively is (Hage 2022a).

Most likely, humans initially assumed that the world existed objectively and that they had an objective image of the world. But this dream cannot have lasted very long. Images of the world that change with the circumstances, or that are different for different persons, cast doubts on respectively ontological and epistemic objectivity. For example, if a stick that seems bent if it stands in a pool of water seems right when it is taken out of the water, the idea that the world objectively exists as it is experienced must be abandoned. Moreover, if well-meaning and well-informed persons seriously disagree about whether some action is right or wrong, the idea that all knowledge reflects the world as it really is, must be abandoned. Apparently, not all knowledge can be objective.

As soon as it is recognized that appearances do not necessarily reflect reality, two questions arise. The first question is what the world is, if it does not have to be what it appears to be. And the second question is what, if any, the role of the world is in producing appearances. In Europe, starting from the Middle Ages, an important development took place: the replacement of a phenomenological account of the world with a realist account.

1.2.3 The phenomenal and the realist account of the world

The phenomenological account of the world takes its starting point in human experience. In our experience, the world contains coloured and heavy objects, good and bad deeds, beautiful and ugly sculptures, ought-facts, and other modal facts.[2]

2 There is a close connection here with the phenomenological work on the notion of a life world (*Lebenswelt*). See for instance Barber 2022 (on Alfred Schutz) and Beyer 2022 (on Edmund Husserl).

Being coloured or heavy are examples of so-called ‘secondary qualities’ (Bolton 2022). These qualities are assumed not to exist in the objective world, but to be the result of how we perceive the world. A red object is an object that, under ideal circumstances, reflects electromagnetic waves that have a wavelength of between 620 and 750 nanometres. In our brains these waves produce the experience of seeing red. A heavy object is an object that has gravitational mass. If we have to carry it, we experience this mass, under the influence of gravity, as the weight of the object.

Being good or bad, beautiful or ugly, are examples of evaluative characteristics. These characteristics are often experienced as resting in the actions or objects that are good, bad, beautiful, or ugly, not in our minds: it is the vase that is beautiful, or this action that was bad. Nevertheless, presently we tend to believe that these evaluative qualities do not rest in the things themselves but are mental additions to the objective characteristics in which they are grounded.

Modal facts are facts that are variants on ‘ordinary’ facts. They come in different types. Necessity and (im)possibility (‘9 is necessarily bigger than 7’) are sometimes called ‘anankastic modalities’ or ‘alethic modalities’ (Von Wright 1963, p. 10; Hilpinen 1971, p. xi). Ought (not) and permission (‘Petra is permitted to drive her bicycle’) are ‘deontic modalities’ (Hilpinen 1971, p. xi), while certainty and, again, but now in a slightly different sense, possibility (‘Possibly, the train will arrive late’) are ‘epistemic modalities’ (White 1975, pp. 59–101). Also modal facts are often experienced as being elements of the world, but it is difficult to find a basis for them that does not include a mind.

In the 17th century, a process began to gain speed in which the phenomenal world—that is: the world as it is experienced—stopped being seen as objective. The developing physical sciences looked for the world as it ‘really’ exists, independent of how it is perceived. In other words: the physical sciences strove for a realist, rather than a phenomenological account of the world. In this process leading from a phenomenological to a realist account, layers of meaning were peeled off the phenomenological world, in search of facts and things that exist independent of human minds. The layers of meaning came to be seen as human (mental) additions to the ‘real’ (objective, mind-independent) world.

In the work of David Hume we can see how this process worked out. Normativity is not a part of the real world anymore, but is added by human minds, in particular by the passions. A direct consequence of this view is that information about the real, objective world by itself cannot suffice to draw normative conclusions. To arrive at these conclusions, it is always necessary to add a normative premise to the information about the objective world. The added premise would contain the mental addition to the ‘real’ world. This necessity has become known as the ‘gap between Is and Ought’, or as ‘Hume’s guillotine’. The existence of this gap has, in the course of centuries, almost become a holy grail of the humanities (Moore 1903; Kelsen 1934; Brecht 1959).

If normativity is a human addition to the objective world, it is not objective and it is tempting to conclude that therefore it must be subjective (Del

Mar 2016). You may believe that abortion is in general wrong, but if I believe that if a mother wants an abortion, this abortion is in principle right, my belief is just as good as yours. Moreover, this goodness depends on our personal preferences and desires, and not on the facts in objective reality, as there are no evaluative facts in objective reality.[3] A similar argument can be given for deontic facts, such as the fact that I ought to refrain from theft, or that my lessee has the duty to pay the monthly house rent. To reasons for action the same story applies: they cannot be found in the objective world and therefore, it seems, they must be subjective.

1.2.4 Smith's constitutivism

The idea that normativity is a subjective matter is not to everybody's taste. Moreover, our social practice, in which we debate on normative issues as if there were a true answer that holds for all opponents in the debate, does not treat normative issues as a subjective matter. This explains why the search for a more solid foundation for normativity has continued, even in a society in which the scientific, realist, image of the world takes a central place. It should therefore not come as a surprise that theories were developed which assign normativity a place which is not merely subjective. The most influential group of these theories rests on the idea that what an agent should, or ought, to do is a matter of reason, rather than of preference or desire. Kantian ethics is a main representative of this rationalist tradition.[4] It focuses on what an agent would do if she were purely rational. Since reason is assumed to be the same for everybody, Kantian ethics abstracts from personal desires or preferences.

In a similar vein, Smith (2015) tries to find an account of what it is for an agent to have reasons for actions in certain circumstances. He suggests that this is a matter of what is desirable relative to the agent in these circumstances. In other words, what an agent has reason to do depends on the circumstances of the case and on the desires of the agent. For example, if the agent is thirsty (circumstances) and does not want to be thirsty (desire), the agent has a reason to drink. However, it is not the actual desires of the agent that count, but the desires of the agent's ideal counterpart (cf. Lewis 1989). To expand the example a bit, suppose that the agent suffers from a disease and that the treatment requires the agent not to drink for half an hour. Then the thirsty agent does not have a reason to drink, even if he actually desires to do so. The ideal counterpart of the agent would not desire to drink and that is decisive.

3 Many readers will have noted that I made the step from normative to evaluative judgments. The distinction between normative (deontic) and evaluative is important, even though it is often ignored (Hage 2016b). However, for the debate on the implications of the step from a phenomenological to a realist account of the world, normative (deontic) and evaluative judgments are on a par.

4 The rationalist natural law tradition, with its main source in the work of Aquinas, is the main alternative for Kantianism.

Smith elaborates. According to him, an agent is the sort of 'thing' whose function it is to realize its desires. She can fulfil this function well, if she fulfils her desires. She fulfils her function badly if she does not succeed in fulfilling her desires. Therefore, an agent as such has reason to fulfil its idealized desires as well as possible.

For any agent, to realize its desires optimally, it must, still according to Smith, have and exercise two capacities. First, it must have and exercise the capacity to have knowledge of that part of the world that is relevant for how the agent can fulfil her desires. And second, the agent must have and exercise the capacity to be at least locally instrumentally rational. In other words, the agent must be able to determine what she needs to do to fulfil her idealized desires and she must use this ability.

This is not all. Smith continues that further capacities that make an agent's ideal naturally spring to mind. And then he continues by listing further capacities and arguing for them. For my argument, the details do not matter. The point that I want to make is that Smith assumes that agents are functional kinds—they are there to fulfil certain functions—and that arguments about how the functions of agents are best fulfilled lead to conclusions about what reasons for action an agent has, whatever the original desires the agent may have had. We see here a move that strongly resembles the move that Kant aimed to make: abstract from all the particular details of a real human being and try to find reasons for action that an agent would have to the extent that she is a purely rational being. The details may differ between Kant and Smith, but the general project is the same: find reasons for action that hold for rational beings as such.

The attraction of this project is clear. If reasons for action cannot be found in the world itself, and if the subjectivity is to be avoided that threatens if reasons for action are made dependent on the preferences and desires of actual persons, it seems necessary to look for universality of reasons outside the world of actual beliefs and desires. It is tempting to believe that universal reason is the place to look for objective reasons for action. But is there such a thing as universal reason?[5]

5 For the main line of my argument it is not important, but it may nevertheless be relevant for a proper understanding of constitutivism to point out that the observation that agency is a functional kind is not about an objective (real) kind of fact. If Smith's project is to arrive at normative conclusions on the basis of objective facts and constitution, the case of agency as a functional kind is not the best possible support. A similar objection would hold against arguments based on the assumption that law is a functional kind (Fuller 1963; Moore 1992). It is not essential for constitutivism, however, that it starts from the fact that something is a functional kind. Therefore, the objection is not an objection against constitutivism as such, but only against the variants that start from functional kinds.

1.2.5 Wrapping up

In Section 1.2, a bird's eye view was given of two radically different views of the world, the phenomenological view, and the realist view. The characteristic of the phenomenological view is the existence of a network of concepts and a corresponding set of characteristics that has its roots in human minds. In this network, the concepts and their corresponding characteristics are closely connected, giving rise to supervenience where the presence of one characteristic presupposes the presence of other characteristics. This leads to the possibility to derive the existence of one characteristic from the existence of other characteristics. One example of this possibility, which became problematic, is the derivation of value judgments from non-evaluative judgments. For instance, the derivation of the conclusion that a heart is good because it succeeds in pumping blood through the body. A second example is the derivation of ought judgments from premises that do not contain an ought. For example, from the fact that this is a heart it can be derived that this ought to pump blood through the body.

Such derivations become problematic if the phenomenological view of the world is replaced by the realist view. In the latter view, everything that is mind-dependent is banned from the 'real' world. This does not mean that value and normativity do not exist, but that their existence is a human addition, 'projection' some would say, on the real world. Value and normativity do not exist objectively.

For many, this is not a palatable conclusion and attempts have been made to show that normativity is more objective than the realist view of the world suggests. A main philosophical tradition has tried to find a foundation for normativity in reason, which is then assumed to have a universal standing. An example would be that there are things than an agent has reason to do, whatever her personal and subjective desires. But is there such a thing as universal reason?

Some would say that deductive logic is the paramount example of what universal reason might be. However, in Section 1.3, I will show that deductive logic, especially in the formal shape it received in the beginning of the 20th century, is not suitable to account for good arguments that reflect constitution. In Section 1.4, I will then investigate to what extent reason can be restored in its role of measure for the quality of practical reasoning by delving into the theory of social reality.

1.3 The boundaries of deductive logic

The purpose of this section on deductive logic is twofold. First, it will show why deductive logic, in the formal shape it received in the first half of the 20th century, is unsuitable for modelling arguments that reflect constitution (Sections 1.3.1 and 1.3.2). This first aim will be pursued at the hand of propositional logic, a relatively simple kind of logic, which makes it especially suitable for dealing with philosophical issues.[6]

And second, it argues that the boundary between logic and factual information about a domain—e.g., the domain of practical reasoning—is fluid and that therefore it is not clear what counts as logic (Section 1.3.3). It also argues that this is relevant for the plausibility of constitutivism (Section 1.3.4).

1.3.1 Logical possibility

Deductive logic deals with inferences that are deductively valid. An argument is deductively valid if and only if it is logically impossible that the premises of the argument are true, while the argument's conclusion is false. The crucial elements of this definition are the truth (or falsity) of the premises and of the conclusion of the argument, and logical necessity. From here on, when I write about validity, I mean deductive validity unless the contrary is explicitly mentioned.

Both premises and conclusion of an argument are propositions. Propositions are either true or false, depending on the facts. Since truth and falsity are determined by the facts in the world, this logical impossibility reflects an impossibility of what is the case in the world.

Logical theory developed so-called 'model-theoretic semantics' to answer the question of what logical (im)possibility precisely is.[7] Logic deals with propositions, such as the proposition that it is raining or the proposition that the sun is shining. These two are examples of elementary propositions, which do not contain a logical operator. There are also compound propositions, which contain one or more logical operators. Examples are that it is not raining, or that either it is raining or the sun shines. It is a bit clumsy to mention the full propositions when discussing logical relations between them. Therefore I will follow the traditional convention to use capitalized letters to abbreviate elementary propositions:

A = It is raining
B = The sun shines

I will use the traditional symbols for the logical operators by means of which elementary propositions can be included in compound propositions:

~A = It is not raining
A ∨ B = It is raining, or the sun shines
B & A = Both the sun shines and it is raining

6 Logicians are requested to overlook the complications in the examples that result from not using quantifiers.

7 The account of model-theoretical semantics that is presented in this chapter is quite philosophical. A more technical account can be found in, amongst many others, Smith 2012.

Every elementary proposition is either true or false, not both. Moreover—and this is very important—the truth values of the elementary propositions are logically independent of each other. So, the combinations

A is true and B is true
A is true and B is false
A is false and B is true
A is false and B is false

are logically speaking equally possible. In the real world, the combination that it is raining while the sun shines may be less plausible, but logically speaking there is nothing wrong with it. Running ahead of the main line of this section's argument, we can already see here that the close connection between states of affairs on which constitutivism is based has no counterpart in propositional logic which treats elementary propositions as independent from each other.

Whereas the truth values of elementary proposition are independent of each other, the truth values of compound propositions are defined in terms of the truth values of their components and their logical operators.

~A is true	if and only if	A is *not* true (false)
A ∨ B is true	if and only if	either A or B is true *or* if both are true
A & B is true	if and only if	A is true *and* B is true

Suppose that we have a set, possibly a very large set, of elementary propositions. Each of these propositions is either true or false. All the states of affairs that match these elementary propositions are compatible with each other, as the truth values of the propositions are independent from each other. The world as the collection of all these states of affairs is logically possible because the truth values of the elementary propositions are independent of each other, allowing every combination.

A very simple world would consist of a single elementary fact: [the sun shines]. This world does not contain the elementary fact that it is raining, and therefore it should also contain the compound fact that it is not raining [~It_is_raining]. In principle it holds that the compound facts in a world depend on the elementary facts in that world. So if a world contains the elementary facts that the sun shines [B] and that it rains [A], it should also contain the compound facts [B & A] and [A ∨ B]. Moreover, it does not contain the compound facts [~A], [~B], or [A~ ∨ ~B].

If the compound states of affairs in a world do not match the world's elementary states of affairs, this world is logically impossible. If the compound states of affairs match the elementary ones, the world is logically possible. A logically possible world contains all those compound states of affairs that it logically ought to contain given the elementary states of affairs and does not contain any compound state of affairs that logically speaking it ought not to contain. The elementary facts in a logically possible world determine all the facts in that world, so also the logically compound ones.

1.3.2 Logical validity

With the notion of a logically possible world in place, it becomes easy to define logical validity. An argument is valid, if and only if there is no logically possible world in which all of the argument's premises are true and in which the conclusion of the argument is false. By constructing the set of logically possible worlds that matches the elementary propositions in an argument, it is possible to determine whether the argument is valid. In this connection the logical operators, by means of which elementary propositions can be combined into compound propositions, play a crucial role.[8] They determine how the truth values of the elementary propositions translate into the truth values of the compound propositions.

As most real-life arguments use compound propositions, the question of which logical operators exist and how they are defined determines to a large extent which real-life arguments count as logically valid. I will use a very simple example to show what I mean.

Jane or Peter took the pencil away
Jane took the pencil away
Therefore, Peter did not take the pencil away

This argument seems valid, but if formalized in propositional logic the matter turns out not to be so easy. Take the following formalization (A stands for 'Jane took the pencil', B for 'Peter took the pencil').

$A \vee B$
A
Therefore, $\sim B$

In the possible world in which both Jane and Peter took the pencil away, both premises are true, and the conclusion is false. So, the argument as formalized is invalid. However, in its original natural language formulation the argument seemed valid. What went wrong?

The usual answer is that the word 'or' is ambiguous. It stands either for a so-called 'exclusive or', which means that precisely one of the two possibilities is realized (either Jane or Peter, but not both, took the pencil away). Or it stands for the 'inclusive or', which means that at least one of the two possibilities is realized, but perhaps even both. The argument in natural language presupposed the exclusive or, while the logical operator used to formalize 'or'

8 This is the method of truth-tables, well-known to logicians.

stands for an inclusive or. Therefore, the argument was incorrectly formalized and that explains why it is invalid in its incorrect formalization. The correct formalization of the argument would have been:

A ∨ B
~(A & B)
A
Therefore, ~B

The premises of this new argument are only all true in the world in which Jane, but not Peter, took the pencil away and in that world, the conclusion is also true. In other words, in its new formalization the argument comes out valid.

1.3.3 The fluid boundary between logic and domain knowledge

The manner in which the seemingly invalid argument about the pencil was shown to be valid after all, namely by adding a premise to the argument that is assumed to be true, represents a technique that can be used to turn any invalid argument into a valid one.[9]

Any invalid argument can be made valid by adding one or more premises to it. Adding the conclusion of the argument to the premises, for instance, will always do the job. If any invalid argument can be made valid by amending its premises, the question arises what the use of logic is. If the set of premises is considered as fixed, logic can distinguish between valid and invalid arguments. However, as soon as it becomes possible to meddle with the premises because the addition of one or more premises does better justice to the argument as it was formulated in natural language, the role of logic becomes less clear. Does it distinguish between valid and invalid arguments, or is it a tool to determine which unmentioned premise(s) are presupposed in an argument as formulated in natural language? Moreover, the vagueness of the role of logic translates into a corresponding vagueness of logic's nature. What counts as logic?

The premises of an argument contain a certain amount of information about the world. Logic is the means by which it can be established whether this information also contains the information of the conclusion (Hage 1994). If it does, the argument is logically valid; if not, the argument is invalid. The premises and the logic together determine what conclusions follow.

If a conclusion does not follow, and the argument is invalid, there are in principle two ways to make the argument valid after all. We have already seen one way: it is possible to add one or more premises, thereby increasing the

9 Strictly speaking, the addition of a premise does not turn the argument from invalid to valid. By adding a premise, the old invalid argument is replaced by a new valid argument. However, psychologically, the mere addition of a premise, especially if this premise is obviously true, will feel as modifying the original argument a bit.

amount of information in the premises. The other way is to make the logic more powerful. In doing so, it becomes possible to derive more conclusions from the information provided by the premises. This may seem strange to some readers who believe that there is just one logic. However, the history of logic in the 20th century has provided abundant examples of different systems of logic, the one more powerful than the other (Haack 1978; Priest 2008). Let us consider an example of an argument that is invalid under propositional logic, but which is valid under a suitable form of deontic logic.

> Laura is not permitted to park her car here
> Therefore, Laura is obligated not to park her car here

Formalized in the language of propositional logic, this argument becomes:

> A
> Therefore B

This argument is obviously invalid, as the truth values of A and B are independent. The argument can be made valid, even under propositional logic, by adding the premise ~A ∨ B. However, it can also be made valid by formalizing it in deontic logic:[10]

> ~Permitted (Laura, park_car_here) Laura is not permitted to park her car here
> Obligated (Laura, ¬park_car_here)[11] Laura is obligated not to park her car here

To make this argument logically valid, the deontic logic in question must have the following constraint on possible worlds:

> ~Permitted (a, b) if and only if Obligated (a, ¬b)

which reads in ordinary language: an agent a is not permitted to perform an action b, if and only if a is obligated to refrain from b. Given the meanings of the words 'permitted' and 'obligated', this is quite 'logical'.

The details of this example do not matter, but its main message does:

> *There can be more than one logic and it depends not only on the premises of an argument whether the conclusion follows, but also on the logic.*

10 For this example it is unavoidable to move from propositional to predicate logic. I hope this move is understandable without additional explanation.

11 The symbol ¬ is used to turn a type of action into the refraining from that type of action. So, ¬park_car_here stands for not parking the car here.

This insight has inspired the adoption of predicate logic, several systems of modal logic including deontic logics, temporal logics, many-valued logics, nonmonotonic logics, and so on …

However attractive this solution of adopting a stronger logic may seem, it immediately raises the question of what systems can still count as logics. By allowing more than one logic, the question of what a logic is, or—better—what can count as a logic, becomes urgent.[12] Take the following example:

Peter is a thief (A)
Therefore, Peter ought to be punished (B)

This argument is invalid under propositional logic. It can be made valid by adding the premise ~A ∨ B (either Peter is not a thief, or Peter ought to be punished). It can also be made valid by adding a constraint on possible worlds to propositional logic, thereby creating a more powerful logic:

B if A

The former solution has the disadvantage that the truth or falsity of the premise that needs to be added can only be established by assuming the truth of the argument's conclusion. Only if we already know that Peter ought to be punished, can we know that Peter, who is a thief either is not a thief or ought to be punished. This necessity to know beforehand that the conclusion of the argument is true does not sit well with our intuition that the argument establishes that Peter ought to be punished. In other words: that Peter is a thief constitutes that Peter ought to be punished. This constitution cannot be modelled by an argument of which one of its premises presumes the constituted fact.

The alternative is to add the constraint on logically possible worlds that if a world contains the fact that Peter is a thief, it must also contain the elementary fact that Peter ought to be punished. However, if this constraint is added, an important starting point of traditional propositional logic is abandoned. This is the assumption that the truth values of elementary propositions are independent of each other. In the examples discussed above about rain and sunshine, it seemed well possible to assume that whether it rains and whether the sun shines are independent of each other. Logically independent, that is, because meteorologically speaking there is a connection between rain and the absence of sunshine. In a similar way, there is a legal connection between being a thief and owing to be punished.

12 For example, the question has been raised, and answered in the negative, whether nonmonotonic logics are still logics or theories about how to adapt the premises of an argument (belief revision). See Israel 1980. Running ahead of the section on social reality, one might argue that whether something counts as logic is a matter of constructivist fact.

Should this legal connection be raised to the level of a logical connection? A clear test of which connections count as logical and which ones as meteorological, or legal, or whatever, is not available. By deciding that a connection, for instance, between being permitted and being obligated counts as logical rather than legal or moral, a choice is made to treat something as a matter of logic.

1.3.4 Back to constitutivism

Constitutivism tries to provide a solution for the problem that results when the phenomenological view of the world is replaced by the realist view and layers of meaning are stripped from our image of what the world includes. If the objective world is devoid of meaning, normative conclusions cannot be based on knowledge of the world alone. The step from hard knowledge about the world as it is independent of human colouring to knowledge of what an agent has reason to do requires the addition of a normative premise. For instance, the premise that an agent who is thirsty has reason to drink. This addition of a normative premise is comparable to making an argument valid by including more information in the premises. Moreover, on the realist view of the world, this information is not information about the world, but a mental addition to the 'hard' facts. If this addition is considered to be subjective, all normativity threatens to become subjective.

However, we have seen that there is an alternative for adding a premise, namely making the logic more powerful. Adopting constitutivism, in any form, is like strengthening the logic. The relation between on one hand what it is to be an agent or to be an action, and on the other hand to what an agent has reason to do is in constitutivism lifted from a contingent and subjective additional premise to a logic-like relation between agency and reasons for action. If this move is made, the logical gap between the hard facts of the objective world and deontic (or other modal) facts has disappeared and normativity is not purely subjective anymore.

Should this move be made? Should constitutivism be adopted and the information about the relation between agency and reasons for action be lifted to a kind of necessity which is very much like, if not a special case of, logical necessity? When should this be done? What relations between kinds of facts are sufficiently 'necessary' to include them in logic, instead of treating them as contingent information? To answer these questions, we must change course, leave the philosophy of logic behind, and turn to the mode of existence of social reality.

1.4 Social reality and constitutivism

Are there any reasons for action that can be derived logically, or which follow in a different way necessarily, from the nature of agency or the nature of action? Constitutivism assumes there are, but how is that possible if the real world only contains objective, in the sense of mind-independent, facts and if reasons for action are not objective in that manner? Perhaps the answer can be found if we do not assume that subjectivity is the only alternative for objectivity.[13]

1.4.1 Objective, subjective, and social

People distinguish between what is objective or subjective, but they also recognize a third category: what is social, or intersubjective. The distinction between objective, subjective, and social can be applied to states of affairs. In that case it is based on two characteristics which may be present or not. The two characteristics are whether the state of affairs is:

1. mind-dependent; and
2. the same for everybody.

Objective states of affairs are (1) not mind-dependent and (2) the same for everybody. An example would be the fact that Mount Everest is a higher mountain than the Vaalserberg (the highest 'mountain' of the Netherlands).

Subjective states of affairs (1) depend on what individual persons think they are and are mind-dependent, and (2) are therefore not the same for everybody.[14] An example would be the 'fact' that Mozart was a better composer than Brahms.

Social states of affairs are somehow in between objective and subjective states of affairs: (1) they depend on what the members of a social group recognize and are in that sense mind-dependent, and (2a) they are the same for the members of a group, but (2b) not necessarily the same between groups. A possible example is the law of a country. The law depends on what the legal subjects of a country recognize as law and is the same for these legal subjects. However, different countries may have different laws, and what is the law for a Frenchman may not be the law for somebody in China.

Social facts come in two main kinds. There are facts which I will call 'conventional'. They depend on their broad recognition in a social group. There are also 'constructivist' facts. They depend on the rationality of their recognition, but indirectly they also depend on what is recognized in a social group.

1.4.2 Conventional facts

The 'social world' is the collection of all social facts for a group. A proper understanding of the social world starts with conventional facts. Conventional facts exist in a social group if most members of that group recognize that they

13 Much of this section on social reality is based on a theory that was developed in a series of papers, three of which have already been published: Hage 2022b, 2022c, and 2023.

14 That is why their status as facts is often contested; many people would not even call subjective facts 'facts' at all.

exist. This collective recognition is the final word about what conventional facts are. For instance, Henrique is the leader of the Maastricht Cycling Club (MCC) if sufficiently many members of that club recognize Henrique as their leader. Another example is that the verb 'rain' stands for a particular meteorological phenomenon. That 'rain' has this meaning is because the speakers of the English language on a large scale recognize it as having this meaning. They might have used a different word, such as 'Regen', but as it is, they use the word 'rain' and therefore 'rain' has this meaning. So, it does not make sense to argue that the convention is wrong. If a state of affairs is recognized as being conventional (see Section 1.4.5), the mere existence of a relevant convention suffices for the state of affairs being a fact, disregarding the value of the convention. The eventual willingness to take the value of the convention into account suggests that the kind of state of affairs is considered to be constructivist, rather than conventional.

In this connection, the notion of recognition is crucial. The notion is used here in a technical sense: a person recognizes a fact if he:

a. believes that the fact exists; and
b. tends to act in accordance with this belief.

Two other conditions for the existence of a conventional fact, which will only be mentioned here,[15] are that:

- the club members should not only recognize Henrique as their leader; they should also believe that sufficiently many other members also recognize Henrique as leader of the group, and that these other members have the same beliefs about their fellow cyclists.
- states of affairs of that kind are considered to be conventional. (This condition will be elaborated in Section 1.4.5.)

Conventional facts are the same for all members of a social group, even for those members who do not recognize them. If Petra does not recognize Henrique as the leader of MCC, she makes a mistake, and other members of MCC may criticize or even sanction her for this mistake. In this respect, conventional facts are very much like objective facts. The only difference is that conventional facts depend on the views of the members of a social group. In this latter respect, conventional facts are like subjective facts. To state it briefly: from within a group, conventional facts are like objective facts, and from the outside, conventional facts are like subjective facts.

15 For a more extensive discussion of the first condition, see Hage 2022c.

1.4.3 Conventions and other rules

Social reality does not only contain facts, but also rules.[16] The most basic form of existence for rules is existence as a convention. It is worthwhile to emphasize the difference between a convention and a conventional fact. A convention is a connection between facts. The formulation of a convention, such as 'Coins count as money', is not a statement. For that reason, it is not true or false. A conventional fact, in contrast, can be expressed by means of a true description, such as 'This (coin) is money'.

A convention exists in a group if sufficiently many members of the group are disposed to recognize the consequence of the convention if they believe the facts of its conditions and if they tend to justify their recognition by mentioning their belief or the convention.[17] For instance, if most people in Belgium are disposed to recognize certain pieces of metal as money and justify this recognition by saying that the pieces of metal are coins, the Belgian people have the convention that coins count as money. Conventions and conventional facts are mutually dependent for their existence. The convention exists because the facts of its conclusions exist as conventional facts. The conventional facts in turn exist because their recognition is dependent on a convention and its conditions. Very simply stated, conventions are rules that exist because they are used.[18]

If a convention exists in a group, this has normative consequences. If the Belgians recognize coins as money and some Belgian refuses to accept coins as money, doubting that they are real money, this person may be blamed for denying the obvious ('everybody' knows that coins represent money), and may even be obligated to recognize payments by means of coins. Analogously, if a group recognizes the convention that if either A or B, then A should be the case, or B, but not both (exclusive or), somebody who claims that A or B is the case, if they are both the case (inclusive or) makes a mistake and may in some circumstances even be accused of misleading others. The meanings of logical operators are conventional, just like money.

We have seen that the motives behind constitutivism include the desire to find a more solid basis for normative judgments than the wishes, preferences, or whatever subjective dispositions of individual persons. Conventions and conventional facts form such a more solid basis. One interpretation of

16 In this contribution I use a broad conception of rules, according to which rules are, in the first instance, mental connections between kinds of facts. More details about this conception of rules can be found in Hage 2015, 2018 chapter V, and 2022c.

17 There are more requirements for the existence of a convention. See Hage 2022c.

18 Other rules exist because their existence is attached to some facts by another rule. These rules are rule-based rules, also called 'institutional rules' (MacCormick and Weinberger 1986). In this chapter, I will not go into details about these institutional rules, which are more important for law than for constitutivism.

constitutivism would therefore be that facts about agents or actions conventionally support facts and judgments about what reasons for action an agent has.

Conventional support is stronger than the merely subjective fact that an agent desires to bring about a particular result, such as quenching her thirst, a desire that turns the fact that drinking water quenches thirst into a reason to drink water. However, conventions are still linked to social groups and a convention that exists in one group may not exist in another group. For example, if one group has the convention that cyclists ought to drive on the right, this leads to a reason to drive on the right in the group that has this convention, but not in another group. Many would like reasons for action not to be relative to social groups. Moreover, many would not like conventions to be decisive for reasons for action, as some conventions might be 'wrong'. Only 'right' conventions should lead to reasons for action, and if they are right, there is not even a need for a convention. If it is right to assist asylum seekers, this would still provide a reason for action even if there is no broad consensus in society about the desirability of providing such assistance. People who think this way will not accept a conventional basis for constitutivism. However, they might be satisfied by a constructivist basis.

1.4.4 Constructivist facts

Not all social facts are conventional. There is a second category, constructivist facts, where an existing broad consensus is, perhaps the first but not the final word on what the facts are. Suppose that the members of MCC take a vote on what was the best cycling trip they made this year. They decide unanimously that the trip to Arcen was the best trip. Does this mean that the Arcen trip really was the best? No, even if all club members agree on what was the best trip, this does not mean that it *really* was the best trip. It remains possible to raise the question of whether all members of the club were mistaken about the best trip.

There appears to be a difference between what most or even all members of the group recognize as the best trip and what really was the best trip. States of affairs such as the fact about what was the best cycling trip of the year are not objective, because they depend on how people 'feel' about things. Neither are they merely subjective, as it makes sense to argue about them. And, finally, they are not conventional either, because a broadly shared belief about them is not the final word. I will call such facts *constructivist facts.*

Constructivist facts are social facts, which are open to serious questioning. This combination is possible if the social practice of a group does not only recognize the existence of these states of affairs, but also the possibility to question them. For instance, prima facie it may be a social fact in MCC that the trip to Arcen was the best trip of the year. However, the members of MCC agree and know that the others also agree that, theoretically speaking, everybody might be mistaken. If somebody came up with convincing reasons that another trip was even better, this other trip would be better. Moreover, it would have been better from the very beginning, not merely because the members of MCC changed their minds. If an argument makes people change their minds about constructivist facts, they change their minds about what the facts already were.

Constructivist facts are characterized by the possibility to have a *serious* debate about them. 'Serious' means in this connection that the participants in the debate believe that it is possible to disagree about these facts without thereby showing a misunderstanding of what the debate is about. They also believe that there is a correct answer to the question of what the facts are, independent of what people actually believe it is. For instance, if Joanna and Frédéric disagree about whether red wine is better or white wine, while they believe it is just a matter of taste, they consider the issue at stake to be a merely subjective one. There is no right answer as to what the best wine is, and their disagreement is not serious. If two members of MCC disagree about whether Henrique is their leader, while both know that practically all members of the club recognize Henrique as their leader, their disagreement is not serious either. The reason is that not believing that Henrique is the leader while also believing that 'everybody' recognizes Henrique as the leader, shows misunderstanding of the conditions for leadership, which is a matter of convention. The example about the best cycling trip of the year illustrates that it is possible to disagree seriously about what was the best trip. The seriousness of the debate becomes manifest in the assumption of all participants that there is a right answer to the question, even though it is not a matter of objective fact, and that this right answer does not change if people merely change their minds about what the answer is.

How is it possible that constructivist facts are social facts, even though broad social recognition is not the final word about what they are? The answer is that constructivist facts are what the best possible argument says they are. This answer seems only to push the issue backward. The question of whether a particular constructivist fact exists—for instance, of whether the trip to Arcen really was the best trip—has no objective answer. How, then, can there be a best possible argument if this argument does not lead to the objectively true answer? There must be a standard that determines what the best possible argument is, and this standard cannot refer to objective truth. This standard can only be found, I claim, in the social practice of the group in which arguments are produced. A constructivist fact is a fact that ought to be recognized as a result of the rational reconstruction of the set of objective facts and of the social facts that are recognized in a social group, including the standards for good argumentation that exist in the group.[19]

19 There is no room in this chapter to further develop the notion of rational reconstruction. As a very short alternative, I suggest that rational reconstruction of a set of beliefs and recognitions is making the set 'integrated coherent' (Hage 2005, 33–68, 2013, 2016a).

Rational reconstruction may involve no change for a particular social fact, and then that fact continues to exist as a social fact in the group because it was already recognized. An example would be that the members of the MCC group believe that the cycling trip to the castle gardens of Arcen was the best trip of 2020 and that this belief survives a rational reconstruction of their belief set, for instance, because nobody sees a reason to question it.[20] Then the belief that the cycling trip to the castle gardens of Arcen was the best trip is an element of the rationally reconstructed belief set, because it was already in the original belief set and nothing changed in this respect. It deserves emphasizing here that if there are no reasons to modify the original belief set, the set as it originally was remains unchanged. So there is a conservative bias in this rational reconstruction, which strengthens the idea that constructivist facts are still social facts, even if they are to a substantial degree determined by reason.

Reconstruction may also involve the inclusion in the belief set of a particular social fact, and then that fact already existed as a social fact in the group because it ought to be recognized according to the rational reconstruction. An example would be that Dutch law initially seemed not to have the right of adopted children to know their birth parents, but that the existence of this right (the 'right to know') is included in the rationally reconstructed set and the right therefore already existed as a matter of constructivist fact.

Finally, reconstruction may involve the removal of a particular social fact from the belief set, and then that fact did not exist as a constructivist fact in the group because it ought not to be recognized according to the rational reconstruction. If the members of the MCC group ought not to have recognized the trip to Arcen as the best one, the belief that the cycling trip to Arcen was the best trip is not part of the rationally reconstructed belief set anymore and the trip to Arcen was, all things considered, not the best trip.

Rationally reconstructing a set of recognitions or beliefs leads to a judgment on what ought to be recognized, *given the original beliefs*. The recognitions in the reconstructed set are what the believer of the original set rationally ought to recognize. Constructivist facts are the conclusions of the best possible arguments. These arguments determine what ought to be recognized, but *ipso facto* they also determine that part of social reality. Perhaps this is the most important thing to remember about constructivist facts: *constructivist reality is what rationally ought to be recognized as real.*

20 Perhaps a better formulation would be: 'if there is no good reason to question it'. The issue at stake here is whether rational reconstruction should be interpreted as an actual procedure, even if it is executed under ideal circumstances, or as a logical operation which takes its input from what the members of a group recognize.

1.4.5 The layered structure of the social world

A conventional fact exists if it is broadly recognized, but only if states of affairs of that kind are in the group considered to be conventional facts. This means that the group members should not consider those kinds of states of affairs to be objective, or merely subjective. Take the following example. Let us assume, perhaps contrary to the truth, that during the early Middle Ages, most people recognized that Earth was flat. This would not mean that Earth was flat as a conventional fact in those days, because even in those times people would recognize that the shape of Earth is something objective.[21] This means that a conventional fact, such as the fact that 'rain' stands for rain, requires recognition on (at least) two levels. First, states of affairs about the meanings of words should be considered to be conventional, and second the word 'rain' should be recognized as standing for rain.

The meta-recognition of conventional states of affairs as conventional does not only mean that conventional states of affairs should be seen as social, and not as objective or subjective, facts. It also means that they are not recognized as constructivist facts.

Constructivist facts are social facts that are open to serious questioning. This combination is possible if the social practice of a group not only recognizes the existence of these states of affairs, but also the possibility to question them and that questions about these facts have a correct answer that is not objectively true, but which does not depend on the opinions of the majority either. Only if these characteristics of constructivist states of affairs are recognized in a group does this group have constructivist states of affairs.[22] Concrete states of affairs of a particular kind, for instance, the moral state of affairs that torture is wrong, can only be constructivist if moral states of affairs are constructivist as a matter of social fact.

The picture that arises from this discussion of how social states of affairs exist is that their existence depends on two levels in the social world. On the more abstract level there are social facts, conventional or constructivist facts, about what kinds of states of affairs are objective, subjective, conventional, or constructivist.[23] This level is self-referring, as it also determines for the meta-level facts themselves to what category they belong. For instance, it is a matter of social fact whether legal states of affairs are conventional. On the more concrete level, social facts exist if they are broadly recognized (conventional

21 People may not have recognized that the shape of Earth is a social fact in these terms, as they may have lacked the necessary conceptual distinctions. People would not need to use the word 'social' for conventional facts, but in the terminology introduced here, the group members should recognize conventional facts as social facts.

22 It is not always a matter of convention to what category a particular kind of state of affairs belongs. It may also be a matter of constructivist fact. In this chapter, there is no room to further discuss this important issue, however. For details, see Hage 2023.

23 For all kinds of states of affairs—not only for social ones—it holds that their existence presupposes that facts of these kinds are recognized as objective, subjective, conventional, or social.

facts), or if they are the conclusions of the best possible arguments (constructivist facts).

1.4.6 Constructivism and constitutivism

The central idea behind constitutivism is that there are some facts which lead necessarily to conclusions about reasons for action or to other normative conclusions. The more popular facts in this connection are facts that deal with the function of an agent and how that function is best realized, or with the nature of actions. The connection between the constituting facts and what they constitute should not be coincidental, or what philosophers call contingent. It should somehow be necessary, perhaps even logically necessary.

Is there such a necessary connection? Objectively speaking not, as necessity is not a part of objective reality. Subjectively speaking also not, as subjective connections between kinds of states of affairs cannot provide the required necessity. If constitutivism is to cut ice, the relation between the constituting facts and the reasons for action, or the normative facts, which they constitute must rest in social reality. It is a matter of social fact whether the relation would exist as a convention, or as a rule that exists as a matter of constructivist fact. The issue is so complicated that the existence of a broad consensus—that is: a convention—about constitution is unlikely. So, it should be a matter of constructivist facts whether the required inference rule exists that allows to conclude from premises about agents or actions to conclusions about reasons for action. Should we, rationally speaking, recognize that, for instance, agents have a reason to collect knowledge about how to fulfil their desires, as Smith claimed? If that is the case, the theory about how social reality exists explains why constitutivism works.

More in general, if a rule exists in social reality, either as a convention or as a matter of constructivist fact, this rule supports logic-like inferences. If the conditions of the rule are satisfied, it is *pro tanto* rational to accept the rule's conclusion. The notion of a rule in this connection is very broad, including legal rules, moral principles, values and other socially accepted goals, inference rules, conceptual rules, and also constitutive rules. Constitutivism works not because it is very special but because it is one of the many cases where connections between kinds of facts exist in social reality. Whether such connections are also called 'logical' in the narrow sense of deductive logic is itself a matter of social (conventional or constructivist) fact.

1.5 The relevance for law

There are many kinds of legal rules, such as rules that impose duties or obligations, rules that assign competences, rules that impose sanctions, or rules that underlie classifications. Many of these rules as such do not lead to reasons for action, although they play a role in a larger system that does provide reasons for action. For instance, a rule that makes the municipality council of Maastricht competent to create bylaws in itself does not provide the council or anybody else with a reason for action. However, the competence can be used by the council to create mandatory rules, which in their turn lead to reasons for action. Mandatory rules typically do provide reasons for action, and it seems that constitutivism can be helpful to understand how at least some legal rules can create normativity.

In this connection it is important to distinguish between two kinds of normativity: legal normativity and the normativity of reason. If a rule of the municipality of Maastricht imposes on all of its inhabitants the obligation to pay a tax to the municipality, the created obligations are so many reasons for action. This is legal normativity.

Next to this legal normativity—what an agent legally speaking has a duty or obligation, or ought to do—we have the normativity of reason. This normativity addresses the issue of what an agent ought to recognize, believe, or desire, given what else he recognizes, believes, or desires. For example, a pupil ought to arrive at the answer 6 when asked what the sum of 4 and 2 is. Or she ought to desire to drink some water if she is thirsty, wants to quench her thirst, and believes that drinking water will do the job.

This normativity of reason also plays a role in law. If a legal subject believes that a particular mandatory rule is valid, for instance, the rule about municipal taxes in Maastricht, and if she also believes that the rule is applicable to her situation, she rationally ought to recognize that she is under an obligation to pay the tax and therefore legally ought to pay the tax. As it is the point of legal obligations to be reasons for action, she rationally ought to believe that she has a reason for action. And this means that it is a matter of constructivist fact that, *pro tanto*, she has this reason. This is how law leads to reasons for action, which is a case of legal normativity. There is a close connection between (the existence of) legal rules and the existence of reasons for action. This connection is not merely contingent, but exists as a matter of social fact, conventional or constructivist. The legal mechanism in question provides an example of how constitution operates in law.

1.6 Conclusion

In the world as we daily experience it there are many connections between different kinds of facts (Tahko and Lowe 2020), and these connections make us recognize the presence of some facts on the basis of recognizing other facts. For instance, we recognize the validity of some legal rule because we believe that the rule was made by means of a statute. We use these connections in argumentation, as when justifying to others what one recognizes. For instance, we justify our belief that it will rain tomorrow by mentioning the weather forecast.

These connections are the products of human minds and do not exist objectively. For instance, it depends on human minds that there is a connection between the fact that a rule was made by means of a statute and the validity of this rule. Moreover, the connections cannot easily be fitted in a system of deductive logic if that system only recognizes the connections based on a small set of logical operators. To return to the example about the rule: it is not a matter of deductive logic that rules made by means of statutes are legally valid.

Both this non-objectivity and not fitting in the system of deductive logic are captured in Hume's guillotine. This metaphorical guillotine separates normativity from what is objective and disallows the deduction of normative propositions from merely non-normative ones. Hume's guillotine sits well in a realist world view, but not in a phenomenological view. It should therefore not come as a surprise that attempts were made to bring back normativity to the place it has in the life world of most people. The Kantian tradition in ethics is a prominent example of a philosophical attempt to do so. The same holds for constitutivism.

The leading idea that underlies constitutivism is that some facts make it the case, constitute, that other facts are the case. If the former facts exist objectively, so would the latter. If the latter facts are normative, while the former are not, it is shown that Hume's guillotine is not always efficacious.

However, constitutivism must still make sense of the idea that some facts 'constitute' other facts. Here the theory about social reality comes into play. Facts in social reality can exist because they are broadly recognized (conventional facts) or because they ought to be recognized, given what is already broadly recognized (constructivist facts). This theory about social reality explains how social facts can be constituted.

It cannot explain why normative facts exist objectively. However, if the possibility is assumed that normative facts exist in social reality (Hage 2022c), we not only have explanations of how normative facts exist, and why they are not subjective, but we can also explain how some facts can constitute other facts and why constitutivism can elucidate how normative facts are grounded in non-normative facts. Whether constitutivism adds much to the theory about social reality is under that assumption a different matter.

References

Barber, Michael. 2022. "Alfred Schutz". In The Stanford Encyclopedia of Philosophy, edited by Edward N. Zalta, Summer 2022 Edition. https://plato.stanford.edu/archives/sum2022/entries/schutz/.

Bargh, John. 2017. *Before You Know It. The Unconscious Reasons We Do What We Do.* London: Windmill Books.

Beyer, Christian. 2022. "Edmund Husserl". In The Stanford Encyclopedia of Philosophy, edited by Edward N. Zalta and Uri Nodelman, Winter 2022 Edition. https://plato.stanford.edu/archives/win2022/entries/husserl/.

Bliss, Ricki, and Kelly Trogdon. 2021. "Metaphysical Grounding". In The Stanford Encyclopedia of Philosophy, edited by Edward N. Zalta, Winter 2021 Edition. https://plato.stanford.edu/archives/win2021/entries/grounding/.

Bolton, Martha. 2022. "Primary and Secondary Qualities in Early Modern Philosophy". In The Stanford Encyclopedia of Philosophy, edited by Edward N. Zalta and Uri

Nodelman, Fall 2022 Edition. https://plato.stanford.edu/archives/fall2022/entries/qualities-prim-sec/.

Brecht, Arnold. 1959. *Political Theory: The Foundations of Twentieth-Century Political Thought.* Princeton: Princeton University Press.

Carnap, R. 1947. *Meaning and Necessity.* Chicago: University of Chicago Press.

Del Mar, Maksymilian. 2016. "The Natural and the Normative: The Distinction, Not the Dichotomy, Between Facts and Values in a Broader Context". In Facts and Norms in Law, edited by Sanne Taekema, Bart van Klink, and Wouter Been, 224–241. Cheltenham: Edward Elgar Publishing.

Fuller, Lon L. 1963. *The Morality of Law.* revised ed. New Haven: Yale University Press.

Haack, S. 1978. *Philosophy of Logics.* Cambridge: Cambridge University Press.

Hage, Jaap. 1994. "Two metaphors of reasoning." In Legal Knowledge-Based Systems: The Relation with Legal Theory, edited by H. Prakken, A.J. Muntjewerff, and A. Soeteman, 127–138. Lelystad: Koninklijke Vermande.

Hage, Jaap. 2005. *Studies in Legal Logic.* Dordrecht: Springer.

Hage, Jaap. 2013. "Three Kinds of Coherentism"". In Coherence: Insights from Philosophy, Jurisprudence and Artificial Intelligence, edited by Michal Araszkiewicz and Jaromír Šavelka, 1–32. Dordrecht: Springer.

Hage, Jaap. 2015. "The (Onto)logical Structure of Law: A Conceptual Toolkit for Legislators". In Logic in the Theory and Practice of Legislation, edited by Michal Araszkiewicz and Krzysztof Pleszka, 3–48. Cham: Springer.

Hage, Jaap. 2016a. "Anything Goes: An Apology for Parallel Distributed Legal Science." *Informal Logic* 36 (3). http://dx.doi.org/10.22329/il.v36i3.4719.

Hage, Jaap. 2016b. "Facts, Values and Norms". In Facts and Norms in Law, edited by Sanne Taekema, Bart van Klink, and Wouter Been, 23–52. Cheltenham: Edward Elgar Publishing.

Hage, Jaap. 2018. *Foundations and Building Blocks of Law.* Den Haag: Eleven International Publishing.

Hage, Jaap. 2022a. "Objectivity of Law and Objectivity about Law." In *Objectivity in Jurisprudence, Legal Interpretation and Practical Reasoning*, edited by Gonzalo Villa-Rosas and Jorge Luis Fabra-Zamora, 31–47. Cheltenham: Edward Elgar Publishing.

Hage, Jaap. 2022b. "Constructivist Facts as the Bridge Between Is and Ought". *International Journal for the Semiotics of Law* 35: 53–81. https://link-springer-com.mu.idm.oclc.org/article/10.1007/s11196-022-09896-4

Hage, Jaap. 2022c. "Rules and the Social World". *L' Ircocervo* 21: 16–35. https://lircocervo.it/?p=5346

Hage, Jaap. 2023. The Nature of Law and Constructivist Facts, In L*egal Reasoning and Cognitive Science: Topics and Perspectives, Diritto & Questioni pubbliche*, edited by M. Brigaglia and C. Roversi. Special Publication, August 2023, forthcoming. Preview. http://www.dirittoequestionipubbliche.org/page/2023_dq-recognise/e-03-Hage.pdf.

Hare, R. M. 1952. *The Language of Morals.* Oxford: Oxford University Press.

Hilpinen, Risto, ed. 1971. *Deontic Logic: Introductory and Systematic Readings.* Dordrecht: Reidel.

Israel, D. J. 1980. "What's Wrong with Non-Monotonic Logic?" In Proceedings of the First National Annual Conference on Artificial Intelligence, 99–101. Los Altos: Morgan Kaufmann Publishers.

Kelsen, Hans. 1934. *Reine Rechtslehre: Einleitung in die rechtswissenschaftliche Problematik*. Leipzig/Wien: Franz Deuticke.

Lewis, David. 1989. "Dispositional Theories of Value". *The Proceedings of the Aristotelian Society* 63: 113–137.

MacCormick, N., and O. Weinberger. 1986. *An Institutional Theory of Law*. Dordrecht: Reidel.

McLaughlin, Brian, and Karen Bennett. 2021. "Supervenience". In The Stanford Encyclopedia of Philosophy, edited by Edward N. Zalta, Summer 2021 Edition. http://plato.stanford.edu/archives/spr2014/entries/supervenience/.

Millgram, Elijah. 2020. "Practical Reason and the Structure of Actions". In The Stanford Encyclopedia of Philosophy, edited by Edward N. Zalta, Winter 2020 Edition. https://plato.stanford.edu/archives/win2020/entries/practical-reason-action/

Moore, G. E. 1903. *Principia Ethica*. Cambridge: Cambridge University Press.

Moore, Michael. 1992. "Law as a Functional Kind." In *Natural Law Theory*, edited by Robert P. George, 188–242.Oxford: Clarendon Press.

Priest, Graham. 2008. *An Introduction to Non-Classical Logic*. 2nd ed. Cambridge: Cambridge University Press.

Richerson, Peter J., and Robert Boyd. 2006. *Not by Genes Alone: How Culture Transformed Human Evolution*. Chicago: University of Chicago Press.

Smith, Michael. 2015. "The Magic of Constitutivism". *American Philosophical Quarterly* 50: 187–200.

Smith, Nicholas J. J. 2012. *Logic. The Laws of Truth*. Princeton: Princeton University Press.

Tahko, Tuomas E., and E. Jonathan Lowe. 2020. "Ontological Dependence". In The Stanford Encyclopedia of Philosophy, edited by Edward N. Zalta, Fall 2020 Edition. https://plato.stanford.edu/archives/fall2020/entries/dependence-ontological/.

Von Wright, Georg Henrik. 1963. *Norm and Action. A logical enquiry*. London: Routledge and Kegan Paul.

White, Alan R. 1975. *Modal Thinking*. Oxford: Basil Blackwell.

2 Ascriptivism, life forms, and recognition. On the social constitution of normativity

Sebastián Figueroa Rubio

2.1 Ascriptivism and constitutivism

Michael Smith presents the philosophical thesis of constitutivism as that according to which "normative facts of certain kinds are explained by facts about the constitutive features of something – that is, the features in virtue of which that thing is the kind of thing it is – where the constitutive features might be those of some person, or some action, or some state of affairs, or something else entirely".[1] This general thesis has evolved into a discussion about how practical normativity can be derived from the constitutive features of agency. For our purposes, this means that "we have to see practical normativity as inherently connected with agency".[2]

Constitutivism invites us to reflect on how some features of our agency and personhood are on the foundations of our normative concepts and judgements. This means, on the one hand, that we might avoid looking outside ourselves for these concepts and, on the other hand, that we should meditate about how we can make sense of the connection between agency and normativity. The invitation, in turn, could be understood in a weak sense, as a fundamental search for an explanation of how some features of agency ground and shape practical normativity without providing an answer to how certain practical problems can be solved. It could also be understood in a stronger sense, according to which the search consists in defining the content of categorical practical norms and the reasons why they should be followed. In this chapter, I will explore a defence of a weak constitutivist view. More specifically, I will explore how some constitutivist ideas might provide a basis for supporting a view developed by H.L.A. Hart, J.L. Austin, and Joel Feinberg called ascriptivism.[3]

Ascriptivism is a thesis within the philosophy of action that defends an internal connection between action and responsibility. In his seminal "Ascription

1 Smith 2018, 371

2 Bertea 2013, 81. For the definition of the thesis and the various views on it, v. Smith 2018; Southwood 2018; Enoch, 2020.

3 v. Austin 1979, ch. 8, 12; Feinberg 1970, ch. 6; Hart 1949.

DOI: 10.4324/9781032670553-3

of Responsibility and Rights",[4] Hart expresses one fundamental thesis of ascriptivism in the following way:

> My main purpose in this article is to suggest that the philosophical analysis of the concept of a human action has been inadequate and confusing, at least in part because sentences of the form "He did it" have been traditionally regarded as primarily descriptive whereas their principal function is what I venture to call ascriptive, being quite literally to ascribe responsibility for actions much as the principal function of sentences of the form "This is his" is to ascribe rights in property.[5]

Ascriptivism advocates a general thesis according to which when we speak about an action, we not only describe an event but also attribute responsibility for what happens. The language of action itself is an attributive language that expresses that we consider a part of the world to be configured by agents. According to Hart, we therefore see our behaviour not just as a mere empirical event to be described, but as an expression of agency.[6] In this sense, ascriptivism contrasts with an influential view on philosophy of action that understands action sentences as descriptions of events (i.e., bodily movements) to which a specific cause (i.e., reasons, understood as mental states, usually a mixture of desires and beliefs) is added.[7] This relationship between action and responsibility links agency with normativity, since it represents an interdependence between the paradigmatic exercise of agency (i.e., actions) and the normative concepts and judgements related to norm violations, guilt, and faultiness (i.e., those related to responsibility). Therefore, we can understand ascriptivism as a theory of action with a constitutivist flavour.

Ascriptivist ideas have been criticized for various reasons. The criticism that concerns us here is that it is not correct to claim that every attribution of action entails an attribution of responsibility. In particular, George Pitcher questions whether it is true that whenever sentences of the type 'he did it' are uttered, someone is said to be a candidate for a typical responsibility response (i.e., punishments, reproaches, praise, etc.). When we attribute actions, we do not always think about or assume the possibility of sanctions, nor do we accuse someone for them or offer excuses or apologies; we often simply say

4 The article has opened discussions on metaethics, legal reasoning, defeasible reasoning, theory of concepts, philosophy of action, and theory of norms (v. Blöser et al. 2013; Duarte d'Almeida 2015; Figueroa Rubio 2024; Sneddon 2006).

5 Hart 1949, 171.

6 According to Ralf Stoecker, ascriptivism in its anylisis of these expressions shows that: 'What makes them action sentences is not what they talk about but what they say about it: they describe the agent as being responsible' (Stoecker 2007, 40).

7 The classical presentation of this model is in Davidson 1980.

that someone did something to point out his or her behaviour without further ado.[8]

For Pitcher, this means not only that we sometimes do not assign responsibility when we attribute an action to someone, but that we never actually attribute responsibility for actions directly. According to the author, it would be more correct to say that we are responsible for the violation of duties by them or for their undesirable effects. In this sense, actions can sometimes be described on the basis of empirical data as events that correspond to what the norms forbid or that have caused what is prohibited.

As can be seen, the critique puts us in the position of abandoning the ascriptivist thesis altogether, but it is worth asking whether it is not possible to rescue, at least partially, the idea that the connection between action and responsibility can be supported. This is the path that Joel Feinberg took and that I would like to defend. To do so, I will first explore the philosophical ground on which it can make sense. The following pages are dedicated to this exploration. More precisely, I will focus my attention on two philosophical insights that emanate from constitutivist views. The first comes from the neo-Aristotelian constitutivist views developed by Philippa Foot and Michael Thompson. Neo-Aristotelians propose to characterize the structure of normativity as (at least partially) anchored in the idea of life and applicable to all living things. In this framework, they propose to discuss the particular case of the character and actions of human agents within their life form. The second insight is the Hegelian idea of recognition, which I will present as an application of the idea that humans are social animals that construct history. It is in interactions with others that the characteristically human form of normativity appears. Although Hegel is not considered a constitutivist, I think that some neo-Hegelian ideas could be useful to argue in favour of a social constitutivist view. The sum of these ideas contextualizes action and agency in sociality. Hence, I will propose what can be called a weak social constitutivist view that relies on the idea that we can find normativity in our social life form.

2.2 Life forms and agency

The constitutivism developed by Foot and Thompson sought the roots of normativity in the context of life. They state that 'Judgements of goodness and badness can have, it seems, a special "grammar" when the subject belongs to a living thing, whether plant, animal, or human being'.[9] Hence, "evaluations of human will and action share a conceptual structure with evaluations of characteristics and operations of other living things".[10] As we can see, these ideas

8 v. Pitcher 1960, 226. Hart himself recognized this criticism as justified (v. Hart 1968, v).

9 Foot 2001, 26

10 Foot 2001, 5. There are three ideas that were discussed after Foot's work, that I will not deal with in this text. The first is whether or not Foot's thesis is a refutation of non-cognitivist

imply placing the concept of agency within the broader concept of life and seeking normativity in this context.[11] In this section, I will explore how the interaction between life and agency can be understood from this perspective.

The concept of agency is based on the distinction between happenings and doings. An agent is the one who has the capacities and powers to intervene in the world by doing things. In this sense, the behaviour of an agent is not accidental, but has a specific direction and follows a certain logic. When we see an agent's behaviour, we can interpret it in such a way that we attribute a purpose or interest to the agent (e.g., to eat, to reach something, to escape) and this interest or purpose defines what is happening (as a *doing*).

Thinking in agential terms produces unity not only in the identification of what takes place, but also in the identification of the one who does it. Thus, even if the body of agents is composed of organic tissue and atoms, it cannot be reduced to the way in which tissues and atoms interact. The unit of agency is the organism (e.g., the animal, the plant), not the set of atoms and cells that compose it. When we refer to behaviour and purpose, we refer to the being as a unity, not to its components.[12]

Furthermore, agential behaviour is recognized and explained within a framework in which behaviour as such makes sense, for example, bearing in mind what the body allows, what the environment allows, and what life itself allows. Thus, we understand the undulating movement of a fish's body in water as if it were swimming, or the movement of a blackbird's wings as if it were flying. These understandings depend on physiological and environmental issues.

The behaviour of agents differs from purely mechanical or random movements; they shape the world through the exercise of their powers and through their interactions. Animals, plants, and other organisms not only perceive their environment, they create, renew, and maintain it. Agency is thus linked to the idea of living beings in the sense that life manifests itself in the existence of animals, plants, and other organisms that, on the one hand, interact with and shape their environment and, on the other hand, deploy these behaviours

---

views on metaethics. The second is whether or not the thesis implies a strong constitutivism based on virtue ethics. The third question is whether the thesis is descriptive rather than normative, i.e., empirical rather than grammatical. I see no reason to suppose that the argument I present here needs to take up some of Foot's views on these issues. For further discussion v. Hacker-Wright 2018.

11 v. Halbig 2020.

12 v. Thompson 2008, 27–28; Figueroa Rubio 2021, 75–78. Hegel and Aristotle have in common that the mental and the practical refer to animals or individuals, not to a part of them. Moreover, it can be said that there are even more similarities between the ideas of both authors and the argumentation of this text. According to Karen Ng: 'Hegel's naturalism can be construed as formal in the following sense: life, as the immediate actuality of the logical idea, provides the minimal form, shape and categorial structure that makes meaning-making and intelligibility available to self-consciousness, expressing the basic form of all minded activity' (Ng 2018, 26).

within a framework that is related to a biologically and historically defined vital trajectory.

As far as the unity of what takes place is concerned, the changes that occur in the presence of living beings are not a mere sequence of events in the sense that they are a purely mechanical correlation between states of affairs or mere causal relationships, as in weather phenomena in which, for example, the temperature, pressure, and chemical composition of the clouds cause the rain. When a living being is involved in a situation, the correct description changes. According to Michael Thompson in his book *Life and Action*, living things interact with their environment in 'a general scheme of "taking and converting"'.[13] Through their activity, living things bind events together through *life processes*. These processes in turn create units of events and changes in the world that can be described as *vital operations* (e.g., reproduction, growth, hunting) and form complex pathways along which the life process develops.

The operations carried out by individual organisms are part of a larger context: the life form (or species). Each life form has its own characteristic way of reproducing, growing, and so on. The paths open to living beings are rooted in the characteristic features of the life form to which they belong.[14] An agent is thus a 'bearer of a specific life form'[15] and the behaviours that can be interpreted and described as actions imply a specific way of organizing the individual not only as an organism but as a bearer of a life form. Thus, there are some verbs that can be applied to some animals and not to others, and their life form is part of this (e.g., eagles fly but cats do not and cats purr but eagles do not). According to Foot, at this point, we can identify evaluative concepts such as 'goodness' and 'defective' and derive some norms relating to the way individuals should be configured. For example, if we look at the life form of owls, we can say that members of this life form must have night vision and that a particular individual that does not have night vision could be judged as a defective owl.[16] Thinking in terms of life forms is therefore a normative way of thinking; individuals can be configured and act defectively, poorly, exemplarily, and so on.

13 Thompson 2008, 43.

14 Thompson points out that: 'Vital description of individual organisms is itself the primitive expression of a conception of things in terms of "life-form" or "species", and if we want to understand these categories in philosophy we must bring them back to that form of description. If this is right, then, of course, we are wrong to think of the concepts of the various life-forms as reached through abstraction from features of their particular bearers. That notion takes for granted a picture of the terrestrial biosphere as offering us a magazine of living individuals, which we then carve up in accordance with certain principles' (Thompson 2008, 59).

15 Thompson 2008, 28.

16 This does not imply that individuals who do not have night vision are not owls, nor does it mean that they cannot lead a good or successful life. Life forms contain different ways in which individuals can develop their lives. As we will see, life forms are also dependent on individuals using vital processes to survive.

Life forms are actualized by individuals through their actions and survive and evolve thanks to their operations and processes. We can see the importance of agency for species. By solving certain problems in their interaction with the environment, individuals actualize their own species. As Michael Tomasello writes: 'Species biology is supplemented by individual psychology'.[17] The interaction between the life form and psychology defines a set of motivations and ways of doing that produce a way of being in the world that the various life forms have developed. In turn, it is the agential capacities of the individual that enable this to become a reality, a possible adaptation and development in a changing reality. The understanding of agency refers both to abilities and to their exercise in a way that is specific to the life form of the species.

Consequently, life forms and agency are closely connected, and understanding one is essential to understand the other. Furthermore, if we take a closer look at the connections, we see that some fundamental normative concepts depend on them. As Foot points out: 'Whether an individual plant or animal actually succeeds in living the life that it is good to live depends on chance as well as on its own qualities. But its own goodness or defect is conceptually determined by the interaction of natural habitat and natural (species-general) "strategies" for survival and reproduction'[18].

2.3 Social agents

In order to survive, agents must be equipped with what is necessary for interaction with their environment. This means that they must not only be capable of recognizing the progression of certain processes, such as temperature changes, but also to recognize and distinguish the behaviour of other agents and react according to what is necessary for success. This leads us to an important concept that has to do with agency: socialization. The existence of many life forms implies that individuals are equipped with social capacities that enable them to interact with other members of the species.[19] Important life processes depend on these abilities. In addition, some behaviours only make sense in the context of socialization, such as communication, protection from predators in some plant species, and breeding in some mammals.

As philosophers and social thinkers have widely argued, socialization is particularly important for understanding the human life form. Foot indicates that: 'We do not need to be able to dive like gannets, nor to see in the dark like owls; but our memory and concertation must be such as to allow us to learn language, and our sight such that we can recognize faces at a glance; while, like lionesses, human parents are defective if they do not teach their young the

17 Tomasello 2022, 2.
18 Foot 2001, 42.
19 This commonly includes interaction with members of other species. This in turn is related to the fact that there are similarities in certain vital processes between life forms.

skills they need to survive. Moreover, in that we are social animals, we depend on each other as do wolves that hunt in packs, with cooperation such as our own depending on special factors such as conventional arrangements'.[20] Our life form is radically social and members of the species are equipped with what is necessary for a good life in this life form. Contemporary studies in cognitive science, social psychology, and evolutionary anthropology have shown how profound this is.[21]

With this in mind, Michael Tomasello developed a series of studies that show that 'what makes human cognition different is not more individual brainpower, but rather the ability of humans to learn through other persons and their artefacts, and to collaborate with others in collective activities'.[22] In his work with Malinda Carpenter, he suggests that these features of the human life form are associated with a set of cognitive skills that we have in common with other primates, but that the type of socialization present in the human life form has its own peculiarities and determines the way in which human agents develop their lives. According to them: 'what [human evolution] did was to take existing skills of, for example, gaze following, manipulative communication, group action, and social learning, and transform them into their collectively based counterparts of joint attention, cooperative communication, collaborative action, and instructed learning – cornerstones of cultural living. Shared intentionality is a small psychological difference that made a huge difference in human evolution in the way that humans conduct their lives'.[23]

The author suggests that this has specific consequences for morality.[24] First of all, human morality goes beyond the sympathetic concern for others that is present in many other life forms. Our sympathetic concern incorporates not just relatives and friends, but also other collaborative fellows. This is related to a second feature: the high rationalization of such collaborative activities. This second feature is expressed in the generation of norms of fairness between participants in these activities and a sense of dependence on collaborators that generates a sense of 'we' that goes beyond the notion of an 'I' and a 'you'. This in turn requires the development of some psychological skills related to the cognitive process of joint attention, the interactive processes of second-personal agency, and self-regulatory processes of joint commitment.[25]

The human life form endows its members with some skills that enable them to develop a specific kind of agency. Human agency is thus shaped by

20 Foot 2001, 15–16.
21 v. Gallagher 2020; Tomasello, 2008; Timpe 2019; Boyd 2018.
22 Tomasello & Carpenter 2007, 121.
23 Tomasello & Carpenter 2007, 124.
24 v. Tomasello 2016, ch. 2–3.
25 These skills are developed in the interaction with others. (v. Gallagher 2020, ch. 5; Honneth 2008, 40–52; Timpe 2019).

the possibility of generating joint attention, defined as a 'truly intersubjective sharing, [that] is critical because it creates a shared space of common psychological ground that enables everything from collaborative activities with shared goals to human-style cooperative communication'.[26] In that sense, for Shaun Gallagher, joint attention 'is itself a kind of *basic joint action*'.[27]

Additionally, according to Tomasello, communication in humans and primates involves different motivations of the individuals. While chimpanzees and other apes gesticulate to manipulate others, humans do so to helpfully inform others or simply to share experiences with them. Sometimes individual motivations are formed for the sake of sharing or cooperation that appear as purely social motives. These motives make it possible to create a common ground where individuals not only experience the same thing at the same time, but also the knowledge that they are doing it together.

Finally, Tomasello distinguishes between individual intentions (or goals) and social intentions. In our interactions, when I have a particular individual goal that is related to the behaviour or knowledge of others, I must communicate to them what I need from them. This implies the necessity of developing a specific intention directed to the other. If we think in our social motives, we usually communicate to others to request things from them, to inform them, or to share (attitudes and feelings) with them. On the other side of the coin, we have the skills not just to form and express our own goals, but to read the behaviour of others in terms of intentions. The reading of another's intentions is mediated by a common ground that is 'necessary for the recipient to determine both what the communicator is directing attention to (his referential intention) and why he is doing it (his social intention)".[28] Consequently, we are able to generate a 'between us' in which actions acquire meaning and are interpreted. In our daily lives, for example, hand movements are perceived as greetings, insults, or commands, depending on how the common ground guides our reading of others' intentions. The very existence of this common ground shows how important a social environment is in shaping our own intentions and how we interpret the intentions of others.

2.4 Recognition and normativity

Probably the philosophical insight that best grasps those human attributes and shows its importance to the understanding of agency and normativity is the concept of recognition, developed in modernity by some influential philosophers such as Rousseau, Smith, Fichte, and Hegel.[29] In this text, I will focus on the Hegelian version because in his proposal, as in Fichte's, recognition serves

26 Tomasello & Carpenter 2007, 121–122.
27 Gallagher 2020, 109.
28 Tomasello 2008, 75.
29 v. Honneth 2020.

to explain two central issues for the topics discussed in this book: the formation of individuals' self-consciousness and the configuration of normativity in the sense of being bound by norms. In these pages, I will focus only on the second of these two issues.[30]

Recognition operates in the configuration of the normative by taking into account the capacities mentioned in the previous section, especially when these are exercised in concrete interactions with others. It is suggested that if we look at the cognitive and attitudinal elements involved in intersubjective exchanges, we can see how objectivity emerges from them.[31] That allows us to see our species as historical, giving rise to what Hegel called *spirit*. It is historical because the human life form is shaped in concrete intersubjective interactions that are settled in time and space and within which meaning is produced and developed. This implies that meaning is transmitted, renewed, and changed over time for those who participate in interactions. In this context, our actions acquire meaning and are in turn a condition for meaning. The concept of spirit appeals to this aspect of the human life form, both as activity and as historicity. In this picture, the concept of recognition plays an important role. Let us see what it consists of.

Mattias Iser proposes to distinguish between four ways of talking about recognition in contemporary debates.[32] The first of these he calls elementary recognition and consists in the mutual identification of individuals as agents who are able to understand what the other says and does, and to say and do something that the other understands; the second he calls recognition as respect, in which the equal dignity of the other is recognized in moral terms; the third, he calls recognition as esteem or regard, in which the value of certain elements of the identity of individuals or groups that are normally denied by the existence of a dominant group is recognized; and the fourth, he calls recognition as love and friendship, which involves the mutual identification of the need for access to certain affective relationships of care. Elementary recognition is presented as the precondition on which the other three forms are based (to make certain moral, political, or affective demands on others), so I will focus on it.

30 Regarding the first v. Brownleee 2022; Pippin 2011; Tughendhat 1986. The importance of this idea can hardly be overestimated, especially when we consider that concepts such as autonomy and life plan depend on self-consciousness. As can be seen, a Hegelian perspective can easily be combined with a relational concept of autonomy (v. MacKenzie 2021; Quante 2013).

31 The different models of recognition also consider the emotions that human beings experience, the habits they develop, as well as phenomena such as the contagion of emotions and attachment, issues that are often of great importance in the formation of personality through socialization and that are maintained throughout life. Although I will focus on the cognitive side, this does not imply to deny the relevance of these elements of the human life form, or defend the idea that there is a qualitative leap between the different types of abilities, and even less that this leads to a superiority of our species. I do not believe that a correct understanding of the human life form can do without these elements.

32 Iser 2019.

Contemporary interpreters of Hegel's view agree that it is worth bearing in mind that Hegel presents his ideas as superseding some of the ideas presented by Immanuel Kant.[33] This is important not only for the history of ideas, but also because the ideas developed by Kant on concepts such as autonomy and self-consciousness underlie much of today's notions of agency. In his interpretation of Hegel, Robert Brandom begins by pointing out that the concept of autonomy is a central concept in Kant's work, as he seeks to change the understanding of the normative, which prior to the Enlightenment was usually understood on the basis of the concept of *obedience*.[34] The Kantian notion results in a concept of positive freedom that consists in 'our *authority* to *make* ourselves *rationally responsible* by *taking* ourselves to be responsible'.[35] In this picture, the normative attitudes of individuals immediately constitute normative statuses. Therefore, it is understood that 'the capacity to be *bound* by norms and the capacity to *bind ourselves* by norms are one and the same'.[36] This idea, a reflection of individual autonomy, serves not only to explain the force of a norm, but also to determine the content of the commitments that one assumes in identifying and applying the norm. But it is precisely this last point that poses a problem, because if it is precisely the attitude of considering oneself as a being with attitudes that makes it possible to determine the content of these commitments, these specific commitments will be correct to the extent that they seem correct to each individual. This makes it impossible to determine common criteria of correctness, or rather criteria of correctness in the strict sense of the word. The point is that the content of a norm that binds an individual cannot be defined by the individual himself.

It is precisely this problem of Kant's proposal that Hegel has in mind. In this respect, he would suggest that statuses like that of authority and responsibility are primarily social statuses in the sense that they are equally dependent on other-regarding attitudes. Accordingly, the focus should be shifted from the rational integration that an individual realizes to the performance of interpersonal exchanges of mutual recognition.

If we consider the logic of obedience that Kant wishes to overcome, the relevant attitudes are external to the one who obeys, since the central role is played by the person who is obeyed. According to this, there are qualitative differences between people, and some have a status that others do not have, a status that empowers them to say what is and what is not in the world and to create the rules that should apply to all. The emancipation proposed by Kant

33 Among the representative authors of this neo-Hegelian thread are Robert Brandom (Brandom 2019), Axel Honneth (Honneth 1995), and Robert Pippin (Pippin 2008). They generally focus on the interpretation of what Hegel said in his 1807 book *The Phenomenology of Spirit*.

34 This notion is common to Kant and Rousseau (v. Brandom 2009, 60–63; 2019, ch.9; Honneth 2014, part A; Schneewind 1998, ch. 22–23).

35 Brandom 2009, 63.

36 Brandom 2009, 63.

places each individual at the centre and gives them equal status as autonomous beings, a status that is independent of what others say or do. For Hegel, both ways of understanding the question are unsatisfactory. For him, one must consider both one's own attitudes and that of others in order to account for both the force and the possibility of determining the content of a norm. This requires two (or more) persons who take the stance towards each other of those who make commitments and are able to create norms, and the stance of those who demand commitments from others and accept them as norm-makers. In this way, they become, in an elementary sense, co-creators of norms and thus of the determination of the commitments they make when acting.

This last form of relationship is exactly what recognition is about. In a basic sense, agents are only responsible if others hold them responsible and only exercise authority if others accept this authority. Recognizing someone means considering her as a subject with normative status and assuming that she can take responsibility and exercise authority. The philosophical point is that the only way to ensure this is through mutual relations (of recognition).

In this context, an individual can attribute many kinds of attitudes to others. In a very minimal sense, which Brandom calls simple recognition, recognition involves attributing to the other the authority to determine how things are. However, there is also a robust notion of recognition in which one attributes to the other the authority to be a recognizer.[37] This step is fundamental because recognizing others as recognizers means accepting the authority of their recognition for oneself by recognizing the one who recognizes.

In relations of recognition, the other is thus seen as someone who can make commitments and demand them from us. This means that we attribute statuses such as 'authority', 'committed', or 'responsible' to them and understand that they can also attribute those statuses to us. This implies that the one who is recognized as having these statuses by saying or doing something is considered capable of saying or doing something correctly (i.e., an authority), which in turn implies that if she says or does something she can be held responsible for it (e.g., she can be called to give answers or she can be reproved for the consequences of what she does). So, when we act, we make commitments to others for which we can be called to respond, which is supported by the fact that we are seen as authorities. In turn, we do the same to others. Thus, in these interactions, we shape the standards that define what actions are right or wrong, what commitments we make, what we are accountable for, and so on.

A central point is that such status do not come with the world. They are not natural in the sense that they do not exist independently of our concrete behaviour in the course of history. We must treat each other as those who can make and claim commitments in order to constitute them. The status are communal.[38]

37 v. Brandom 2019, 253–258.

38 This does not mean that it is not part of a life form, as we have seen.

At the same time, it is the exercise of our agency that produces this form of normativity. Thus, the kind of interaction involved in this agential dynamic becomes a constitutive element of ideas such as responsibility and authority and helps to form the 'between us' in which the behaviour of others becomes intentional actions.[39]

As I have already mentioned, a key element of the Hegelian proposal is historicity. This is related to two things that are important for understanding some of the institutions and normative structures in which we live. The first point is that the determination that something is correct, as well as the making of a commitment is not something that is plucked out of the air, but is formed in our exchanges. This can be understood as a general thesis about normativity, but it can be clearly seen in four phenomena of our normative lives: social norms, promises, forgiveness, and apologies.[40] The first is grounded in attitudes that we repeatedly adopt in relation to patterns of behaviour, the second is based on the existence of future actions to which we commit ourselves, and the last two are grounded in the existence of past events that are seen as a violation of a norm and an attempt to prospectively restore the relationship between the parties involved. These structures and phenomena are in turn behind legal institutions such as precedents, legal customs, contracts, and pardons.[41] These concepts make sense when there is more than one agent and require a series of actions that take place within historically intersubjective relations.

The second insight that emerges from the inclusion of historicity is that the meaning of the actions we perform and the judgements we make are embedded in a socio-historical background of interactions in which meaning and personal identity take place. Honneth refers to institutions of recognition (e.g.,

39 As Robert Brandom points out: 'To recognize someone is to take or treat that individual in practice as a self: a knowing and acting subject, hence as subject to normative assessment as potentially committed, responsible, authoritative, and so on' (Brandom 2019, 246). If I treat the other as an authority and see that the other does this to me, it makes sense to define together what there is and what there is not, as well as what we are. This gives rise to the idea of self-consciousness when applying such categories to oneself, a self whose actions are limited by the norms that define what there is and who we are. Thus, the self is partly presented as something confirmed (or to be confirmed) by others. Hegel argues that this can be understood on the basis of a struggle for recognition that arises from the need for two consciousnesses to interact in a characteristic way: one (can) question the claims of the other as consciousness presenting itself to the world, creating a conflict that opens up the need for mutual corroboration of the claims being made. In this interrelation, both constitute themselves through mutual exhortation and understand themselves as individuals with normative claims (v. Honneth 1995, ch. 1–3). A further consequence of this is that individuals develop self-authorization as soon as they are recognized by a recognizer, which has consequences for the configuration of autonomy (v. Mackenzie 2021).

40 v. Anscombe 1991; Gilbert 1996, ch. 13; Radzik 2009; Brennan et al. 2013. For a more comprehensive project on various aspects of morality, see Wallace 2019.

41 v. Brandom 2013; Kimel 2005; Gilbert 1996; Bratman 2022; Brennan et al. 2013; Radzik 2009; Nedelsky 2012.

language) to explain the social context that generates the conditions for the production of meaningful interactions. These institutions form the context in which individuals are educated and develop their lives.[42] The members of the human life form are born into a social world that is already in progress and develop their personality by using their social skills in interaction with others, by integrating themselves and shaping history. The social background offers limits on what can be the subject of disagreement and makes it possible to distinguish between different types of judgements and actions and attribute them to others and to oneself.

Simultaneously, the background is reproduced through the actions of the participants. As José Medina emphasizes: 'This background agreement is incessantly renewed by the repetitive agency of speakers. There is a constant performative regeneration of the underlying consensus shared by the members of a linguistic practice. According to pragmatic contextualism, meanings are as stable as the background consensus that sustain them'.[43] Such interactions are sustained by the skills, attitudes, and actions that form the elementary recognition. The norms that form the background depend on their actualization by agents who recognize the authority of these norms, submit to them, and apply them. This application does not have to be always conscious or intentional, yet it is configured by the behaviour and attitudes of the agents. In this sense, this background is not immutable and some normative categories such as 'oppression' and 'resistance' are meaningful precisely for this reason.[44]

The adoption of the so called 'we-mode' in social ontology[45] can easily be accommodated in a social model of agency such as the one presented here. The ability both to form and recognize social motives and to interpret behaviour in terms of social intentions enables the realization of a multiplicity of joint activities, including the possibility to act in agreement with others, to be seen as an authority, and to be held responsible. Looking at language as a model of practical normativity, Brandom argues that language can be seen as a model of freedom, in the sense that we can potentially create infinite combinations of words and new expressions within language, but this is only possible if we are bound by norms in a structure of mutual recognition with others.[46] This has the political consequence that the loss of negative freedom that results from being bound to social norms is constituted as an increase in positive expressive freedom. This in turn makes it possible to add elements to the language and make changes that form a linguistic history. Much more work is needed to explain in detail how this works. For now, it suffices to point out the fruitfulness of this approach.

42 v. Honneth 2014, 45.
43 Medina 2006, 30.
44 v. Khalidi 2014; Cudd 2006.
45 Gilbert 1996; Bratman 2022.
46 v. Brandom 2019, 514–523

2.5 Action and responsibility

On the basis of the neo-Aristotelian and neo-Hegelian ideas presented so far, I would now like to revisit the problem of the relationship between action and responsibility presented in Section 2.1. Let me first briefly return to the relationship between agency and socialization.

Interaction with others is of great importance in shaping the various facets of agency. Kevin Timpe has developed an ecological theory of agency that takes this into account. He points out that many of the individual abilities associated with agency depend on social factors. The author illustrates this idea with studies that show how akinesia manifests in different ways in people diagnosed with Parkinson's disease, depending on the context in which the movements are performed. If the person has to initiate the movements herself, they have much greater difficulty than if they are performed on command or in other contexts involving socially mediated interactions. Shaun Gallagher points to a similar issue in relation to certain ideomotor apraxias, where motor control improves in contexts in which actions have a social significance.[47]

For our purposes, however, it is important to point out that the role of socialization goes beyond this, because it is not only about the development of motor and linguistic skills, but also about the organization of an entire symbolic framework that is shaped by society and which individuals internalize through various socialization processes. The interactions within a society generate the content of how one interprets one's own actions and those of others. By sharing and talking about our own behaviour and the behaviour of others, we learn how to perform and interpret actions. In doing so, we apply concepts and name what is done: 'walking', 'eating', 'promising'. When we say that someone has acted intentionally, this attribution is supported by the way we interpret the behaviour of others on the basis of the social norms that are part of both the explicit agreements and the background against which we act. When we say that someone has done something with a certain intention, we tie their behaviour into a narrative which includes their intentions and plans. Thus, we use terms such as 'lying', 'caring', and 'cheating' that give meaning to what we do by framing it within a social context that allows us to attribute intentions based on the significance of the behaviour in that context. This narrative, in turn, generates the space in which it makes sense to ask about the reasons that lead individuals to adopt one course of action over another. This is related to the development of exchanges in which actions can be explained and justified. This leads to the formation of practical commitments that shape our

47 v. Timpe 2019; Gallagher 2020, ch. 2. This is related to something very important: If we understand that our abilities depend heavily on society, it is our social responsibility to create the conditions for their development. So, when we talk about a good life, we do not necessarily mean a life that disabled individuals cannot achieve. On the contrary, by recognizing our weaknesses, vulnerabilities, and dependencies as part of our life form, we can face ableism (v. Taylor 2017; Shoemaker 2022).

personality. The intentions, reasons, and practical commitments that agents develop are therefore formed through socialization.[48]

Now we can recall the ascriptivist idea that to attribute an action is to attribute responsibility. After what we have said about recognition, it is easy to see that there is a very basic idea behind the connection proposed by the asciptivists: since actions are meaningful behaviour in interpersonal contexts, if our behaviour is understood as an action, we are treated as responsible individuals. This is a very important idea, but it is also very general. It does not clearly state the implications of the kind of responsibility that is involved. The answer to this last concern is given by the ascriptivists, as we saw in the first section. For Hart, the relevant sense of responsibility is the moral and legal idea of liability, in which a person is accused of having done something wrong in order to be sanctioned for it. The problem with this thesis is that there seem to be ways of attributing actions that are not related to this kind of context.

To cover a wider range of contexts, Joel Feinberg distinguishes five meanings that the expression 'ascription of responsibility' can have: as ascriptions of causal responsibility, as ascriptions of causal agency, as ascriptions of simple agency, as ascriptions of faulty actions, and as liability. They all represent ways in which agency is associated with responsibility. The last two seem to be included in Hart's proposal. They imply the evaluation of the action as morally or legally wrong and are associated with the imposition of a sanction. An important point is that in these two types of ascription we attribute agency and at the same time assign responsibility. Thus, a faulty action, then, is an action that occurs through a defective exercise of agency. And the norms that are used for this judgement are those that have arisen historically to signify our behaviour. To explain this, Feinberg says that these attributions can be understood as entries in the agent's record.[49] For example, if someone says, 'Sarah cheated', they are adding an entry to Sarah's record as a player that tarnishes her reputation and probably warrants punishment. Sarah can defend herself by saying that what happened was not cheating, but a valid move in the game. If Sarah is successful, the action will not be recorded on her record.

The other three meanings seem to be relevant in order to go beyond Hart's original idea. As for the first, straightforward ascriptions of causality, it does not seem to be specifically linked to actions, but to occur in the context of responsibility when something happens that violates a norm. This type of attribution allows us to assign responsibility for the consequences of wrongdoing in cases where the link to agency is not defined by a direct exercise of agential powers, but can be associated to the practical commitments of people.[50]

In cases where causal agency is ascribed, the attribution of causality takes on a special significance. According to Feinberg, it is very common to attribute

48 v. Haslanger 2020; Vargas 2020; Webster 2021.
49 v. Feinberg 1970, 124.
50 v. Figueroa Rubio 2024.

complex causal relations between events to agents as a unit. To do this, we use verbs that express that these complex relationships are meaningful. So, for example, if a person lights a match and throws it into a pool of petrol, causing a combustion that results in a house burning down, it makes sense to say that the person burnt the house down. We describe what happens as a single occurrence (e.g., 'Sarah burnt the house down'), even though there are many events that are causally connected. We use our concepts and use verbs to express this unity. For Feinberg, the way our concepts are expressed in verbs generates an accordion effect, as they expand and contract the number of events and relevant factors considered in order to talk about an action without it losing its unity. In his words 'because of the accordion effect, we can usually replace any ascription of causal responsibility to a person by an ascription of agency or authorship' (Feinberg 1970, 134). Accordingly, the attribution of responsibility in terms of causation can imply the attribution of authorship, and this means not only describing events, but speaking in agential terms. Finally, in ascriptions of simple agency are attributed actions which do not involve complex causal scenarios, but actions that are directly identified by the individual's behaviour, such as smiling. On this point, Feinberg says that: 'to be responsible for one's simply actions is only to be properly identifiable as their doer' (Feinberg 1970, 139). As we can see, in the last two meanings, we ascribe responsibility for actions without implying that we accuse the agent of a wrong or that she is sanctioned for it. Nevertheless, in both cases we can see how actions, intentions, and responsibility are linked.

We attribute actions in different contexts and thereby express that someone is responsible for them: as a causal agent, as a faulty agent, as a liable agent, etc. These attributions are conveyed through our language. So, when something happens, we have linguistic tools to attribute it to ourselves and others (as *doings*). This generates a space for discussion in which disagreements about what happened are possible.[51]

The key idea is that our language of responsibility works not only in contexts involving accusations and sanctions, but also when we want to make sense of what happens in causal terms and this is also related to agency and action. Feinberg shows that we use the concepts that refer to types of action (expressed in verbs) as glue for reality. When we do this, we simultaneously attribute agency and responsibility, thus rescuing Hart's original idea about the internal connection between action and responsibility. Feinberg concludes that 'for all kinds of action sentences, there is some context in which they can be used adscriptively, that is, to identify "the author"'.[52] This is a response to Pitcher's concerns by applying a pluralist view to the relationship between

51 For example, there could be disagreement about whether what happened can be registered in someone's records and under what name, or there could be a disagreement between the individual intention and the social intention expressed in the behaviour.

52 Feinberg 1970, 139.

action and responsibility that opens the door to different ways of talking about the terms related to responsibility, such as 'taking responsibility', 'assigning responsibility', 'making responsible', 'culpability', 'blame', 'exceptions', and 'excuses'.[53]

Finally, we can identify a series of actions and activities that are expressed in our verbs and represent part of what constitutes the human life form, socially and culturally configurated. Humans eat, dress, walk, promise, burn houses down, discuss, and so on. By identifying these manifestations of our life form, we can assess the performance of individuals and identify different types of deficiencies and excellences. For example, individuals can eat, walk, and dress better or worse, and they can fail in their intention to do these things. When these actions are interpreted in the context of liability responsibility, they can be interpreted as faulty actions, as violations of a norm, or as failures of the person's character. This introduces new evaluative verbs that show how action and responsibility interact and shape the normative landscape in which our actions are understood as actions. Furthermore, the diversity of ways of talking about being responsible for the exercise of agency grounds more complex normative phenomena such as joint commitments.

On these pages I have proposed a plural ascriptivist model supported by a weak constitutivism based on the social aspects of agency. The model is modest in the sense that it can probably only explain some normative concepts (e.g., promises, commitments, oppression, resistance), but at the same time it allows us to understand that these concepts cannot be understood outside of sociality. Moreover, the model is useful to see how our normative concepts operate at different levels within sociality.

Not only can this model account for a weak constitutivist view that supports the ascriptivist thesis, as I have argued, but it can also provide arguments in favour of the idea that 'we cannot but be agents, that agency is not optional' (Ferrero 2009, 304).[54] This is supported by the fact that the exercise of agency is a manifestation of our historical life form. In this sense, if an individual chooses not to identify intentions or manifest them in their behaviour, and furthermore chooses to be outside any kind of elementary relationship of recognition, we can hardly speak of her as someone who performs meaningful actions, and a central part of our life form would be missing, leading to a difficulty in developing her personality and identity. We can hardly say that this kind of life is optional given the kind of animal we are. On the other hand, if we see and treat somebody as incapable of participating in an exchange characterized by recognition, we run the risk of reifying her and treating her as an object, and that can be seen as a socially defective way of treating others (by

53 The discussions surrounding these concepts also characterize the way we understand personality. v. Quante 2013; Figueroa Rubio 2024.

54 This argument is related to the *agency/shmagency* objection presented by David Enoch (Enoch 2006).

denying their agency and personality).[55] In this way, a social constitutivism can not only refer to the conditions under which it makes sense to speak of human agency (and how it is shaped in normativity as it shapes it), but also help us to think about normative institutions and concepts whose content is only possible if we understand ourselves within a social life form.[56]

References

Anscombe, Gertrude Elizabeth Margaret. 1991. "On Promising and its Justice". In *Collected Philosophical Papers, vol III: Ethics, Religion and Politics.* Anscombe, Gertrude Elizabeth Margaret, 61. Minneapolis: Wiley-Blackwell.

Austin, John Langshaw. 1979. *Philosophical Papers*, edited by J. O Urmson and G. J. Warnock. 3rd ed. New York: Oxford University Press.

Bertea, Stefano. 2013. "Constitutivism and Normativity: A Qualified Defence". *Philosophical Explorations: An International Journal for the Philosophy of Mind and Action* 16 (1): 81–95.

Blöser, Claudia, Mikae Janvid, Hannes Ole Matthiessen, and Marcus Willaschek, eds. 2013. *Defeasibility in Philosophy: Knowledge, Agency, Responsibility, and the Law.* New York: Editions Rodopi.

Boyd, Rrobert. 2018. *A Different Kind of Animal.* Princeton: Princeton University Press.

Brandom, Robert. 2009. *Reason in Philosophy.* Cambridge, London: Belknap Press.

Brandom, Robert. 2013. "A Hegelean Model of Legal Concept Determination. The Normative Fine Structure of the Judges´ Chain Novel". In *Pragmatism, Law and Language*, edited by G. Hubbs, and D. Lind, 19–39. Abingdon: Routledge.

Brandom, Robert. 2019. *A Spirit of Trust.* Cambridge, London: Harvard University Press.

Bratman, Michael. 2022. *Shared and Institutional Agency: Toward a Planning Theory of Human Practical Organization.* Oxford: Oxford University Press.

Brennan, Geoffrey, Lina Eriksson, Robert E. Goodin, and Nicholas Southwood. 2013. *Explaining Norms.* Oxford: Oxford University Press.

Brownlee, Timothy. 2022. *Recognition and the Self in Hegel's Phenomenology of Spirit.* New York: Cambridge University Press.

Cudd, Anne. 2006. *Analyzing Oppression.* New York: Oxford University Press.

55 v. Honneth 2008; Brandom 2019; Gallagher 2020, 198. This point was made by P.F. Strawson in his famous essay 'Freedom and Resentment' (v. Hieronymi 2020, who identifies this perspective as social naturalism).

56 The author would like to thank Carlos González Bellene and Matilde Rey Aramendia, as well as the audiences in Madrid and Santiago, where some of the ideas contained in the text were discussed.

This article has benefited from Project N. 2024/00209/001, *Justicia ecológica y nuevas vulnerabilidades: desafíos jurídicos globales* funded by the State Research Agency, Spain (Agencia Estatal de Investigación, AEI), as well as from Project N. 101086202 (Speak4Nature), HORIZON-MSCA-2021-SE-01, funded by the European Union. Views and opinions expressed are, however, those of the author only and do not necessarily reflect those of the European Union. Neither the EU nor the granting authority can be held responsible for them.

Davidson, Donald. 1980. *Essays on Actions and Events.* Oxford: Oxford University Press.

Duarte d'Almeida, Luis. 2015. *Allowing for Exceptions. A Theory of Defences and Defeasibility in Law.* Oxford. Oxford University Press.

Enoch, David. 2006. "Agency, Shmagency: Why Normativity Won't Come from What Is Constitutive of Action". *Philosophical Review* 115 (2): 169–198.

Enoch, David. 2020. "Constitutivism: On Rabbits, Hats, And Holy Grails". In *The Routledge Handbook of Practical Reason*, edited by Ruth Chang and Kurt Sylvan, 336–348. New York: Routledge.

Feinberg, Joel. 1970. *Doing and Deserving.* Princeton: Princeton University Press.

Ferrero, Luca. 2009. "Constitutivism and the Inescapability of Agency". In *Oxford Studies in Metaethics 4*, edited by Russ Shafer-Landau, 303–333. Oxford: Oxford University Press.

Figueroa Rubio, Sebastián. 2021. "Acción, expresión y atribución de estados mentales". In *Razonamiento jurídico y ciencias cognitivas*, edited by Arena, Federico, Pau Luque, and Diego Moreno, 54–99. Bogotá: Universidad Externado de Colombia.

Figueroa Rubio, Sebastián. 2024. "Ascriptivism, Norms, and Negligence". In *Oxford Studies in Agency and Responsibility Volume 8: Non-Ideal Agency and Responsibility*, edited by David Shoemaker, Santiago Amaya, and Manuel Vargas, 126–148. Oxford: Oxford University Press.

Foot, Philippa. 2001. *Natural Goodness.* Oxford: Oxford University Press.

Gallagher, Shaun. 2020. *Action and Interaction.* Oxford: Oxford University Press.

Gilbert, Margaret. 1996. *Living Together.* New York: Rowan & Littlefield Publishers.

Hacker-Wright, John, ed. 2018. *Philippa Foot on Goodness and Virtue.* London: Palgrave MacMillan.

Halbig, Christoph. 2020. "Aristotelian Naturalism as Metaethics". In *Martin Aristotelian Naturalism*, edited by Martin Hähnel, 81–90. Cham: Springer Nature.

Hart, Herbert Lionel Adolphus. 1949. "The Ascription of Responsibility and Rights". *Proceedings of the Aristotelian Society* 49: 174–194.

Hart, Herbert Lionel Adolphus. 1968. *Punishment and Responsibility.* Oxford: Oxford University Press.

Haslanger, Sally. 2020. "Practical Reason and Social Practices". In *The Routledge Handbook of Practical Reason*, edited by Ruth Chang and Kurt Sylvan, 68–82. New York: Routledge.

Hieronymi, Pamela. 2020. *Freedom, Resentment & The Metaphysics of Morals.* Princeton: Princeton University Press.

Honneth, Axel. 1995. *The Struggle for Recognition.* Oxford: Polity Press.

Honneth, Axel. 2008. *Reification.* Oxford: Oxford University Press.

Honneth, Axel. 2014. *Freedom's Right: The Social Foundations of Democratic Life.* Columbia, New York: University Press.

Honneth, Axel. 2020. *Recognition. A Chapter in the History of European Ideas.* Cambridge: Cambridge University Press.

Iser, Mattias. 2019. "Recognition". In The Stanford Encyclopedia of Philosophy, edited by Edward N. Zalta, Summer 2019 Edition. Accessed May 14, 2024. https://plato.stanford.edu/archives/sum2019/entries/recognition/.

Khalidi, Muhammad Ali. 2014. "Three Kinds of Social Kinds". *Philosophy and Phenomenological Research* 90 (1): 96–112.

Kimel, Dori. 2005. *From Promise to Contract Towards a Liberal Theory of Contract.* Oregon: Hart Publishing.

Mackenzie, Catriona. 2021. "Relational Autonomy". In *The Oxford Handbook of Feminist Philosophy*, edited by Kim Q. Hall and Ásta, 374–385. Oxford: Oxford University Press.

Medina, José. 2006. *Speaking from Elsewhere*. Albany: State University of New York Press.

Nedelsky, Jennifer. 2012. *Law's Relations: A Relational Theory of Self, Autonomy, and Law*. New York: Oxford University Press.

Ng, Karen. 2018. "Life and Mind in Hegel's Logic and Subjective Spirit". *Hegel Bulletin* 39 (1): 23–44.

Pippin, Robert B. 2008. *Hegel's Practical Philosophy*. Cambridge: Cambridge University Press.

Pippin, Robert B. 2011. "On Hegel's Claim That Self-Consciousness Is "Desire Itself"". In *Recognition and Social Ontology*, edited by H. Ikäheimo and A. Laitinen, 53–84. Leiden: Brill.

Pitcher, George. 1960. "Hart on Action and Responsibility". *The Philosophical Review* 69: 226–235.

Quante, Michael. 2013. "Being Identical by Being (Treated as) Responsible". In *Autonomy and the Self. Philosophical Studies Series*, edited by M. Kühler and N. Jelinek, vol. 118, 253–271. Dordrecht: Springer.

Radzik, Linda. 2009. *Making Amends. Atonement in Morality, Law, and Politics*. New York: Oxford University Press.

Schneewind, Jerome B. 1998. *The Invention of Autonomy: A History of Modern Moral Philosophy*. Cambridge: Cambridge University Press.

Shoemaker, David. 2022. "Disordered, Disabled, Disregarded, Dismissed: The Moral Costs of Exemptions from Accountability". In *Agency in Mental Disorder: Philosophical Dimensions*, edited by Matt King and Joshua May, 33–62. Oxford: Oxford University Press.

Smith, Michael. 2018. "Constitutivism". In *The Routledge Handbook of Metaethics*, edited by Tristram McPherson, and David Plunkett, 371–384. New York: Routledge.

Sneddon, Andrew. 2006. *Action and Responsibility*. Cham: Springer.

Southwood, Nicholas. 2018. "Constructivism about Practical Reasons". In *The Oxford Handbook of Reasons and Normativity*, edited by Daniel Star, 342–346. Oxford: Oxford University Press.

Stoecker, Ralf. 2007. "Action and Responsibility – A Second Look at Ascriptivism". In *Intentionality, Deliberation and Autonomy. The Action-Theoretic Basis of Practical Philosophy*, edited by Sandro Nannini and Christoph Lumer, 35–46. London, Vereinigtes Königreich: Routledge.

Taylor, Sunaura. 2017. *Beasts of Burden: Animal and Disability Liberation*. New York: The New Press.

Thompson, Michael. 2008. *Life and Action*. Cambridge, MA: Harvard University Press.

Timpe, Kevin. 2019. "Moral Ecology, Disabilities, and Human Agency". *Res Philosophica* 93 (4): 767–796.

Tomasello, Michael. 2008. *Origins of Human Communication*. Cambridge, MA: MIT Press.

Tomasello, Michael. 2016. *A Natural History of Human Morality*. Cambridge, MA: Harvard University Press.

Tomasello, Michael. 2022. *The Evolution of Agency*. Cambridge, MA: MIT Press.

Tomasello, Michael, and Carpenter, Malinda. 2007. “Shared intentionality”. *Developmental Science* 10 (1): 121–125.

Tugendhat, Ernst. 1986. *Self-Consciousness and Self-Determination*. Cambridge, MA: Mit Press.

Vargas, Manuel. 2020. “Negligence and Social Self-Governance”. In *Surrounding Self Control*, edited by Alfred Mele, 400–420. Oxford: Oxford University Press.

Wallace, R. Jay. 2019 *The Moral Nexus*. Princeton: Princeton University Press.

Webster, Aness K. 2021. “Socially Embedded Agency: Lessons from Marginalized Identities”. In *Oxford Studies in Agency and Responsibility 7*, edited by David Shoemaker, 104–129. Oxford: Oxford University Press.

3 Moral ignorance, wrongness, and responsibility for negligent actions that arise due to ‘belonging to a group’

Steps towards an Aristotelian constitutivism

Veronica Rodriguez-Blanco[1]

3.1 Introduction

In this chapter, I extrapolate two important theories of responsibility for negligent actions that apply to individual actions to explain the character of responsibility in relation to an action that takes place in the context of group ‘belonging’, i.e., the ‘reasonable expectations’ view and ‘the responsibility as answerability’ conception. These theories might seem promising as a means of explaining the problem of responsibility for negligence that arises due to moral ignorance resulting from ‘group belonging’. I will show, however, that they fail to explain the phenomenon in an adequate way. I also reflect on the lessons we can learn from our *via negativa*.

3.2 John, the son of a slave owner in the 19th century

Let us think about the following example. John is the son of a slave owner living in an imaginary land in the 19th century. He has just inherited his father’s landed estate and chattels, including the slaves. However, John chooses neither this style of life nor born into these particular circumstances and social context. When he was young slavery abolitionists started to propagate ideas of freedom, dignity, and equality for all human beings. Furthermore, John achieved a decent level of education as his father insisted on giving him the best possible opportunities and education through private tutors and attendance at university. John’s father’s idea was that educating John would give him good returns, i.e., John could successfully continue his business, which concentrated on the cultivation and production of tobacco.

1 I am grateful to Herlinde Pauer-Studer, Nathan Biebel, Niels de Haan, Olof Leffler, Lars Moen, Grace Patterson, and Anne Schwenkenbecher for comments and discussion on the topic of the paper. This research was funded by the European Union’s Horizon 2020 research and innovation programme under grant agreement No 740922, ERC Advanced Research Grant “The Normative and Moral Foundations of Group Agency”, University of Vienna.

DOI: 10.4324/9781032670553-4

One day, one of John's slaves, Betty, committed a misdemeanour, i.e., she stole a precious watch, and John imposed on her a strict punishment, i.e., more than 30 lashes. On that day John decided to carry out the flogging himself and, blinded by his anger and the circumstances, put too much strength on the whip as his anger took him over. Betty survived the chastisement but after a few days her wounds became infected, she developed a high fever and died. John killed Betty negligently, but not intentionally. At that time and in that place John was not considered to be legally responsible for Betty's death as slaves were chattel and therefore his property, and he could do what he liked with his property. However, is he ethically responsible? John belonged to a group, slave owners, who possessed a set of firm convictions and beliefs regarding the ownership and treatment of slaves. At that time and in that place slaves were chattel and, like cattle or other things in the land, could be used, sold, destroyed, and moved around as the owner wished. John did not know and, arguably, *could not have known better.*

3.3 A satisfactory account of negligent action

A satisfactory and sound account of John's negligent actions needs to provide a reasonable and powerful picture of the basic features of the phenomenology of inadvertent actions, which can be formulated as follows:

Inattention/inadvertence

1) Cases of pure negligence are grounded on inattention or inadvertence
   Non-intentional
2) The agent is engaged in the performing of the action and her deliberative stance is crucial, but paradoxically, she brings about a state of affairs that is non-intended
   Trivial
3) At the moment of performing the action, the part of the action that involves the inadvertence or error is seen as trivial from the perspective of the agent

Blameworthiness grounded on failing to act according to a standard

4) Blameworthiness is grounded on the idea that there are objective standards or a right action and that the negligent action falls below the standard or involves a wrong action

Failure to grasp the objective standard or the right action

5) At the moment of the performance of the action, the agent fails to grasp the objective standard or the right action.

John's actions while flogging Betty were grounded on inattention. He started the action by being angry and his anger took over; unintentionally he put too much strength on the whip. At the moment of the action John sees his movements as trivial. He or his men apply this chastisement to slaves as part of a routine and it is rare for a slave to die from a flogging. However, features 4 and 5 are not straightforwardly applicable to John's negligent action and therefore the standard of right action as both guidance for John's action and to determine responsibility for negligent action are not present. Somehow John's responsibility for negligence that arises due to moral ignorance is not detachable from his belonging to a certain group. The group possesses false beliefs and his moral ignorance cannot be severed from the group and their false beliefs. The group of slave owners falsely believed that human beings could be owned and therefore that adjectives such as 'unjust' or 'just' could not be applied to actions in the context of these human beings. It seems that our judgements of responsibility for John's negligence are closely connected to judgements of responsibility concerning the group. His failure to grasp an objective standard of action, e.g., respect for all human beings, arises *because he belongs to a group that thinks and engages with the world in specific ways.* This is a strange thought but one that possesses a force and an appeal. It is strange to say that a judgement about his ethical responsibility, something that is *essentially individual*, for a negligent action which arises because John 'could not have known better', applies to everyone belonging to a certain group. Let us say that John, Peter, Steve, Frank, Thomas, Alexander, William, and Samuel are all sons of slave owners and have inherited their fathers' land and their respective chattels, including the slaves. Their wrong could not have been committed but because of their belonging to a group where certain beliefs and traditions were shaped. We need to determine what this idea entails.

These men are morally ignorant, arguably, but they have committed these wrongs due to the fact that their moral ignorance was shaped by 'belonging to a certain group'. The standard theories of collective action are grounded on the idea of shared knowledge and/or shared intention; however, in the case of John's action and his potential ethical negligence there is a lack of knowledge and moral knowledge. Precisely, the key feature of negligence is that there is *no knowledge*, *no intention*, and therefore, no shared intention. Consequently standard theories of collective responsibility do not help with this case.

To explicate negligence for actions that arise due to moral ignorance by 'belonging to a group' we look at two theories which were not explicitly advanced to address the question of responsibility qua belonging to a group, but which can be extrapolated from for these purposes without much modification. We demonstrate that they are deficient and through this *via negativa* we show the potential theoretical underpinnings of responsibility for negligence due to moral ignorance that arise from 'belonging to a group'.

3.4 The 'reasonable expectations' solution

William Fitzpatrick (Fitzpatrick 2008) defends the view that in cases of responsibility for negligent actions due to moral ignorance what we need to identify is the *normative* element of the action within the temporality of the agency instead of the *cognitive* aspect of this same temporality. For him the key to unlocking responsibility for negligence is to understand what agents are *reasonably expected to do prior* to acting to address or remedy their normative ignorance. The problem is that in many cases of alleged pure negligence, in which the wrong is not present for the agent, the agent is immersed in a moral outlook or vision that keeps him ignorant of any moral or normative knowledge regarding the action in question. In other words the agent has no opportunities to improve his moral position. Thus, for example, young people educated under the *Hitlerjugend* programme were morally ignorant of the value of tolerance of other races; the son of a dictator in a totalitarian regime is morally ignorant concerning the freedom of speech of others; and a woman educated by the Taliban, which is a repressive and extremely traditional society, is ignorant of women's rights. These are all examples of people immersed in and educated under a narrow normative landscape and, if we follow Fitzpatrick, we cannot reasonably expect them to do something to remedy their moral ignorance. If they act due to their moral ignorance we cannot expect them to act in a different way and, therefore, they are not responsible.

We only need, however, according to Fitzpatrick, to establish that the agent could have *reasonably* been expected to do something to address or remedy his moral or normative ignorance. In this way we could have reasonably expected her to act differently to the way she did. The example provided by Fitzpatrick illustrates his point. Mr Potter is a successful businessman and a ruthless capitalist. He is the product of a bad moral education, but his life was normal in other ways. He has normal capacities and has been exposed to normal social and intellectual development, and opportunities to learn about moral visions that oppose his own. There have been plenty of opportunities for him to learn about better ways of behaving and to appreciate other moral perspectives. Potter, however, engages in negligent actions that are harmful towards his employees. Unlike the case of the young Nazi, the son of the dictator, or the women brought up under the Taliban regime, we can reasonably expect him to do something to remedy his moral ignorance. Nevertheless, Mr Potter did not take these opportunities and as a consequence his behaviour shows vices. Fitzpatrick tells us that Mr Potter is responsible for these vices because we could reasonably expect people to take the given opportunities and acquire moral knowledge. He should have remedied his moral or normative ignorance. Note, however, that these vices are conceived as epistemic vices that might or might not result from vices of character. Following our example, John is not an isolated case. Peter, Steve, Frank, Thomas, Alexander, William, and Samuel are all sons of slave owners. We could argue that we reasonably expect them to take opportunities to learn and acquire moral knowledge. John, for example, is an educated man and during his time at university he met a number of abolitionists and attended a meeting where ideas on freedom and the equality of all human beings were intelligently discussed. We expect John, who was brought up in normal conditions, to take this opportunity and change his beliefs.

Socrates's view on *tecnne* or skills is the key constitutive feature to acquire moral knowledge. According to this view, the focus of change and transformation is true beliefs and, more specifically, the acquisition of true moral beliefs and therefore, moral knowledge (Plato 1976). The 'art of measurement' as a skill can save us and Socrates believes that this art can be taught. Like Socrates, Aristotle thought that reason and moral knowledge play a key part in learning to be good, but also emphasized that we need to transform our character, desires, and passions. However, like the Socratic view on moral knowledge, Fitzpatrick offers us a *non-realist* psychological picture of learning and becoming good. Mr Potter's development of a vicious character is due to his lack of engagement with opportunities *to learn moral propositions or true moral beliefs.* This depicts a conception of agency far from our own experience and phenomenology of learning to be good. One potential interpretation of Fiztpatrick's view would be that it is through *will* that we choose or decide to engage or not with moral truth and acquire the required cognitive and moral knowledge. He states, '*I will defend an alternative view that appeals instead to facts about personal capabilities, social opportunities for acquiring knowledge, and the role of voluntary exercises of vices in certain failures to fulfil epistemic obligations*' (Fitzpatrick 2008, 590). This is a voluntarist position concerning vices and virtues (Fitzpatrick 2008, 608).[2] The problem with any voluntarist explanation is that it simplifies the process of deliberation and practical reason. Will is informed by beliefs but has its own force. Virtue can be taught as we teach skills, but our 'will' also needs to engage with moral truth and knowledge to replace moral ignorance with moral knowledge. This proposal does not seem to consider the role that Mr. Potter's passions and desires, e.g., greed, play in overlooking the opportunities that could have saved him from his moral ignorance. Fitzpatrick recognizes that Mr Potter's epistemic vices[3] might have led

2 Fitzpatrick asserts that character traits are the result of our choices from the point of maturity onwards.

3 Fitzpatrick resorts to Aquinas who attributes responsibility for negligence when the person does not consider what she ought to consider (Fitzpatrick 2008, 605, footnote 34). Aquinas distinguishes between 'acting in wrongly choosing' and 'ignorance of right principles' and for Aquinas both cases are cases of negligence. The cited text in Aquinas states: 'It is present when a person does not actually attend to what he could and should consider; the technical term is "ignorance in wrongly choosing", and it may result from passion or a settled attitude. Or again, a person may have made no effort to acquaint himself with the proper notions; the technical term is "ignorance of right principles". It is voluntary as not knowing of what one should know and as resulting from negligence' (Aquinas 2006, I-II, Q6, art. 8). Fitzpatrick recognizes that the negligent agent commits intellectual or epistemic vices and that they are voluntary. It might be unclear whether these intellectual vices have led the agent to either 'wrongly choosing' or 'ignorance of right principles'. However, since the former would involve non-clear eyed akrasia, we can infer that he aims to adhere to an account of negligence in which the agent fails to act according to the right principles. Therefore, Mr Potter is ignorant of the right principles. In my forthcoming monograph, *The Grammar of Negligence in Law and Ethics*, however, I problematize the idea that we access 'right principles' through our deliberations and practical reason.

him astray from moral knowledge, but does not recognize that other passions and desires play a transformative role in our thinking and practical knowledge.

We have discovered in the voluntarist reading of Fitzpatrick the idea that it is a matter of finding a *locus* within the temporality of agency, i.e., the point(s) at which Mr Potter refused to take on others' moral outlooks and learn from them, to determine and attribute the agent's responsibility for negligence. However, Fitzpatrick insists that his strategy does not involve tracing and arguably there is no such *locus* of responsibility. The agent is responsible because of his epistemically debilitating choices and not '*because he was even earlier responsible for something else that led to them*' (Fitzpatrick, 2008, 609). In the case of Mr. Potter, he is acting in light of his epistemically debilitating choices. However, arguably, we can only assess the 'reasonability' of expectations if we look at his past life and past choices, if we search for a *locus* within the temporality of Mr. Potter's agency. Responsibility can still be direct and we do not need to assert that Mr. Potter's failure to seek moral knowledge and engage with changing his moral outlook *effectively caused* and is closely connected to his derivative responsibility of acting in light of his epistemi cally debilitation view. Contrast this seeking for a *locus of responsibility* with a more complex account of the temporal history of Mr. Potter's agency and development, which is also richer and more appealing from the point of view of psychological realism, i.e., the way we experience the phenomenology of becoming good and of negligence and our attributions of responsibility.

Fitzpatrick's view might not escape sceptical positions and might lead to the fallacy of infinite regress. Since he argues that Mr Potter is responsible for his negligence due to his epistemic vices which are voluntary, we need a clear notion of what voluntariness entails and the only way to clarify this notion might be through either 'choice' or the idea of 'clear-eyed akrasia'. Fitzpatrick rejects both strategies and aims to stop passing the buck of responsibility to a prior choice or knowing sin (clear-eyed *akrasia*). Fitzpatrick argues that it is reasonable for us to expect that Mr Potter will not exercise vicious or debilitating epistemic choices given 'his capabilities and culturally available opportunities' (Fitzpatrick 2008, 606). There is, therefore, for Fitzpatrick, neither clear-eyed akrasia nor choice, but only our 'reasonable' expectations due to the agent's normal capacities and social environment. For Fitzpatrick, there are, arguably, two conditions of responsibility for negligence, which are: a) our reasonable expectations and b) the capabilities and appropriate environment of the agent. For now I will address the idea of 'reasonable expectations'.

It seems that that the 'reasonableness' of our expectations depends on whether agents in general *can and do* behave as Fitzpatrick thinks they do. The characterization of agency offered by Fitzpatrick is insufficient and lacks psychological realism. Epistemic virtues seem insufficient to guarantee that we will engage with acting not negligently due to confusion about the content of the values connected to the action, or due to the unequal development and transformation of our desires. To be fair, Fitzpatrick insists that Mr Potter has been *socialized normally* and that he could apply his critical thinking skills, which are evidenced by his knowledge of finances, to morality (Fitzpatrick 2008, 607–608). However, our concern is that if this were to happen, Mr Potter's epistemic engagement with the right principles would not be sufficient.

I aim to show that we need to understand how we choose, deliberate, and engage with values at the immersive level and how we can engage with aspirational conceptions transforming our lower level desires and more sophisticated desires, e.g., in the case of Mr Potter, the value of money, its accumulation, and its place in his life. Beliefs, according to Fitzpatrick, have a key role in acting virtuously and rightly and becoming good. According to this view our defective engagement and responsibility for wrong actions is '*where there is ignorance of balance of reasons against it*' (Fitzpatrick 2008, 609).

But I will argue that Fitzpatrick's model is of no use for the case of John, the son of the slave owner. John was brought up under 'normal conditions', e.g., a beloved son, who was given educational opportunities and the opportunity to flourish within his social and cultural context. Our attributions of responsibility to John cannot be detached from his 'belonging to a group' and our judgements of responsibility. I will argue that his responsibility for his negligent act depends on what the group believed and did at the time, but, arguably, there is a guiding standard of conduct, though, *contra* Fitzpatrick, it is not a matter of 'reasonable expectations'. Let me explain. Imagine that there is another son of a slave owner, Alexander, who is as well educated as John and was also brought up under normal conditions. One afternoon Alexander decides to attend abolitionist meetings. He reads and reflects and starts to understand that corporeal chastisement is barbaric, and starts to change the rules regarding the disciplining of the slaves in his plantation. What is exactly the account that would enable us to establish that Alexander has started to transform himself? The voluntaristic idea that mere beliefs have made a transformation in Alexander but not in John is not sufficiently realistic. Both Alexander and John are equally intelligent, reflexive, educated, and virtuous within their social context. They are both decent, honest, beloved sons and fathers, and so on. It is yet unclear what has made possible the transformation or the *becoming* of Alexander. It seems somehow insufficient and unrealistic to just say that, 'We reasonably expect John and Alexander to know better, but only Alexander has a better management of his beliefs'. Therefore, we could have reasonably, Fitzpatrick would say, expected John to acquire correct moral beliefs.

Elizabeth Harman has also argued that Fitzpatrick's portrait of the learner moral agent is implausible (Harman, 2011, 454). According to Harman, Fitzpatrick's claim that Mr Potter is *not* a hard case and, therefore, that we could reasonably expect him to manage his beliefs is mistaken. For Harman, *all cases are hard cases*, it does not matter if the subject is government ethics or business ethics, or the case of young people indoctrinated under the *Hitlerjugend* programme. Thus, she aims to demonstrate that there are many cases in which the agent has false moral beliefs without mismanagement of her beliefs; '*they have thought long and seriously about the relevant moral question, have considered opposing views, and have come to false moral beliefs*' (Harman,

2011, 456). They have not violated *any procedural epistemic* norms. Harman puts the example of a businessman who justifies his reprehensible ruthless behaviour as permissible within the practices of competitive business. His brother criticizes his behaviour and, after reflection, he comes to the view that his behaviour is justified by the needs of the economy; if his business maximizes profits, the economy will be better off. This case also extends to, for example, people brought up in a Mafiosi family, sexist society, or under the dominance of an inner city gang, in which extremely selfish and discriminatory practices are common. Harman argues that these agents have 'implicit' moral beliefs that in their view justify their actions and make them permissible. Harman points out that these agents are morally responsible because they '*have violated some moral norms that apply to beliefs themselves, not to the management of one's beliefs*' (Harman, 2011, 459). Thus, she tells us that we are morally obligated to believe moral truths. The *locus* of our moral responsibility is the false moral belief (Harman, 2011, 459) and she endorses the view that our beliefs need to connect to truth and caring attitudes and actions that link to what is morally true. Let us apply these reflections to the case of John and Alexander. We could say that John is not able to connect to what is morally true and this contrasts with Alexander's engagement with sound values, truth, and caring attitudes.

However, Harman *does not explain how we can achieve this*, how this operates within the framework of a psychologically realistic picture of agency, or whether it is even possible to achieve it. Her thoughts on the importance of tracking moral truth, i.e., values, is sound. However, as she seems to work within the idea of the mere balancing of 'beliefs', she is anxious to show that there is a *locus* of responsibility and that beliefs are present in the agent, though in the form of 'implicit' moral beliefs. Her reliance on mere beliefs as a *locus* of responsibility leads her to ignore the role of desires and emotions and the way thinking shapes them and vice versa. Let me explain.

Let us analyze closely Harman's example of the businessman who has 'long and seriously' thought about his moral beliefs and the permissibility of his ruthless and aggressive behaviour. Harman tells us, expanding on her example of the businessman, that the businessman's brother has criticized him and that, after reflection, he thinks that it is better for the economy if his business practices focus on maximizing profit. Thus, aggressively competitive and ruthless behaviour helps to optimize business and the prosperity of the economy. We could defend a model of ethical constituvism, according to which agents engage with values when they deliberate at the substandard or narrow level.[4] Let us see how this proposal applies to Harman's businessman, let us call him Mr Potter II. Mr. Potter II owns a car dealership that sells used vehicles and

4 We have elsewhere fully defended an Aristotelian-inspired model of ethical constitutivism with two levels, i.e., narrow or immersive deliberation and aspirational deliberation (see Rodriguez-Blanco 2022).

a few years ago he decided on the company's policy with regards to disclosing the defects of cars to potential purchasers. According to this policy, the company and its employees who are engaged in negotiation with clients and sales have no duty to disclose that, for example, a car has been damaged[5] and Mr Potter II and his employees have developed a number of tactics and strategies to avoid disclosing the defects of cars they are selling. When Mr Potter II started his business he engaged with business practices that gave too much value to competitive behaviour and success to the detriment of transparency and honesty. When his brother criticizes him, Potter reflects on this but reaches the conclusion that his brother is ignoring the importance of strong profits for the prosperity of the economy. However, if we can transition from narrow deliberation through our thoughts about our relationships and use these thoughts, i.e., descriptions and re-descriptions of our values, these reflections arguably can have an impact on our desires and emotions. *In this way, we can change our moral vision.* However, through our relationships with others, through either avoidance or recognition, we can either avoid or inhabit a deliberative-aspirational perspective. This entails not only changing our beliefs through imagination, descriptions, and re-descriptions of our particular circumstances and embedded values, but it also entails the change, transformation, and becoming of our entire self, including our desires and emotions, towards a different perspective. Imagine another businessman, Mr Potter III, who deliberated in a different way to Mr Potter II. He created a policy of complete disclosure (in compliance with the legal duty to disclose) and informed himself of his legal duties, but he and his employees also engaged with the value of understanding why it is important to adhere to legal duties and to follow the respective values on this matter. Through this engagement they learnt the values of honesty, transparency, and trust in dealing with their clients. After a few years of doing business, the company has gained a fabulous reputation for being reliable, trustworthy, and honest, and the staff who work there pride themselves on this. They feel empowered by working for a company that not only makes a strong profit, but is also honest.

Similarly, we could argue that in the case of John, his descriptions and re-descriptions of values play the key role in his avoidance or recognition of an aspirational perspective. For example, we could say that John would have the following thoughts, 'the value of property extends to slaves as it has been created by tradition'. On the other hand, his children play with the children of the slaves, he goes hunting with the slaves, and John considers his slaves to have good characteristics, but John deprives them of the space of justice precisely because this contradicts the requirements of tradition. These descriptions and re-descriptions of these values transform John's desires and make the conditions for his avoidance of inhabiting an aspirational perspective possible. If he were to inhabit an aspirational perspective, he could track sound values

5 In the example I will isolate Mr Potter's moral duties from his legal duties.

and actions in the particular circumstances. By contrast, Alexander's reflections and descriptions of values tend to go in the opposite direction. Alexander starts to re-describe the value of tradition as inevitably intertwined with sound moral judgement. He reflects on the criticism that is presented to him by abolitionists. He describes the value of property in a more limited manner and starts to grasp the value of equality in his daily interactions with his slaves. In this way, he transforms his desires and emotions in light of these new descriptions and re-descriptions of values.

I reject the idea that there is a *locus* of responsibility or that our task as philosophers of responsibility is to identify and explain it. On the contrary, the idea presented here is that changes of the self are due to emotions, desires, and beliefs, and how these interact when we engage in both narrow and aspirational deliberation. Unlike Harman's and Fitzpatrick's proposals, we explain agency in cases of alleged moral ignorance which arises by 'belonging to a group' in a psychologically realistic manner. Thus the deliberations and performances of Mr Potter II and Mr Potter III are temporally located, and the engagement with values and perspectives is presented in a complex and rich way. If there is responsibility for negligence it is not because we can identify the *locus* at which Mr Potter II or Mr Potter III disregarded their epistemic duties. On the contrary, we argue that Mr Potter II acts negligently because there is an uneven development of character and thinking due to the incorrect interaction of beliefs and desires. Mr Potter II does not *choose* to ignore the guidelines on disclosure because, if this is the case, his action is either intentional or reckless (clear-eyed akrasia). Nor is it the case that only his beliefs guide his actions, or that his beliefs are just something that happens to him. The core argument is that Mr Potter II determines the answer to the question, 'What shall I do?'. His general ends are indeterminate and he cannot know what shape they will take prior to engaging in both substandard or narrow deliberation, and deliberative-aspirational deliberation. When Mr Potter II tries to settle the question, 'What shall I do?' in the context of creating a policy on disclosing damaged and defective vehicles, he establishes that the value of maximizing profit is more important than the value of fair dealing and transparency. But this view has been shaped through past substandard or narrow deliberations, i.e., engaging with misconceptions of wealth and greed, or perhaps as the avoidance of engaging with different values and inhabiting a deliberative-aspirational perspective, e.g., the importance of truth, transparency, and honest business practices. But Mr. Potter II's actions are negligent and involve ignorance, though a more complex story that includes an understanding of deliberation and practical reason is required.

Similarly, John reflects on what the value of tradition requires of him and transforms his desires accordingly. Alexander re-describes the value of tradition in his engagement with other values, i.e., moral truth, and transforms his emotions and desires accordingly.

John's negligence is due to changes and transformation, but *not due to his beliefs* only, either passive or active, i.e., the active duty to discharge his epistemic duties. His changes are due to the fact that his desires are transformed because of his thinking about and engagement with the respective values, i.e., the value or tradition and, for example, seeing truth as a matter of 'degrees'. At the same time his vision and understanding of the respective values are revised in light of the re-described desires. Arguably, Mr Potter is also engaged in a similar process of avoidance of inhabiting an aspirational perspective. Thus, Mr Potter II desires to maximize profit and accrue wealth before he is 40 years old in an easy manner, but this is still an indeterminate end. According to his thinking, seeing truth as a matter of 'degrees' will be the *how of maximizing profit soon*. He develops the thought that truth comes in degrees and that omitting to say the truth is justifiable when negotiating in business. In light of his engagement with or avoidance of values, he thinks that disclosing details of the accidents that his cars have been in is not necessary. The value of truth is avoided and, as he sees it, it is the purchaser's duty to ask for all the relevant information when negotiating the purchase of a vehicle. It is the purchaser who should take all reasonable steps to be informed whether the car has been involved in an accident or has been damaged in the past. As he sees the matter, he has no duty of disclosure to future purchasers. The *what?*—What he shall do?, i.e., become wealthy—is determined by his answer to the question *how?*, i.e., become wealthy through the value, as he sees it, of truth as a simple matter of degrees, and imposing a duty on the purchaser. Mr Potter II does not act intentionally, he does not 'choose' to lie in order to deceive his clients and maximize profit and become wealthy. Similarly, in the case of John, the value of ethical truth is avoided, he re-describes tradition in such a manner that there is complete avoidance of re-describing other values such as personhood, property, and so on. The reasonings of both of Mr Potter II and John are different and I think this is what Harman wishes to emphasize. Mr Potter II is truthful in other spheres of his life; he is transparent in his relationships with his friends, family, and relatives and in other matters too he is an honest man and decent human being. It is only in the sphere of business practices that he endorses the policy of non-disclosure to his clients. He slips into this thinking of truth 'by degrees' and due to his desire to become wealthy at a young age without too much effort. Contrast Mr Potter II with Mr Potter III, who reaches exactly the opposite conclusion, but the process is a similar one, i.e., an interaction of beliefs and desires and the transformation of his thinking. However, Mr. Potter III engages with changing and transforming his beliefs and desires towards a deliberative-aspirational perspective. Similarly, John is a good and honest man in other spheres of his life, i.e., he is a good son, an honest man in his business dealings, a loyal friend, and a good father and husband. However, in dealing with his slaves he aims to *follow tradition* and what his father has taught him is never questioned. John, in contrast to Alexander, avoids the becoming or transformation of his desires and emotions towards a more aspirational perspective. Our proposal can explain the multiplicity of changes and transformations through a realistic picture of the phenomenology of our moral experiences and the changes in our moral vision and the role that groups may play in our moral ignorance. But let us examine again Fitzpatrick's 'reasonable expectations' account further.

Levy (Levy 2009) advances a potential objection that Fitzpatrick raises against his own view on reasonable expectations. The objection is as follows: Mr Potter's early upbringing has determined his later choices. Due to his background and beliefs he cannot revise and change his moral outlook (Levy 2009, 734). According to Levy the objection turns into a question about *what is rational for Mr Potter to do.* Thus, given his background and beliefs, and given that culpability and reasonable expectations are a function of our actual capacities, we cannot reasonably expect Mr Potter to do something that is beyond his actual capacities. He tells us, 'Potter, I argue, could not rationally have taken advantage of the opportunities for moral improvement that were (in some sense) available to him' (Levy 2009, 735). For Levy, internalism for reasons should prevail when we are dealing with blameworthy action and, therefore, when Mr Potter considers alternative choices he conceives them from his internal standpoint, i.e., beliefs and desires (what Levy calls pro attitudes). Mr Potter III sees himself as managing well his reasons and beliefs. Levy tells us that what is rational for me to do *is settled by my mental states.* I have a reason to p-ing only if I believe that p-ing. He remains neutral on whether these reasons are motivating, and emphasizes that they are actual representations and pro-attitudes. He acknowledges that a moral outlook is more than a set of beliefs, it also includes what he calls a 'moral world' (Levy 2009, 737). However, Levy does not expand on this and states that this moral world is the perspective from which we 'assess moral claims'. From his view that internal reasons are representations and that what is rational to do is *the settling of mental states,* we can infer that the moral world is mainly about *representations.* Mr Potter cannot access other ways of assessing his own actions due to his representations, i.e., beliefs, and therefore he cannot change or transform his moral world. '*The opportunities of moral improvements that he encounters – say, editorials by Paul Krugman in the New York Times – are seen as the whining of socialists or sissies.*' (Levy 2009, 737). Fitzpatrick, by contrast, insists that we could reasonably expect these opportunities to be taken on by Mr Potter.

We see in this dispute the predominance of the balancing view on deliberation. This means for Levy there are only internal reasons characterized predominantly by beliefs that we weigh against other beliefs,[6] but these beliefs are our own representations and we cannot change them. For Fitzpatrick, by contrast, it is a matter of vices, but, arguably, his argumentation involves the implicit assumption that vices are chosen and that we can transform our false

6 'Our moral views are constitutive of our outlook: we assess evidence in terms of our views. We weigh the evidence in ways that are a function of these views; moreover, we give different sources of evidence different weight in ways that are responsive to our views (e.g., dismissing critics as motivated by the "politics of envy"' (Levy 2009, 738).

moral beliefs by simply learning other moral outlooks and taking the opportunities to revise, modify, and change our false moral beliefs. If we refuse to do so, it is because our will 'hangs on', so to speak, to vices, mainly epistemic vices, e.g., arrogance, overconfidence in what we can achieve, and so on. Fitzpatrick also assumes the truth of the bifurcation thesis and its corollary. Beliefs and vices and presented to us and in our deliberations we engage with choosing or rejecting vices, and with beliefs. There is no account of transformation and change due to the process of deliberation itself. If our account is the sound model of deliberation, then it is evident that the dispute between Levy and Fitzpatrick relies on mistaken premises about how we engage with values, beliefs, and desires in our deliberations.

Fitzpatrick's arguments are more embedded in a character account of vices. Mr Potter's moral ignorance is the result of his own vices. If he could have avoided exercising his vices in the way he did, he could have avoided his moral ignorance (Talbert 2017, 51). However, it seems that alternative choices are a 'live option' for Mr Potter. For example, Talbert tells us that we need to trace back the bad character of Mr Potter to early choices and to bad starting points, though 'a bad starting point is not something that one can reasonably be expected to avoid' (Talbert 2017, 52). It is, therefore, not reasonable to expect him to change his moral outlook or moral vision. Talbert argues that we can explain Mr Potter's potential responsibility in terms of an attributionist theory of responsibility, and we now turn to the different and complex theories that are called 'attributionist'.

3.5 Attributionism as answerability

Smith has defended a view of responsibility that minimizes the role of *choice and control* and focuses instead on attributions of responsibility that arise from the third-person or observer perspective, and perhaps also the second-person perspective, when the latter aims at grasping the *underlying* unreflective patterns of awareness of the evaluative judgements of the agent and demands justificatory responses for the agent's actions or attitudes.

Smith's criticism of the control condition centres on the fact we cannot control the agent's states that are sensitive to our judgements, i.e., the presence or absence of reasons in the circumstances, emotions such as fear, and other relevant states. Since attitudes depend on judgements about reasons and the former cannot change until our judgements change, we are not free to choose our attitudes. In other words, Smith tells us, '*we are not free to adopt, control or modify our attitudes in any way we choose*' (Smith 2015a, 123). Her positive position relies on the Scanlonian conception (Scanlon 2000)[7] that

7 In her earlier work she relied on Watson's aretaic responsibility but in later work she has come closer to Scanlon's conception of judgement-sensitive. In her earlier work she says that her account is self-expressive, which is the expression used by Watson.

establishes that there is a class of judgement-sensitive attitudes which an ideally rational agent will come to have or reject depending on their judgement of sufficient or insufficient reasons (Scanlon 2000, 20). Thus, judgement-sensitive attitudes are a set of dispositions that makes the agent react or act in certain ways. Furthermore, these judgement-sensitive attitudes make the agent disposed to patterns of *unreflective* thoughts which, according to Smith, underly our evaluative judgements. Smith concentrates less on the Scanlonian ideally rational agent and places more emphasis on the dispositional aspect together with the resulting patterns of underlying unreflective patterns of awareness (Smith 2005, 241).

Smith's name for her own account varies; in some texts she calls it the 'rational relation' view (Smith 2008, 369; Smith 2005, 240, 244–45) as it focuses on the rational connection between the agent's actions, her attitudes, and evaluative judgements. For example, if Mr Potter II acts in a way that overlooks truth and transparency in his relations with his clients, then this is an indication that Mr Potter II does not accept the evaluative judgement 'truth and transparency are important values when dealing with clients'. According to Smith, arguably, Mr Potter II does not 'choose' to act in a rude and inconsiderate manner, rather it is the case that his rude actions show, manifest, or express an unreflective pattern of awareness that underlies his evaluative judgements, i.e., indifference to truth and transparency. Smith oscillates between i) an *expressivist* interpretation of this rational connection, i.e., the unreflective pattern of awareness *expresses* underlying evaluative judgements; ii) a *constitutive* interpretation (Smith 2005, 244 footnote 14) of this rational connection, i.e., the unreflective pattern is *constitutive* of an evaluative judgement, and iii) an *inferential* interpretation, i.e., an evaluative judgement reflects a particular mental state and in light of the agent's spontaneous attitude and other explicit beliefs and judgements, an observer *can infer* that she has a particular evaluative judgement (Smith 2005, 255).

In some of her work Smith calls her position the 'answerability' view as it focuses on the potential answers or responses that an agent could give if she were to ask why she is doing what she is doing (Smith 2015b). More precisely, these are a set of answers that would emerge from moral criticism (Smith 2008, 374). Furthermore, Smith believes that the answerability view of responsibility is basic (Smith 2015b, 102 footnote 11)[8] and that reflections on adequate accountability towards, or sanctions or punishments directed to, the agent's actions depend on attributions of underlying evaluative judgements, i.e., attributivism as answerability.

8 See also Gardner 2003, who defends responsibility as answerability as primary or basic. Smith rejects the distinction defended by Watson between accountability responsibility and aretaic responsibility. The former involves the legitimacy of punishment and sanction. For Smith, any punishment, moral criticism, or sanction can be assessed once we have attributed basic responsibility in the sense defended by her, responsibility as answerability (Smith 2008, 379).

The gist of responsibility, according to Smith, is that when we act, we need to confront others and answer in a justifying manner *for* our actions and this is possible because we are the kind of beings that have dispositions to act according to evaluative judgements. Our actions, however, do not depend on beliefs or other control mechanisms that we exercise over our bodily actions. On the contrary, our actions depend on our evaluative judgements and on emerging and *underlying unreflective patterns of awareness.* Not surprisingly, the temporality of the agent is irrelevant. For Smith, it does not matter how our prior choices, valuing, and experiences determine our reasons for actions and beliefs, and how the latter shape our desires, values, and choices (Smith 2005, 239, 251; Smith 2008, 389). Judgements are presented as a matter of self-discovery. We find ourselves surprised by our reactions, emotions, and attitudes (Smith 2005, 252). Consequently, one might infer that there are two steps in grasping the relevant action and responsibility for the particular in Smith's account. First, the observer[9] or the second-person, i.e., the person who has a claim on the actions and responses of the agent,[10] grasps the unreflective patterns of awareness that underlie the agent's evaluative judgements. Second, the observer or second-person could potentially ask, or at least the agent is capable of being asked, for a justificatory response or answer for her action or pattern of awareness.

In early work Smith does not seem to endorse the view that attributivism as answerability can be extended to non-intentional actions. Even cases of inattention are not interpreted as non-intentional but rather as cases in which the agent intends '*to treat something with a particular form of (in)attention or (dis)respect*' (Smith 2005, 242). According to Smith what a person notices and neglects has an expressive significance. My interpretation is that intention for Smith is a dispositional mental state directed to an object. This line of thought is similar to Scanlon's view as for him, '*actions are the kind of things for which normative reasons can be given only insofar as they are intentional, that is, are the expression of judgement-sensitive attitudes*' (Scanlon 2000, 21).

Contrary to her early position, Smith in recent work (Smith 2017) has attempted to show that attributivism can be applied to non-intentional omissions[11] or as she calls them 'unconscious' omissions. Her point of departure is Patricia Smith's view (P. Smith 1990) which aims to establish that we are responsible for our non-intentional omissions because they involve a violation of or deviation from reasonable expectations according to a contextual

9 I use the terms 'observer perspective' and the 'third-person perspective' as interchangeable.

10 For further examination of the second-person perspective, see Darwall 2009. The second-person view is the perspective of the individual who has a claim on the agent's actions. For example, if you step on my foot I have a claim on you and can demand that you provide reasons for your actions.

11 To keep the discussion simple I will use inadvertent actions, non-intentional omissions, and non-intentional actions as interchangeable. For a view that it does not make much sense to distinguish between actions and omissions, see Sandis 2022.

standard. For Patricia Smith it is a standard based on the community standard, i.e., the pattern of conduct of the community. Patricia Smith's understanding of reasonable expectations is in terms of what is probable or likely, though she recognizes the distinction between the probabilistic sense and the normative sense. However, she tends to dilute both senses and argues that these grounds are difficult to keep separated. Smith's concern with Patricia Smith's account is that it does not explain the rational connection between the agent and the omission. We do not know which omissions are truly attributable to the agent as failures of her acting and seeing as an active agent. For example, I can bite my nails when I am nervous, and my friends can reasonably expect me to bite my nails when I am nervous. However, one day when I am nervous, against all reasonable expectations of my friends, I do not bite my nails. Have I committed an omission? According to Angela Smith this and many similar cases show '*that people can fail to act in ways that it was reasonable (in an epistemic sense) to expect them to act without thereby committing omissions*' (Smith 2017, 50). What is really doing the work, according to Angela Smith, is not a reasonable expectation, but rather that omissions depart from practical norms that give agents reasons for actions.

Following Angela Smith's view on responsibility in terms of attributionism as answerability, we could say that the position aims to establish that we first need to determine whether non-intentional omissions can be attributed to agents. This type of responsibility is basic. After assessing basic responsibility we can then engage in the question whether the omission warrants a negative or critical response, i.e., sanction, punishment, moral criticism. We need to show: a) that the non-intentional omission is attributable to the agent in a rational manner, i.e., we can establish a connection between the omission, we can grasp that this is a failure to comply with the practical norms that give reasons for actions, and that the omission reflects the agent's underlying evaluative judgements; and b) that the omission is susceptible to moral criticism and that the agent is susceptible to provide justificatory responses for her omissions (Smith 2017, 52–53). Furthermore, according to Angela Smith, the practical norm gives the agent reasons that either require or favour doing a specific action and the agent knows or should know this (Smith 2017, 52). In this way, Smith expands her model of attributivism as answerability to inadvertent actions or non-intentional omissions.

Smith wants to emphasize that we are not passive victims of our characters (Smith 2008, 369), and therefore the fact that atributionism cannot distinguish the bad agent from the blameworthy agent is an advantage (Smith 2008, 390). However, the attributionist theorist cannot understand why the agent is not passive concerning her character. It only assumes it because it sees her action, performance, attitudes, feelings, and character as having a rational underpinning and therefore belonging to her. But this is only an inference or conjecture, and character development and the way we are active concerning our characters remains a mystery within Smith's model of attributionism. Within the confines of Smith's proposal, *reason is not seen in its operation but only in its effect.* There is no real account of reason. It is mysterious whether it establishes boundaries or connects contingently to emotions and desires. Smith argues that there is a correlation between the mental state, emotion, attitude, intention, and the evaluative judgement, reason. But this correlation is imposed by the observer or third-person perspective. Within this view *reason cannot shape emotions, desires, or intentions.* They only *correlate.* When the state of mind is present, then the evaluative judgement *must* be present. It is unclear why this is so. Maybe it is because we are rational creatures, which explains why there are 'patterns', but the nature of these patterns remains unexplained.

Arguably, for Smith, reasons for belief or action (following Scanlon's position) are distinguished from desires, i.e., attitudes, emotions, and passions. However, since the concept of reasons for actions requires spontaneity to show that reasons are involved with something we do, in Smith's model spontaneity is assumed and explained as *unconscious or unreflective* patterns of awareness which underlie evaluative judgements or reasons. Smith asserts, '*We remember some things and forget others, particular considerations strike us as being relevant to the issue at hand, and we are moved spontaneously by various desires and inclinations*' (Smith 2005, 246). Desires and emotions are created spontaneously, but they are judgement-dependent and Smith presents them as if they are *reducible* to reasons and evaluative judgements.[12] They express themselves together with evaluative judgements as dispositions in our actions but Smith does not consider how we shape and transform these desires and emotions through our judgements. For Smith desires and emotions do not have an independent or partially independent existence from evaluative judgements. There is no explanation on how this reduction of desires to reasons operates and what is the interaction between beliefs and desires *prior* to this reduction, let alone the complex interaction between values, reasons, and desires.[13] Smith

12 Smith points out, 'Attitudes such as contempt, jealousy, and regret seem to be partially constituted by certain kinds of evaluative judgements or appraisals. To feel contempt toward some person, for example, involves the judgement that she has some feature or has behaved in some way which makes her unworthy of one's respect, and to feel regret involves the judgement that something of value has been lost' (Smith 2005, 250).

13 This bifurcation between desires and reasons, and the ultimate reduction of desires to reason, is also present in Scanlon. Furthermore, he believes that desires play no role in practical reasoning or thinking. Scanlon asserts, 'I will argue that desires, insofar as they are distinguished from the recognition of reasons, have a much less fundamental role in practical thinking than is commonly supposed. Indeed, I have become convinced that insofar as "having a desire" is understood as a state that is distinct from "seeing something as a reason", it plays almost no role in the justification and explanation of action' (Scanlon 2000, 18). He also has defended the view that there is no distinction between practical and theoretical reasoning (Scanlon 2000, 23). Thus, desires motivate action because action has a belief-like component and he regards cases of *akrasia* as the failure to give weight to specific reasons. Negligence is considered to be what happens when the agent ignores normative reasons and fails to make connections (Scanlon 2000, 23, 30–51). He acknowledges that his position is similar to Davidson's view on weakness of will (Scanlon 2000, 377, footnote 18). Scanlon fails to explain the puz-

presents us with a 'black box' picture where we have the input, i.e., the evaluative judgements of the agent and emotions and desires that are part of the evaluative judgement. On the other hand, we have the respective output, the expressions or manifestations of these evaluative judgements via unreflective patterns of awareness and the potential demands from either the third-person or second-person perspectives.

Smith's account misses something important, which is that responsibility plays a crucial function in our *becoming* and therefore in inhabiting an aspirational perspective. When we demand responses from others and when we express moral criticism, we express our reactive attitude ***but also intend that the agent is able to inhabit a different perspective*** concerning her actions, judgements, emotions, and desires, and take this new perspective into account in her future actions. We also desire that the agent reassess her entire self and explores new ways of looking at her actions and conduct. I have defended the view that changes and becoming are possible through our judgements and the transformation of our desires.

However, let us go back to and reflect on the criticism advanced by Wolf (Wolf 1990) that Smith's attributivism seems to be too close to a shallow conception of responsibility. She does not explain the structure of thinking and valuing of the agent and this aspect remains obscure. Arguably, we can attribute unreflective patterns of awareness to children, but they are not responsible in a deep or robust sense. Thus, let us suppose the following example. A young child, Pedro, acts in an indifferent manner towards other children, i.e., he is rude, cruel, and inconsiderate. He has behaved like this for a number of years and when he is eight years old he stabs a friend at school. According to attributivism he is responsible as he has shown a pattern of unreflective awareness which underlies his evaluative judgements. However, somehow we do not make him responsible in the same way that we think Mr Potter II is responsible for his rude and inconsiderate conduct and John is morally responsible for the death of Betty. Pedro is responsible, arguably for his pattern of unconscious awareness only but not for his actions. Mr Potter II is responsible for both, his underlying pattern of unreflective awareness and for his actions. John is responsible for both his underlying reflective awareness and for his actions. The expression or manifestation of an underlying pattern of unreflective awareness cannot be the feature that guides us on what responsibility is. Smith could argue that Pedro does not have evaluative judgements in the proper sense and that his pattern of unreflective awareness does not reflect evaluative judgements in the proper sense. But this is difficult to defend. Thus, Pedro considers that he has reasons to be rude, he knows that in this way he can be feared and powerful among his friends. Smith could also

zling phenomenology of *akrasia*. For a discussion on Davidson's view on akrasia, see my forthcoming monograph, *The Grammar of Negligence in Law and Ethics: Aspiration, Perspective and Civic Maturity*.

argue that it is not reasonable to demand justificatory responses from Pedro as to why he has done what he has done. True, but this means that it is only the answerability feature that enables us to distinguish between Pedro and Mr Potter II together with John. It seems, therefore, that the first step of Smith's account, i.e., attribution in terms of underlying unreflective patterns of evaluative judgements, plays no role in demarcating the cases of Pedro and Mr Potter II/John. It is only the second step of Smith's account, i.e., that we are responsible if it is reasonable to ask for justificatory responses for our actions and conduct, that plays the crucial role in demarcating the cases of Pedro and Mr Potter II/John.

Smith's account of basic responsibility for non-intentional omissions is also unsatisfactory and reflects the difficulties of her view on responsibility as attributionism for actions in general. Thus, the idea that the agent ought to have known the practical norm generating reasons for action that apply to her does not illuminate the case of responsibility for negligent actions. Because Smith assumes a bifurcation between beliefs as reasons for actions and desires, her view is that the agent simply needs to engage with the *respective beliefs as evaluative judgements* to understand how the practical norm generates the respective reason for action. The position of the first-person perspective, the temporality of her agency, her struggles between reason and desires, her development and learning are ignored. Furthermore, ignoring the complexity of the interaction of desires and beliefs and focusing on a backward-looking perspective, i.e., attribution of underlying unreflective patterns of awareness, have further consequences for the understanding of negligent action that arise by 'group belonging'. A mismatch between a) the underlying pattern of awareness of evaluative judgements, b) the violation of the practical norm, and c) potential answers to the question of why the agent did what she did or omitted to do what she ought to have done arises. Thus, we can correctly interpret that the agent has violated a practical norm that gives reasons for actions, and say that she can be asked to answer for her omissions. Despite this, however, there could be a mismatch between her evaluative judgements and *our* attribution of the underlying pattern of awareness of evaluative judgements; consequently, there would be no rational connection between *her* evaluative judgement and the violated practical norm that grounds reasons for actions that apply to her. For example, the case *State v Williams*[14] where the poorly educated native American parent was ignorant of the son's gangrenous infection as signalled by fever, and since they did not seek medical advice, the son died. The parents violated the practical norm of 'caring for their child' and therefore failed to follow the respective normative reason for actions that apply to them. We can grasp the fact that when Mr Williams's child initially got ill, Mr Williams did not seek medical advice, days passed and the child's fever continued up to the point that it was dangerously high, but Mr Williams still did not look

14 *State v Williams*, 484 P.2d 1167 (Wash. App. 1971).

for medical advice. From these facts we can *attribute* to Mr Williams an unreflective pattern of awareness that reflects or underlies the evaluative judgement 'I do not care about the health of my child'. Following Smith's account, Mr. Williams ought to have known that a high temperature combined with other symptoms can be indicative of a gangrenous infection. However, Mr Williams's evaluative judgement was that, 'I profoundly care for and love my child. I care for his health'. Thus, in this example, it is false that the so-called unreflective pattern of awareness expresses or underlies Mr Williams's evaluative judgement. It is unclear the way that Smith would defend the idea that Williams's agency is rationally connected to the violation of the practical norm and its respective normative reasons for actions.

The problem lies in that Smith is not interested in the deliberative process, or the choices and engagement of the agent in its temporality. Her focus is on attribution and the backward-looking perspective. Due to this limited focus, the complexity of both the agency and the first-person deliberative stance are lost. The only perspective that we can appreciate is the observer or second-person perspective to the detriment of the first-person perspective and the forward-looking view.

Smith emphasizes the importance of our interactions and relations with other persons, and the importance of recognizing normative reasons in our interactions with other human beings. Thus, she asserts that to fail to see the value of jazz or philosophy is different than to fail to recognize or care about reasons that flow from the value of other people (Smith 2008, 387). I can be criticized if I poorly perform a piece of jazz music, but this kind of criticism is different from the criticism that arises from treating others rudely, inconsiderately, unkindly, and so on. Thus, when I attribute to others cruel conduct, I am not only saying that this person is bad in the way that I am saying that the jazz performer is performing poorly. I am not only attributing a trait, but I am also making a demand of a justificatory response for her attitudes and conduct. Smith asserts: '*This demand is by its very nature implies responsibility, for it is directed at his judgmental activity, activity for which we must regard him as responsible if we are to regard him as a moral agent in any case*' (Smith 2008, 388). However, this seems to make a stark separation between activities and relationships or interactions with others. It overlooks the fact that the way we treat others, assess their values, develop and learn valuing *is through our activities.* Aristotle establishes an analogy between craft and practical reason (Aristotle 1934, 1094a6-14;1105b12-16;1138b26-32), and showed that this analogy breaks down when we look at ethical or moral actions. In the case of craft, the standard of excellence is external to the crafter, e.g., for every carpenter there is a standard of excellence in working with wood, for a jazz performer there is a standard of excellence in performing a specific piece of music. In ethics, however, the end is indeterminate and Aristotle only tells us that in ethics the right end is determined by the person who exercises practical reason. Arguably, when the agent deliberates in a narrow way she is engaging with understanding and grasping the particular value in the circumstances, but there are also medium and large scale indeterminate ends and values that we are required to integrate. We are asked, therefore, to occupy a deliberative-aspirational perspective that will shape what we have learnt in our substandard or narrow deliberation. The picture that is therefore presented is dynamic and complex, in which through our activities we also learn about the values that flow from other people. There is no stark separation between our activities and our relationships with others. If I am performing a jazz piece with a friend, I am learning to play the piece according to the standard of excellence, but I am also grasping the values of friendship, respect, consideration, and kindness. The standard of my ethical actions are internal and I am trying to give content and shape to my life according to the indeterminate conception of 'living well'. The standard of my performance of jazz is external, i.e., there is a clear and external way of performing this piece in an excellent way. But both activities and relationships are intertwined. I may ask to put aside the demand to reach the external standard of excellence in performing this piece of jazz because the value of friendship and kindness demands it particular situation. In this way, I acquire a depth in valuing other people through my activities. The stark contrast between relationships and activities seems unjustified.

In his reply to Talbert's atributionism, Fitzpatrick makes a distinction between fittingness and deservingness. In the former case we evaluate someone's moral views and in virtue of this evaluation we criticize, react, and respond to them; in the latter case, we say that the agent deserves a sanction, e.g., a reprimand, because of the way she has behaved (Fitzpatrick 2017, 33). Thus, Fitzpatrick tells us, attributionists cannot capture the second sense of responsibility when we not only respond or react to moral flaws and errors, but when we also think that the actor deserves a punishment or sanction. Fitzpatrick also rightly points out that Scanlon denies this and argues that his attributionism is about deservingness (Scanlon 2000, 188). Fitzpatrick doubts that this position is coherent and pressing further on this point asks, '*how can we say that he deserves blame if he couldn't have helped being as he is?*' (Fitzpatrick 2017, 34). Fitzpatrick tells us that the attributionist account gets wrong results in two key cases: a) cases of indoctrination when there were no opportunities to learn and improve one's values and evaluations; and b) cases of 'pure' negligence when the agent cares about and values the activity she is engaged with and/or takes care to avoid harm, but simply forgets to take the necessary precautions to avoid the harm. For example, a mother who forgets to change the battery of the smoke alarm and a house fire subsequently kills her family. She cares deeply about her family and their safety but attributionists will say that her judgement shows the contrary, which is counterintuitive. The first set of cases is illustrated by Daniel who has been indoctrinated by a sect and develops strong homophobic views. But we also can use the previous cases of the women indoctrinated by the Taliban or the young man indoctrinated by the *HitlerJugend* programme. In all these cases, Fitzpatrick tells us, attributionist accounts collapse together deservingness and fittingness. For Fitzpatrick the indoctrinated individuals do not *deserve* to be punished or sanctioned because they had no opportunity to develop and improve their moral judgements. For a correct judgement of deservingness we need to show that at some point there was an opportunity for moral improvement that was not taken. By contrast, attributionists will say that these people deserve punishment and it is fitting to reprimand them or react against them because they acted on *the basis of their values and wrong evaluations.* Fitzpatrick's core argument is that an explanation and understanding of the temporal history of agency is fundamental if we want to take responsibility for negligence or moral ignorance seriously and give a sound account of it. However, Fitzpatrick's idea that there is a *locus* at which the agent could reasonably expect to choose and improve his conceptions of values and moral beliefs relies on a simplistic model of deliberation and fails to capture the process of development and learning to become good.

Let us examine again the cases of negligent action due to moral ignorance that arise from 'belonging to a group'. So far I have tried to show that there is insufficient complexity in the cases offered by both attributionists and 'reasonable expectations' theorists. According to our proposal the agent engages in narrow or substandard deliberation, the determination of *what* through determining the *how,* and it is through this engagement that she grasps *what* the end-value or end-desire looks like. This realization illuminates further deliberations, but also through criticism, friendship, *engagement with other people who belong to one's group and people who belong to other groups*, and her own thinking, i.e., her description and re-description of her actions and valuing, she has the opportunity to avoid or recognize an aspirational perspective. In the case of John, the son of the slave owner, for example, he would have to decide 'What shall 'I do?' regarding the disciplining of his slaves. His children play with the slaves' children, including Betty's children, he hunts with his slaves, and he considers them to be good people; he has grasped the value of the slave being a person at a basic level. When Betty steals the watch he needs to decide whether to follow tradition and punish her with lashes, or whether to change the rules and consider a different sort of punishment. John avoided inhabiting an aspirational perspective through a description or re-description of what tradition really requires of him.

Within my proposal we more accurately say that the agent needs to inhabit the deliberative-aspirational perspective and avoid or recognize the value of truth in connection to moral truth. John needs to engage in thinking, and describe and re-describe the situation and the positioning of his values, including other connected values within his indeterminate vision of 'living well'. He can avoid the aspirational perspective and say to himself that loyalty to traditions and ways of living as he has been taught are what matters. He could also take the deliberative-aspirational perspective and, like Alexander, say that tradition cannot require obscure moral truths and distorted religious beliefs and faith. John could take the view that tradition cannot demand ignoring intelligible and powerful understandings of the value of justice and equality. My point is that, *contra* Fitzpatrick and Smith, my proposal shows the complexity of deliberation, it shows how our desires and thinking are transformed while we decide what we should do, and while we succeed or fail to inhabit a deliberative-aspirational perspective. This account of how practical reason operates is richer and presents the different layers of our immersion in values and the exercise of our reasoning and thinking.

3.6 Conclusion

The case of pure negligence has also been explained by our conception where it was shown that in cases of negligence, Condition 4—'*Blameworthiness grounded on failing to act according to a standard*' and Condition 5—'*Failure to grasp the objective standard or the right action*', can both be satisfied if we rethink what the idea of standard of action and guidance entails. I have shown that two standard theories of responsibility for negligent action fail; but we also have learnt the elements that are missing in such theories.

My proposal demonstrates how our intelligent thinking transforms desires and vice versa. In this way we create a new conceptual space between attributionism and voluntarist accounts of responsibility for negligence, and moral ignorance.

My proposal acknowledges the key insight of the 'reasonable expectations' view that we should not collapse deservingness and fittingness, and that we need to explain the process of becoming good. But I also argue that we need to take into account a more psychologically realistic view of our practical reason and deliberation. On one hand I acknowledge the role that values play in our lives and recognize attributionists' emphasis on the significance of valuing, but on the other I reject the view that we can grasp the richness of the interaction between reasons, values, and desires through mere attribution from the observer's or second-person point of view.

Our emphasis is on the first-person perspective and I argue that mere attribution misses the process of reasoning and *the becoming of agency within a group*, which involves an engagement with the thinking of people who belong to one's group and also those who *do not* belong to one's group. Our belonging to groups is inevitable. It can help us in grasping the good and the values of our life and community, but it can also misguide us in the essential task of soundly describing what really matters in the particularities of our actions. If we think in merely attributionist or voluntaristic terms, we tend to miss the richness and complexity of our aspirational perspective, and we misunderstand the phenomenon of negligent action that arises due to moral ignorance by 'group belonging'.

This account of agency within a group, in which desires and beliefs interact and shape each other, and we can transform our lower desires through thinking and sound descriptions of values, allows us to inhabit an aspirational perspective. This is an outline of essential steps towards 'Aristotelian constitutivism'.

References

Aquinas, St. T. 2006. *Summa Theologicae, I-II.* Cambridge: Cambridge University Press (English translation Thomas Gilby).

Aristotle. 1934. *Nicomachean Ethics.* Cambridge, MA: Harvard University Press, the Loeb Classical Library, translated by H. Rackham).

Darwall. 2009. *The Second-Person Standpoint.* Cambridge, MA: Harvard University Press.

Fitzpatrick, W. 2008. "Moral Responsibility and Normative Ignorance: Answering a New Skeptical Challenge". *Ethics*, 118: 589–613.

Fitzpatrick, W. 2017. "Unwitting Wrongdoing, Reasonable Expectations, and Blameworthiness". In *Responsibility: The Epistemic Condition*, edited by P. and Wieland, J. W. Robichaud, 118: 29–46. Oxford: Oxford University Press.

Gardner, J. 2003. "The Mark of Responsibility". *Oxford Journal of Legal Studies*, 23: 157–171.

Harman, E. 2011. "Does Moral Ignorance Exculpate?" *Ratio*, 24: 443–468.

Levy, N. 2009. "Culpable Ignorance and Moral Responsibility: A Reply to Fitzpatrick". *Ethics*, 119: 729–741.

Plato. 1976. *Protagoras.* Translated with Notes by C.C.W Taylor. Oxford: Clarendon Press.

Rodriguez-Blanco. 2022. "Ways of Inhabiting the Deliberative-Aspirational Point of View: Practical Reason and Objective Goods". *American Journal of Jurisprudence*, 67: 1–35.

Sandis, C. 2022. "What Is It To Do Nothing?". In *Agency, Negligence and Responsibility*, edited by V. Pavlakos and G. Rodriguez-Blanco, 187–204. Cambridge: Cambridge University Press.

Scanlon, T. M. 2000. *What We Owe To Each Other.* Cambridge, MA: Harvard University Press.

Smith, A. 2005. "Responsibility for Attitudes". *Ethics*, 115: 236–271.

Smith, A. 2008. "Control, Responsibility and Moral Assessment". *Philosophical Studies*, 138: 367–392.

Smith, A. 2015a. "Attitudes, Tracing and Control". *Journal of Applied Philosophy*, 32: 115–132.

Smith, A. 2015b. "Responsibility as Answerability". *Inquiry*, 58: 99–126.

Smith, A. 2017. "Unconscious Omissions, Reasonable Expectations, and Responsibility". In *The Ethics and Law of Omissions*, edited by D. K. Rickless and S. Nelkin, 36–62. Oxford: Oxford University Press.

Smith, P. 1990. "Contemplating Failure: The Importance of Unconscious Omissions". *Philosophical Studies*, 59: 159–176.

Wolf, S. 1990. *Freedom Within Reason.* New York: Oxford University Press.

Legal Case

State v *Williams*, 484 P.2d 1167 (Wash. App. 1971).

4 Constitutivism and the normativity of social practices

The case of law

Triantafyllos Gkouvas

4.1 Introduction

There is a plethora of occasions where we feel the intuitive urge to say that the fact that one is a participant in some sort of conventional or institutional practice is a reason to abide by its rules. A more sophisticated urge might also include the thought that the fact that one is a participant in some sort of conventional or institutional practice is a reason to abide by its rules *because that is just what it is to be a practice participant.* Thus, if I engage in the practice of etiquette, I should not put the wine glass on the left side of the plate because that is just what it is to be a participant in such a practice. This is a more complex sample of thinking. A fact about membership of some social practice appears to be both a reason *for* acting in a certain way and a reason *why* one should act in this way. One and the same fact, it so seems, has both a prescriptive and justificatory quality.

The same piece of reasoning applies to cases of status possession as when the fact that someone is a citizen of a state is (treated as) a reason to abide by the laws of said state. In the latter case the static property of having been accorded a particular status takes over the reason-giving role that the dynamic property of participating in a practice has played in the first example. Thus, if I decide to move my bishop sideways one may retort that this is not how chess is played and that I should reconsider my move. The property of being a bishop is a status in the qualified sense that it is a higher-order property of a lower-level property such as the property of having a particular shape.

A similar argument is frequently used in jurisprudential debates: legal systems *qua* abstract entities are the mirror image of a set of immanent (hence, not purely abstract) legal practices and being a participant (official or subject) of a legal practice just is to be governed by its rules. Accordingly, the fact that someone holds a legal office or is subject to a legal jurisdiction is (treated as) a reason to act in some ways but not in others. Moreover, in the legal case, the reason-giving force is equally attributed to facts about participation as well as to facts about status possession (legal official or law subject).

The question then becomes: how are we to explain the normative pressure exerted in such cases? Membership of or participation in a practice comes with

DOI: 10.4324/9781032670553-5

practical requirements whose defiance can sometimes be deemed a sufficient reason to chastize or expel someone from the practice or, if this is normatively inconceivable, suboptimal, or counterintuitive, to compel someone to comply or make amends for failing to meet the practice requirements. On the other hand, there can be weighty or even overriding practice-extrinsic reasons (ethical, moral, prudential, 'iusnatural', or a combination thereof) to discard such requirements. If keeping the knife on my lap is the only way to prevent a toddler from grabbing it during dinner, then it seems reasonable to say that there is no genuine practical dilemma in displaying bad table manners. The problem, however, is that even if I have extremely weak reason or no reason at all to engage in a practice, the practice itself seems to generate very rigid requirements: failing to abide by said requirements counts as a violation of the rules of the practice. *Tertium non datur.*

Leaving variations aside, rigid reason ascriptions of the type under discussion display the following form:

> *The fact that a person X bears status Y is a reason to Z or a reason in favour of being treated by others as allowed or required to Z (in C) because that is just what it is to be (or be treated as) a Y*

Whereas Z is always a type of action (e.g., to move the bishop diagonally, to put the wine glass on the right side of the plate, or to pay taxes in France), it need not always be the direct complement of a 'the fact that X counts as Y'-type of reason. Depending on which level of abstraction we choose in order to regiment our talk of such rules, Z-type actions can also be embedded under state-of-affairs-like reason complements such as the reason in favour of '*being treated* as allowed or required to Z'.[1] At any rate and bracketing the ramifications of this nuance, all reason ascriptions of this kind have an interesting underlying logical structure: they are, I want to suggest, fusions of constitutive *rules* and constitutive *norms* where such fusion showcases their reason-giving 'aspirations', so to speak. Being fully aware that in the relevant literature such a distinction is not canonical (at least not in the sense I am about to explain), I should be more precise from the very beginning regarding how I intend to understand this distinction. I will suggest that constitutive rules have the form 'X counts as Y (in C)' and constitutive norms have the form '*Z-ing* (or being treated by others as allowed or required to Z) is just what it is to be a Y (in C)'. In their fusion a constitutive 'rule-norm' displays its reason-giving function

1 Treating someone as being in a certain normative predicament or position is not, however, purely attitudinal. Treatment-like attitudes are standardly expressed through various types of physical or illocutionary action.

within the form 'the fact that X is a Y is a reason for X to Z because that is just what it is to be a Y'.[2]

The *for*-reason (the fact that X is a Y) has the canonical logical structure of a constitutive rule as this concept has been exhaustively rehearsed in debates on social ontology and normativity. The *why*-reason (the fact that *Z-ing* is just what it is to be a Y) which normatively explains the obtaining of the *for*-reason has the normative flavour of a constitutive norm in the less familiar sense that we encounter in debates on the nature of practical normativity. Talk of constitutive norms in the latter domain of inquiry is usually centred on deriving the demands of practical reason from the norms that govern the bearing and exercise of agency *qua* practical power or capacity. Leaving aside the ontological discord between practical constitutivists of a neo-Kantian (Korsgaard 2009; Velleman 2009), a neo-Humean (Leffler 2016), a neo-Nietzschean (Katsafanas 2013), and a neo-Aristotelian (Silverstein 2016) bent, their vision remains crucially common: the reason-giving force of practical norms emanates from standards that are constitutive of what it is to be an agent.[3]

In this chapter, I shall argue that this way of accounting for the normativity of conventional requirements is one step ahead of what needs to be accounted for in the first place which is the following: is the normative force of practice-based requirements a matter of practical *reasons*? If practical reasons are indeed the kind of entity that do the requisite work, then constitutivism about such practical reasons *may* indeed be a promising contender for the normativity of social practices. But settling the question of whether a constitutivist account of practice-immanent reasons is explanatorily potent is methodologically prior to settling the question of whether reasons *as such* are the most suitable normative concept for making sense of the normative mechanics of social normativity. This prior question is rarely treated as a conceptual precursor to any discussion about the normativity of social practices. My timid proposal will be to consider the possibility that the normativity of social practices is more akin

2 My constitutive rules are Frank Hindriks's 'base rules' and my constitutive norms are Hindriks's 'status rules' and, obliquely, John Searle's (2010) status functions. In Hindriks's words, 'it will be useful to break Searle's formula in two parts, introducing the twin notions of "base rule" and "status rule". A status rule explicates what it means to have a certain status. The status rule of money, for instance, is "money is a medium of exchange". A base rule specifies what it takes to have a certain status. In certain contexts, an item has to be a shell in order to be money; in others it has to be a disc of metal, and so forth. In more theoretical terms, base rules concern the ontological basis or constitution base of statuses. Status rules, in contrast, are meaning rules and concern the definition of status terms. They concern the behavior that the status regulates, or the rights and obligations that the status entails' (Hindriks and Guala 2015, 470–471). For an early formulation of the same distinction see (Ransdell 1971).

3 Depending on one's further meta-normative allegiances, the latter gerundive expression ('being an agent') can be further specified as being engaged in a certain type of proto-activity (e.g., deliberation), being an agent of a certain kind (e.g., a rational agent), or being the holder of certain agential powers (abilities).

to the normativity of formal rationality than to the normativity of practical reasons.

The structure of the chapter will be simple. In the first part I shall give a brief overview of the current meta-normative inquiry. This section is more or less dedicated to painting a relatively informative map of some important distinctions operative within the domain of normative metaphysics. The key elements in this section include the alleged metaphysical primitiveness of reasons and the nature of normative explanations. Particular emphasis will be placed on the structure of constitutive explanations as they figure prominently in arguments regarding the normativity of social practices. In the second part I shall put forward the claim that 'the normativity of all that is normative' may not be exhausted by the concept of reasons. I intend to keep my claim weak enough so as to allow space for a more quietist understanding of normativity. More precisely, I shall focus on two classes of rational requirements—requirements of coherence between mental states and explanatory requirements—that seem to be recalcitrant to reasons analysis and yet are capable of providing informative explanations as to how various normative phenomena operate.

The remainder of the chapter serves to elaborate on the relevance of two points. The first point regards the distortive impact of constitutive explanations in the domain of social practices. The second point serves to amend the inadequacy of constitutivism as an explanatory tool. The suggestion I hope to be able to take through is that the normative nature of participatory social practices like games or etiquette is better thought of as inviting the application of requirements of rational coherence between two different types of 'sense' by which participatory requirements apply (the 'property sense' and the 'source sense'), whereas legal normativity is properly understood as governing the explanatory relation between two different species of the same type of 'sense' (namely, the 'source sense') by which requirements apply, namely, between non-legal and legal *sources* of requirements. If this strategy is shown to have some purchase, then many interesting conclusions may follow regarding the nature of normativity *tout court* and its relation to institutional normativity.

4.2 The normativity of all that is normative

4.2.1 Reasons

Our most intuitive grasp of normativity is, queerly enough, 'descriptive'. What I mean by descriptive is that our usual affirmative appeals to the normative are enumerative in the sense that we attach normativity to anything that stems from our use of concepts like norms, values, oughts, reasons, goodness, rightness, correctness, rationality, etc. A more philosophically nuanced approach to normativity tries to bring some order into the normative universe by drawing a wedge between evaluative and deontic properties. The former are typically instantiated in judgements about what is good or valuable whereas the latter are usually understood as introducing constraints in our judgements about what is the right thing to do, believe, or feel.

Another classificatory construal divides the normative repertoire into thick and thin properties. A mark of thick concepts is, as Bernard Williams (1985, 129–132) has suggested, that they seem to be simultaneously both evaluative and descriptive. Trait concepts like 'courageous' or 'lewd' are typically classified as bearing a thick structure. The thought is that the property of being courageous has two different by nature yet interdependent components. It's not just the case that a courageous man is brave and good, but brave and good for being brave. In that sense the descriptive part is rendered intelligible in light of the attitude that is deemed fitting for the bearer of such a property. By contrast thin properties like that of being right, wrong, good, or desirable, are considered as lacking the descriptive depth or specificity of thick predicates in the sense that we use them across widely variable contexts to evaluate all sorts of persons, states of affairs, or actions.

So far talk about normativity is more like swirling around the core of a concept whose essence remains uncapturable. I do not aspire to put an end to this agonizing quest. Nevertheless, it is possible to gain further insight into the metaphysics of normativity by exploring the possibility of adding, at least, some structure to the normative universe on the basis of relations of derivative properties to a fundamental normative category. Many philosophers tend to answer the primitiveness or fundamentality question by accepting a more or less robust version of the claim that the ultimate source of normativity consists in an intricate network of relations to reasons for actions and/or for attitudes. This latter claim need not amount to the purely analytical remark that the concept of a reason is definitionally primitive in the sense that all other normative concepts can be defined in its terms. Defining one concept in terms of another does not always settle the question of what is the direction of metaphysical dependence in the bi-conditional with the concept of a reason as *definiens*. The claim is rather metaphysical in that the nature of normative properties—not just normative concepts—consists in their relations to reasons. Although I shall not espouse the optimism of those who defend the metaphysical primitiveness of reasons, I shall expand on this reductive hypothesis as it provides the most powerful contrast with the picture I wish to develop.

Assuming for the moment that reasons enjoy metaphysical priority in the normative cosmos a few remarks are in order regarding the logical structure of reason statements of the form 'A has a reason to φ in C' or 'there is a reason for A to φ in C'. There is near consensus that the property of being a reason is relational in the sense that it denotes a relation between a proposition or a fact, a set of contextual conditions, and an action or attitude.[4] Reason-giving facts can have non-normative as well as normative contents. They can be facts about our world—as when the fact that my best friend is sick is a reason for me to visit her, they can be facts about our conative, affective or propositional attitudes—as when the fact that I desire to eat ice cream is a reason to buy some, or, they can be

4 For a systematic overview of reasons ascriptions and reasons explanation see (Väyrynen 2013).

normatively laden facts—as when the fact that it would be good to be friendly to a new colleague is a reason for me to assist her.

4.2.2 Two types of reasons-based explanation

Nevertheless, facts do not merely figure as a convenient placeholder in the left-side of the reasons relation. It is a further question whether the normative fact that something is a reason for something else is *itself* an item that calls for some further normative explanation (Väyrynen 2013). It is an almost common conviction that reason statements are not true *simpliciter* but hold in virtue of some other more fundamental truths or grounds. What is important to notice is that the relation of a fact about the obtaining of a reason relation to a grounding fact or proposition is not merely metaphysical but explanatory. To illustrate my point, when we say such things as that the fact that John promised to return the book he borrowed from Peter is a reason to do so because promises ought to be kept, we are naturally taken to suggest that the moral principle that *ceteris paribus* promises ought to be kept does not merely make it the case that giving the book back to Peter is what John has most reason to do but also that it makes it intelligible why this is the case.

What matters the most for our purposes, however, is not what figures as the proper content of a normative explanation. Rather it is the way the explanans is related to the explanandum that calls for attention. Put more succinctly, figuring out what explains the fact that killing people is wrong might be cashed out in terms of a further reason statement or evaluative verdict depending on our favoured metaethical perspective. By contrast, the issue I am addressing is, so to speak, meta-explanatory in the sense that the way we formalize an explanatory relation may significantly impact the adequacy of our explanans. Although I do not profess to be capable of providing an exhaustive map of explanatory modalities, I am confident enough that the two modes of normative explanation I am about to describe can more than adequately enhance our grasp of normative phenomena including social practices.

The first type of normative explanation is *subsumptive* (Schroeder 2005, 10–15; Schroeder 2007, 293–302). On this approach, the fact that there is a reason for me to φ is explained in virtue of its being subsumable under some categorical generalization that requires to ψ (for instance, one ought to exercise regularly) such that φ-ing (for instance, swimming) is an instance of the generic activity of ψ-ing prescribed in the explanans. On this view, the normative fact that one is required to ψ must be prior to and independent of any psychological (dispositional or motivational) or phenomenological fact on pain of vicious circularity.[5]

5 Adopting this explanatory model is not without consequences; a psychologistic theory of practical reasons like Williams's account of internal reasons is incapable of accommodating this mode of explanation. To figure out why, recall that an internal reasons proponent believes

The second type of normative explanation is *constitutive* (Heathwood 2012, 9–14; Schroeder 2005, 17–23). The constitutivist strategy aims at explaining the normative authority of reasons or values in terms of the nature or essence of a generic property or state of affairs. To illustrate my point, proponents of moral constitutivism try to explain the binding force of rational principles by interpreting them as standards of correctness derivable from the nature of agency or intentional action. On this model explaining the normative validity of a principle or norm is not a matter of subsuming it under an independently valid categorical rule; rather it comes down to showing that the relevant norm is a *partial description* of agency itself. On this construal constitutivism is reductive by default in the sense that by saying that being under an obligation to φ is just what it is to be an agent one is committed to the idea that normative principles can be explained in terms of other normative—or non-normative—notions.

4.2.3 Constitutive explanations of social normativity

A seemingly straightforward application of the constitutivist model of reasons-based normative explanation to the case of social practices comes down to the claim that, to recall our familiar variables X, Y, and Z, *Z-ing* (e.g., a bishop's being moved diagonally) is a partial description of being a Y (e.g., a bishop). You simply cannot count as a Y if you do not Z or if others do not deem you as allowed or required to Z. Accordingly, the more inescapable it is for someone to be a Y the more rigid is the reason for her to Z or to be deemed as allowed or required to Z. To illustrate, a castle's being moved in a straight line is just what it is to bear the status of 'castle' such that moving in a straight line is a partial description of bearing the status of a castle. If the bearing of such a status is an inescapable consequence of bearing the status of a chess player, then being deemed by one's fellow players as being allowed to only move in a straight line is what all game participants have a reason to do, namely, to deem me as thus and so allowed. One might stop here thinking that this is the most comprehensive answer one can get on this matter.

But the normative question still lingers and this can be easily shown by reformulating it as: 'In virtue of what do I have a reason to abide by the rule

that one's having a reason to do something holds in virtue of the content of her psychological attitudes that she would come to acquire if she deliberated properly. To put it more graphically, Keith has an internal reason to help his financially devastated friend in virtue of the fact that he has acquired the desire to help him and has no false beliefs about the actual conditions of his friend's destitution. For this explanation to fit the subsumptive type of normative explanation, it must appeal to some further thing that everyone has a reason to do, such that *ceteris paribus* everyone ought to provide assistance to friends and not just because one has acquired the desire to do so. Appealing to the latter fact makes the explanation circular. A Williams-like reasons internalism cannot accommodate universalizable imperatives, hence the subsumptive explanatory model is unlikely to work in this case.

that licenses my moving the castle only in a straight line?' Why does the fact that moving the castle in a straight line is a constitutive of playing chess operate as a reason to conform to it? One plausible reply is to say that literally speaking there is no *real* reason to act in accordance with this rule; it's just a game. But if this is our best answer, we thereby abandon the intuitive idea that there is something non-trivially normative (albeit non-moral and non-prudential) in the case of playing chess. Another answer could be that insofar as it is somehow valuable to play chess (e.g., leisure or competition) in the first place you have a reason to play by its rules. But this reply is at pains to explain the intuitive asymmetry between the defeasible value of play (i.e., there are other infinitely more exacting values than enjoying one's free time playing chess or winning a competitive game) and the putative conclusiveness or verdictiveness of practice-based requirements.

The alternative answer I tend to favour is premised on the remark that the way in which a set of rules is constitutive of a conventional practice like chess is not reducible to the way a proper constitutive normative explanation works. The point is that being a constitutive rule is a metaphysical property of abstract objects (rules) that has no explanatory function vis-à-vis the normative implications of being a practice participant. To be a constitutive rule is not an elliptical answer to the question of why I ought to follow the rule; it is a property that partially makes it the case that this practice is chess and not checkers.[6] It is precisely because a constitutive rule has no independent normative explanatory power that it is perfectly intelligible to ask whether I have an overriding or sufficiently weighty reason to participate in the practice in the first place. Trying to mold the normativity of practice-immanent requirements in the likeness of ordinary ascriptions of practical reasons is an otiose task if one wants to preserve the relevance of ordinary intuitions about the variable weight of regular reasons and the categorical appeal of constitutive rules.

4.3 Normativity beyond reasons

4.3.1 Rational requirements and the bootstrapping problem

The view that normativity is more or less amenable to the operation of reasons that carry a proper amount of 'normative weight' is not unobjectionable. Apart from arguments internal to the normativity debate, I am particularly

6 I say 'partially' because it is inaccurate to claim that only rules determine the identity of a practice. As Andrei Marmor explains, 'the identity of such a practice, like chess, is partly path dependent' (Marmor 2009, 42). There is always a 'metaphysical residue' that is extraneous to the concept of a rule that specifies how the behaviour in accordance with those rules is to be regarded. A Wittgensteinian proper way to say this is to refer to the 'grammar' of a practice as that which determines what sorts of things it makes sense to say with respect to chess. This meta-rule dimension is particularly relevant in strategic utterances like 'that was a silly move' or 'well played'. For an incisive approach see (Schwyzer 1969).

inclined to feel suspicious of the tenability of this thesis as it seems to generate grossly unintuitive results when applied to the domain of social practices. The alternative view I would like to entertain favours a kind of normative pluralism in the sense that it postulates the existence of mutually irreducible normative concepts each one performing a distinct practical and/or epistemic function. Granted that a theory of normativity amenable to being characterized as plural could be any theory that postulates the existence of at least two mutually irreducible normative concepts, I shall try to keep things as simple as possible by choosing to employ one theoretical version of normative pluralism according to which apart from the concept of a reason there are rational requirements that serve a distinct normative function.

Rational requirements are standardly (Broome 2013) taken to specify which conflicts between our various cognitive attitudes ought to be resolved or avoided if we are still lacking one of the conflicting attitudes. A typical example is the rational requirement not to have inconsistent intentions or beliefs, as in the case of someone who simultaneously believes that she ought to attend a class reunion and she does not intend to attend it. Another case is when someone does not intend what she believes to be the necessary means to her intended ends. In the cases above as well as in various others, rationality requires a certain kind of coherence among mental states. Some of our acquired attitudes will intuitively not fit to our current shape of mental states and thus need to be properly adjusted or even abandoned if one is to avoid conflict.

The leading intuition behind the theory about the distinctness of rational requirements is that the ways we exercise our mental capacities are frequently the source of rationally incoherent or morally objectionable claims. Philosophers of normativity tend to describe the relevant phenomena as 'bootstrapping'. Typical cases of bootstrapping include paradigmatic instances of immoral instrumental reasoning as when I desire to kill my mother-in-law and believe that a sufficient means for achieving this end is to hire an assassin. Is it intelligible—the 'bootstrapping' objector goes—to say that I have a reason of some kind to hire an assassin? To put it differently, it's simply not the case that simply by holding a desire or a normative belief we thereby acquire a respective reason as a matter of metaphysical necessity.

Just how precisely a rational requirement is normative is a highly contestable issue. My main concern is not to provide a comprehensive map of candidate accounts defending the normativity of rational requirements. I am more interested in showcasing the structural dimension of the relevant controversy. It is rather accurate to say that proponents of the normative nature of rational requirements generally tend to favour the so-called wide-scope interpretation (Brunero 2010; Way 2010), whereas those wishing to debunk their normative import usually employ a narrow-scope interpretation (Kolodny 2005; Schroeder 2004). To cut a long story short, 'wide-scopers' believe that an indispensable step towards vindicating the normativity of rational requirements is to offer a plausible solution to the bootstrapping problem while retaining a normative story about the norms of rationality.

The solution offered by wide-scopers as a means of avoiding unwanted reasons detachments amounts to the claim that one can equally satisfy a rational requirement by revising any one of the relevant conflicting attitude-states. There is no preference either as to what outcome among the permissible ones should be brought about or as to what is the ideal means for reaching an outcome. All that rational requirements call for is the avoidance of certain combinations of mental states no matter what means one employs in trying to satisfy the requirement. The normativity—thin as it may be—of a rational requirement is not of the same genre as the normative guidance provided by all-things-considered reasons. Wide-scope requirements perform the more modest task of specifying the permissible ways of resolving rational inconsistencies. Or conversely, their normative function is negative in the sense that it only forbids the joint holding of certain attitudes leaving it up to the deliberator to choose the alternative ways of resolving the tension.

On the contrary, 'narrow-scopers' try to account for the apparent normativity of rational requirements by explaining it away. That is, they offer an eliminative reduction base for requirements of coherence by cashing them out in terms of descriptive claims about the beliefs we have about what there is a reason to do, feel, or believe. On the narrow-scope view, having a state-given reason—a normative belief or a desire-based reason—has no genuine normative implications. If the bearer of such a reason still experiences a sentiment of rational failure by desisting from acting on her believed reason, that fact merely amounts to a failure *from a point of view*. Perspectival failures are not normative in any robust sense though. Hence, for a narrow-scoper the normativity of rational requirements is not simply superfluous, it is non-existent.

4.3.2 *Types of rational requirement*

Insofar as one is willing to subscribe to the view that there is a point of substance in preserving a function for rational requirements, there arises the further question of what serves as a criterion in classifying rational requirements. A large—maybe the largest—class of rational requirements contains requirements of formal coherence among mental states. Coherence requirements are normatively symmetric (Way 2011) in the sense that they do not guide our deliberation as to what pair of attitudes to choose among other alternatives. The intuitive idea is that formally incoherent attitudes generate some kind of normative tension which can be resolved by revising one of the conflicting attitudes. Hence, understanding the non-contradiction principle in terms of formal coherence entails that one is rationally required to avoid believing that p and non-p at the same time. It is equally coherent to say that one satisfies this requirement by dropping her initial belief that p or by not believing that not-p. So, on this construal, formal coherence does not amount to the virtue of achieving the best possible combination of attitudes. Consequently, formal coherence is content-independent or deliberator-neutral in the sense that it is not conditional on one's particular situation.

The second class of rational requirements (Broome 2013, 186–191) deals with another type of normative problem which seems to remain unresolved by merely applying a requirement of formal coherence. There are some cases of relations between attitudes that we are intuitively guided to regard as introducing a certain kind of *asymmetry* between the relata. For instance, the instrumental requirement to intend what one believes is a sufficient means for achieving an intended end provides a characteristic example of asymmetric rational relations between attitudes. Suppose that I intend to φ. Intuitively, it would be rational to intend ψ because I believe that ψ is a means for achieving φ, but irrational to drop the belief that ψ is a means to φ just because I do not intend to ψ. The asymmetry refers to the way one attitude is explained by another; it does not refer to the quite different 'asymmetry' that seems to emerge when, absent some independent reason to drop my intention to φ, I stop intending to φ rather than considering the possibility of acquiring the intention to adopt ψ as a means to achieving my initial end.

The later apparent asymmetry concerns the intuitive unequal distribution of 'compelling pressure' among the two ways of satisfying the wide-scope instrumental requirement.[7] To return back to my preferred understanding of the relevant asymmetry, explanatory requirements seem to disfavour a particular explanatory connection. That is to say, I may disbelieve ψ is a means to φ, but I am not to disbelieve it because I do not intend to ψ. Consequently, explanatory requirements are by definition narrow-scope *because* they are normatively asymmetric as opposed to requirements of coherence which are wide-scope *because* they are normatively symmetric.

4.3.3 Formal coherence and participatory practices

The incongruence between the bearing of practice-extrinsic reasons to conform or not conform with the rules of a practice and the rigidity with which the practice rules apply to their participants is a matter that often invites deflationary responses either in the direction of denying that conventional rules are bearers of any distinct kind of normativity or in the direction of ascribing semantic incompetence to those who go about applying the rules of a game on the basis of reason-giving considerations. A non-deflationary way to move forward is—I believe—to reformulate the structure of the incongruence described above and try to see whether it can be interpreted *in the likeness* of wide-scope readings of requirements of rational coherence. A promising way to proceed is by utilizing an ingenious distinction suggested by John Broome with regard to the logical properties of requirements in general rather than just rational requirements. Broome (2013, 109–119) distinguishes between

7 This different kind of asymmetry has been considered by defenders of the narrow-scope view as a fatal flaw of the wide-scope formula. See (Schroeder 2004, 352) and (Bedke 2009, 687–689).

the property sense and the source sense of requirements (moral, rational, or prudential).

The property sense of moral requirements manifests itself explicitly in utterances such as 'humans ought to be moral'. In this sense the property of being moral denotes an attainment of some sort which is ascribable to a person. So, when we understand morality in the property sense a statement like 'Morality *requires* of John that he φ' entails that, necessarily, if John bears the property of being moral, he φ-s.[8] Property requirements display an interesting gradability in the sense that it is intelligible to say that there are more or less morally proper ways of achieving this end. What is interesting about the degrees of property requirements is that they do not provide guidance as to what one ought to do in a given case. Broome uses a very illustrative example to depict this incongruity. If I can be moral either by using less energy or by giving more money to Oxfam, a property understanding of the relevant requirement could legitimize the statement that it is not the case that morality requires that I use less energy. But as Broome remarks, that is intuitively wrong. It is rather the case that morality requires *both* that I use less energy and that I give more money to Oxfam.

What counterbalances the unintuitive implications of the property construal of requirements is the source approach or, as I would like to term it, the 'action-guiding' approach. Source requirements are better understood as individual propositions specifying what is required in a particular circumstance. Thus, source requirements are operative within a particular possible world at which the corresponding required proposition is true. So, whereas at the actual world *w* I am required—in the source sense—to be kind to strangers, at another possible world where I am not a sociophobe, it is not the case that I am required to be kind to strangers. On the source construal, requirements I am under may not be the same at all worlds. This is a feature that the property construal cannot capture. Being moral is too 'insatiable' a property to guide us in particular situations—where we are inevitably fallible somehow—in the sense that what is required of me is an infinite set of propositions that are necessary conditions for my qualifying as being moral.

How can we utilize this distinction in the quest for explaining the normativity of (some) social practices? First of all, I have to designate somehow the corresponding terms for the property and source sense for practices of the sort we've been discussing so far. I will choose to use the property term 'being a participant'

8 Notice that the meaning of the necessity operator does not cover every metaphysical possibility but is context-dependent. That is to say, it is not the case that necessarily if John does not φ, he is immoral. There might be a context within which φ-ing is a morally sub-optimal choice. This is something that a strong counterfactual interpretation of the property sense of a requirement cannot capture. A reverse implication of this strictly modal interpretation is that the possibility of being moral has to be secured in the sense that it would be counterintuitive to address a requirement to someone when it is counterfactually impossible for her to bear the respective property.

in order to provide a generic characterization for members of a practice. The property of being a participant can be more 'thickly' described depending on the particular practice we are dealing with. So we can say that by following the rules of chess one bears the property of being a chess player and so forth. We can further thicken those properties by adding some reference to the value of the practice or some features that rigidly designate it. For instance, we can say that by playing chess well one bears the property of being a 'competent chess player'. As for the source sense it suffices to talk about practice requirements.

What makes the property-source distinction particularly useful for our purposes is a very interesting disanalogy between the standard uses of this distinction for sources of requirements like morality, prudence, or rationality, and its potential use in the domain of social practices. In the former case the source sense and the property sense are necessarily co-instantiated in the sense that when morality requires of you, in the source sense, to φ, it follows—by strict implication—that morality also requires, in the property sense, to φ. Otherwise put, you cannot satisfy each particular requirement without bearing the property of, say, being moral. But that is not the case in practice requirements. I can get rid of the property of being a participant without so failing to satisfy a practice requirement. For example, I may decide not to play chess without violating in any sense its rules. Whereas in the former case source requirements necessarily set the boundaries of their property correlatives, in the case of a participatory practice the source and property sense come entirely apart without incurring criticism of any kind.

Now I would like to argue that this is not a trivial remark; on the contrary it serves as the major incentive for applying a wide-scope formula in order to explicate the normative function of a large set of practices, namely those that are *participatory* in some substantive sense. To see how this works allow me once again to contrast our case with the domain of formal rationality where the wide-scope strategy is more explicitly deployed. In the latter case the wide-scope formula does not *directly* govern the relation between the source and the property sense of rational requirements. As previously noted, these two senses are inseparable. The disjunctive ways of satisfying a rational requirement refer, instead, to our *cognitive attitudes*, not to the requirement itself that regulates their relation. To recall a classical example, I can satisfy the instrumental requirement either by dropping my intention to fulfill an end or by intending to take the appropriate means for its achievement. By sharp contrast, I can satisfy the chess requirement either by conforming to its local source requirements (rules) or by not participating or withdrawing participation, that is, by not bearing or renouncing the property of being a participant.

On this new picture, a plausible answer to the normative question with regard to participatory practices comes down to this:

CohR: *one is practice-required [either to follow its rules or to cease being a participant]*

CohR has wide scope in the sense that it can be satisfied in two ways. The normative prohibition implied by this proposition is that one should not be a participant and, at the same time, not abide by the relevant rules. This negative proviso is the core of the normativity of participatory practices. On this construal, requirements pertaining to participatory practices like chess or etiquette are requirements of formal coherence just like the majority of requirements of formal rationality. In the case of participatory social practices formal coherence is understood as coherence *between the source and the property sense* of a practice requirement as opposed to the case of formal rationality where formal coherence is supposed to govern the relation between our relevant *attitudes*.[9]

4.3.4 *Law as a source of explanatory requirements*

Is the previous analysis somehow informative as to how law performs its normative operation? My aspiration is to show that the preceding analysis was not an unnecessary digression but an indispensable background against which I might be able to advance an original argument about the social normativity of legal rationality. The three key concepts I shall be employing throughout this last section are already familiar: the wide-scope formula, the distinction between coherence and explanatory requirements, as well as the distinction between the property and the source sense of requirements.

I shall begin my analysis by examining whether it is possible to apply in a similar fashion the property-source distinction to the legal case and, consequently, assume that legal normative requirements are, just like participatory practice requirements, requirements of coherence between a legal property sense and a legal source sense. My answer will be negative: there is no such thing as the property sense of legal requirements, only a source sense. If I were to pick out one specific property that is distinctive of law that would most plausibly be the property of *being legal*. Thus, we say, for example, that this is the legal way to notarize a contract or that it is illegal to drive under the age of 16. I deliberately choose to keep the property of legality as thin as possible in order to avoid question-begging commitments regarding the nature of law. That is, if I were to choose a thicker property as that of being lawful, law-abiding, or fair I would be presupposing something that I had not presupposed in the previous cases.

In the case of morality or rationality the property sense of their respective requirements is not informative in any robust sense as to what is the nature of morality or rationality. Being moral or rational is just the property correlative of being under a moral or rational requirement. A more informative approach would be to 'thicken' the respective properties by saying something

9 Whether coherence between the source and the property *sense* of a requirement is also a type of coherence among attitudes is a further question that I am inclined to answer in the affirmative. The source sense is or corresponds to the attitude of considering oneself bound by the applicable practice requirements and the property sense is or corresponds to the attitude of considering oneself a practice participant.

like 'being such that maximizes utility' or 'being such that preserves coherence'. But these descriptions do not seem to follow immediately from the concept of being moral or rational. They are further *substantive* conceptions of the initial, generic property of being moral or rational. Likewise, in the case of law, choosing to thicken the property of legality is to presuppose too much already. Therefore, I shall stick to the initial thin version of being legal as interpreted in the examples mentioned above.

Now, supposing that what I have said so far is more or less unobjectionable I move to a crucial observation that follows from my last remark. Once again John Broome has astutely remarked that law is never the name of a property that can be possessed by a person. Being legal is always the property of acts or normative propositions but it cannot be informatively ascribed to a person. A point of caution is in order: one could respond to this remark by saying that being law-abiding is the respective property possessed by law subjects. But that is plainly wrong. The latter property is simply trivial as it is a mere adjectivization of the respective *source* requirement. To say that one is a law-abiding citizen is just to say that she satisfies the relevant legal requirements. But, as explained above, to be a requirement in the property sense is much more 'global' than merely satisfying the requirements one is under in a particular situation. Therefore, law-abidingness won't work as an informative property correlative of legal source requirements.

The crucial point then is: what follows from the fact that law can be understood only as generating requirements in the source sense? I believe that what ensues from this remark is far from trivial. Firstly, the fact that persons cannot claim the property of being legal as being entailed by the respective source requirements reveals a conceptual truth about law that many political and legal philosophers tend to recognize. Law is not a participatory conventional practice in the sense that the acquisition or loss of legal status *qua property* is not a genuinely voluntary act of individuals. The status of a citizen or a legal person within a certain legal jurisdiction is constituted by the law and cannot be freely disposed of irrespective of the relevant rules governing one's legal status. It is important to notice that this is not a moral truth about law but a conceptual feature about its institutional operation.

Secondly, the fact that legal requirements are requirements only in the source sense makes available for exploration the hypothesis that law may be *meta-normatively* potent if there apply certain normative standards on the proper explanatory order that holds between legal source requirements and some non-legal source requirements. In other words, legal practices may be normative in the higher-order sense that their function necessitates the adoption of certain standards on how legal source requirements bear upon the explanation of non-legal source requirements. This is a more abstract way of referring to law's celebrated (or lamented, depending on how one reads the history of this debate) relation to extra-legal sources of requirements such as virtue, morality, prudence, and natural law.

To see how this line of reasoning can work it is advisable to entertain a distinction which is likely to be seen by many as *ad hoc* or artificial. The distinction I invite the reader to consider as plausible or worthy of further exploration is between practical deliberation and adjudication.[10] My intention is to use this to map this distinction on a less unfamiliar distinction between all things considered requirements and legal requirements. All things considered requirements of which moral requirements is the most paradigmatic case, I would like to suggest, are deliberative in the sense that they are ascertained or discovered through deliberative reasoning. Conversely, legal requirements are adjudicative in the sense that they are derived through a special (namely, distinctly juridical) form of inferential reasoning.

Deliberative requirements serve as the termination point of episodes of practical deliberation, namely, deliberation about what to do. Deliberative requirements are about what one ought *to do all things considered* and serve as conclusive answers to practical deliberative questions ('what should I do?'). Such requirements are final instructions for how to conduct oneself in or respond to a given type of situation. Virtue, morality, prudence, and natural law are sources of practical requirements that naturally seem to vie for this role in the sense that the ordinary outcomes (conclusions) of practical deliberation are statements of what virtue, morality, prudence, or natural law require all things considered. To say that virtue, morality, prudence, or natural law require of me to φ is to say that the requirement to φ is the right thing *to put an end* to thinking about what I ethically, morally, prudentially, or iusnaturally ought to do.[11]

Perhaps contrary to folk and academic intuition alike, I would like to suggest that law is not a source of deliberatively ascertained but a source of adjudicatively ascertained practical requirements. Adjudicatively ascertained requirements are not about what one ought to *do* all things considered but rather about which *eventualities* ought to *be deemed* as one's own to deal with.[12] If someone suffers a loss as the result of my own wrongdoing, dealing with this loss is my problem—I am liable to damages—not the person's who suffered the loss because of me. In the absence of an appropriate insurance policy, ending up with a broken leg after having slipped in my bathtub is a

10 For a very illuminating defence of this distinction in a different context see (Valentini 2022, 8–11) and (Bello-Hutt 2017, 83).

11 For someone to be required to φ in the deliberative sense is for the question of what to do to be settled in a some more or less conclusive way. Moreover, being required to φ in the deliberative sense entails that one's duty to φ does not conflict with a duty not to φ or with a duty whose fulfillment requires of me not to φ.

12 Arthur Ripstein (Ripstein 2004) develops an account of tort law along these lines but goes a step further in suggesting that solutions to adjudicative disputes presuppose answers to corresponding moral questions of the form 'how should we treat each other'. Whether such questions are deliberative in the sense I develop here and whether their relation to adjudicative questions ('which affairs are my responsibility?') are issues that I leave aside for future discussion.

predicament that I have to deal with by paying the medical bills on my own dime. If my reckless driving results in someone's losing her life, the latter loss is my problem to deal with—I am civilly liable to compensate the statutorily defined close relatives and criminally liable to punishment. If I end up being much worse off financially as a result of my competitor's luring my customers away by providing a better combination of product quality and price this my problem to deal with.[13] My competitor is not liable for not providing me with a favourable market context in which to run my business. This sums up to the hypothesis that being adjudicatively required to φ is jargon for saying that seeing to it that φ is my responsibility.

Accordingly, the suggestion I would like to make is that, whereas deliberative reasoning concerns the settling of first-personal *questions* about which actions are due ('what should I do?'), adjudicative reasoning concerns the resolution of *disputes* about which practical predicaments are fittingly deemed to fall within the domain of my responsibility *instead of someone else's*. Deciding whose problem an unwelcome situation or eventuality should be deemed is the bread and butter of judicial practice which, in its turn, is the institutional amalgamation of this type of reasoning. Legal disputes can indeed be and often are formalized in terms of first- or second-personal questions about what I should do or what you should do, but that does not make them first- or second-personal questions in a purely deliberative or dialogical respectively sense because they are neither mine nor yours but a third party's (the judge's) to answer.

Such disputes can be of a private (civil), public (criminal), or hybrid (administrative) nature but their common core is that the impartial resolution of a dispute by means of a predetermined procedure is *allocative* in nature: following this procedure determines which consequences are to be deemed as properly left to whom they befall and which ones are to be deemed as admitting of removal from one's domain of responsibility and, subsequently, as admitting of reassignment to someone else's domain of responsibility.[14] The distinction I have just drawn suggests that deliberatively ascertained requirements relate agents to actions by specifying which actions are due, whereas adjudicatively ascertained requirements relate agents to practical predicaments by specifying which situations or events are fittingly deemed as one's own to deal with or, equivalently, as falling within one's own domain of responsibility.

With this distinction on board, the next step is to shoulder the hypothesis that the relation between deliberatively ascertained requirements and adjudicatively ascertained requirements is governed by certain explanatory constraints. In other words, there are proper and improper ways of relating the explanation of why I ought to φ all things considered with the issue of which practical predicaments ought to be deemed as mine to deal with. My way

13 I owe this example and its underlying rationale to (Ripstein 2009, 49–50).

14 For an allocative understanding of legal justice see (Gardner 2000).

of understanding the propriety of this relation is to exclude facts about the obtaining of legal requirements (in short, legal facts) from contributing to the explanation of why, all things considered, one ought to do this instead of that. Contributing to an explanation is a matter of adding a consideration to the list of considerations whose combination in a successful episode of practical deliberation will provide an all things considered justification of why I ought to φ.[15]

The exclusion of legal facts from playing the role of reasons that bear on genuinely deliberative questions lies on the opposite side of those who admit of constitutive explanations of legal authority of the form 'I ought to φ *because Rex said so*' where 'because Rex said so' is treated as analytically equivalent with 'because the Law so requires'.[16] Such explanations purport to be constitutive in the aforedescribed sense that for Rex to obligate me to φ is just what it is for it to be the case that I ought to φ. Rex's authoritative edict, in other words, is a partial description of what it is to be under a legal duty to φ.

My counter-response to this model of explanation is that locutions of the form 'I ought to φ because the law so requires' are normatively ill-formed because they premise the explanation of the obtaining of a deliberative requirement ('φ-ing is the right thing to do') on the obtaining of an adjudicative requirement ('φ-ing is my responsibility'). The latter requirement falsely appears to operate as a reason that contributes its normative weight to the justification of a practical decision. The fact that φ-ing is my responsibility is not a reason that fully explains why φ-ing is the right thing to do. At best it may *enable* other facts to explain why I ought to φ in the sense that it qualifies as eligible reasons that otherwise could not contribute to the explanation of why I ought to φ.[17]

These two types of requirement, I want to insist, form two orthogonally related types of practical reasoning and that makes their interaction less smooth or straightforward than what the locution 'I ought to φ *because the law says so*' appears to suggest. To appreciate why this is so I would like to take one final step by paraphrasing the clause 'because the law so requires or says' into the clause 'because I $\text{ought}_{\text{ADJ}}$ to φ' and reparse the previous statement as follows:

15 For an account of reasons as contributive explanantia see (Dancy 2004, 15–37).

16 Mark Greenberg outlines this type of explanation (which he dubs 'the command paradigm') in terms of the property of explanatory directness. In his words, '[in] the complete *constitutive* [my emphasis] account of the obtaining of a given legal norm…there are no explanatory intermediaries between the authoritative pronouncement's being made and the norm's obtaining' (Greenberg 2011, 44).

17 An analogy with promissory requirements might help. The fact that my promise was not given under duress enables the fact that I uttered the sentence 'I promise to φ' to contribute *qua reason-giving fact* to the explanation of why I ought to φ. Accordingly, one may intelligibly assume that the fact that I was not forced into promising to φ is nothing but the negative correlative of the positive fact that I assumed the responsibility for seeing to it that φ. For the notion of enabling an explanation see (Dancy 2004, 38–52).

(1) I $ought_{DEL}$ to φ because I $ought_{ADJ}$ to φ

What I want to suggest is that $ought_{ADJ}$ cannot be a normative explanans of $ought_{DEL}$ because the first-personal pronoun 'I' on the left-hand side of the statement is intensional, whereas the same pronoun on the right-hand side is extensional. To say that the deliberative 'I' is intensional in this case is to say that it is semantically opaque in the sense that it is not intersubstitutable *salva sensu* (namely, without a change in meaning) with other pronouns like 'you' or 'he/she' or with proper names like John or Mary. On the contrary, the adjudicative 'I' is extensional in precisely the opposite sense: nothing in the meaning of 'I $ought_{ADJ}$ to φ' changes if we replace 'I' with 'You' or 'John'. Self-ascriptions of adjudicative requirements are not robustly experiential in a phenomenologically or psychologically first-personal way and for quite a plausible reason: the procedure (adjudication) by which they are ascertained and eventually ascribed is transpersonal *because* followed from an impersonal *because* impartial point of view, namely, the point of a view of a mediator or judge (actual or idealized).

Accordingly, precisely 'because the law so requires' can only pick out an adjudicatively ascertained requirement or ought, (1) can be reparsed as:

(2) I $ought_{DEL}$ to φ because John $ought_{ADJ}$ to φ

which reads nonsensical, or so I dare to believe. Granted that I *am* John, I, nonetheless, cannot feature in an episode of practical deliberation in the third-personal mode of 'I am thinking about what John (me) ought to do'. The metaphysical explanation for this runs deep, perhaps deeper than I can currently fathom. One such possible explanation could be that actions are intrinsic properties of self-conscious individuals (in short, subjects) rather than of individuals *tout court*.[18] Conversely, and quite revealingly, unwelcome eventualities that can or ought to be deemed as falling within the domain of someone's responsibility are not—at least not without further argument—*intrinsic* properties of (conscious) agents. Whether these eventualities are *my* problem or someone else's problem is a question that is not settled solely by virtue of how I reflect upon myself as an agent. Responsibility for how these eventualities are to be dealt with is conferred upon an agent *within the context of a social practice* of holding others responsible that regulates the allocation of the burdens and benefits among members of a politically organized society.

That brings me to my final and hopefully modest point which is that there obtains a rational explanatory constraint on the relation between law as a source of adjudicative requirements and virtue/morality/prudence/natural law as sources of deliberative requirements. Law is not an autonomous normative domain in precisely the sense that it cannot settle *in and of itself* the

18 For a similar account see (Schroeder 2011, 24, 33). Schroeder does not refer to actions as intrinsic but as 'non-trivial' (ibid, 24).

first-personal, deliberative question of what I ought to do. Whether it is a mirror or modifier of what other domains of normativity require is a further, distinct jurisprudential question. Regardless of how this further question is settled, legal requirements cannot, I want to suggest, operate as explanantia of deliberative requirements and that is a minimal, yet important *normative* constraint.

Acknowledging the normative pull of this constraint is enough to disqualify the constitutive-explanatory model from accounting for the normativity of legal authority. Law is *not* normative in the sense that it guides practical deliberation in an authoritative way. It is rationally improper, I claim, to say that there are occasions where I ought in the deliberative sense to φ because that is (part of) what it is to be obligated by a legal authority. Exercises of legal authority, I dare to insist, cannot engage my agency in a deliberative, first-personal way.[19] They *do* engage my agency in an adjudicative way (namely, in a responsibility-implicating way) and when they do so they seem to exert a normative pressure of their own but this pressure, whenever and however intensely it applies, is not the pressure of practical reasons.

The thesis I have just put forward is minimal in the sense that it does not specify the kind of normative force exerted by requirements resulting from the exercise of legal authority. I remain charitably or, perhaps, embarrassingly agnostic about that. The thesis simply states that, whatever force they are left with, legally authoritative requirements do not operate as *reasons* because they cannot directly bear on the *deliberative* question of what I should do. Whatever else they are, practical reasons are considerations that bear on deliberation about what I should do all things considered. Adjudicatively invoked considerations are not fit for playing this role, hence they are barred from bearing directly on the respective explanation of why I should act in a particular way. This explanatory normative constraint can read as follows:

ExR: *Rationality requires of me [not to settle the question of what I ought to do on the basis of ascertaining what I am responsible for seeing to it that it happens]*

'Because the law requires of me to φ' is elliptical for 'because I am legally responsible for seeing to it that φ'. The latter locution cannot properly serve as a reason that helps to settle a practical question ('what should I do?') or a practical dilemma ('should I do this or that?'). ExR tells me that I should not decide what to do on the basis of which affairs are fittingly deemed as my responsibility. Morality, for instance, may occasionally require that I treat other people's problems *as if* I were responsible for their solution or it may

19 Whether exercises of legal authority can nonetheless engage my agency in a *second*-personal way is an open question that an analogical application of Stephen Darwall's second-personal account of moral authority may answer in the affirmative. For this analogical application see (Darwall 2007).

allow that I treat others as answerable if they fail to provide me with a favourable context in which to pursue the ends that I value. The same (perhaps even more acutely) can apply in the case of virtue.

Conversely, I cannot decide for myself and on the basis of the reasons that I reflectively endorse which losses I happen to impose on other members of society are theirs to deal with and which are mine or which gains I derive from my co-existence with others are mine to process and which are to be shared with or conceded to others. It is the job of law *qua* 'allocator' of the burdens and benefits of social co-existence to determine which losses or gains are up to me to deal with. Accordingly, it is irrational to treat answers to irreducibly first-personal practical questions about what to do as if they were solutions to interpersonal disputes about whose problem it is to deal with a potential or actual predicament.

References

Bedke, Matthew. 2009. "The Iffiest Oughts: A Guise of Reasons Account of End-Given Conditionals". *Ethics* 119 (4): 672–698. https://doi.org/10.1086/600130.

Bello-Hutt, Donald. 2017. "Deliberation and Courts: The Role of the Judiciary in a Deliberative System". *Theoria* 64 (152): 77–103. https://doi.org/10.3167/th.2017.6415204.

Broome, John. 2013. *Rationality Through Reasoning*. Malden, MA: Blackwell Publishing.

Brunero, John. 2010. "The Scope of Rational Requirements". *Philosophical Quarterly* 60 (238): 28–49. https://doi.org/10.1111/j.1467-9213.2008.596.x.

Dancy, Jonathan. 2004. *Ethics Without Principles*. Oxford, UK: Oxford University Press.

Darwall, Stephen. 2007. "Law and the Second-Person Standpoint." *Loyola of Los Angeles Law Review* 40 (3): 891–910. https://digitalcommons.lmu.edu/llr/vol40/iss3/2.

Gardner, John. 2000. "The Virtue of Justice and the Character of Law". *Current Legal Problems* 53 (1): 1–30. https://doi.org/10.1093/clp/53.1.1.

Greenberg, Mark. 2011. "The Standard Picture and Its Discontents." In *Oxford Studies in Philosophy of Law: Volume 1*, edited by Leslie Green and Brian Leiter, 39–106. Oxford, UK: Oxford University Press.

Heathwood, Chris. 2012. "Could Morality Have a Source?". *Journal of Ethics & Social Philosophy* 6 (2): 1–19. https://www.jesp.org/index.php/jesp/article/view/62.

Hindriks, Frank, and Francesco Guala. 2015. "Institutions, Rules, and Equilibria: A Unified Theory." *Journal of Institutional Economics* 11 (3): 459–480. https://doi.org/10.1017/S1744137414000496.

Katsafanas, Paul. 2013. *Agency and the Foundations of Ethics: Nietzschean Constitutivism*. Oxford, UK: Oxford University Press.

Kolodny, Niko. 2005. "Why Be Rational?". *Mind* 114 (455): 509–563. https://doi.org/10.1093/mind/fzi509.

Korsgaard, Christine. 2009. *Self-Constitution: Agency, Identity, Integrity*. Oxford, UK: Oxford University Press.

Leffler, Olof. 2016. "The Foundations of Agency – and Ethics?." *Philosophia* 44: 547–563. https://doi.org/10.1007/s11406-016-9702-2.

Marmor, Andrei. 2009. *Social Conventions: From Language to Law*. Princeton, NJ: Princeton University Press.

Ransdell, Joseph. 1971. "Constitutive Rules and Speech-Act Analysis". *The Journal of Philosophy* 68 (13): 385–400. https://doi.org/10.2307/2025037.

Ripstein, Arthur. 2004. "Philosophy of Tort Law." In *The Oxford Handbook of Jurisprudence and Philosophy of Law*, edited by Jules L. Coleman, Kenneth Einar Himma and Scott J. Shapiro, 656–686. Oxford, UK: Oxford University Press.

Ripstein, Arthur. 2009. *Force and Freedom: Kant's Legal and Political Philosophy*. Cambridge, MA: Harvard University Press.

Searle, John. 2010. *Making the Social World: The Structure of Human Civilization*. New York, NY: Oxford University Press.

Schroeder, Mark. 2004. "The Scope of Instrumental Reason". *Philosophical Perspectives* 18 (1): 337–364. https://doi.org/10.1111/j.1520-8583.2004.00032.x.

Schroeder, Mark. 2005. "Cudworth and Normative Explanations". *Journal of Ethics & Social Philosophy* 1 (3): 1–27. https://jesp.org/index.php/jesp/article/view/15.

Schroeder, Mark. 2007. "Reasons and Agent-neutrality". *Philosophical Studies* 135: 279–306. https://doi.org/10.1007/s11098-007-9087-y.

Schroeder, Mark. 2011. "Ought, Agents, and Actions". *Philosophical Review* 120 (1): 1–41. https://doi.org/10.1215/00318108-2010-017.

Schwyzer, Hubert. 1969. "Rules and Practices". *Philosophical Review* 78 (4): 451–467. https://www.jstor.org/stable/2184198.

Silverstein, Matthew. 2016. Teleology and Normativity. In *Oxford Studies in Metaethics*, 11, edited by Russ Shafer-Landau, 214–240. Oxford, UK: Oxford University Press.

Valentini, Chiara. 2022. "Deliberative Constitutionalism and Judicial Review: A Systemic Approach". Revus 47: 1–27. https://doi.org/10.4000/revus.8030.

Väyrynen, Pekka. 2013. "Grounding and Normative Explanation". *Proceedings of the Aristotelian Society* 87: 155–178. https://www.jstor.org/stable/23482055.

Velleman, David. 2009. *How We Get Along*. Oxford, UK: Oxford University Press.

Way, Jonathan. 2010. "Defending the Wide-Scope Approach to Instrumental Reason". *Philosophical Studies* 147 (2): 213–233. https://www.jstor.org/stable/40542491.

Way, Jonathan. 2011. "The Symmetry of Rational Requirements". *Philosophical Studies* 155: 227–239. https://doi.org/10.1007/s11098-010-9563-7.

Williams, Bernard. 1985. *Ethics and the Limits of Philosophy*. Cambridge, MA: Harvard University Press.

5 Robustly enough

A constitutivist explanation of legal normativity

Jorge Silva Sampaio

5.1 Introduction

According to the Portuguese legal system, everyone is *forbidden* to kill.[1] No one questions the existence of a legal norm that prohibits killing—and, from another perspective, that confers a right to life—but am I *really* forbidden to kill and what exactly does that mean?[2] To put it differently, despite the existence of *this* legal norm, why should I comply with it?[3] Well, perhaps I should comply with it because, considering that the Portuguese law contains severe sanctions for non-compliance, *prudence* advises it. Or perhaps I should comply with it because I have a *moral* reason not to kill. It is no coincidence that this discussion has been related with the question of whether legal norms and legal systems can produce or change *moral* obligations or reasons for action.[4]

Despite numerous theoretical disagreements regarding the nature of law, there is some agreement that law is, on the one hand, a *social* practice and, on the other hand, it has a *practical* nature as it is functionally designed to guide human behaviour, making it plausibly *normative* qua reason-giving. But do legal norms actually make any difference to the structure or content of institutional and non-institutional agents' practical deliberation?[5] Alternatively, do legal norms serve as *motivational* guides for these agents (Shapiro 1998, 490)? In essence, what type of *normativity* does the law possess?

1 Of course, the norm in question has constitutional pedigree, but that fact is irrelevant for the present purposes. What is relevant is the fact that this norm is a member of the Portuguese legal system.

2 I adhere to the prevailing linguistic convention in the legal field, particularly in continental Europe and South America, where the term 'norm' is commonly used instead of 'rule' to denote legal normative contents. Additionally, legal norms are often classified as either 'rules' or 'principles' based on their specific or generic structure.

3 Unlike certain antipositivist authors and others, I clearly distinguish between the 'existence' (or 'validity', although I consider them distinct) of law and its 'normativity', as I believe they have different conditions.

4 On the obligation to obey the law, for example, see Bix 2023, 161 ff.

5 This is, of course, a reference to the 'practical difference thesis'. On the subject, among others, see Shapiro 1998; Coleman 2001; Waluchow 2000.

DOI: 10.4324/9781032670553-6

Traditionally, law is considered to be a mere source of *formal* normativity, while morality and prudential rationality are viewed as sources of *robust* normativity.[6] In this sense, many legal philosophers argue that:

(1) Law's normativity is identical to games' normativity.

For instance, Bix (2018, 40) recently argued for an 'unambitious view of legal normativity', suggesting that the law does not necessarily make moral claims on its subjects. He posits that assuming practical reasoning is not a unified practice, legal normativity is confined to a particular domain.[7] In an influential paper, Enoch (2011) claimed that it is far from clear whether robust normativity is a non-contingent feature of legal systems.[8] From this perspective, it can be inferred that formal normativity would be the only non-contingent property of law, akin to games. This implies that the robustness of law's normativity would depend, for example, on factors such as the moral authority of law or the presence of coercive mechanisms to induce compliance, which are contingent facts.[9] Accordingly:

(2) Legal normativity can be boosted by morality or prudence.

While proposition (2) appears true, proposition (1) seems implausible. The statement that one is only *bound* to play by the legal norms if one chooses to participate in the legal practice remains counterintuitive, to say the least.[10] The primary objective of this chapter is to propose an account of the nature of legal normativity that explains the intuition that law's normativity cannot be equated with that of games, regardless of the moral or prudential reasons it may instantiate. This account of the *distinctive* authority possessed by legal norms in practical reasoning will be grounded in a constitutivist framework.[11]

The argument runs as follows. Through a constitutivist lens, I argue that law can be viewed as a necessary means to achieve one of our ends related to

6 See Section 5.2.
7 On a similar vein, see Redondo 2019.
8 Seemingly agreeing, see Toh 2019, 226.
9 For instance, according to Copp's (2019, 58) 'legal teleology' thesis, in the circumstances faced by modern societies, there is a 'pro tanto moral obligation to do what is required by laws that are not unjust'.
10 Criticizing Bix for this reason, see for example Bertea (2019, 11), who says that 'etiquette, fashion, and games are circumscribed practices by their own nature; by contrast, the law constitutively concerns general and essential dimensions of our existence and so purportedly impacts on the reasoning about how we ought to act period. This is why the practical claims the law makes cannot be compared with the practical claims etiquette, fashion, and games make'.
11 According to Lindeman (2019, 88), constitutivism is a metaethical account well-positioned to provide a general explanation of diverse normative domains.

action. Specifically, drawing from evolutionary theory, I propose that humans are inherently disposed to cooperate for survival, indicating a general motivational attitude towards abiding by laws. The drive for survival thus emerges as a constitutive end of law, because law is an essential means to further cooperation for survival. Given law's indispensable role in fulfilling this end, as an objective matter of normative practical rationality, individuals are rationally compelled to comply with law. Consequently, legal norms establish non-optional universal reasons for action, showcasing robust normativity independent of moral or prudential reasons, which appears as a non-contingent feature of legal systems. Moreover, the argument highlights a clear distinction between the normativity of law and that of games, asserting that law possesses an inherent normative force transcending mere formal correctness criteria.

I will proceed as follows. In Section 5.2, I will briefly analyze the concept of normativity, emphasizing the role of motivating reasons, and introduce how can legal normativity be accounted. In Section 5.3, I will analyze the concept of constitutivism to assess whether the potential robustness of law's normativity can be explained based on its constitutive features, particularly its conceptual function. Then, in Section 5.4, building upon a soft constitutivist framework, I will argue that law's normativity transcends mere game-like normativity because we possess an attitude towards obeying law, serving as the motivational trigger for legal reasons. Specifically, I will posit that the behavioural disposition to rule-following humans show imbue law with an overlooked *motivational normativity*. Finally, in Section 5.5, I will address some possible objections, to which I offer some brief rebuttals.

5.2 The concept of normativity

As the main objective of this paper is to contribute to explaining *legal* normativity, it is important to begin by explaining the general concept of normativity. We use various terms to describe and evaluate behaviour, emotions, and people, such as 'obligatory', 'illegal', '(in)appropriate', 'good', 'bad', 'permitted', and 'required'. These terms serve different practical purposes: they prescribe, justify, recommend, advise, praise, censure, and evaluate actions, thoughts, and feelings. They display *normativity* (Baker 2018, 567), indicating the standards by which we judge and guide behaviour and attitudes.

Moreover, different normative systems apply to different domains.[12] For example, epistemic norms govern cognitive attitudes, legal norms regulate behaviour, and moral norms potentially influence both behaviour and conative attitudes (Baker 2018, 567). This diversity suggests that normative terms are relative to standards from various domains—moral, prudential, legal—highlighting the existence of varieties of normativity (Wodak 2017).

12 Which seems to suggest the 'fractionation' of practical reasoning. Claiming this, see Redondo 1996.

There appears to be a widespread agreement that language (including words, sentences, and speech acts such as utterances) and thought (involving concepts and mental acts such as judgements) can be *normative* (Finlay 2019, 190 ff; Wedgewood 2018, 24; Copp and Morton 2022). Even if some question the existence of normative facts, few would dispute the presence of normative thoughts. For instance, the common belief that certain actions are wrong demonstrates the existence of normative concepts within those thoughts. One area where philosophers commonly direct their attention is towards normative judgements and the language used to express them (Finlay 2019, 196). Specifically, this focus centres on the role of normative judgement in practical deliberation—the process by which we make decisions and take action (Finlay 2019, 197). Normative concepts play a vital role in this deliberative process and are thus believed to psychologically influence our actions to some extent.[13]

There is general agreement that normative concepts primarily serve an *action-guiding* function. However, the nature of normativity is a subject of debate among philosophers, particularly between cognitivist realists and noncognitivist antirealists. Cognitivist realists argue that a sentence or judgement is normative if it represents something normative in the world (e.g., facts, entities, properties, functions, or normative relations). In contrast, noncognitivist antirealists reject the existence of normative facts or properties, instead claiming that normativity is a property of the concepts or terms themselves. They contend that normative sentences and judgements do not directly represent reality[14] but instead suggest that their normativity arises from their non-representational functions thought and discourse, such as expressing the speaker's conative attitudes or motivating attitudes or behaviour (Finlay 2019, 192). Furthermore, while some cognitivist realists are naturalists who tie normativity to 'natural' properties, others, known as non-naturalists, deny this connection. Non-naturalists tend to argue that normativity is the special property of what one 'ought' to do, is 'obligated' to do, is 'correct' to do, is 'valuable' to do, or has 'reason' to do (Finlay 2010, 334 ff; Finlay 2019, 201; Wedgewood 2018, 24 ff).[15]

13 And regarding this a non-naturalist cognitivist such as Enoch (2011) would be in agreement with a noncognitivist such as Gibbard (2003). The good thing about keeping the explanation of normativity at the conceptual level is that no one calls into question the idea that we have and use concepts and normative language, even though there may be disagreement regarding their content and which terms and concepts are considered normative.

14 Hybrid theorists admit normative sentences and judgements are representational, but claim they are normative not because of representing some normative fact or property, but due to their noncognitive function. See, for example, Ridge 2014, 79–80.

15 Wedgewood (2018, 35) considers we apply normative concepts not only to actions, but also to other performances such as ways of thinking and states of affairs, suggesting to broaden the scope of application from actions to *reasoning*. Additionally, Copp and Morton (2022) mention a broader view according to which the normative realm also extends to guiding *attitudes*.

This last idea is gaining traction among philosophers, with many suggesting that there is a foundational normative concept that underpins all others: normative reason. Specifically, the 'logical space of reasons' encompasses two classes of reasons: (a) epistemic and (b) practical reasons. The former ones are considerations that count in favour or against believing in some proposition, while the latter ones are considerations that count in favour or against some action (Himma 2020, 102). Practical reasons and practical normativity are the ones relevant in accounting law's normativity. In the pursuit of understanding normativity's nature, realist perspectives often assert that facts concerning *reasons* hold normative primacy (Raz 1999; Dancy 2004; Parfit 2011; Scanlon 2014).[16] Under this account, normative facts, such as the ones about goodness, obligation, or virtue, are facts that are, or depend on, facts about reasons (Copp and Morton 2022).[17] In short, if someone *ought to do* something, there must be a (grounding) reason for it, which is a reason for action. However, 'reasons fundamentalism' may stay at the conceptual level, proposing that the concept of reason itself serves as the fundamental concept of normativity.[18]

The discussion regarding the term 'normativity' also reveals an ambiguity between two distinct types: (a) formal (or minimal) normativity and (b) robust (or substantive) normativity.[19] Formal normativity, which is ubiquitous, pertains to the existence of norms or standards against which actions, attitudes, agents, or events can be judged, essentially reflecting 'norm-relativity' (e.g., if a legal norm prohibits killing, the act of killing is *legally* incorrect or wrong) (Finlay 2019, 206).[20] Thus, games, etiquette, language, fashion, or law would

16 Differently, Broome (2013) refers to '*normative requirements*', which involve ensuring consistency in agents' attitudes and are thus linked to instrumental rationality. However, it remains unclear whether instrumental normativity can be adequately explained using the concept of reason, particularly through the distinction between objective and subjective reasons. Wedgewood (2018, 34; 2017) also questions whether 'reason' is the primitive normative concept, suggesting that ambiguous or context-sensitive terms such as 'ought' may express 'parallel' concepts.

17 Others argue, for example, that normative facts are, or depend on, facts about value (Maguire 2016). Or even that normative facts are not normatively fundamental (Wodak 2020).

18 This approach to determining normativity raises questions about what makes facts about reasons normative. If reasons fundamentalism is correct, normatively fundamental facts about reasons likely pertain only to robustly normative reasons. Therefore, reasons fundamentalists may need to refine their perspectives, suggesting that a fact is normative because it is either a robustly normative reason itself or depends on such reasons. See Copp and Morton 2022.

19 On the distinction, see, for example, Copp 2007, 257 ff; Copp 2019, 46 ff; McPherson 2011, 232 ff; Baker 2018, 567 ff; Plunkett, Shapiro 2017, 48 ff; Plunkett 2019, 113 ff; Enoch 2019, 69 ff.

20 In different terms, normativity is related to a 'norm'. However, the term norm is ambiguous, as it can be used in at least three ways: (i) to denote something serving as a standard, guiding people's behaviour and thoughts, and allowing judgements of correctness or incorrectness; (ii) to refer to a social norm, that is, a regularity in behaviour of a set of subjects, which finds explanation in the approval of behavioural conformity and the disapproval of behavioural nonconformity; and (iii) as a 'general principle' about how people ought to think, feel, or act,

have this type of normativity. On the other hand, robust normativity involves situations where norms or oughts provide definitive or all-things-considered reasons for action, feeling, or thought, going beyond mere comparison against standards. This form of normativity appears to be unconditional (or universal), in that it applies to all human beings regardless of their will. Assuming it is possible, philosophers often advance two possible sources of robust normativity: (b1) moral reasons or (b2) prudential reasons.[21]/[22]

Hence, law could be qualified as a normative phenomenon if, and only if, it is capable of *providing* reasons for action (Bix 2018, 25 ff; Bix 2021, 585 ff).[23] Additionally, and more importantly, one must ask: does law, like games but unlike morality, possess only formal normativity? In other words, within the pluralistic realm of the normative, which encompasses various types of reasons such as moral and legal (Copp 2019, 48), can one speak of robust legal reasons?

In my view, answering this question requires distinguishing between two types of reasons: (a) justifying reasons and (b) motivating reasons. Justifying reasons refer to considerations in favour of an action, such as those that justify a behaviour as correct or rational. Motivating reasons, on the other hand, are causal factors that prompt agents to act, serving as premises of practical reasoning guiding their action (Raz 1999; Smith 1994; Dancy, 2000; Alvarez, 2017). When considering law's normativity, motivating reasons appear to be the relevant ones. Law is seen as practically normative if and only if it can persuade rationally competent subjects to comply with (at least some of) its requirements (Himma 2020, 99, 112–113).[24]

otherwise being subject to serious criticism. The use of 'principle' here also displays ambiguity, as it can refer to a linguistic item, a general fact or state of affairs, or a proposition or thought. See Wedgewood 2018, 24; also stressing the ambiguity of the term 'norm', see Finlay 2010, 332.

21 We can distinguish between (a) incomplete reasons, which alone are unable to justify an action, and (b) complete reasons, which have the normative capacity to justify an action on their own (Raz 1999; Pino 2021, 85). Apparently, only moral reasons and prudential reasons are examples of complete reasons, capable of justifying actions (Himma 2018, 67). However, moral reasons can justify the actions of *all* individuals, making them general, while prudential reasons are specific to the agent and aim to maximize personal interests (Pino 2021, 85). Consequently, obligations imposed on all agents could derive only from moral reasons.

22 It's worth noting that the assertion that moral reasons constitute robust normativity seems to rely on certain metaethical assumptions, particularly some form of moral realism. For instance, if error theories are true, then robust normative facts and normativity itself would be undermined. Regarding skepticism about robust normativity, see Baker 2018, 577 ff. Interestingly, Copp (2007, 280) also expresses doubts about morality's robust normativity.

23 In an alternative, less demanding formulation, law is considered normative if citizens *believe* that it provides reasons for action. Criticizing this possibility, see Rosati 2019, 69 ff.

24 It is also important to consider the distinction between subjective and objective reasons when accounting for normativity. Subjective reasons are considerations mentally regarded by rational competent subjects, as a descriptive matter of contingent fact, as favoring *p*, being therefore internal reasons arising from the subject's experienced mental states. In turn, objec-

According to Finlay's (2019, 207) naturalist objectivist stance, robust normative judgements are the ones made from a '*relevantly motivated perspective.*'[25] Specifically, he argues that judgements with end-relational content, which concern the possibility of a certain outcome, are considered 'robust' when the agent 'desires' the end in question. For instance, legal judgements are deemed 'robust' if the agent 'accepts' the rule at stake as a guide for conduct. In Parfit's (2011, 363) disconsolate words: '[f]or the philosophical naturalist, concerned to place normativity within the natural order, there is nothing plausible for normative force other than motivational force'. But I think this is already something.

Crucially, according to internalism, there is an internal connection between our mental and linguistic usage of 'ought' and our conative attitudes, which holds particular significance in elucidating normative claims (Wodak 2017, 270). In legal theory, however, according to the Hartian thesis commonly embraced by positivists, the existence of legal systems depends on the internal acceptance by legal officials of a rule of recognition, which defines the criteria other norms must meet to be considered *legal*, that is, to be members of the legal system. Yet, individual acceptance of norms identified as legal by the rule of recognition is not necessary, and, as Hart contended, compliance with legal norms can stem from various reasons. However, the question remains: is there an internal connection between humans and legal oughts? If so, does it align with the proposition put forth by noncognitivist expressivists—that our normative language serves to express the speaker's conative attitudes—or does the nature of this internal connection differ?

At this point, it is important to reiterate the question and taking stock: what does it mean for a community to regard laws as providing reasons to act in specific ways and to criticize those who deviate? Perhaps there is nothing distinctive in legal norms qua legal norms that distinguishes them from rules of games. From this perspective, the normativity of law is no more substantial than that of games. But the claim that law encompasses formal normativity is a trivial one. More contentious, and interesting, is to explore whether law entails robust normativity in a meaningful sense (Plunkett 2019, 114).

Undoubtedly, the law is intertwined with sources of robust normativity—individuals may comply with legal norms because they are convinced about the moral or epistemic legitimacy of the legal authority that created them, or perhaps simply to avoid sanctions. In other words, compliance with legal directives can stem from moral or prudential reasons. However, a more interesting

tive reasons are considerations that, in accordance with mind-independent standards of normative rationality, should be regarded by rationally competent subjects as good or bad. See Himma 2020, 106–107.

25 According with Finlay (2019, 207), this would correspond to Hart's distinction between internal and external legal judgements or statements. Distinguishing between the psychological, behavioural, and normative senses of legal normativity, see Zaluski 2013, 168 ff.

inquiry is whether there is a non-contingent connection, and therefore in some sense robustness, between normativity and law. In simpler terms, does law possess an intrinsic robustness in its normative nature?[26]

To answer this question, what I am to investigate further, within the framework of constitutivism, is whether there is some general connection between agents and actions when they make first-personal normative judgements relative to legal norms, particularly whether they are motivated to comply with the law. More broadly, can the robustness of law's normativity be explained based on constitutive characteristics of what the law is, such as its aim?[27]

5.3 The promises of constitutivism

Assuming that law is functionally designed to guide human behaviour through legal norms for resolving practical uncertainty (Shapiro 2000), such as the one arising from certain contingent features of the human condition, can we ground the normativity of law in its constitutive features? Insofar as law's conceptual function is normative governance, any legal institution must engage in normative governance to qualify as such. This raises the question: are we rationally committed to enter in legal activity in a way that we are not regarding activities like games? The existence of law simultaneously presupposes agency and purports to domesticate practical reasoning, which immediately distinguishes it from activities such as games. But is that all? Enter constitutivism.

According to constitutivism, 'normative facts' such as the reasons we have to perform certain actions, the comparative value of different outcomes of actions, and virtuosity (or lack of it) of individuals can be explained by facts about the *constitutive features*—the features that define the nature or essence of a person, action, or state of affairs.[28] In other words, constitutivists argue that normative claims about persons, actions, or states of affairs can be derived from claims about their constitutive features, which are *more fundamental* (Smith 2018, 371).

This approach suggests that it is possible to move from descriptive facts or claims to normative ones. For instance, in the case of functional kinds, the constitutive function of something—such as a biological organ or a social

26 In a way, what I am suggesting is that there is a special robustness in law, even if it does not coincide with other senses of robust normativity. Precisely noting that might not be one single thing all philosophers are after when they refer to 'robust', see McPherson and Plunkett 2017.

27 While Lindeman (2019) acknowledges that Shapiro's 'moral aim thesis' could be interpreted as constitutivist due to its teleological nature, which attributes to the law the aim of resolving substantial moral disagreements, it should be distinguished from the argument presented here.

28 Of course, one might question the existence of normative facts. A less compromising view would be that robustly normative facts may not be entirely independent of the mind or agency, but rather constituted by actual or hypothetical psychological facts, or at least bear some modest connection to agents' minds. See Paakkunainen 2017.

institution—implies certain normative facts. Describing the function of something involves understanding what *properly* functioning entities of that kind do, what *defective* entities fail to do, and what they *ought* to do (Smith 2018, 372). For example, the function of a heart is to pump an adequate supply of blood around the body, which implies certain normative claims about what a properly functioning heart should and should not do. As articulated by Smith (2018, 373), constitutivist accounts explain normative facts in terms of 'goodness-fixing kinds' and are fully reductive when it can specify the ordering generated by that kind in wholly non-normative terms.

More specifically, constitutivist accounts aim to derive substantive accounts of normative reasons for action from the structure of *action* (Millgram 2020). They seek to demonstrate that action possesses a particular feature—namely, a constitutive aim or principle—that is universally present in all instances of action and thus establishes a standard of success for action. Law serves as a pertinent example. Let's assume for the sake of illustration that law inherently serves an aim, such as keeping societal peace.[29] Instances of law that lack this aim would fail to fulfill the fundamental purpose of the legal institution. Of course law may have various other aims, such as deterring undesirable behaviour and securing desirable behaviour, providing facilities for private arrangements between individuals, providing services and redistributing goods, or settling disputes.[30] But if law does not aim at keeping the peace, it would not be law. In essence, if there is such an aim, it will hold a special significance among legal participants.

We can define a constitutive aim as follows:

(3) There exists a constitutive aim if and only if every instance of attitude or event A is directed towards the goal G. (Katsafanas 2018, 369)

For instance, if A represents a legal system and G signifies keeping peace, then law would possess the constitutive aim of maintaining peace if every token of law is oriented towards this aim. From this premise, we can derive a minimal normative claim:

(4) If X aims at G, then G is a standard of success for X, thereby generating normative reasons for action.

If law aims at preserving peace, then we can evaluate law based on whether its instances contribute to this aim. There would be reasons for creating certain legal contents if they further the goal of maintaining peace, while there would be reasons against institutional actions that undermine peace. Of course,

29 Arguing keeping the peace is law's conceptual function, see Himma 2018, 2020.
30 Stating these as the primary functions of law, see Raz 2009, 169 ff.

applying (3) to the realm of law, concerning whether law possesses a constitutive purpose, remains a subject of considerable debate.

If this could be generalized to action, as some constitutivists claim, there would be a 'standard of success pertaining to all actions', regardless of the particular goals or motives agents could pursue or have. This would generate universal reasons for action, that is, normative reasons for all agents, despite their contingent goals or attitudes (Katsafanas 2018, 370). The question is how we can demonstrate that action has constitutive aims. There are many constitutivist accounts attempting to show this, such as Velleman's (2009) idea that actions are immediately known and Korsgaard's (2008, 2009) conception that action is distinct from mere behaviour because it is issued from a 'unified agent'. However, for the purposes of this chapter, I will assume what is usually called the 'standard theory of action', according to which action is simply an event qua goal-directed movement that is responsive to or caused by the occurrence of specific mental states and events, such as desires, beliefs, and intentions (Piñeros Glasscock and Tenenbaum 2023; Schlosser 2019). This allows to argue for a minimal constitutivist account, from which requirements of practical rationality can be derived from the constitutive features of action or agency (Ferrero, 2009, 303 ff).

Action, on the thin account assumed, is aimed at bringing about changes in the world to align with our desires—I desire end X, I see that I could achieve X by doing Y, so I do Y.[31] This understanding of action leads to the formulation of the *instrumentality principle*, which advises us to select the necessary means to achieve our ends (Katsafanas 2018, 378).[32] In other words, we have instrumental reasons to choose actions that are conducive to achieving our desired aims.[33]

An important advantage of a constitutivist account, like the one presented here, is its potential to transcend the debate between internalists and externalists.[34] As Katsafanas (2018, 380) puts it:

31 This presupposes a Humean constitutivist view, insofar as it tries to infer reasons from constitutive aims (and not from 'principles', as Kantians do).

32 Arguing that we can move from this extremely thin conception of action to a constitutivist account of the instrumental principle, see Korsgaard 1996; Smith 2010; Katsafanas 2013. This thin conception is very different from thick conceptions such as Korsgaard's (1996, 123), according to which all moral code can be extracted from the constitutivist features of agency, or Velleman's (2009) one, according to which some moral norms can be given a constitutivist explanation.

33 In a similar vein, Copp (2019, 48–49) argues that what he terms the 'problem of autonomy', related to human biases and temptations, can be mitigated by subscribing (that is, by having an intention to conform to it and being disposed to experience a negative emotional response when failing to conform to it) to a 'standard of prudential rationality'. This standard advocates for behaviour that serves our values and fulfils our needs. See also Copp 2007, 309 ff.

34 On the debate, see Finlay and Schroeder 2017.

> both externalism and internalism have attractive features, yet incur substantive costs. Traditional internalism grounds normative claims in familiar features of our psychologies, yet for that very reason has trouble generating universal normative claims. Externalism generates universal normative claims with ease, yet encounters the problems of practicality and queerness.

Constitutivism occupies a middle ground between internalism and externalism, capturing the grain of truth of each position.[35] Similar to internalism, it asserts that normative claims are contingent upon agents' aims. However, in constitutivist accounts, this aim is constitutive and non-optional, thereby enabling the derivation of universal reasons for action, akin to externalism.

Furthermore, constitutivism provides a straightforward response to the 'authority problem': 'as long as you are committed to an activity with constitutive standards, you are committed to those standards' (Katsafanas 2018, 381). For instance, consider the normative statement that 'you should obey the legal prohibition against exceeding 120km/h on highways'. Now, imagine someone questioning why they should comply with this standard. While one could cite prudential reasons, such as avoiding financial penalties or preventing car accidents, or moral reasons, such as minimizing risks to the lives of innocent people, these reasons are *external* standards tied to other aims the agent accepts or desires. In contrast, constitutive aims do not necessitate external standards, as they are inherent to the phenomenon or activity in question.

This framework appears to require minimal theoretical commitments—at least for a thin account such as the one described—by deriving normativity from the agent's aims or principles and relying on a mere structural conception of rationality, without necessitating subscription to substantive (and potentially more problematic) aims (Katsafanas 2018, 381).

If action indeed possesses a constitutive aim—that is, an aim that constitutes its nature—and given the significant role of action in the realm of law (where it is undisputed that law and legal norms concern human action), exploring this relationship could provide deeper insights into the nature of law, particularly its normativity (Bertea 2013).[36] The aforementioned constitutivist account will be applied to the legal domain by starting to test the view of *law* as an artefact-kind functionally directed at guiding *action*, whose conceptual function furnishes a standard of success.

From this perspective, law can be understood as a means designed to guide the behaviour of members within a legal community towards achieving certain ends (Green 2023). This conceptualization of law is broad in scope because despite being functionally aimed at guiding human behaviour, it acknowledges

35 That is why some call constitutivism 'meta-internalism' and 'quasi-internalism'. See Wallace 2006; Enoch 2006, 172.

36 Arguing the same regarding morality, Paul 2021, 101. In turn, Leiter (2013, 5–6) is skeptical regarding the appeal to constitutive functions of legal institutions to understand legal normativity.

the variability of the content of law, which is shaped by the evolving and potentially open-ended goals that are accepted or valued by society and thus incorporated into legal systems. Moreover, it is *instrumentalist* in nature, as the value of law is contingent upon its efficacy in achieving these goals rather than possessing inherent worth (Green 1998, 121 ff; Green 2023, 77 ff). Even if many instrumentalists are antipositivists,[37] the instrumentalist view here described is not incompatible with positivist theories of law (Green 2023).[38]

If this understanding holds true and law is considered a necessary means to achieve one of *our* ends that is related to action, then we should regard law, as an objective matter of normative practical rationality, as a standard to be complied with. This perspective would explain the intuition that legal requirements have some authority over us, unlike arbitrary rules in games. Therefore, for all of this to be valid, it is essential to demonstrate that (a) humans inherently desire an end X, and that (b) law is a necessary means to achieve X. I will next attempt to demonstrate that regarding (a), humans are disposed to cooperation for survival, and that regarding (b), law, with its function of guiding human behaviour, is a necessary means to achieve this end.

5.4 More than a game: a law-abiding attitude as the motivational trigger of legal reasons

5.4.1 The conceptual function of law

It's commonly understood that law, as a human artificial institution, has a function, such as guiding human behaviour (Hart 2012, 78 ff; Shapiro 2000, 127 ff; Himma 2020, 82 ff; Fuller 1969; Finnis 1980). Furthermore, in recent times, law has been increasingly perceived as a social artefact (Burazin et al. 2018, 2022). The function of a thing can be understood more broadly as an intended consequence or effect of that thing (Green 1998, 117). Artefacts are usually defined as something intentionally made for some purpose or end. This is so, because unlike organisms, artefacts are created to serve human purposes. Therefore, when considering the function of artefacts, human intentional states must be taken into account. Various theories exist regarding the role of intentions in establishing functions (Preston 2022), with some emphasizing intentions (Neander 1991; Baker 2009; Dipert 1995) and others emphasizing the role of evolution (Millikan 1984; Houkes and Vermaas 2010; Preston 2013). As Green (1998, 118) puts it:

37 For the sake of example, just recall Fuller (1969), according to whom the function of law is to guide human behaviour, which it can do only by conforming to what he calls the 'inner morality of law', or Finnis (1980), according to whom the function of law is to coordinate action for the common good.

38 On this and more demanding conceptions of action, such as Korsgaard and Velleman's conception, see in general Schapiro, 2001; Millgram, 2020. On the legal domain, Bertea 2025. For the problems of robust conceptions of action, see Paul 2021, 102 ff.

> Conscious selection or choice figures in the best explanation of the existence of artifacts: they were designed for a job. But other things might also have an explanatory role, for there are also mechanisms of unconscious or unintended selection.

For accounting an artefact such as law, it seems that mixed or pluralist theories about functions—stressing both intentions and evolution—are better placed.[39] Accordingly, the function of law can be defined as the intended purpose or end for which it was created, which may have been influenced, to some extent, by human evolution. Also note that these 'agentive' functions may and usually are ascribed through collective acceptance.[40] Hence, according to this theory, the minimal functional explanation of law suggests that it is essentially a tool, which was at least partly intentionally designed to regulate human behaviour, even though it may sometimes fail in this regard.[41] Consequently, law is considered useful as a means to the end of normative governance and has been utilized in pursuit of that end (Dipert 1995, 121). In essence, law's proper function is *normative governance*.[42]

Furthermore, artefacts may have accidental and conceptual functions, with the latter defined as '[functions] that something of a certain kind must be capable of performing in virtue of the nature of things of that kind' (Himma 2018, 144). Therefore, it follows that for all x and all artefactual kinds K, an x is K if and only if it is used to perform Ks conceptual function. However,

39 For example, Green (1998, 117) highlights two limitations in applying intention-based analysis to law: (a) it cannot be applied to laws created non-intentionally (e.g., customary law); and (b) it cannot be applied to law as an entire legal system, as legal systems are the result of collective social actions over time, lacking clear social rules for ascribing intentions to them, unlike what happens with specific legal statutes. The mixed theory of functions being employed here allows us to overcome both limitations.

40 See Searle 1995. According to Searle, for example, money functions, such as serving as a medium of exchange or a measure of value, are imposed on their physical bearers through our collective acceptance of them as money. The intentional states constituting this collective acceptance create an 'institutional fact', which depends on collective human agency. Stressing that artefacts necessarily have an author and thus depend on intentional agency, see Hilpinen 2018.

41 Which is normal because failure is necessary for something to have a function. See Ehrenberg 2016, 28–29.

42 Talking about *proper* functions, using Ruth Millikan's terminology, see Ehrenberg 2016, 21 ff. Following Raz (2009, 169 ff), one can distinguish between 'primary functions', which relate to guiding human behaviour, and 'secondary functions', which pertain to enabling and maintaining the legal system. These secondary functions include the creation, application, and coercive enforcement of legal norms. It's important to note that these functions serve as instruments in achieving the primary function of regulating human behaviour. Additionally, one can differentiate between 'regulatory functions', which encompass both human and institutional conduct, and 'constitutive functions', such as the constitution of legal conducts, concepts, or meanings. While secondary functions are related to constitutive functions, they are not reducible to them.

determining the conceptual function of an artefact category is not without problems. One possibility for identifying conceptual functions is to determine the specific problems that artefacts are needed or used to solve (Himma 2018, 145). Until now, I assumed guiding behaviour was the conceptual function of law. However, normative governance itself doesn't appear to be the problem to solve—regulating behaviour isn't inherently valuable for its own sake (Himma 2020, 78 ff).[43] So, what problem does law aim to address? What purpose was law intentionally designed and evolved to serve or pursue? To frame it in constitutivist terms: what is the ultimate *end* for which law is utilized as a *means*? The answer to this question, if there is one, will reveal the *conceptual function of law*.

We usually view law as fulfilling several social functions, such as maintaining order, settling disputes, and providing benefits and services.[44] More interestingly, Himma (2020) outlines various ultimate purposes for which legal systems are employed to govern human behaviour through legal norms, including morally justifying the state's exercise of police power, directing individuals towards right reasoning to enhance compliance with moral standards, resolving disputes regarding moral obligations, and establishing objective moral requirements.[45] However, he argues that none of these functions adequately address the fundamental problem that legal systems aim to solve. According to him, humans are passionately self-interested subjects that live in acute material scarcity, which hampers legal norms' compliance.[46] From here he infers that rationally competent subjects are disposed to violate law. Within this context, he suggests considering the hypothetical scenario of rational, competent, self-interested individuals existing in a world devoid of a regulatory system akin to law. By employing the Hobbesian State of Nature concept, Himma (2020, 83 ff) concludes that the core problem necessitating a legal system is the maintenance of peace among human subjects.[47] Accordingly:

43 Also arguing that behaviour-guiding can be seen as a means to coordination-solving, see Ehrenberg 2016, 183 ff.

44 Green 1998, 117.

45 Ehrenberg (2016, 180 ff) provides a comprehensive list of the primary explanatory functions of law found in various theories: (a) justifying the state's use of force; (b) implementing or enforcing community-held moral and political principles; (c) facilitating general coordination and dispute resolution; (d) organizing behaviour to solve coordination problems and promote the common good; (e) establishing order through general rules; (f) guiding human behaviour and providing standards for evaluating it; (g) creating new reasons through communication of legal intentions; (h) incentivizing behaviour for economic efficiency; (i) specifying, recognizing, and protecting contextual rights and duties. But as noted by Rábanos (2024a), some of these functions seem instances of other, more general functions (e.g., (d) and (e) seem instances of (c), and (g) and (h) seem instances of (f)).

46 Precisely because of this, Himma (2020) argues that coercion is a conceptual feature of legal systems.

47 With some similarities, Copp (2019, 52, 58) affirms his 'legal teleology' thesis according to which law has a purpose, and should be understood as an answer to what he calls the 'problem

(5) The conceptual function of law is keeping the peace among humans.

And his pessimistic perspective on human nature leads him to argue that law *necessarily* requires a coercive apparatus to offer practical incentives that induce compliance with legal norms governing non-official behaviour.

At this juncture, it's worth asking: is (5) true, that is, are humans naturally inclined to engage in actions prohibited by law? For instance, are we disposed to disregarding legal norms such as stopping at a red light? Does this encompass the entirety of human behaviour in relation to the law?

While acknowledging that law is commonly employed to pursue peacekeeping, I am not convinced that this defines law's conceptual function.[48] As Coleman (2001, 93) seems to suggest when assessing the nature of the rule of recognition, in a Hobbesian scenario, law could serve to solve the state of nature prisoner's dilemma situation.[49] Following this suggestion, perhaps a less committing and broader, although also substantive, claim is that law is functionally contrived and utilized to facilitate cooperative survival. Similar to language (Railton 2019, 9), law is ubiquitous wherever humans reside because it serves a variety of vital interests and makes possible a wide range of activities—as recognized by Hart (2012, 191, 193 ff)—primarily fostering cooperation for survival.[50] Consequently:

(6) The conceptual function of law is cooperation for survival.

Proposition (6) is justified by three main reasons.[51] Firstly, beginning with a Hobbesian model, which suggests that humans are egoistic and non-coop-

of security', which is the risk of conflict and discord among human beings.

48 Also rejecting peacekeeping as the conceptual function of law, see Green 1998, 119.

49 It's true that Coleman then claims law does not have to be 'a solution to any sort of problem at all—let alone one that can be modeled game-theoretically', because law may serve several purposes, such as 'to make more determinate the requirements of a shared political morality or to organize society in a way that enables individuals to be responsible for the lives they lead. Or law can create an efficient scheme of production and distribution'. However, as Himma (2018, 146, note 28) notes, these purposes seem to be intended to solve some kind of problem.

50 Arguing that 'law constitutively concerns general and essential dimensions of our existence and so purportedly impacts on the reasoning about how we ought to act period', which immediately distinguishes it from normative but circumscribed practices such as etiquette, fashion, and games, see Bertea 2019, 11; also stressing law's 'broad scope' and 'wide reach', see Green and Adams 2019, 4.2.

51 Ehrenberg (2016, 197) claims that ends such as behaviour guidance, social ordering, predicting the state's response to personal choices, communicating the society's values, mitigating the demands of the individual upon others, and mitigating the demands of others upon the individual can be viewed as instances of solving coordination problems. However, as cautioned by Rábanos (2024a, 6), the inclusiveness of coordination as a purpose depends on the definition being employed. But she also tends to see coordination as the primary function of law (Rábanos 2024a, 13 ff). It's also crucial to note that the purpose outlined in (6) is broader than coordination.

erative, that the state of nature was characterized by social chaos driven by individual pursuit of self-interest, and that the origins of law stem from a social contract forming the state, and then inferring that law was devised by egoistic yet rational individuals for the objective of maintaining peace is problematic. This perspective seems overly pessimistic and consequently probably false. A more nuanced perspective, such as the Darwinian model, portrays humans as narrowly altruistic, where the state of nature was not chaotic but rather orderly, and law can be viewed as an expression of our natural cooperative dispositions and as a tool to pursuing them.[52] Secondly, while maintaining peace is indeed an instance of cooperation for survival, it does not seem necessary for it. In reality, as history shows, cooperation for survival can sometimes be achieved through conflict, such as war, which may challenge the claim that peacekeeping is the conceptual function of law. As expressed by Hart (2012, 192), 'an overwhelming majority of men do wish to live, even at the cost of hideous misery'. Thirdly, considering cooperation for survival as an overarching end of law might garner broader acceptance among diverse perspectives.[53] In sum, cooperation for survival seems to have an important explanatory role in understanding some feature of law.

However, as Green (1998, 118) broadly posits, this purpose would be 'a function if and only if the disposition to produce the relevant consequence [or purpose] figures in the best explanation of the existence or persistence of that feature or item'.

Given the falsity of (5), and in order to demonstrate (6), what I will endeavor to show next is that, as a matter of contingent descriptive fact, humans have a *disposition* towards cooperation to ensure survival. Cooperation for survival is an innate end that we desire, and as I will illustrate, law emerges as a necessary means to achieve this end—largely crafted for this purpose. Consequently, as matter of objective normative practical rationality, we should conform to law. This will underscore a clear distinction between the normativity of law and that of games.

5.4.2 Law as a means for cooperation to survival

According to Kelsen (2006, 20), 'law is a means, a specific means, not an end'. Hart (2012, 248 ff) also seems to agree that we cannot ascribe significant ends to law 'as a whole'. However, this instrumentalist thesis strongly asserts both

52 I draw heavily on Zaluski 2009, 61 ff; Zaluski 2013, 155 ff. This is also expressly acknowledged by Hart (2012, 196), when he claims that 'men are not devils dominated by a wish to exterminate each other', which does not mean they are angels. In a word, human altruism is limited.

53 As Green (1998, 119) argues, when trying to identifying the functions of law, 'The difficulty lies in pitching the necessary functions of law at a level which is sufficiently abstract to be plausible—there is no point in saying that legal systems necessarily guarantee human rights, since many of them do not—but not so abstract as to be unilluminating'.

that law can only serve as a means for some ends, and that it can never be a universal end in itself (Green 2023, 58).[54] As Green (2023, 60 ff) notes, both positivists and antipositivists agree that law constitutes a means. The disagreement lies in the strong 'instrumental conception of law', (Raz 2009, 226) which denies the existence of universal ends among or unique to all legal systems (Green 1998, 123; Gardner 2012, 207–208). Accordingly:

(7) Law is only a means, never an end.

I want to argue that (7) is false because it is possible to identify a generic end common to all legal systems that is not too vague to be useless. This is not to say that law isn't like a 'Swiss-Army knife', serving as a multi-purpose tool handy for various ends (Green 2023, 75), but rather that cooperation for survival can be viewed as law's conceptual function.

Evolutionary psychologists posit that a significant portion of human behavioural mechanisms are adaptations—biological dispositions that evolved through natural selection in response to the conditions of our ancient Stone Age ancestors' environment, known as the 'environment of evolutionary adaptedness' (EEA).[55] Assuming every organism struggles for existence—a process that naturally selects variations conducive to the survival and reproduction of their bearers (Gildenhuys 2024)—these psychological adaptations were favoured by evolution because individuals possessing them had a greater likelihood of surviving in the EEA and passing on their genetic traits to future generations. If this portrayal of human nature holds merit,[56] it warrants serious consideration by legal theorists (Załuski 2009; Dyevre 2014; Zaluski, Bourgeois-Gironde, and Dyrda 2024).

It is widely acknowledged that humans are inherently social creatures reliant on cooperation for survival and prosperity (Bowles and Gintis 2011). Evolutionary psychologists suggest that human psychology has evolved over time to support larger, more cooperative societies characteristic of modern humans.[57] Cooperation is one of the most important ends human beings value and law is one of the paradigmatic means they have designed to facilitate cooperation. In essence, evolution appears to have disposed humans to cooperate, and given that law is a primary form of cooperation, it is reasonable to infer that humans are disposed to create and comply to legal systems. And legal

54 On different interpretations of the claim that law is a means for solving collective action problems, see Zaluski 2013, 152 ff.

55 For a more detailed presentation of the foundations of EP, see Tooby and Cosmides 1992, and 2005. See also Załuski 2009, 24 ff.

56 According to Dennett (1984, 153 ff), views claiming that human agency is genetically and behaviourally impaired are moderate views.

57 For example, stressing that cultural adaptation is a key factor in these changes, see Boyd and Richerson 2009, 3281 ff.

theorists have become increasingly aware of the potential relevance of human evolution in understanding some aspects related to the nature of law.

In his analysis of the essential conditions for the effectiveness of law, Hart (2012, 192–193) explicitly acknowledged that the group and respective members have a purpose of strive for survival, which is made possible through cooperation, noting that this is even something 'reflected in whole structures of our thought and language'.[58] Building on this premise, the British philosopher claimed that legal systems *must* ensure the survival of at least some members of the community. Consequently, he asserted that, as a matter of natural or nomological necessity—the so-called and somewhat misleading 'minimum content of natural law' (Dyevre 2014, 374)—legal systems should restrict the free use of violence because of the vulnerability of the human body; protect some form of property given the scarcity of resources; allow for the exchange of goods and so on since individuals are not self-sufficient; and impose sanctions of some sort for the breach of legal commands, because humans possess only 'limited understanding and strength of will' (Hart 2012, 194 ff).[59]

A possible interpretation of Hart's argument suggests that, by assuming a universalistic conception of human nature, individuals are biologically disposed 'to engage in violent behaviour, appropriate the fruits of others' labor, and exploit their partners in economic exchanges. (Dyevre 2014, 374).[60] Alternatively, one might interpret Hart's perspective as suggesting that our desire for survival predisposes us to be more cooperative, and that the establishment of law is a natural outcome of this inclination. Furthermore, as societies evolve and become more intricate, the probability of disagreements, conflicts, and diverse needs among people increases, thereby heightening the necessity of law for the survival of society. Thus, law arises as a nomological necessity stemming from these innate human behavioural traits.[61] Moreover,

58 And also mentioned the 'perennial need for co-operation' (Hart 2012, 197).

59 Criticizing Hart's view on the evolution of law, see MacCormick 2008, 118 ff. Reconstructing both theories in accounting for the evolution of legal systems, see Rábanos 2024b.

60 This interpretation is coherent with Himma's thesis previously mentioned.

61 Which was also acknowledged by Hume—see Zaluski 2013, 157 ff. According to Green (1998, 120), the minimum content thesis fails to demonstrate that law can be classified as a functional kind due to two primary reasons. Firstly, the thesis is limited in its application, as it pertains only to legal systems that aim to comprehensively regulate the behaviour of natural persons. However, certain legal systems, such as some religious legal systems, only apply to specific realms of behaviour. Moreover, there exist legal systems that solely regulate the behaviour of artificial persons, such as states, companies, and trade unions, where the truisms about human nature will not be applicable. Regarding the classification of religious systems as legal, it could be argued that they are more appropriately categorized as normative systems rather than legal systems. Similarly, while legal systems governing artificial persons exist, their existence ultimately hinges on the practices and attitudes of natural persons. Secondly, the minimum content thesis does not establish that law possesses distinctive functions; rather, it suggests that law shares certain functions with other institutions such as custom and morality. The rules governing social survival, if indeed that is their purpose, vary significantly in nature. Concerning the relationship between social customary norms and legal norms, it's not entirely

given the apparent immutability of these traits, the implementation of sanctions also becomes relevant (Dyevre 2014, 374).[62] The history of law seems to account for its function, that is, to show its 'etiological function' (Lindeman 2019, 96 ff; Zaluski 2013, 154 ff). In sum, as Hart (2012, 193 ff) argues, legal systems typically aim to regulate aspects such as violence, property, kinship, and promises. And in my view these specific aims are essentially instances of the broader, non-contingent goal of cooperation for survival.[63]

In the domain of metaethics, 'evolutionary explanations' have also been proposed to elucidate moral judgements (Leiter 2007, 209), particularly by antirealists like Blackburn (1988) and Gibbard (1990), who aim to construct a naturalistic account of moral judgement.[64] Gibbard (1990, 108 ff), in particular, suggests analyzing normative judgements as expressing states of norm-acceptance and explaining this capacity in terms of its contribution to 'coordination', which he views as a 'biological function' selected by evolution.[65] While this remains a speculative proposition, if evolutionary biologists have demonstrated selection for altruistic behaviour, it seems reasonable to assume 'it also selects in favor of the normative practices that support that behaviour' (Leiter 2007, 209).

In conclusion, according to evolutionary theory, humans are hard-wired for survival, and more precisely, we are *disposed* to cooperate to survive.[66] The desire to survive is therefore a constitutive aim of human beings and it can be seen as figuring in the best explanation for the emergence of law. As law serves as a means to achieve this end, we are rationally compelled to comply with

clear-cut that they are mutually exclusive. Additionally, regarding morality, as I will elaborate on in the conclusion of the chapter, law encompasses a much broader scope and often serves to resolve moral conflicts.

62 Also giving this explanation for the Hartian thesis of the residual moral content of legal systems, see Toh 2021, 572–573.

63 Of course, being a natural or nomological necessity, it applies to all *actual* legal systems, but not necessarily to all *possible* legal systems.

64 Street (2006) also suggests that natural selection has played a significant, though not exclusive, role in shaping the moral beliefs we hold.

65 Critically, see Sturgeon 1995, 412 ff.

66 It is often asserted that one of the primary functions of law is to resolve coordination problems. See Shapiro 2011, 105 ff; Zaluski 2013, 153 ff. However, what some theorists claim is that it is the rule of recognition, rather than law itself, that addresses the coordination problem essential for the existence of law. See Postema 1982; Green 1998, 43 ff; Coleman 2001, 93. It's important to note that I am not suggesting that solving coordination problems represents the conceptual function of law. Instead, viewing coordination as a form of cooperation, law sometimes also serves as a means to coordinate.

law.[67] But there's more to it. As I'll try to demonstrate below, humans appear to possess a *law-abiding attitude*.[68]

5.4.3 The law-abiding attitude and legal normativity

Attitudes refer to mental phenomena concerning an object, such as propositions or actions. They encompass cognitive elements (perceptions, concepts, and beliefs about the object), affective aspects (emotions or feelings elicited by the object), and conative components (disposition to act in a certain way towards the object) (Gur 2019). Moreover, attitudes exhibit a *degree of persistence*, albeit varying in intensity. They are, therefore, mental states that maintain a certain hold in the mind of the individual over time (Gur 2019, 145). It's important to note that attitudes differ from personal traits, which are more persistent and less prone to change. While attitudes may have a genetic basis, individuals retain the capacity to form, develop, modify, and discard them over time. This capacity is influenced by external factors such as socialization (family, school, peers, media) as well as individual reflection, including contemplation on the value of legal systems (Gur 2019, 152–153). It's essential to distinguish attitudes from propositional attitudes, which involve beliefs or desires towards propositions (Branddon-Mitchell and Jackson 2006, 171) and are sometimes referred to by philosophers of mind as 'occurring' beliefs or desires (Schwitzgebel 2013, 92 ff). In essence, the attitudes discussed here, as described by Gur (2019, 146), possess continued existence and a relative tendency to persist.

In turn, dispositions (also referred to as 'causal powers', 'capacities', 'abilities', or 'propensities') serve as the conative component of attitudes. These are properties that predispose an object to exhibit a specific state or behaviour, typically observable under specific conditions (Mumford, 1998). For example, a glass possesses the disposition to break when struck or colliding with another object or hard surface, indicating the *possibility* for breakage contingent upon certain conditions (Choi and Fara 2021).

After examining the concepts of attitude and disposition, I proceed to clarify the content of what I refer to as the 'law-abiding attitude' (LAA).

I previously rejected the idea that humans are always inclined to violate the law. Instead, as discussed earlier, I proposed that evolution ingrained in humans a disposition to cooperate for survival, leading to the formation of a law-abiding attitude. Now, let's delve into the content and structure of this attitude. Firstly, the LAA encompasses a cognitive element, recognizing legal

67 It is worth noting that my argument differs from Green's (2023) criticism that assumes it's always bad to lack law and makes an inference from 'ought' to 'is'. Instead, I argue that the pervasiveness of law may be explained by our disposition to cooperate to survive.

68 It should be clear that the existence of this LAA does not mean that human nature is a 'society of angels'. On this society, see Raz 1999, 157 ff.

institutions as authorities entitled to issue directives and demand compliance.[69] Secondly, albeit contingent, the LAA may include an affective component, such as feelings of gratitude towards officials or pride in the virtues of a legal system. Thirdly, the LAA comprises a conative element, representing the disposition to abide with legal systems and, more specifically, to comply with legal norms (Gur 2019, 148, 151).

The LAA imbues legal reasons with motivational force. Consequently, legal reasons are not merely inert formal reasons; although they are content-independent (Sciaraffa 2009, 233 ff), they can be seen as constituting (more) robust reasons for action. When determining what we ought to do, there is a tendency to follow legal norms, driven by the desire to cooperate for survival. The force of the LAA transcends contextual reasons qua considerations or the merits of the prescribed action, as it is deeply ingrained in human subjects.

It is crucial to clarify that I am not proposing, as Gur (2019) does, that when legal systems instantiate some properties, such as moral ones, we have reasons to endorse the LAA.[70] Rather, I argue that we possess an embedded natural disposition to obey the law.[71] Hence, the LAA is not a conscious decision but rather a product of natural selection and evolution. What may be (partly) attributed to an intentional nature is law as an artefact. This suggests that, on the one hand, rational individuals, as a matter of descriptive fact, are disposed to cooperate for survival. On the other hand, because law is an essential means for cooperation to survival, as an objective matter of normative practical rationality, we should engage in legal practices and obey the law.[72]

Additionally, I am not advocating for a presumption of universal compliance with law. On the contrary, my argument posits that humans have evolved to possess, by default, a general disposition to accept legal norms from an internal perspective. This perspective differs significantly from the Hartian idea that individuals accept legal norms when they believe there is a reason to do so; rather, I claim that individuals are generally disposed to follow legal norms.[73]

69 The human inclination to obey authority figures is widely recognized, as evidenced by Millgram's (1998) experiments, which appeared to validate Arendt's (2006) insights into our responses to authority directives.

70 A problem with Gur's interesting proposal is that it is not easy to distinguish between the LAA and motivating moral attitudes.

71 This may also be related to the 'law of least effort', as simply following the law would be the least demanding course of action. See Kahneman 2013.

72 With this, as Zaluski pushed me to clarify in private correspondence, I am not claiming that the LAA can be completely reduced to cooperative dispositions, because the former is broader, as we also evolved to be disposed to accept social hierarchies (everyone knows the fate of our ancestors who did not).

73 This is not to say that we *only* have a general disposition to cooperate and, therefore, to obey the law. As Zaluski noted to me, it makes sense to argue (and is not incoherent with my claim) that we may also have more specific dispositions, such as property instincts, the tendency to keep promises, and the inclination to not harm others. However, this would have to be addressed in another chapter.

It's important to note, however, that the existence and strength of the LAA are independent of the existence of reasons for action. On one hand, the LAA bolsters the robustness of legal reasons. On the other hand, its disposition implies a heightened resistance to reasons against compliance, although it's not absolute and consequently can be overridden (Gur 2019, 156 ff). Humans possess many other dispositions and answer to contrary reasons for action, which explains why they may intentionally violate legal norms in certain circumstances. For instance, when individuals perceive legal norms as irrational or morally objectionable, other attitudes and reasons come into play. Moral judgements about the legitimacy of a legal system can incline individuals to disobey certain legal norms, while perceptions of moral justification can reinforce the LAA.[74] Moreover, the history of revolutions and civil disobedience highlights the significant influence of moral considerations on human behaviour, sometimes even overriding the coercive power of law.[75] Ultimately, the existence of the LAA does not necessarily determine our practical deliberation and does not prevent resistance to irrational or unjust laws, as it is subject to change and may be defeated by other factors (Gur 2019, 180).

This doesn't imply that it's meaningless to create prudential reasons through sanctions to deter individuals who may be tempted to break legal norms when they believe it serves their interests.[76] On the contrary, it underscores the necessity of providing legal systems with coercive mechanisms, such as civil and criminal sanctions, to enhance legal compliance.[77] Law enforcement has the capacity to generate prudential reasons, which are essential for ensuring the overall effectiveness of legal systems (Gur 2019).

Furthermore, it's important to emphasize that the thesis proposing the conceptual function of law as cooperation for survival doesn't imply that law is purely a functional entity, wherein its nature is solely defined by its function. Thus, I'm not suggesting that the nature of law—particularly if interpreted as its mere existence—can be fully understood by identifying its function alone.

74 Arguing that one of the reasons people invoke when obeying law is its moral legitimacy, that is, our moral perceptions contribute for the formation of the belief about a legal system's legitimacy, see Tyler 2006.

75 Copp (2019, 54) even claims that since 'a well-functioning legal system that includes Hart's minimum content of natural law can help to ameliorate the problem of sociality by reducing the risk of discord and conflict and by facilitating cooperation', 'then the ideal moral code for a society would contain, inter alia, a norm calling us to comply with the law—provided it is not unjust'.

76 As Hart (2012, 196) notes, even if men are not devils, 'human altruism is limited in range and intermittent, and the tendencies for aggression are frequent enough to be fatal to social life if not controlled'.

77 While I am advocating for the existence of an LAA, it's important to acknowledge that Hart's (2012, 232) assertion remains valid regarding the various reasons that may lead normative subjects to accept legal reasons created in each legal system. These reasons may include considerations such as long-term interest calculations, moral principles, the preservation of traditions, or altruistic concerns for others.

In different words, I don't think it is possible to identify law solely based on considerations of function (or content). Rather, I think the end of cooperation for survival can help in distinguishing legal systems from other normative systems,[78] and, more importantly, I contend that understanding its function is crucial for determining the nature of normativity inherent in law.[79]

What I have been claiming can be encapsulated in the Dispositional Constitutivist Thesis (DCT):

> (DCT): As human subjects possess a law-abiding disposition and law serves as an essential means to further the aim of cooperation for survival, these subjects should, as an objective matter of normative practical rationality, be committed to complying with the law.

In conclusion, within a thin constitutivist framework, pinpointing the conceptual function of law as cooperation for survival, which is intertwined with our disposition to obey it, the argument presented reveals that law possesses an inherent normative force beyond mere formal correctness-setting criteria. More ambitiously, legal norms establish non-optional universal reasons for action, showcasing robust normativity independent of moral or prudential reasons—they show the 'marks of robust normativity'.[80]

5.5 Some final objections and rebuttals

So far, I have argued that legal normativity differs from mere formal normativity, as observed in games, due to our disposition to obey the law. However, this does not imply that the creation of prudential legal reasons, through sanctions for non-compliance with legal norms, is irrelevant. Additionally, the moral legitimacy of a legal system significantly enhances the overall effectiveness of a legal system. Given this, we can question whether the intuition that

78 Arguing the same regarding what he called the 'minimum content' of natural law, see Hart 2012, 193 ff.

79 Of course, as noted by Marmor and Sarch (2019), one may say that contemporary legal theories about the nature of law have two main interests: (a) the question about the conditions of legal existence (validity as membership) and (b) the question about the normative aspect of law. In this case, being specially related to (b), my thesis would be also related to the nature of law.

80 Similarly, concerning the case of morality, one might argue that moral requirements are *objective* for two main reasons: (i) they are metaphysical aspects of the natural world and are not contingent upon the human mind, or (ii) they are inescapable for the beings to whom they apply, meaning that all such beings must adopt a practical perspective from which these demands are inherently viewed as authoritative. This implies that a rational agent will inevitably be motivated by the dictates of morality, in stark contrast to phenomena such as fashion or etiquette. Why should one care about acting morally? Because the property of moral rightness is authoritatively linked to something that one cannot help but care about or be moved by. See Paul 2021, 110–111.

we are disposed to follow the law is not a mistake. Rather, such motivation would result precisely from prudential and/or moral reasons in favour of compliance with the law.[81]

Regarding prudential reasons, my answer to this possible objection is that even if the creation of law-enforcement mechanisms, such as criminal, civil, or administrative sanctions, is important for guaranteeing the general effectiveness of legal systems,[82] it is unable to explain legal normativity by itself. If there were no disposition to abide with law, it seems to me that law-enforcement mechanisms would have to be much more vigorous than they usually are. However, Schauer claims that coercion does all the work in inducing law compliance, seriously doubting about the existence of an LAA and, at least in American society, about the relevance of its causal contribution for legal compliance (Schauer 2015, 46 ff, 52, 55 ff, 74, 167 ff). I think Schauer is right in underlining the importance of prudential reasons in explaining legal compliance, which has been considerably neglected by legal philosophers. However, he wrongly disregards the empirical evidence for the existence of the LAA.[83]

According to Tyler's (2006, 57 ff) work, individuals who ascribe greater legitimacy to legal authorities less frequently violate individual legal norms. Additionally, people's assessments of the moral merits of legal directives also influence legal compliance; they were generally inclined to comply with law, but the inclination seemed much stricter whenever the law was morally relevant and more prone to violate law if the moral relevance was smaller (Tyler 2006, 59 ff). These conclusions are corroborated in many other empirical studies.[84] Tyler (2006, 65) concludes that there is a 'predisposition toward following law'. Among other criticisms,[85] Schauer (2015, 60 ff) and Claus (2012, 66 ff) mention a pair of examples of legal rules—namely, a parking meter scofflaw and a tax on self-reported income—with high rates of non-compliance as evidence for the inexistence of the LAA. The problem is that this seems to be a generalization from cases related to legal rules that involved the payment

81 Note that even if my further analysis bears some similarities with Gur's (2019, 170 ff) analysis, I am not analyzing if prudential and moral reasons are better suited to do the work of the LAA. To put it differently, his argument seems normative, while mine aims to be descriptive, since I think we are disposed to comply with law, regardless if that is a good or a bad thing.

82 In this sense, one could argue that law is ***pragmatically dependent*** of coercion ('*a* properly works in virtue of *b*'). See Miotto 2021, 75 ff.

83 Sometimes, Schauer's claims are more qualified, seeming to focus only on compliance with laws human subjects disagree with.

84 Mentioning a bunch of them, see Gur 2019, 186.

85 There are, nevertheless, criticisms to Tyler's findings. For example, Schauer (2015, 160 ff) claims the perceived legitimacy of laws exerts a weaker influence on human subjects' acts of compliance. Green (1998) and Schauer (2015, 60 ff) argue that the questions used in the survey were not sufficiently fine-grained to support his conclusions about the predisposition to comply with law, as well as sometimes they do not exclude the possibility of responses based on the existence of prudential reasons arising from legal sanctions. Critically, see Gur 2019, 189 ff.

of fees—which triggers countervailing self-interest reasons not to comply—in which around half of the people still complied. The fact that the LAA does not always tip the balance for rule-following deliberation whenever other prudential and/or moral reasons are at stake does not mean that the LAA is irrelevant in that case and cannot be decisive in other cases (Gur 2019, 191–192).

Regarding moral reasons, one may ask if we do not possess moral dispositions to act in some ways, for example, not to kill or assault other people; or perhaps we are morally disposed to comply with law if it is just. In this case, the idea that we have an LAA would be a mistake; in fact, what *motivates* our law compliance actions would be this moral disposition.

Firstly, it's widely acknowledged that moral reasons do not exhaust the universe of actions regulated by legal norms. Far from it. Even though we might be generally morally disposed towards certain behaviours, the 'motivational reach of moral dispositions' is quite limited compared to the extensive reach of the law, and in some cases its influence is very peripheral (Gur 2019, 176). In addition, as a means of cooperation for survival, law actually functions as a framework providing practical solutions for human subjects' disagreements, such as the ones arising from the 'differing moral outlooks among members of society', which 'track ideological and political orientations, religious beliefs, ethnic backgrounds, and other affiliations'. (Gur 2019, 177–178)

In addition, even in situations of manifest immorality, there is empirical evidence that human beings are disposed to obey what authorities order them.[86] This seems to suggest that moral reasons, by themselves, are not able to explain our disposition to obey law and, therefore, legal normativity.

A different objection concerns the claim that a formal normative system such as law is not a necessary instrumental means to promote the end of human survival, given the existence of non-formal normative systems such as moral and social ones.[87] According to Mackie (1977, 121), morality is best understood as a 'device' necessary to address a 'problem' stemming from 'certain contingent features of the human condition'. Does this imply that law is not an essential means to our survival? While law is instrumental in promoting our survival, there may be other mechanisms (e.g., a lawless anarchist society) that could achieve the same result. Thus, it may not be possible to rely on the instrumental principle to ground the robust normativity of law. This is because it would not be instrumentally irrational to rely on those other mechanisms, instead of relying on law, to cooperate to survival. Which means that the normative governance of law would not necessarily be rational in quality and, thus, would lack the robustness of legal normativity I am after. In sum, it is necessary to vindicate the *essential* survival-functionality of law for being able to rely on the instrumental principle to ground the robust normativity of

86 I recall again Millgram's (1998) experiences of authority and obedience and Arendt's (2006) philosophical analysis of the banality of evil.

87 Distinguishing formal and non-formal normative systems, see Brennan et al. 2016, 40 ff.

law.[88] I think my previous answer to the first objection already anticipates the rebuttal to the second one.

Concerning morality, it appears to me that it cannot serve as a substitute for law for two main reasons. Firstly, it is widely acknowledged that legal norms extend their governance to actions far beyond what moral principles or reasons dictate. The domain of morality is significantly narrower compared to the broad range of subjects covered by law, which encompasses nearly every aspect of human interaction. Additionally, disagreements arising from diverse moral perspectives, influenced by factors such as ideology, politics, religion, or ethnicity, often lead to escalating conflicts.[89] Law functions precisely as an artefact designed to facilitate the orderly and peaceful operation of societies, promoting human cooperation for survival. In short, even if ideal morality exists, the contingent human condition renders epistemic access to morality so difficult, leading to great disagreements and conflicts, and makes the creation of law necessary for us to survive.

One might also argue that cooperation for survival can occur even without a formal legal system, relying solely on social norms. While social normative systems, such as etiquette, have a limited scope in regulating human conduct and cannot replace law in fostering cooperation for survival, the case for broad customary social normative systems is worth considering. Hart (2012, 91 ff) explores the possibility of a society governed solely by 'rules of obligation', like those restricting violence. He concedes that in a small, stable society, a 'regime of unofficial rules' might suffice. However, the development of legal systems as societies expanded and became more complex appears to be more than coincidental.[90] This is because social normative systems often lack the capacity to address issues related to the functioning of systems, including the identification, creation, application, and enforcement of legal norms. Additionally, in modern societies, social pressure alone would likely be insufficient to ensure compliance. Consequently, it also does not appear that possible social normative systems constitute true alternatives to legal systems.

5.6 Conclusion

This chapter challenges both the unambitious view of legal normativity, which equates law's normativity with that of games, and the view that the robustness of law's normativity depends solely on moral and prudential reasons, making robust normativity a contingent feature of legal systems. Contrary to these theses, I argued from a constitutivist perspective that law is a necessary means

88 I thank Stefano Bertea for pressing me on this point.

89 Copp (2019, 55) admits what he calls the 'problem of security' can be exacerbated by moral disagreements, which is precisely one reason societies need law. In turn, it is because Shapiro (2011, 169 ff) recognizes this that he affirms the 'moral aim thesis', according to which law has the aim of resolving substantial moral disagreements.

90 Hume also acknowledges this fact. On this, see Zaluski 2013, 157 ff.

to achieve certain ends related to action. Drawing on evolutionary theory, I proposed that humans are inherently disposed to cooperate for survival, indicating a general motivational attitude towards abiding by laws. The drive for survival thus emerges as a constitutive end of law, as it serves as an essential means to facilitate cooperation for survival. This supported the affirmed Dispositional Constitutivist Thesis, according to which as human subjects possess a law-abiding disposition and law serves as an essential means to further the aim of cooperation for survival, these subjects should, as an objective matter of normative practical rationality, be committed to complying with the law. Consequently, legal norms establish non-optional universal reasons for action, showcasing robust normativity independent of moral or prudential reasons. As a result, it does not seem that possible social normative systems can serve as true alternatives to legal systems.

Acknowledgements

I am grateful to Stefano Bertea, Marco Brigaglia, Julieta Rábanos, Wojciech Zaluski, as well as to the audiences at the XXVIII Seminario Hispano-italiano-franco-luso de Teoría del Derecho, which took place in Alicante, and at the Belgrade Legal Theory Group for helpful comments and discussion of a preliminary version of this chapter.

References

Alvarez, Maria. 2017. "Reasons for Action: Justification, Motivation, Explanation". In The Stanford Encyclopedia of Philosophy, edited by Edward N. Zalta. https://plato.stanford.edu/archives/spr2017/entries/reasons-just-vs-expl/.

Arendt, Hannah. 2006. *Eichmann in Jerusalem: A Report on the Banality of Evil.* New York: Penguin.

Baker, Lynne Rudder. 2009. The Metaphysics of Malfunction. *Techné: Research in Philosophy and Technology* 13 (2):82-92

Baker, Derek. 2018. "The Varieties of Normativity". In The Routledge Handbook of Metaethics, edited by Tristram McPherson and David Plunkett. London: Routledge.

Bertea, Stefano. 2013. "Constitutivism and Normativity: A Qualified Defence". *Philosophical Explorations* 16 (1): 81–95.

Bertea, Stefano. 2019. "A Problem for the Unambitious View of Legal Normativity". *Revus* 37: 9–16.

Bertea, Stefano. 2025. "Constitutivism about Practical Reasons and the Idea of Legal Norm". In Metaethical Issues in Contemporary Legal Philosophy: A Constitutivist Approach, edited by Stefano Bertea and Jorge Silva Sampaio. London: Routledge.

Bix, Brian. 2018. "Kelsen, Hart, and Legal Normativity". *Revus* 34: 25–42.

Bix, Brian. 2021. "The normativity of law". In The Cambridge Companion to Legal Positivism, edited by Torben Spaak. Cambridge: Cambridge University Press.

Bix, Brian. 2023. *Jurisprudence: Theory and Context.* 9th ed. London: Sweet & Maxwell.

Blackburn, Simon. 1988. "How to Be an Ethical Antirealist". *Midwest Studies in Philosophy* 12: 361–375.

Bowles, Samuel, and Gintis, Herbert. 2011. *A Cooperative Species: Human Reciprocity and Its Evolution*. Princeton: Princeton University Press.
Boyd, Robert, and Richerson, Peter J. 2009. "Culture and the Evolution of Human Cooperation". *Philosophical Transactions B* 364(1533): 3281–3288.
Braddon-Mitchell, David, and Jackson, Frank. 2006. *Philosophy of Mind and Cognition*. 2nd ed. Oxford: Blackwell.
Brennan, Geoffrey, Lina Eriksson, Robert E. Goodin, and Nicholas Southwood. 2016. Explaining Norms. Oxford: Oxford University Press.
Broome, John. 2013. *Rationality Through Reasoning*. Hoboken, NJ: Wiley.
Burazin, Luka, Himma, Kenneth Einar and Corrado Roversi, eds. 2018. *Law as an Artifact*. Oxford: Oxford University Press.
Burazin, Luka, Kenneth Einar Himma, and Corrado Roversi. The Artifactual Nature of Law. Cheltenham: Edward Elgar Publishing.
Choi, Sungho and Fara, Michael. 2021. "Dispositions". In The Stanford Encyclopedia of Philosophy, edited by Edward N. Zalta, 2021. https://plato.stanford.edu/archives/sum2021/entries/dispositions/.
Claus, Laurence. 2012. *Law's Evolution and Human Understanding*. Oxford: Oxford University Press.
Coleman, Jules. 2001. *The Practice of Principle*. Oxford: Oxford University Press.
Copp, David. 2007. "Moral Naturalism and Three Grades of Normativity". In Morality in a Natural World: Selected Essays in Metaethics, 279–303. Cambridge: Cambridge University Press.
Copp, David. 2019. "Legal Teleology: A Naturalist Account of the Normativity of Law". In Dimensions of Normativity: New Essays on Metaethics and Jurisprudence, edited by David Plunkett, Scott J. Shapiro and Kevin Toh, 127–153. Oxford: Oxford University Press.
Copp, David and Justin Morton. 2022. "Normativity in Metaethics". In *The Stanford Encyclopedia of Philosophy*, edited by Edward N. Zalta and Uri Nodelman, 2022. https://plato.stanford.edu/archives/win2022/entries/normativity-metaethics/.
Dancy, Jonathan. 2000. *Practical Reality*. Oxford: Oxford University Press.
Dancy, Jonathan. 2004, *Ethics Without Principles*. Oxford: Oxford University Press.
Dennett, D. 1984. *Elbow room: The varieties of free will worth wanting*. Oxford: Clarendon Press.
Dipert, Randall R. 1995. "Some Issues in the Theory of Artifacts: Defining "Artifact" and Related Notions". *Monist* 78: 119–135.
Dyevre, Arthur. 2014. "Law and the Evolutionary Turn: The Relevance of Evolutionary Psychology for Legal Positivism". *Ratio Juris* 27(3): 364–386.
Ehrenberg, Kenneth E. 2016. *The Functions of Law*. Oxford: Oxford University Press.
Enoch, David. 2006. "Agency, Shmagency: Why Normativity Won't Come from What Is Constitutive of Action". *Philosophical Review* 115 (2): 169–198.
Enoch, David. 2011. *Taking Morality Seriously: A Defense of Robust Realism*. Oxford: Oxford University Press.
Enoch, David. 2019. "Is General Jurisprudence Interesting?" In Dimensions of Normativity: New Essays on Metaethics and Jurisprudence, edited by David Plunkett, Scott J. Shapiro, and Kevin Toh, 65–94. Oxford: Oxford University Press.
Ferrero, Luca. 2009. "Constitutivism and the Inescapability of Agency". *Oxford Studies in Metaethics* 4: 303–333.

Finlay, Stephen. 2010. "Normativity, Necessity and Tense: A Recipe for Homebaked Normativity". In Oxford Studies in Metaethics, Vol. 5, edited by Russ Shafer-Landau. Oxford: Oxford University Press.
Finlay, Stephen. 2019. "Defining Normativity". In Dimensions of Normativity: New Essays on Metaethics and Jurisprudence, edited by David Plunkett, Scott J. Shapiro, and Kevin Toh, 137–158. Oxford: Oxford University Press.
Finlay, Stephen and Schroeder, Mark. 2017. "Reasons for Action: Internal vs. External". In The Stanford Encyclopedia of Philosophy, edited by Edward N. Zalta. https://plato.stanford.edu/archives/sum2017/entries/reasons-internal-external/.
Fuller, Lon F. 1969. *The Morality of Law*. New Haven: Yale University Press
Finnis, John. 1980. *Natural Law and Natural Rights.* Oxford: Oxford University Press
Gardner, John. 2012. "The Supposed Formality of the Rule of Law". In Law as a Leap of Faith: Essays on Law in General, 194–223. Oxford: Oxford University Press.
Gibbard. Allan. 1990. *Wise Choices, Apt Feelings: A Theory of Normative Judgement.* Cambridge, MA: HUP.
Gibbard Allan. 2003. *Thinking How to Live.* Cambridge, MA: Harvard University Press.
Gildenhuys Peter. 2024. "Natural Selection". In The Stanford Encyclopedia of Philosophy, edited by Edward N. Zalta and Uri Nodelman. https://plato.stanford.edu/archives/sum2024/entries/natural-selection/.
Green, Leslie. 2023. "Law as a Means". *The Germ of Justice.* Oxford University Press
Green, Leslie. 1998. "The Functions of Law". *Cogito* 12 (2): 117–124.
Green, Leslie and Adams, Thomas. 2019. "Legal Positivism". In The Stanford Encyclopedia of Philosophy, edited by Edward N. Zalta. https://plato.stanford.edu/archives/sum2019/entries/legal-positivism/.
Gur, Noam. 2019. *Legal Directives and Practical Reasons.* Oxford: Oxford University Press.
Hart, H. L. A. 2012. *The Concept of Law.* 3rd ed. Oxford: Oxford University Press.
Hilpinen, Risto. 2018. "Artifact". In The Stanford Encyclopedia of Philosophy, edited by Edward N. Zalta. https://plato.stanford.edu/archives/fall2018/entries/artifact/.
Himma, Kenneth Einar. 2018. "The Conceptual Function of Law: Law, Coercion, and Keeping the Peace". In Law as an Artifact, edited by Luka Burazin, Kenneth Einar Himma, and Corrado Roversi, 143–161. Oxford: Oxford University Press.
Himma, Kenneth Einar. 2020. *Coercion and the Nature of Law.* Oxford: Oxford University Press.
Houkes, Wybo and Vermaas, Pieter E. 2010. *Technical Functions: On the Use and Design of Artefacts.* Dordrecht: Springer.
Kahneman, Daniel. 2013. *Thinking, Fast and Slow.* New York: Farrar, Straus and Giroux.
Katsafanas, Paul. 2013. *Agency and the Foundations of Ethics: Nietzschean Constitutivism.* Oxford: Oxford University Press.
Katsafanas 2018 Constitutivism about Practical Reasons". In The Oxford Handbook of Reasons and Normativity, edited by Daniel Star, 367–394. Oxford: Oxford University Press.
Kelsen, Hans. 2006. *General Theory of Law and State.* London: Routledge.
Korsgaard, Christine M. 1996. *Creating the Kingdom of Ends.* Cambridge: Cambridge University Press.
Korsgaard, Christine M. 2008. *The Constitution of Agency.* Oxford: Oxford University Press.

Korsgaard, Christine M. 2009. *Self-Constitution*. Oxford: Oxford University Press.
Leiter, Brian. 2007. *Naturalizing Jurisprudence: Essays on American Legal Realism and Naturalism in Legal Philosophy*. Oxford: Oxford University Press.
Leiter, Brian. 2013. "Why Legal Positivism (Again)?" *University of Chicago Public Law Working Paper No. 442.*
Lindeman, Kathryn. 2019. "Legal Metanormativity: Lessons for and from Constitutivist Accounts in the Philosophy of Law". In Dimensions of Normativity: New Essays on Metaethics and Jurisprudence, edited by David Plunkett, Scott J. Shapiro, and Kevin Toh, 87–104. Oxford: Oxford University Press.
MacCormick, Neil. 2008. *H.L.A. Hart*. 2nd ed. Stanford: Stanford Law Books.
Mackie, J. L. 1977. *Ethics: Inventing Right and wrong*. New York: Penguin Book.
Maguire, Barry. 2016. "The Value-Based Theory of Reasons". *Ergo* 3: Article 9.
Marmor, Andrei and Sarch, Alexander. 2019. "The Nature of Law". In The Stanford Encyclopedia of Philosophy, edited by Edward N. Zalta. https://plato.stanford.edu/archives/sum2019/entries/law-nature/.
McPherson, Tristram. 2011. "Against Quietist Normative Realism". *Philosophical Studies* 154 (2): 223–240.
McPherson, Tristram and Plunkett, David. 2017. "The Nature and Explanatory Ambitions of Metaethics". In The Routledge Handbook of Metaethics, edited by Tristram McPherson and David Plunkett, 1–28. London: Routledge.
Millgram, Elijah. 2020. "Practical Reason and the Structure of Actions". In The Stanford Encyclopedia of Philosophy, edited by Edward N. Zalta. https://plato.stanford.edu/archives/win2020/entries/practical-reason-action/.
Milgram, Stanley. 1998. *Obedience to Authority: An Experimental View*. London: Pinter & Martin.
Millikan, Ruth Garrett. 1984. *Language, Thought, and Other Biological Categories: New Foundations for Realism*. Cambridge, MA: MIT Press.
Miotto, Lucas. 2021. "Law and Coercion: Some Clarification". *Ratio Juris* 34(1), 74–87.
Mumford, Stephen. 1998. *Dispositions*. Oxford: Oxford University Press.
Neander, Karen. 1991. "The Teleological Notion of 'Function'". *Australasian Journal of Philosophy* 69(4): 454–468.
Paakkunainen, Hille. 2017. "Normativity and Agency". In The Routledge Handbook of Metaethics, edited by Tristram McPherson and David Plunkett. London: Routledge.
Parfit, Derek. 2011. *On What Matters*. Vol. 2. Oxford: Oxford University Press.
Paul, Sarah K. 2021. *Philosophy of Action*. London: Routledge.
Piñeros Glasscock, Juan S., and Sergio Tenenbaum. 2023. "Action". In The Stanford Encyclopedia of Philosophy, edited by Edward N. Zalta and Uri Nodelman. https://plato.stanford.edu/archives/win2023/entries/action/.
Pino, Giorgio. 2021. "Normativity for Positivists". In Contemporary Perspectives on Legal Obligation, edited by Stefano Bertea, 82–97. London: Routledge.
Plunkett, David and Shapiro, Scott. 2017. "Law, Morality, and Everything Else: General Jurisprudence as a Branch of Metanormative Inquiry". *Ethics* 128 (1): 37–68.
Plunkett, David. 2019. "Robust Normativity, Morality, and Legal Positivism". In Dimensions of Normativity: New Essays on Metaethics and Jurisprudence, edited by David Plunkett, Scott J. Shapiro, and Kevin Toh. Oxford: Oxford University Press.

Postema, Gerald J. 1982. "Coordination and Convention at the Foundations of Law". *The Journal of Legal Studies* 11(1), 165–203.

Preston Beth. 2022. "Artifact". In The Stanford Encyclopedia of Philosophy, edited by Edward N. Zalta and Uri Nodelman. https://plato.stanford.edu/archives/win2022/entries/artifact/.

Preston, Beth. 2013. *A Philosophy of Material Culture: Action, Function, and Mind.* New York: Routledge.

Rábanos, Julieta. 2024a, "Coercion and the (Functions of) Law". In Sanctions: An Essential Element of Law? edited by N. Bersier, C. Bezemek, and F. Schauer. Springer.

Rábanos, Julieta. 2024b. "On an 'Evolutionary' Theory of Legal Systems". In Research Handbook on Legal Evolution, edited by Wojciech Zaluski, Sacha Bourgeois-Gironde, and Adam Dyrda, 130–148. Edward Elgar Publishing.

Railton, Peter. 2019. "'We'll see you in court!': 'The Rule of Law as an Explanatory and Normative Kind". In Dimensions of Normativity: New Essays on Metaethics and Jurisprudence, edited by David Plunkett, Scott J. Shapiro, and Kevin Toh. Oxford: Oxford University Press.

Raz, Joseph. 1999. *Practical Reason and Norms.* Oxford: Oxford University Press.

Raz, Joseph. 2009. *The Authority of Law: Essays on Law and Morality.* Oxford: Oxford University Press.

Redondo, Maria Cristina. 1996. *La noción de razón para la acción en el análisis jurídico.* Centro de Estudios Políticos y Constitucionales.

Redondo, Maria Cristina. 2019. "Legal normativity as a moral property". *Revus* 37: 57–68.

Ridge, Michael. 2014. *Impassioned Belief.* Oxford: Oxford University Press

Rosati. Connie S. 2019. "Bix on the Normativity of Law". *Revus* 37: 69–74.

Scanlon, Thomas. 2014. *Being Realistic about Reasons.* Oxford: Oxford University Press.

Schapiro, Tamar. 2001. "Three Conceptions of Action in Moral Theory". *Noûs* 35 (1): 93–117.

Schauer, Frederick. 2015. *The Force of Law.* Cambridge, MA: Harvard University Press.

Schlosser, Markus. 2019. "Agency". In The Stanford Encyclopedia of Philosophy, edited by Edward N. Zalta. https://plato.stanford.edu/archives/sum2019/entries/agency/.

Schwitzgebel, Eric. 2013. "A Dispositional Approach to the Attitudes". In New Essays on Belief: Constitution, Content and Structure, edited by Nikolaj Nottelmann, 75–99. Palgrave.

Sciaraffa, Stefan. 2009. "On Content-Independent Reasons: It's Not in the Name". *Law and Philosophy* 28 (3): 233–260.

Searle, John. 1995. *The Construction of Social Reality.* New York: Free Press.

Shapiro, Scott. 1998. "On Hart's Way Out". *Legal Theory* 4 (4): 469–507.

Shapiro, Scott. 2000. "Law, Morality, and the Guidance of Conduct". *Legal Theory* 6 (2): 127–170.

Shapiro, Scott. 2011. *Legality.* Cambridge, MA: -Harvard University Press.

Smith, Michael. 1994; *The moral problem.* Oxford: Blackwell.

Smith, Michael. 2010. "Beyond the Error Theory". In A World Without Values, edited by Richard Joyce and Simon Kirchin. New York: Springer.

Smith, Michael. 2018. "Constitutivism". In The Routledge Handbook of Metaethics, edited by Tristram McPherson and David Plunkett. New York: Routledge.

Street, Sharon. 2006. "A Darwinian Dilemma for Realist Theories of Value". *Philosophical Studies* 127: 109–166.

Sturgeon, Nicholas L. 1995. "Critical Study of Gibbard's Wise Choices, Apt Feelings". *Noûs* 29 (3): 402–424.

Tooby, John and Cosmides, Leda. 1992. "The Psychological Foundations of Culture". In The Adapted Mind: Evolutionary Psychology and the Generation of Culture, edited by Jerome Barkow, Leda Cosmides, and John Tooby, 19–136. Oxford University Press.

Tooby, John and Cosmides, Leda. 2005. "The Conceptual Foundations of Evolutionary Psychology". In The Handbook of Evolutionary Psychology, edited by David M. Buss, 5–67. Hoboken, NJ: Wiley & Sons.

Toh, Kevin. 2019. "Legal Philosophy à la carte". In Dimensions of Normativity: New Essays on Metaethics and Jurisprudence, edited by David Plunkett, Scott J. Shapiro, and Kevin Toh. Oxford: Oxford University Press.

Toh., Kevin. 2021. "Legal Positivism and Metaethics". In The Cambridge Companion to Legal Positivism, edited by Torben Spaak. Cambridge: Cambridge University Press.

Tyler, Tom R. 2006. *Why People Obey the Law*. Princeton: Princeton University Press.

Velleman, J. David. 2009. *How we get along*. New York: Cambridge University Press.

Wallace, Jay R. 2006. *Normativity and the Will*. Oxford: Oxford University Press.

Waluchow, Will. 2000. "Authority and the Practical Difference Thesis: A Defense of Inclusive Legal Positivism". *Legal Theory* 6(1): 45–81.

Wedgewood, Ralph. 2017. The value of rationality, Oxford: Oxford University Press.

Wedgewood, Ralph. 2018. "The Unity of Normativity". In The Oxford Handbook of Reasons and Normativity, edited by Daniel Star. Oxford: Oxford University Press.

Wodak, Daniel. 2017. "Expressivism and Varieties of Normativity". *Oxford Studies in Metaethics* 12: 265–293.

Wodak, Daniel. 2020. "Who's on First?" In Oxford Studies in Metaethics, edited by Russ Shafer-Landau, 49–71. Oxford: Oxford University Press.

Zaluski, Wojciech. 2009. *Evolutionary Theory and Legal Philosophy*. Cheltengam: Edward Elgar Publishing.

Zaluski, Wojciech. 2013. *Game Theory in Jurisprudence*. Kraków: Copernicus Center Press.

Zaluski, Wojciech, Sacha Bourgeois-Gironde, and Adam, Dyrda. eds. 2024. *Research Handbook on Legal Evolution*. Cheltenham: Edward Elgar Publishing.

6 Closure of normative competence in legal systems

María Beatriz Arriagada and Jorge L. Rodríguez

This chapter focuses on the thesis, supported by public law scholars and by some legal theorists, according to which systems of power-conferring norms of public authorities require for their closure of rule-prohibiting lower ranked authorities from performing any normative action that has not been expressly permitted by higher ranked authorities. The first goal of the chapter is to raise two objections to this thesis if power-conferring norms are reconstructed as constitutive rules: (i) such a closure rule cannot be regulatory in character and, (ii) its enactment would be superfluous since power-conferring normative systems are closed for logical reasons. The second goal is to offer, following a suggestion of von Wright and some of the ideas defended by the constitutive approach to practical normativity, an explanatory hypothesis for the belief in the need for such closure rule. It consists in the suggestion that power-conferring norms can be viewed from two different perspectives and, as a consequence of this, they can assume a constitutive character from one of these perspectives and a regulative character from the other. The chapter suggests that, if we assume this last perspective, the thesis that is examined and discussed in the chapter makes sense.

6.1 A first approach to the problem[1]

Public law scholars usually contend or assume that public authorities can only do that which has been explicitly authorized or permitted.[2] This widespread

1 This work is the result of a project (no. 1200549) titled *La clausura de los sistemas de normas jurídicas de competencia*, funded by the Fondo Nacional de Desarrollo Científico y Tecnológico (FONDECYT). We are grateful for the observations and critiques made on a draft of this work by those who attended the Seminar *La clausura de los sistemas jurídicos competenciales* II, held on 27 March 2023 at the law school of the University of Diego Portales. We are especially grateful to Professor Pablo Navarro and Professor Juan Pablo Mañalich who, in that instance, were invited as commentators on our work.

2 For example, (Merkl 1927, 217); (Varas 1940, 17); (García de Enterría 1994, 127–128); (Verdugo, Pfeffer and Nogueira 1994, 136); (Moraga Klenner 2008, 278); (Soto Kloss 2012, 178); and (Bermúdez 2014, 90 et seq.).

DOI: 10.4324/9781032670553-7

idea, closely linked to the rule of law, finds support in general legal theory, where many believe that the acts of normative authorities that have not been explicitly permitted by a superior normative authority are prohibited.[3]

A paradigmatic example of this position can be found in von Wright, who is also particularly clear about the fact that the principle 'what is not permitted is prohibited' corresponds to a norm that closes up normative systems that determine the competent authorities to issue and cancel norms.

Von Wright contends that the acts through which norms are given or cancelled can themselves be obligatory, prohibited, or permitted, and he calls the norms whose contents are said *normative acts* 'norms of higher order'. These norms deal with prescriptions because the normative action consists in issuing or cancelling prescriptions, but they are prescriptions themselves.[4]

Norms of *the first order* are, then, norms whose contents are non-normative acts. A norm of higher order is a norm of the second order if the normative act which is its content is the act of issuing or cancelling certain norms (prescriptions) of the first order. A norm is of the third order if the normative act which is its content is the act of issuing or cancelling certain norms (prescriptions) of the second order, and so on and so forth. The subjects of norms of higher order, that is, the agents at whom these norms are addressed, are, in turn, authorities of norms of lower order, such that different authorities of first order, second order, etc., can be distinguished. And if the normative act of issuing a certain norm were not, in turn, the content of any norm of higher order, the agent performing such an act would be acting as sovereign or supreme authority of the norm in question.[5]

While among norms of the first order commands and prohibitions hold the most prominent position, among norms of higher order permissions are of a particular interest and importance. According to von Wright, a *competence norm* is a permissive norm of higher order through which the superior authority of higher order delegates power to a sub-authority of lower order. 'Power' or 'normative competence' here means competence, by virtue of a norm, to act as an authority of norms.[6]

Von Wright claims that it is essential for the delegation of power the permissive character of delegating norms, in the sense that the sub-authority must be free to issue or not the norms within its competence. However, the delegation of power to a sub-authority is often combined with an order to this authority to issue norms about certain types of acts. Thus, it is beyond the sub-authority's competence to decide if there should be regulations of certain

3 (Guastini 2001, 124; 2016, 148; 2014, 146–147 and 422–424); (Redondo 2006, 317, note N° 20 therein); (Mazzarese 2000, 45).

4 Unless they are considered as moral norms (von Wright 1963a, 189–191).

5 (von Wright 1963a, 191–192).

6 (von Wright 1963a, 192).

kinds of acts, but it is within its competence to decide which regulations these might be.[7]

In turn, the limits of the delegated power are usually determined by certain prohibitions. According to von Wright, the authority may issue norms of a certain kind, but must not issue norms of certain other kinds. And although it could be argued that the authority is barred from issuing norms whose enactment is not explicitly permitted, this could not be deduced from the nature of the permission as such. The prohibition, if it exists, would be a norm in its own right.[8]

Von Wright also points out that a theory of higher-order norms helps to clarify the notion of validity. In order to avoid ambiguities, he opts to understand that the validity of a norm means that the norm exists and that, in addition, there exists another norm which permits the authority of the first to issue it. In that sense, the validity of a norm refers to the legality of the act issuing it and, as such, it would be a relative notion: a norm is valid, if at all, relative to another norm permitting its issuing or its coming into existence. To this notion of validity corresponds a notion of invalidity; a norm is invalid if the issuing of that norm by a certain authority is forbidden to this authority by virtue of some higher-order norm. And under this view, sovereign norms could not be valid or invalid.[9]

Finally, and in what matters for the purposes of this chapter, von Wright contends that, in contrast with first order norms, where it seems natural to adopt the point of view that everything which is not prohibited is permitted, as far as norms of higher order are concerned it seems far more natural to think that 'whatever is not permitted is prohibited'.[10]

In this context, von Wright clarifies that the prohibition of issuing norms for which there is no explicit permission to enact could not be addressed at the sovereign authority delegating power in a sub-authority. Such a prohibition could be only addressed to sub-authorities. Only their normative acts could consistently be regarded as forming a normatively closed field of acts, in the sense that these authorities are solely allowed to exercise such normative power as has been delegated to them, and no other.[11]

7 (von Wright 1963a, 192–193).
8 (von Wright 1963a, 193).
9 (von Wright 1963a, 194–198).
10 (von Wright 1963a, 193–194).
11 (von Wright 1963a, 194). The conclusion is the opposite to the principle *nullum crimen sine lege*. Once it has been ruled out that this principle can be considered as a logical principle in the sense that everything that is not prohibited is therefore *ipso facto* permitted, von Wright admits its consideration as a permissive norm closing up the system of norms to which it belongs by conferring normative status to every human action not subject to norm. The content of the permissive rule *nullum crimen sine lege* is, so to speak, the total sum of every action and abstention not already prohibited. If this rule belongs to a normative system, it would be closed because it would have no gaps. Cfr. (von Wright 1963a, 87 and 193–194)

We thus encounter here the thesis that will be the object of analysis of this work. It posits that legal systems are, from the point of view of norms assigning competence to public authorities, closed systems because they contain a closure rule establishing that every normative action by an authority that has not been explicitly permitted by a superior authority is prohibited.

6.2 The closure of first order systems

The analysis of closure in legal systems has been one of the most debated topics in legal philosophy. One of the most important contributions made by Alchourrón and Bulygin is, precisely, their analysis of the problem of gaps in law. Harnessing their own breakthroughs in logic as applied to the field of norms, in particular the distinction between a genuine *logic of norms* and a *logic of normative propositions*, that is, of descriptive propositions about norms, Alchourrón and Bulygin reject one of the most widespread arguments to attempt to justify that completeness is a necessary property of normative systems. Hans Kelsen's position is a good example of this point of view.[12] His main argument for grounding the thesis that there are no gaps in the law is based on the principle establishing that everything that is not legally prohibited is legally permitted. This principle would prevent the existence of gaps and would also be an analytical truth.

Alchourrón and Bulygin[13] show that this argument is fallacious and a product of an ambiguity hiding behind the principle 'Everything that is not legally prohibited is legally permitted'. According to their analysis, when the expression 'permitted' appears in genuine norms, it is equivalent to not prohibited. However, when 'permitted' appears in a normative proposition, its meaning becomes ambiguous because there are two senses in which the negation of a proposition such as 'the action of *A* is prohibited in normative system *S*' can be interpreted. It may mean that: (i) within the normative system under consideration there is no norm prohibiting that action—negative or weak permission, or (ii) a norm that does not prohibit (authorizes) said action belongs to the system under consideration—positive or strong permission (for the sake of simplicity we will henceforth refer simply to positive or negative permission).

Negative permission: $P^{-}_{S}A = PHA \notin S$
Positive permission: $P^{+}_{S}A = \sim PHA \in S = PA \in S$

With the aid of these conceptual distinctions, it is possible to appreciate that the principle 'Everything that is not legally prohibited is legally permitted' admits different readings. In the first place, if the principle is understood as a genuine norm permitting those actions that have not been prohibited, it

12 Cfr. (Kelsen 1960, 245–250).
13 Cfr. (Alchourrón and Bulygin 1971, 121–125).

cannot be said that it is an analytical truth simply because it is more than debatable that truth values can be attributed to norms. On the other hand, there is no reason warranting that such a norm must necessarily belong to every conceivable legal system.

In the second place, if the principle is interpreted not as a norm but as a normative proposition—which is the sense Kelsen appears to assign it when he deems that it is a necessary truth with respect to any legal system—the expression 'permitted' contained therein can be read as a positive permission or as a negative permission. Thus, in this descriptive sense there would still be two versions of the principle that have to be differentiated: one negative and one positive.[14]

If 'permitted' is interpreted as a negative permission, the principle would express that, for all legal systems, if the system does not contain (or it cannot be derived from it) a norm prohibiting the conduct *A*, whatever this may be, then *A* is permitted in the negative sense within the system. The negative permission is tantamount to the inexistence of a prohibitive norm with regards to the conduct in question, thereby in this version the principle would simply state 'Everything that is not legally prohibited, is not legally prohibited'. In this sense, the principle corresponds indeed to an analytical truth and, therefore, is true with respect to every legal system since it is simply a particular manifestation of the principle of identity. But under this interpretation, the principle cannot preclude the possibility of gaps since it says nothing about how to solve a case to which no solution has been attached. It simply states the trivial truth that, if the legislator did not solve a case, she did not solve it, which is obviously compatible with the existence of gaps.[15]

If, conversely, 'permitted' is interpreted as a positive permission, the principle would express that, for all legal systems, if the system does not contain (or it cannot be derived from it) a norm prohibiting a conduct *A*, whatever this may be, then *A* is permitted in a positive sense within the system. Since the positive permission is equivalent to the existence in the system of a norm authorizing the performance of an action, in this version the principle would guarantee the inexistence of normative gaps for it would be tantamount to asserting the existence of a permission to perform any non-prohibited action. But far from being necessarily true, it would be a contingent statement: only with regards to those legal systems containing a norm to this effect, this is, a norm residually authorizing any action that has not been prohibited, the principle would become true under this interpretation.[16]

In conclusion, the principle under analysis cannot fulfill in every case the functions that authors such as Kelsen assign to it. Either in its negative version it would indeed constitute an analytical truth, yet trivial and insufficient

14 Cfr. (Alchourrón and Bulygin 1971, 125).
15 Cfr. (Alchourrón and Bulygin 1971, 125–126).
16 Cfr. (Alchourrón and Bulygin 1971, 126–127).

to close up normative systems, or in its positive version it would be used to preclude the possibility of normative gaps, but it would become contingent, its truth depending on the existence of a norm of closure within the given system. The appearance of plausibility of the argument appealing to the principle in question derives exclusively from a fallacy of ambiguity stemming from the two meanings that may be given to the expression 'permitted', and as such it cannot justify the conclusion that *every* legal system is *necessarily* complete.

Thus, for example, although article 19 of the Argentinian National Constitution in its second sentence ('No inhabitant of the Nation shall be obligated to do what the law does not mandate, nor deprived of what is does not prohibit') seems to express a norm of closure that residually permits the conducts that have not been prohibited by the legislator, it is incorrect to suppose that every legal system must necessarily have such a norm. In fact, many authoritarian legal systems do not contain this principle of legality, and so certain conducts may be considered illegal though they have not been expressly prohibited. Furthermore, the principle enshrined in article 19 of the Argentinian Constitution does not even apply in every field of Argentinian law. It only works undoubtedly in the field of criminal law, thus it would be wrong to contend that in Argentinian law there is a norm generically permitting any non-prohibited conduct. That is why Alchourrón and Bulygin highlighted the normative importance of the principle of legality in criminal law as a political conquest:

> The rule "nulla poena", when seen as a directive to judges, typifies the expression in penal law of a political ideology. A liberal penal law may be characterized as one than contains this rule.[17]

6.3 Two objections to the principle 'Everything that is not permitted is prohibited' as a rule of closure of systems of norms of competence

If the preceding analysis is accepted it may be concluded that, given that completeness and closure are contingent properties of normative systems in general, the same would apply for the systems of norms of competence, whose closure requires a rule establishing so. At any rate, the idea that the rule of closure of such systems 'of second order' would prohibit every normative action that has not been expressly permitted, in the reverse sense of the rule of closure of the systems of 'first order' in von Wright's understanding of them, would still be in need of a proper justification.

In what follows we shall examine two different objections to the thesis under consideration. The ground for both critiques is, however, the same: the idea that norms of competence are a type of so-called constitutive rules.

17 Cfr. (Alchourrón and Bulygin 1971, 142).

6.3.1 Norms of competence as constitutive rules

When von Wright identifies the central meanings of the word 'norm' he rules out that the meaning of 'normative' should be restricted to the prescriptive domain. In this context, he clearly distinguishes those norms that prescribe or regulate (order, prohibit, or permit) conduct from those norms that, instead, define different social practices or institutions by determining the patterns to perform (correctly) certain activities,[18] which he calls 'determinative rules'.[19] It could be said that those are two different *species* or *types* of norms.

A similar contrast is famously drawn by Searle through the distinction between regulative and constitutive rules.[20] Regulative rules regulate conducts whose existence is independent of those rules, whereas constitutive rules regulate conducts whose existence is not independent of those rules, that is, they regulate new forms of conduct constituted by those very rules. Refining the distinction as a result of the critiques addressed to this way of presentation,[21] it could be formulated in the following terms:[22]

i) Regulative rules regulate conducts in the sense that they qualify them normatively as mandatory, prohibited, or permitted. Constitutive rules regulate conducts in the sense that they define or determine certain ways of interpreting the conduct, without introducing deontic modalities;
ii) Regulative rules regulate conducts whose description is independent of said rules. Constitutive rules make it possible to describe conducts in a way that would not be possible without them.

A classic example of a regulative rule is the norm that prohibits smoking in public spaces. A classic example of a constitutive rule is a rule establishing how bishops should move in chess. Note that the first normatively qualifies as prohibited the action of smoking in public spaces, an action whose execution is conceivable with total independence of whether or not there exist norms normatively qualifying its execution. In contrast, the second is not a norm that obligates, permits, or prohibits moving the bishop in a certain way, but it determines what counts as a valid move by a bishop in the game of chess, an action that would not be possible to perform without such a rule. If according to it we say that the bishop 'can' only move in a straight diagonal forward or backward, and that it 'cannot' jump over other pieces, here 'can' and 'cannot' do not amount to permissions and prohibitions. If we were to move a bishop in a different way, we would not be executing a valid move in the game, since

18 Such as playing a game, speaking a language, or calculating; (von Wright 1963a, 1–8; 1971, 151–153).
19 Cfr., for example, (Bulygin 1992) and (Rodríguez 2021, 42).
20 Cfr. (Searle 1964, 1969, 1995, 2018).
21 In this regard, for example, (Raz 1975, 108–111).
22 (Orunesu and Rodríguez 2022, 198).

to move a bishop in the game of chess is an action that may only be performed in accordance with its rules.[23]

Analytical legal theory has shown the importance of this distinction in the law. Hart, even before von Wright and Searle, distinguished, first, between rules imposing obligations and rules conferring powers and, second, between primary rules and secondary rules.[24] Primary rules are precisely those which impose obligations, while secondary rules are mainly rules conferring powers to certain subjects to produce or apply other rules.[25] As it is well known, Hart's most important argument is that while a rule imposing an obligation is conceptually separable from the punishment (which is the consequence of breaching that rule), a rule conferring powers is conceptually inseparable from nullity or invalidity (which is the consequence of not following that rule).[26]

Norms of competence, as constitutive rules and, unlike regulative rules, present us with new ways of thinking and acting.[27] This is due to the fact that they create meanings in conjunction with other constitutive rules. They determine certain conditions and certain normative consequences for the constitution of competence as a significant element within the practice. In addition, constitutive rules determining specific modes of behavior limiting the use of competence also contribute to constitute this meaning.[28]

The distinction between regulative rules and constitutive rules has had an importance that is hard to overstate. Not only it is used to explain the elements of the law in general,[29] but also the functioning of different legal institutions, such as, for example, constitutional norms,[30] fundamental rights,[31] and judicial precedents.[32]

On account of this explanatory power, and given that it is a distinction that, as we have seen, is considered by von Wright when distinguishing between

23 Following Searle, the characteristic logical structure of constitutive rules answers to a scheme of the type '*X* counts as *Y* in the context *C*'. Strictly speaking, this is incorrect since that would be the structure of a normative proposition referring to the existence of a constitutive rule. The constitutive rule itself ('such and such moves count as a play by the bishop') does not include a reference to the context, but it is a rule *within* a certain context.

24 (Hart 1961, 27–42 and 79–99).

25 The so-called 'rule of recognition' that defines the ultimate criteria of validity of legal systems is also a secondary rule. The fact that it is a secondary rule, even though it does not confer any power (Cfr. Ferrer 2000, 79–80) (Vilajosana 2010, 104–105) allows us to argue that the distinction 'primary rules and secondary rules' is tantamount to the distinction 'rules imposing obligations and rules conferring powers'.

26 (Hart 1961, 33–35). A similar view is held by (Ross 1968, 53–57, among others).

27 (Roversi 2018, 141).

28 We apply to norms of competence what Roversi argues about constitutive rules (Roversi 2010, 226–228).

29 Cfr. (Atienza and Ruiz Manero 2004, 45 et seq); (Moreso and Vilajosana 2004, 65 et seq.); (Guastini 2014, 41–71).

30 For example, (Ruiz Manero 2007); (Orunesu and Rodríguez 2022).

31 For example, (Arriagada 2015a; 2015b; 2015c).

32 For example, (Núñez 2018; 2021); (Arriagada 2021b).

prescriptions and determinative rules, his account of norms of competence as prescriptive rules of a permissive nature is particularly noteworthy. However, the arguments in favour of considering norms of competence as constitutive rules are convincing and, certainly, it is no accident that subjects at whom the norms are addressed and that exercise the different functions of state power are called '*constituted* authorities' or '*constituted* powers'.[33]

Before venturing into the reasons that might justify von Wright's position, it is necessary to examine the critiques that may be levelled against the thesis that competence systems are closed by a rule establishing that every normative action by an authority that has not been explicitly permitted by a superior normative authority is prohibited.

6.3.2 *First objection: the rule of closure of a competence system cannot be regulative or prescriptive*

We have seen that, according to Alchourrón and Bulygin, the statement 'Everything that is not legally prohibited is permitted' admits of an interpretation as a normative proposition affirming the existence of a rule that permits any action that has not been prohibited by the norms of the system under consideration.

It must be, however, emphasized that this rule: (i) closes up the system, insofar as it authorizes to infer, from the sole fact that the norm prohibiting certain conduct does not belong in the system (negative permission), that an implicit norm permitting that conduct (positive permission) belongs in the system;[34] (ii) is a second level rule, as it refers to the system's norms constituting the first level and is not included itself in this reference; and (iii) it has a supplementary character, inasmuch as its use is restricted to those situations where no solution to the case in question may be inferred from ordinary rules.[35]

If norms correlate generic cases with normative solutions,[36] the generic case (or condition of application) of this second level rule is no other than the verification of a case not solved by first level norms, and its normative solution is the qualification of the given action as permitted. From this it follows that the ability of this second level rule to close up the system depends on it being *of the same kind* as first level rules. This means that it must be a norm correlating a case with a normative solution, that is, a regulative norm.

Under the same logic, if norms of competence are not regulative but constitutive, the rule that closes up a system of norms determining the competences of constituted public authorities would have to be constitutive, not

33 (Carré de Malberg 1922, 249, note 1); (Troper 1994, 204); (Guastini 2014, 171).
34 (Alchourrón and Bulygin 1971, 126–127; 1984, 355) and (Bulygin 2010, 285).
35 (Alchourrón and Bulygin 1971, 135–136).
36 Cfr. (Alchourrón y Bulygin 1971, 15 and 28–29).

regulative.[37] An adequate understanding of this thesis requires to analyze in more detail the constitutive nature of norms of competence, and in particular the way in which these norms constitute or determine normative actions.

That competence norms constitute or determine normative actions means that they establish the conditions under which those actions are valid, that is, legally possible. A normative action is valid or invalid depending on whether it complies or not with the norms of competence constituting or determining it. Among the norms of competence constituting the sphere of action of constituted normative authorities there are usually different kinds: (i) those conferring competences to certain authorities, (ii) those defining the procedures to exercise said competences, (iii) those circumscribing the *object* of the competences (the *cases* that can be solved by those authorities), and (iv) those limiting the *way* in which that object may be disciplined (the *solutions* that can be connected to the cases that may be regulated).[38]

Norms of types (i) and (ii) define the *form* of *normative actions.* Norms of types (iii) and (iv) refer to the *content* of the *norms* produced by those actions. Although the invalidity arising from the breach of type (iv) norms is deemed independent from the invalidity stemming from the breach of type (iii) norms,[39] the existence of type (iv) norms presupposes the existence of type (iii) norms. Type (iv) norms limit the *solutions* that can be attached to the cases that are defined by type (iii) norms.[40]

Based on the foregoing, we may consider the possibility of stipulating that a 'normative solution' is not only the qualification of a class of actions or omissions (factual or normative) as *legally mandatory or permitted*, but also the qualification of a class of normative actions as *legally possible/valid or impossible/invalid*.[41] Yet, these categories are not strictly analogous.

As mentioned before, a normative action is *valid* if it complies with the norms of competence constituting/determining it, and a normative action is *invalid* if it does not comply with the norms of competence constituting/determining it. But, analogously, an action or omission (factual or normative) that complies with the norm regulating it (because it complies with an obligation/prohibition or uses a permission) is *licit.* An action or omission (factual

37 (Arriagada 2021a, 74–75); (Mañalich 2021, 14–15).

38 (Guastini 2017, 51–55); (Prieto Sanchís 2009, 76–78).

39 Whereas the breach of type (iv) rules gives rise to a material unconstitutionality, the breach of type (iii) norms would be a subspecies of formal unconstitutionality due to an infraction of type (i) norms, as the latter attribute to certain organs the power to produce legal norms within certain limits relative to the subjects that can be regulated by said organs, (Ezquiaga 2001, 68) and (Prieto Sanchís 2009, 77). In fact, it is usually admitted that the personal and material aspects of competence are always united (Carrió 1994, 254) and (Ferrer 2000, 124–125).

40 A different matter is that the distinction between types (iii) and (iv) can be considered to be vague because the description of the solution entails, to an extent, the description of the case, (Ross 1968, 96, 107–108 and 130).

41 Cfr. (Arriagada 2021a, 65, note N°28; 2022a, 269–270; 2022b, 129–133).

or normative) that does not comply with the norms regulating it (because it breaches an obligation/prohibition or a permission exceeding its limits) is *illicit*.[42]

As it is widely known, W.N. Hohfeld[43] attempted to clarify the meaning of some of the basic legal concepts by showing their reciprocal relations of opposition and correlativity, according to the following scheme:

Opposite concepts:		Correlative concepts:	
Right	No-right	Right	Duty
Privilege	Duty	Privilege	No-right
Power	Disability	Power	Liability
Immunity	Liability	Immunity	Disability

The pairs of concepts that Hohfeld calls 'opposites' are contradictory, that is, one is the negation of the other. For example, the claim that *x* has a right with respect to *y* with regards to certain action is equivalent to the negation that *x* has a no-right with respect to *y* with regards to that action; the claim that *x* has a power with respect to *y* with regards to certain normative action is equivalent to the negation that *x* is disabled with respect to *y* with regards to that normative action, etc. The pairs of concepts that Hohfeld calls 'correlative' are equivalent notions when the order of the subjects is inverted: the claim that *x* has a right with respect to *y* with regards to certain action is equivalent to claiming that *y* has a duty with respect to *x* with regards to that action; the claim that *x* has a power with respect to *y* with regards to certain normative action is equivalent to claiming that *y* is liable to *x* with regards to that normative action, etc.[44]

In this reconstruction, the concept of liberty or privilege corresponds to that of permission. Now, as Hohfeld himself points out, a privilege or liberty is the negation of a duty of a content precisely opposite to that of the privilege in question.[45] What is 'opposite' to a duty of *x* with respect to *y* with regards to action *A* is not a liberty of *x* with respect to *y* with regards to action *A*, but a liberty of *x* with respect to *y* with regards to the *abstention* of *A*. In turn, the 'opposite' of a duty of *x* with respect to *y* with regards to the abstention of *A* is a liberty of *x* with respect to *y* with regards to the *performance* of *A*.

Hohfeld's object of analysis are judicial opinions and legal theory materials, but it is not clear if the discourses formulated in those documents are considered to be in the level of norms or in the level of normative propositions. For that same reason, Hohfeld's analysis has been understood as referred to

42 For example, (MacCormick 2007, 114).

43 Cfr. (Hohfeld 1913; 1917).

44 (Hohfeld 1913, 38–39, 55–60); (Williams 1956, 1144–1145); (Ross 1968, 154); (Rainbolt 1993, 95; 2010, 2 and 4); (Kramer 2000, 8, 24, 26, 30–31, 35, 40); (Cruz Parcero 2007, 33–34, note N°19).

45 (Hohfeld 1913, 39). See also (Williams 1956, 1135–1142) and (Ross 1968, 119).

norms,[46] to normative propositions,[47] or both.[48] But more important that this is the consideration that Hohfeldian notions can be used both to formulate norms as well as to describe them.[49]

In what matters here, if those notions are used in normative propositions, following Alchourrón and Bulygin, it is possible to differentiate two concepts of liberty or privilege, one positive and one negative, which can be derived from the two senses in which we can interpret the negation of the proposition '*x* has a duty with respect to *y* with regards to certain action or abstention.' Correlatively, we may distinguish two concepts of no-right, one positive and one negative, which can be derived from the two senses in which we can interpret the negation of the proposition '*y* has a right with respect to *x* with regard to certain action or abstention'.[50]

It may be thought that the same can be said of the concepts of disability and immunity that are, respectively, opposite to the concepts of power and liability, assuming, of course, that norms of competence ascribe relations of power-liability and of disability-immunity. Thus, Guastini argues that a subject's disability can stem from the mere absence of a norm conferring power (negative disability) or from the existence of a norm depriving them of a power previously bestowed (positive disability). Likewise, immunity can stem from the absence of a norm imposing a liability (negative immunity) or from the existence of a norm exempting from a previous liability (positive immunity).[51]

However, it must be noted that Guastini collapses the positive and negative concepts of disability and immunity due to the way in which he characterizes positive disability and immunity. A norm depriving a subject of a previously conferred power is a norm that derogates the norm that had conferred that power. As a result, the subject becomes disabled in the negative sense, as there is no norm conferring power upon him. Analogously, a norm that exempts a subject from a previous liability is a norm that derogates the norm instituting

46 For example, (Ross 1958, 208); (Biasetti, 2015).
47 For example, (Carrió 1991, 8–9); (Kurki 2017, 138).
48 For example, (Wellman 1978, 2013).
49 See, for example, (MacCormick 1977, 150); (Guastini 2014, 83–84); (Rodríguez 2021, 292). To these possibilities it may be added Hart's proposal according to which the expressions 'subjective right', 'liberty', 'power', and 'immunity' that are used in statements with the form 'A has a right', have the function of extracting a legal conclusion from a relevant rule and the relevant facts. According to Hart, the person formulating these statements does not enunciate the aforementioned rule nor enunciate or describe the aforementioned facts (Hart 1953, 28 and 35). This proposal may be seen as a preview of what he later called 'internal statements' (Hart 1961, chapter V).
50 Strictly speaking, all deontic concepts become ambiguous when they appear in normative propositions and, therefore, also those of duty and right in Hohfeld's reconstruction. Cfr. (Rodríguez 2002, 190–191).
51 Cfr. (Guastini 2014, 86–87).

the liability. As a consequence, the subject becomes immune in the negative sense, because there is no norm establishing the liability.[52]

But there is a different way in which the distinction between the negative and positive meanings of '*x* is disabled with respect to *y* with regards to normative action *NA*' may be drawn, avoiding this objection to Guastini's distinction: (i) in the system of reference there is no norm attributing *x* the power with respect to *y* in relation to normative action *NA* (negative sense), and (ii) in the system of reference there exists a norm establishing the disability of *x* with respect to *y* with relation to normative action *NA* (positive sense). Accordingly, it may be said that the proposition '*y* is immune with respect to *x* in relation to the normative action *AN*' can be interpreted in a negative sense or in a positive sense: (i) in the system of reference there is no norm establishing the liability of *y* with respect to *x* in relation to normative action *NA* (negative sense), and (ii) in the system of reference there exists a norm establishing the immunity of *y* with respect to *x* in relation to normative action *NA* (positive sense).[53]

Thus characterized, the positive concepts do not collapse with the negative ones. A norm establishing a disability and the correlative liability is not necessarily a norm derogating another norm that has established a previous power–liability relation. Very often it is a norm limiting the scope of another norm that, synchronically, establishes a power–liability relation. Let us examine this in more detail.

The sovereign or constitutive authority usually circumscribes the object of the competences of authorities by using *intensional* (connotative) definitions, whose insufficiency makes necessary to complement with *extensional* (denotative) definitions in mere lists of *matters* or *themes* which, in addition, are closed up through residual clauses establishing that everything (generically) not included in them falls within the sphere of competence of another constituted authority.[54] Such lists may not be exhaustive but merely indicative, and as a result constituted authorities are competent to issue norms on any matter without limits.[55] It is even possible that the constitutive authority does not

52 Cfr. (Rodríguez 2021, 297).

53 Similarly, see (Arriagada 2021a, 72).

54 Thus, for example, in the Chilean Constitution, intentional definitions of the legislative functions of co-legislatives bodies (articles 32 N°1 and 46) are complemented by a list of legal subject matters (article 63). In turn, article 32 N°6 confers to the President of the Republic the power to dictate regulations in all the matters not belonging to the legal domain.

55 Thus, for example, as to the catalog of subject matters that can be regulated by legislative authorities under the Chilean Constitution (Ribera 2001, 477–478 and 480–481). In the same vein, it is argued that it is not possible to establish *a priori* all the subject matters that are to be regulated by the legislator, which is why it is they, and not the constitutive authority, who determine which aspects of social life are legally relevant; (Cordero 2009, 433). Highlighting again the unlimited normative capacity of the Chilean legislator, it is argued that there is a 'material gap' of legal regulation that is translated in a problem of determination of the realities able to be regulated; (Kazor 2013, 63 and 71). To this it is added that

define the competences of constituted authorities in terms of their object, but through exclusively formal criteria.[56]

Thus, the limits of constituted competences usually are established through norms limiting the content of the norms those authorities are competent to issue by establishing disabilities and immunities.[57] The positive concepts of disability and immunity are then used for indicating that the powers and liabilities established by norms are ascribed and limited both through norms establishing power–liability relations as well as norms establishing disability–immunity relations.

According to this, it makes no sense for the rule of closure of a system of norms of competence to be formulated in terms of permissions and prohibitions. It would have to be formulated in terms of powers and disabilities or in terms of liabilities and immunities:[58]

(i) Constituted normative authorities are disabled to execute normative actions that have not been explicitly subjected to their competence by a superior authority;
(ii) Every individual not explicitly subjected to the normative actions of a normative authority constituted by a superior normative authority has an immunity vis-à-vis the constituted normative.

6.3.3 Second objection: systems of competences are necessarily closed up

The proposal of distinguishing two concepts of disability and immunity in analogy with the two concepts of permission, when those expressions appear in normative propositions, seems very interesting and shows a lot of potential to explore. There is, nonetheless, a problematic point that seems to hinder the delineation of a perfect analogy with the notions of positive and negative permission.

In the analysis of Hohfeldian concepts there is, as we have seen, a very important difference between the group including right, duty, liberty, and no-right, on the one hand, and the group comprising power, disability, immunity, and liability, on the other. Assuming that Hohfeldian notions are used in

---

the attributive sphere of the legislative function is a power of attribution not constitutionally closed up; (Kazor 2016). On the non-exhaustive nature of the aforementioned catalogue, see also (García Pino and Contreras 2014, 640–641). This is remarkable if we consider that the lack of exhaustiveness seems more characteristic of the dogmatic parts of constitutions usually characterized for being the product of wide political consensus; for example, (Atria 2016, 274–281 and 285; 2005, 27).

56 (Carré de Malberg 1922, 257; 1931, 35–37). For example, the legal reserve contained in the sixth transitional clause of the Chilean Constitution is not material, but formal; (Kazor 2016, 23).

57 (Arriagada 2021a, 105).

58 Similarly, (Arriagada 2021a, 59 and 81–82).

normative propositions, the first group of concepts derives from the existence within a normative system of *regulative rules*, whereas the second group of concepts derives from the existence of *constitutive rules*.

If the reconstruction of norms of competence as regulative rules of a permissive nature[59] *were* correct, it would be perfectly natural to discriminate between a positive and a negative sense of immunity and disability, in analogy with the notions of positive and negative permission. In fact, the very notion of power to perform a normative action (*NA*) would admit a positive and a negative sense:

> Negative power: In *S* there is not a norm prohibiting *x* to perform *NA*.
> Positive power: There is in *S* a norm permitting *x* to perform *NA*.
> Negative disability: In *S* there is not a norm permitting *x* to perform *NA*.
> Positive disability: There is in *S* a norm prohibiting *x* to perform *NA*.

But if the arguments in favour of reconstructing norms of competence as constitutive rules are correct, the analogy of the distinction between the concepts of positive and negative disability/immunity and the concepts of positive and negative permission must be reconsidered.

Let us examine this first with the example of the game of chess. The current regulations of the International Chess Federation establishes that the bishop can move to any square of the diagonals in which it is placed and that, while so moving, it may not jump over any other piece.[60] It may be conceivable to reconstruct these rules as follows:

> RB1: If the bishop moves onto any of the squares of the diagonals in which it is placed, that counts as a valid move.
> RB2: If the bishop jumps over a piece in its trajectory, that amounts to an invalid move.

According to these rules, it could be said that the bishop is 'disabled' in the positive sense to jump over pieces in its trajectory, as RB2 so establishes explicitly, whereas it is 'disabled' in a purely negative sense, for example, to castle, as there is no rule establishing it may do so. However, this interpretation is seriously debatable, basically because according to it, RB1 does not exclude the possibility that the bishop executes other valid moves (moving horizontally and vertically, castling, taking out pieces in a different direction than that of its movement, etc). Thus, such a formulation does not allow to determine

59 Besides (von Wright 1963a, 189 et seq.), see, for example, (Lindahl 1977, 194 et seq.).

60 Articles 3.3 and 3.5 of the regulations approved in the *88 Congress of FIDE, Göynük (Turkey)*, in force since 1 January 2018.

adequately the way bishops move in chess. A more satisfactory reconstruction would be to say something along these lines:

> RB: The bishop moves validly if and only if it moves to any square of the diagonals in which it is placed without jumping over any other piece in its trajectory.[61]

Constitutive rules about the movements of bishops in chess specify the *set of necessary and sufficient conditions to establish what counts as a valid move* by that piece. The aptitude or 'power' of a bishop to move on the board is determined by the constitutive rules defining its movements. Any movement not authorized by such rules simply does not count as a valid move, since 'moving a bishop' in chess is not a natural action subject to regulative rules, but an institutional action, this is, a certain interpretation of an action within a certain context and according to certain constitutive rules defining it.[62] Of course, rules may exist that explicitly refer to what a piece 'cannot' do in a game. Such rules determine their 'disability' to move in a certain way, such as the one establishing that bishops 'cannot' jump over pieces in their trajectory and, in that sense, are 'disabled' to do so by virtue of an explicit rule. But this rule only specifies a negative condition within the set of necessary and sufficient conditions to determine what is a valid move by a bishop. In other words, *every and only those* moves determined by the game's constitutive rules count as valid moves by a bishop.[63]

Let us now consider norms of competence. Suppose there is a norm in a legal system *S* establishing that 'The President may issue decrees on the basis of necessity and urgency when exceptional circumstances make impossible to follow the ordinary procedures set forth by the Constitution for the sanction of laws', and another one establishing that 'The decrees of necessity and urgency may not regulate criminal, tax, or electoral matters'.[64] These rules may be reconstructed as follows:

61 This would not truly be a complete formulation of the bishop's moves, as they say nothing of how the bishop 'takes out' pieces, for when it does it can come to occupy the square formerly occupied by an enemy piece. We omit this for the sake of simplicity.

62 Cfr. (Searle 1969, 33-36; 1995, 43–45).

63 The above does not mean that the rules of a game cannot be formulated in a deficient way. For example, it may happen that in the formulation of the rules of chess it is not clear whether bishops may or may not jump over pieces in their trajectory. Now, such a deficiency would not give rise to a gap but to an ambiguity: by not making it clear whether or not bishops can jump over pieces in the trajectory there would be two alternative ways in which to play chess, either admitting or not that bishops jump over pieces.

64 These rules partially correspond to the text of article 99.3 of the Argentinean National Constitution.

DR1: If exceptional circumstances make impossible to follow the ordinary procedures set forth in the Constitution for the sanction of laws, the President may validly issue a decree of necessity and urgency.
DR2: If it regulates criminal, tax, or electoral matters, the decree of necessity and urgency is invalid.

According to these rules, it may be said that the President is incompetent in a positive sense to issue decrees of necessity and urgency regulating criminal, tax, or electoral matters, as DR2 so establishes explicitly, whereas she is disabled in a purely negative sense to, for example, issue decrees of necessity and urgency in exceptional circumstances that, however, do not impede the normal functioning of the legislature,[65] as even though there is no norm authorizing such a decree of necessity and urgency, there is also no norm stating that this would constitute an invalid decree of necessity and urgency. However, this interpretation is seriously debatable, basically because according to it, DR1 does not exclude the possibility that other things count as decrees of necessity and urgency beyond the verification of the conditions stipulated therein. Therefore, such a formulation does not allow to determine in an adequate manner how to produce a valid decree of necessity and urgency. A more satisfactory reconstruction would amount to saying something like:

DR: A decree of necessity and urgency is valid if and only if it is issued by the President when exceptional circumstances make it impossible to follow the ordinary procedures set forth in the Constitution for the sanction of laws, and they do not address criminal, tax, or electoral matters.

The constitutive rules determining how to issue a decree of necessity and urgency must specify the *set of necessary and sufficient conditions for establishing what counts as a valid decree of necessity and urgency*. Generalizing this, to say that an agent *x* has, according to the norms of the legal system *S*, a legal power with respect to an agent *y* to perform certain normative action *NA*, i.e., an action whose result is the modification of certain consequences derived from *S* (in the example, a decree of necessity and urgency), is equivalent to saying that a constitutive rule that is a consequence of *S* establishes that the performance by *x* of certain action *A* is one of the conditions for the production of a valid instance of *NA*, to which at least another norm derived from *S* attaches certain normative consequence with respect to *y*. Thus, the power to issue decrees of necessity and urgency is determined by the constitutive rules of a legal system that determine what counts as a valid decree of necessity and urgency. Any conduct not authorized by such rules simply does not count as a valid decree of necessity and urgency, since to issue a decree of necessity and urgency is

65 As it actually occurred in Argentina with the decrees of necessity and urgency during the Covid-19 pandemic.

not a natural act but an institutional act. Of course, there may be rules that explicitly determine the disability to perform certain normative action, such as the rule establishing the disability to issue decrees of necessity and urgency on certain matters. But this rule merely specifies a negative condition within the set of conditions that are necessary and sufficient to determine what is a valid decree of necessity and urgency. In other words, *all and only* those acts determined by the constitutive rules of a legal system count as valid decrees of necessity and urgency.

It seems incontrovertible that a subject *x* is disabled vis-à-vis another subject *y* with respect to certain normative action (and *y* would have, correlatively, an immunity vis-à-vis *x*) if there is no norm issued by a normative authority of a superior hierarchy bestowing power on *x* to perform such a normative action. And it may of course happen that there are in a legal system explicit norms instituting the disability of certain authorities to perform certain normative actions or instituting the immunity of certain individuals vis-à-vis the normative actions of an authority. Yet, such norms only establish negative conditions within the set of necessary and sufficient conditions to determine what counts as a validly issued normative action by a certain authority.

What are the consequences of this fact for the distinction of the two considered senses of disability/immunity? A first possibility would be to assert, as mentioned before, that an agent *x* has a power with respect to an agent *y* to perform certain normative action *NA* if and only if a constitutive rule that is a consequence of *S* establishes that the performance by *x* of certain action *A* is one of the conditions for the production of a valid instance of *NA*, to which at least another norm derived from *S* attaches a certain normative consequence with respect to *y*. This being the case, there would be a unique sense in which *x* can be disabled to perform the normative action *NA*: when according to the constitutive rules derived from *S* the actions of *x* do not count as a condition for the valid production of an instance of *NA*. This could be the result of the presence of an explicit rule so establishing it or from the absence of a rule so establishing it.

Therefore, instead of distinguishing two senses of disability/immunity, we should here differentiate two different ways, one express and another tacit or, in other words, one explicit and another implicit, in which a subject can be disabled or have an immunity. Accordingly, an authority would be disabled in the same sense, both when she performs a normative action with respect to which there is an explicit norm declaring that disability, and when she performs any other normative action beyond the limits of her power as defined by the constitutive norms conferring it. But then, if norms of competence are adequately reconstructed as constitutive rules, the principle '*Authorities are disabled to perform normative actions that have not been subject to their power*' would become analytically true, because there would not be two senses of disability and because, since those constitutive rules would determine the necessary and sufficient conditions for a normative or institutional action to count as valid, any action that does not meet those conditions (because a norm so explicitly excludes or because no norm so establishes) would be invalid.

A second possibility would be to keep the distinction as delineated, i.e., to claim that there are two notions of disability/immunity, a positive one according to which a subject *x* would be disabled in a positive sense with respect to *y* with relation to certain normative action *NA* if in the system there is a hierarchically superior norm establishing that disability of *x* with respect to *y*, while she would be disabled in a negative sense with respect to *y* if there is not within the system a hierarchically superior norm ascribing her power with respect to *y* and with regards to the normative action *NA*.

In this case, it could be argued that the principle '*Authorities are disabled to perform normative actions that have not been subject to their power*', interpreted as a normative proposition, admits two readings: it would be analytically true if 'disability' is interpreted here in a negative sense, and it would be contingent if 'disability' is interpreted in a positive sense, depending on the existence or not of a rule of closure determining explicitly the disability to perform every normative action for which there is no norm conferring a power. However, what would be the point to issue such a rule of closure? Formally it could not be ruled out that a person is disabled in a negative sense according to the norms of *S* to perform *NA* because there is no norm in *S* that affords her the power to perform that action and, nevertheless, would not be disabled in a positive sense to do so because there is also not in *S* a norm declaring the subject disabled to perform *NA*. But would I be sound to say in this case that the system is in any way incomplete? And what would be this incompleteness about?

In the case of regulative rules, it may happen that a certain normative system does not qualify normatively either as prohibited or as permitted a certain conduct *A*, which is conceptually possible to perform or not regardless of what is the normative qualification it merits, and in that case we would say that the system is incomplete with regards to *A*. Of course, it may happen that the normative authority of system *S* has no interest whatsoever in regulating *A*, but even in this case it may be said that a conduct that is conceptually possible to perform is indeterminate according to *S* with respect to its normative qualification. Now, in the case of disability, although it may happen that in a given normative system there is no norm bestowing power upon someone to perform *NA*, as well as no norm declaring her disabled to perform *NA*, *NA* is a conduct that is not conceptually possible to perform simply if the first condition is met, that is, if there is no norm conferring power upon someone to perform it. In other words, it is not possible to say that an action *NA*, which is conceptually possible to perform, is indeterminate in the system with regards to the power or disability to perform it, or that that system is incomplete in any sense with respect to the power to perform *NA*: in the face of absence of norms conferring power to someone to perform *NA*, that action is conceptually impossible to perform because such rules create the very possibility of performing *NA*.

In conclusion, if the rules establishing disabilities or immunities are interpreted as constitutive, there is here a significant difference between the notions of positive and negative permission and of positive and negative disability/immunity, whether because in that case the distinction between the notions of positive and negative disability/immunity should be reshaped into one between an express and a tacit modality (or explicit and implicit) of a sole notion of disability/immunity, or whether because, even if the original distinction is kept, there would be no need for a rule of closure establishing the disability to perform certain normative actions with respect to which there is no rule affording such power. Therefore, from the perspective of the norms establishing the powers of public authorities, the closed nature of our legal systems would not be a consequence of a certain concrete configuration of their positive norms, but a conceptual consequence of conceiving norms of competence as constitutive.[66]

6.4 An explanatory hypothesis of the principle 'Everything that is not permitted is prohibited' as a rule of closure of competence systems

We have seen that both public law jurists and some legal theorists agree that for constituted public authorities the principle applies that only the normative actions that have been explicitly permitted may be performed, any other action being prohibited. As we can conclude from von Wright, this principle is an authentic rule that closes up the systems of second order rules.

In the previous section we have presented the two objections to which this thesis is exposed and evidenced that both are grounded on a common base: that norms of competence are a species of so-called constitutive rules. With the purpose of exploring an explanatory hypothesis of why such a thesis is usually assumed, a different reading of the problem of the closure of the systems determining the competences of public authorities shall be tested.

For that we propose to begin by revisiting an outstanding point, that is, that the consideration of norms of competence as permissive regulative rules is especially noteworthy in von Wright, since this author clearly differentiates prescriptive or regulative rules from determinative rules that, as we have seen, are generally called constitutive rules. Taking into account the explanatory potential that the distinction of these two types of norms has had, as well as the arguments in favour of the consideration of norms of competence

66 'The second possible answer to the irrelevancy of the distinction between strong and weak disabilities/immunities is that systems of competences are necessarily closed. This reason of conceptual nature is the same justifiying that powers/liabilities and disabilities/immunities cannot be primary and are necessarily relational. The object of these relations is constituted by normative acts whose performance according to norms of competence constituting them makes it possible that certain individuals validly alter the normative status of other individuals also determined. Therefore, no individual may validly alter the status of another but in accordance with the norms defining its execution and the consequences following from it' (Arriagada 2020, 26).

as constitutive rules, it is time to probe the reasons that might justify von Wright's position.

6.4.1 Two points of view on constitutive rules

When von Wright characterizes the rules *determining* the patterns to (correctly) execute certain activities, he points out, as later the analytical legal theory has, that the rules of a game are the prototype and standard example of this class. In this context, he introduces an important distinction: (i) from the point of view of the game itself, the rules of the game determine which are the correct moves; and (ii) from the point of view of the activity of playing, the rules of a game determine which moves are 'permitted', 'prohibited', and 'mandatory' for the players of the game. From this last point of view, that is, when the game is being played and under the view of its players, the correct moves are understood as 'permitted' and the incorrect moves as 'prohibited'. Additionally, if one move is the only correct one in a specific situation within the game, it are understood as 'mandatory'.[67]

It is hard to overstate the importance of these observations. To begin with, the distinction of two different points of view from which constitutive rules may be understood could be viewed as an answer to the thesis affirming that rules that determine or make possible an activity cannot also regulate it.[68] This opens the door to the reexamination of Searle's proposal. Specifically, the thesis holding that while regulative rules regulate conducts whose existence is independent of said rules, constitutive rules regulate conducts whose existence is not independent of said rules, that is, they regulate new forms of conduct that the same rules constitute.

Thus, for example, as González Lagier argues, for von Wright definitional (constitutive) rules have a double dimension: (i) a properly constitutive or ontological dimension, in the sense that without said rules the game or activity in question would not exist, thus logically depending on the rules; and (ii) a regulative dimension, in the sense that the player is limited by the rules defining the game, if they want to play it; these rules indicate which are the permitted and prohibited moves.[69] According to González Lagier, this definition is similar to Searle's according to which constitutive rules constitute but also regulate an activity whose existence is logically dependent on the rules.[70]

More precisely, the apparent Searlean suggestion that constitutive rules are, at the same time, regulative could be interpreted from a perspective like von Wright's who—instead of suggesting that the same rule constitutes and

67 (von Wright 1963a, 6).
68 (Bertea 2013, 7).
69 (González Lagier 1995, 247).
70 (González Lagier 1995, 248).

regulates at the same time—proposes that the same rule can be viewed from two different points of view.

Schauer appears to point in this direction when he sustains that, although sets of constitutive rules establish institutions, they lose their constitutive character within these institutions, serving instead to regulate antecedently defined behavior.[71] Refining this idea, Schauer proposes a new way of understanding what the law does by constituting the possibilities that otherwise would not exist. In his view, once legally constituted forms of conduct supplant the forms of conduct that are independent of the law, that is, once we are 'within the game', rules lose some of their constitutive character and *seem* regulative and coercive. 'The coercive aspect of constitutive rules thus becomes a phenomenological matter, and the power of those who make, change, and enforce the constitutive rules may well appear coercive to those who are inside the institutions that the constitutive rules constitute.[72]

In the same vein, Bertea argues that von Wright allegedly remarked precisely that constitutive rules play both roles at once (constitutive and regulative), but in the following specific sense: (i) from the point of view of the practice as such, as a framework within which to engage in an activity, constitutive rules establish the conditions that make the practice possible and meaningful and that would be their primary role; and (ii) from the point of view of the users (who move within, make use of, and rely on that framework practice), constitutive rules state what is permitted, prohibited, or what is mandatory as a condition for staying within the framework practice, which means that, unless one plays according to the rules shaping the practice as it is constituted, one would not engage in the practice at all.[73]

In this second sense, by performing their conceptual role, constitutive rules fulfill, also and secondarily, a deontic function since, by working ultimately as directives, they partake of the properly normative dimension.[74] This does not mean—Bertea remarks—that the two concurrent roles of constitutive rules are simultaneously engaged, for the normativity they can exert comes into play only when an agent is acting and the rule in question is applied. In this point Bertea[75] connects his analysis with the theoretical framework presented by Roversi, to whom the context, that is, the practice within which

71 (Schauer 1991, 6–7).
72 (Schauer 2015, 28–31).
73 (Bertea 2013, 7).
74 Thus, for example, by determining what counts as valid reasoning (setting out conditions for the possibility of a reasoned argument), the rules of logic also state which inferences may or may not be made. Likewise, in defining the game of chess (making it possible to play chess), the constitutive rules of chess state as well what moves the players may or may not make, and ultimately, when they ought to concede victory. (Bertea 2013, 7–8).
75 (Bertea 2013, 8–9).

constitutive rules are framed, helps to clarify how they constitute and regulate simultaneously.[76]

Roversi's proposal begins distinguishing two kinds of questions in relation to the game of chess: (i) How is it that castling is a possibility in chess? and (ii) How is it that players must attempt to win in chess? The answer to the first question lies in the constitutive rules on castling and that are part of the rules of chess. Instead, the answer to the second question resides not in the rules of chess but in a feature of this game, namely that it is the practice of competitive game-playing. This difference lays bare the distinction of two separate, although overlapping 'layers' of the game. On the one hand, there are moves, pieces, and events constituted by rules determining conditions, consequences, and modes of behavior specific to the game. On the other, there are the general features of the game as a practice and that form the context within which constitutive rules are framed. From this it does not follow that we are in the presence of two different things because those who follow the rules of the game are involved/committed in the practice of playing competitively, and there would not be a way to become involved in the practice but by following the rules of the game.[77]

Thus, the game of chess may be seen: (i) *from a close-up view,* as a system of distinct constitutive rules defining a group of elements connecting as parts of a formal system, without reference to the context in which these rules are framed, and (ii) *from a panoramic view,* as the practice of competitive game-playing, without considering the specific elements constituted by constitutive rules. While the close-up view tends to put all the elements defined by those rules on the same level, only from a panoramic view it would be possible to appreciate how the connections established in such rules can create meaning. Only in the context of an already meaningful practice could the function for which an element of the system is used confer meaning to that element[78].

Faced with the question 'Why must the players try to win in chess?' Roversi argues that a player who clearly and deliberately moves their pieces with the intention of losing is not really a player. Players in competitive games could be considered as such only if they participate—or at least appear to participate—in them to win. The panoramic view allows, therefore, to highlight two distinct elements of the practice: on the one hand, *the goal of winning* by which every person must abide who enters the practice, and on the other, the *necessary mediation of rules* in the attempt to achieve this goal. These two elements are internal to the practice. The first may be described as *teleological* as

76 (Roversi 2010, 224).

77 Another example of the second kind of question is 'How is it that player mustn't cheat in chess or must follow the rules of chess?' (Roversi 2010, 229–230). We shall return to it at the end.

78 (Roversi 2010, 231–233).

it establishes an objective, and the second as *technical* since it establishes the procedural conditions that must be satisfied in the effort to reach this goal.[79]

If the close-up view is combined with the panoramic view, it would be possible then to appreciate that the different constitutive rules comprising the system are not on the same level as they are not all functionally equivalent: (i) on the *bottom* level we find those that, by defining the pieces themselves—their conditions and modes of behavior—represent the game's rules of opening; (ii) on the *intermediate* level we find the rule that, by establishing the consequence common to the different pieces in connection to the concept of capture, establishes the game's basic mechanics. The mechanics of a capture links the rules of opening to the superior level of the game, where the concepts of attack and checkmate are defined. In fact, the concept of capture is essential to establish what it means to attack a piece and, therefore, what it means to attack the king. And, through the constitutive rule establishing the conditions for checkmate, the attack plays an essential role by establishing what counts as checkmate; and (iii) on the *topmost* level we find the constitutive rules establishing the conditions and consequences of checkmate. These rules establish the conditions under which a player wins a game, that is, the specific content that chess assigns to the teleological element of the practice and that explains their place as 'rules of closure'. In particular, the constitutive rule determining the consequences of checkmate, establishing the conditions of victory in chess, acts as a 'bridge rule' connecting the technical element with the teleological element of chess as the practice of a competitive game. This rule establishes, within the technical element, the conditions of victory demanded by the teleological element of the same practice. In addition, it connects the system of constitutive rules and its context, and through this connection, ultimately, it would assign meaning to every element of the system.[80]

Roversi concludes that, for the elements of an institution to have meaning, at least one of those elements must already have a meaning not dependent on the constitutive rules of the system. Victory would be one of these elements as it is not a concept exclusive to chess, as checkmate or castling, but a concept that qualifies this game as a form of competition. In this competitive context and, therefore, from the perspective of the teleological element, constitutive rules acquire the functional differentiation that we saw under the combined view and would create meaningful elements by establishing a more or less direct connection between these elements and victory.[81]

This argument could, in Roversi's view, be enunciated tentatively as a general thesis: the meaning of an institutional element depends on whether its importance is ultimately (more or less directly) relevant to the goal (the teleological element) of the practice within which the institution is framed

79 (Roversi 2010, 232).
80 (Roversi 2010, 233–234).
81 (Roversi 2010, 234–235).

and the process of construction of meaning with constitutive rules cannot achieve its objective unless it is framed within an already meaningful and specific context.[82]

Now, the combined view not only allows us to better appreciate how constitutive rules can create meaning, that is, how they can be properly constitutive. Context also helps to clarify how constitutive rules can regulate an activity. That would not be a syntactic or semantic matter since it would not refer to the structure of constitutive rules or their meaning. It is rather a matter of the pragmatic role of such rules.[83]

The combined view shows, according to Roversi, that all the rules of the game, as parts of the technical element of a practice of a competitive game, are regulative, even if they do not appear so because they resemble definitions. They are regulative because they establish what must be done in order to play the game of chess and, thus, to achieve the goal of that practice, even if they do so by defining elements whose role is essential to make playing the game possible in the first place. The close-up view—which considers constitutive rules in isolation—would then become what impedes to see their pragmatic nature and, therefore, their regulative character that may only be observed taking into account the context to which these rules belong.[84] In other words, constitutive rules, in light of certain purposes, admit a regulative character, defining how individuals must behave in order to obtain normative results.[85]

In Bertea's words, and considering especially von Wright's distinction, the moves that integrate the technical component are translated into a deontic set, specifying everything that can and cannot be done, as well as which actions are required and under which conditions. Such practical possibilities and restrictions work as directives. In sum, the how (technical component) would not make sense without the why (teleological component). As the why (teleological component) gives us a reason to partake in the practice, along with a corresponding goal, we would not have a way to achieve that goal unless we know how to do it (technical component), that is, unless we have rules framing the practice.[86]

These considerations not only allow us to reinterpret Searle's thesis in the proposed sense. They also allow us to shed light on what analytical legal theory obscures when it focuses on a certain perspective of legal institutions. In this sense, it is no accident that the interpretation of the distinctions proposed by von Wright and Searle in terms of two mutually exclusive types of norms favours the conclusion that constitutive legal norms (among which there are some as important as norms of competence) do not guide conduct directly,

82 (Roversi 2010, 235).
83 (Roversi 2010, 236).
84 (Roversi 2010, 236–238).
85 (Roversi 2018, 270–271).
86 (Bertea, 2013, 10–11).

but contribute to guide it in an indirect manner, that is, from their connection to regulative rules.[87] This could be true from a technical perspective, but it would not be so from a teleological perspective.

The conclusion that constitutive legal rules—which, according to Alchourrón and Bulygin, correlate cases with cases—do not guide conduct directly presupposes the stipulation according to which norms qualifying certain classes of factual or normative actions or omissions as mandatory, prohibited, or permitted—which, according to Alchourrón and Bulygin correlate cases with solutions—guide conduct directly.[88] Clearly stated, as determinative rules do not regulate behavior, they are deprived of the normative force of prescriptions.[89]

In order to avoid this conclusion, it may be stipulated, as we have suggested, that a 'normative solution' is not only the qualification of a class of actions or omissions (factual or normative) as *legally mandatory or permitted*, as Alchourrón and Bulygin argue, but also the qualification of a class of normative actions as *legally possible/valid or impossible/invalid*.[90] More precisely, as these categories are not strictly analogous, and focusing on the legal norms of competence, we have suggested that, within the notion of normative solution, based on Hohfeld, we must distinguish between normative actions with respect to which a certain subject is competent, and normative actions with respect to which a certain subject is incompetent or disabled. However, we still need to explain the way in which constitutive norms, and especially norms of competence, guide normative actions, that is, their normative force.

The relevant question seems to be whether, from the perspective of the participants of the legal practice, norms of competence regulate actions in the same sense that regulative norms regulate them. The answer to this question would have to be affirmative from the perspective of the normative solution, as the thesis under consideration asserts that, from the point of view of participants of the legal practice, norms of competence obligate, prohibit, or permit. In von Wright's terms, the character of these norms (seen from the point of view of their subjects) would be the same as that of prescriptions.

87 For example, (Moreso and Vilajosana 2004, 72–74); (Ruiz Manero 2007, 64–65); (Rodríguez 2021, 55); (Orunesu and Rodríguez 2022, 197).

88 Cfr. (Arriagada 2021a, 65, note N°28; 2022a, 269–270; 2022b, 129–133).

89 (Rodríguez 2021, 55).

90 This is not the time to develop a full explanation of how the nuance introduced in the notion of normative solution is applied to all kinds of norms legally constituted. Suffice it to say that they determine the necessary and sufficient conditions to perform, validly, normative actions such as (i) using certain expressions of the legislator (legal definitions), (ii) interpreting normative provisions (interpretive norms); (iii) considering as constituted certain facts or institutional results or including certain facts under certain kinds of institutional facts (purely constitutive norms); (iv) producing, modifying or derogating legal norms (norms of competence). Cfr. (Arriagada 2021a, 65, note N°28; 2022a, 269–270; 2022b, 129–133).

A different matter is that regulative norms and constitutive norms (the latter as they are seen by their subjects) are different, not from the perspective of their normative solution, but from the perspective of the generic case that is correlated with the normative solution. In von Wright's terms, from the perspective of the condition of application.[91] Our argument is that the generic case or condition of application of (constitutive) norms of competence as they are seen by their subjects (as regulative norms) includes the circumstance that the subject of the norm wants to obtain the objective of performing a valid normative action and, therefore, the corresponding normative result. What we are suggesting is that, taking into account the point of view of the subjects at whom norms of competence are addressed and applied, we could reconstruct those norms as 'autonomous prescriptions', which are practical necessities.

In order to explain this it is necessary to consider, first, that, according to von Wright, it can be said, although only in a secondary or analogical sense, that an agent gives prescriptions (commands, permissions, prohibitions) to himself and, therefore, that there are autonomous prescriptions (self-commands, self-permissions, and self-prohibitions) if the norm-authority issuing them is the same as the norm-subject.[92] Second, it must be noted that, in this exact sense, an autonomous norm is but the conclusion of a first-person practical syllogism.[93] Third, it must be considered that, in this kind of sillogism, the first premise is a person's want of a certain end or aim, the second premise is the belief/knowledge/understanding that a certain condition is necessary to the fulfilment of that want, and the conclusion is the decision to act or the fact of acting.[94]

According to von Wright, while heteronomous prescriptions can be disobeyed, autonomous prescriptions come to be from—or consist of—the fact that the agent acts directed by their wants and beliefs. Thus, in a sense, autonomous norms are ipso facto obeyed, that is, the notions of obedience or disobedience are not applied to them.[95] Taking all of this into account, it could be said that individuals subject to the law are only *obligated* to the normative actions set forth in norms of competence if they want to achieve the aim of performing those actions validly and, therefore, the corresponding normative result.

Certainly, the last word has not been spoken on this matter, but for the purposes of this work it becomes of interest how the two points of view from

91 Cfr. (von Wright 1963a, 70).

92 The issuing norm-authority would be, conversely, different from the norm-subject of heteronomous prescriptions. To this it must be added that it can also be considered that an autonomous norm is that not given by any authority, but from this perspective, no prescription could be autonomous. (Von Wright 1963a, 11 and 76–77; 1963b, 159; 1963c, 10).

93 (Von Wright 1963b, 162, 171–173).

94 (Von Wright 1963b, 168–170; 1963c, 8–9). For a reading of the conclusion of this type of reasoning as a reasoned decision to act, see (Navarro 2024).

95 (Von Wright 1963b,173–174).

which constitutive rules may be seen could be useful to offer a plausible explanation of the consideration of norms of competence as permissive norms, a basis to attribute meaning to the idea that competences systems are closed because they contain a rule of closure, as well as a justification of the formulation of this as a regulative rule prohibiting every normative action not expressly permitted.

6.4.2 Two perspectives of norms of competence and a justification of the belief in the existence of a competence-related rule of closure

For Roversi, as we have seen, the question '"Why must players try to win at chess?' makes sense from the panoramic view that focusing on the objective of the game of chess allows us to identify it as the practice of a competitive game. Accordingly, a similar kind of question is, according to this author, 'Why must chess players not cheat in chess?' or in other words 'Why *must* players follow the rules of chess?'.[96]

Roversi argues that chess players do not think that a victory claimed by a declared cheater counts as a victory. The declared cheater could not be *strictly* considered a chess player, since players partaking in a competitive game must follow the rules to try to win or at least appear that they follow them.[97] The panoramic view thus allows us to appreciate, on the one hand, the objective of winning anyone participating in the competitive game must have (teleological element) and, on the other, the *necessary mediation by rules* in the attempt to achieve that goal, that is, the procedural conditions that must be satisfied in that effort (technical element). These two elements are, as we have seen, internal to the practice, but equally internal is the relation between them: the objective must be achieved by following the rules, as nobody can win if they do not respect them. Conversely, the point of this breach is to work towards the goal of winning.[98]

According to Roversi, this internal relation between the technical and teleological components of a game is expressed through the following rule: 'When playing in a competitive way, you must follow the rules in order to win'. It would amount to the *first rule* of the competitive game, the one followed by all honest players and breached by all cheaters.[99]

We may thus think that this rule is similar to the rule of closure that public law scholars and some legal theorists suppose exist in legal systems, if we

96 (Roversi 2010, 229).
97 (Roversi 2010, 232).
98 (Roversi 2010, 232 and 236).
99 (Roversi 2010, 236). Later, Roversi delves into the different perspectives from which an institution can be seen, distinguishing the structural, teleological, axiological, strategic, and sociological perspectives. In this context, he considers that while the objective of winning the game may be appreciated from the teleological perspective, the duty to play following the rules of the game may be appreciated from the axiological perspective. (Roversi 2018, 143–148).

substitute the objective of winning the game with the objective of executing valid normative actions in the law. The relevant question would then become 'Why *must* authorities performing normative actions do so by following norms of competence?' This question could be answered affirming that constituted normative authorities do not think that normative actions performed without following norms of competence count as valid normative actions. And by stating that from the moment we learn that a normative authority that does not follow the rules does not act as an authority, we know that normative authorities must follow the rules or at least pretend to follow them.

This first rule of legal practice of performing normative actions, as a second level rule, would have to be expressed then not in terms of powers and disabilities or in terms of liabilities and immunities, but by affirming that every normative action by an authority that has not been explicitly permitted by a superior authority is prohibited.

The matter, however, must be examined with more care, considering the two points of view from which norms of competence of the first level can be seen reconstructing them as constitutive rules. Thus, an admissible reading of the permissive character that von Wright attributes to norms of competence could be to understand that such an attribution depends on the adoption of the perspective to whom said norms are addressed and applied.

As we have seen, the analysis of what von Wright calls 'norms of higher order' focuses precisely on the subjects to whom norms of competence are addressed, delegating in them the power to act as authorities of norms. From the point of view of these authorities, norms of competence can be understood as permissive rules, in the sense that the delegation of the power to issue and cancel norms supposes that the delegated authority has the liberty to decide to do so or not, although within certain limits. Such limits can be, therefore, seen as prohibitions of issuing norms of certain kinds, and even as an order to issue norms on certain types of acts. In line with this, the validity of a norm is considered as relative to another norm permitting its issuing and it is considered that a norm is invalid when its issuing is prohibited to the authority issuing it by virtue of a norm of higher order.

None of von Wright's observations are, in principle, incompatible with the consideration of norms of competence as determinative or constitutive rules, if we admit that the latter can be seen from two different points of view: that of the legal practice of delegating power to issue and cancel norms and that of the system of rules determining the set of necessary and sufficient conditions to issue and cancel norms.

Note, therefore, that in this reading it continues to be true that norms of competence determine the necessary and sufficient conditions to perform valid normative actions. Therefore, from the point of view of these norms that, as constitutive rules, institute disabilities or immunities, the distinction between the concepts of positive and negative disability/immunity can be maintained, but at the cost of recognizing that there is no need for a rule of closure establishing disability/immunity with relation to any normative action in regard to which there is no norm instituting power/liability relations.

Now, if by assuming that norms of competence are constitutive rules we accept that, from the point of view of those accepting them, they regulate the normative actions they constitute, there would be grounds for attributing meaning to the idea that competence systems require a rule of closure prohibiting every normative action not expressly permitted. In this hypothesis, this second level rule, seen from the point of view of those individuals at whom they are addressed and to whom first level norms of competence apply, it would have to be of the same kind as that of first level norms.

In a different sense than Roversi's, Feis and Scofienza object to what is called the 'inviolability dogma', this is, that constitutive rules possess a merely definitional nature ('almost tautological', as Searle expresses[100]). This dogma would become clear in the fact that it would make no sense to talk about the violation of constitutive rules, since those not complying with such a rule simply fall outside of the activity defined by them. These authors offer the following example: the fact that someone moves a chess piece in an invalid way in order to cheat shows that constitutive rules can be violated, because in that case we would not say they are playing a different game, but they are playing chess, only violating its rules by executing a prohibited conduct.[101]

Thus formulated, the example of these authors fails to show what they pretend. Let us consider, first, and in general, the conduct of those who perform an invalid move: it may occur that in this case the subject has made an involuntary mistake, due to a lack of attention or to a lack of adequate knowledge of the rules of the game. In this case, the move obviously will not count as valid, but beyond that we would not reproach the subject's conduct, but we would point out to them that they have made a mistake: 'That is not a valid play' or 'It is not permitted to move that piece in this way'. But here 'cannot' or 'not permitted' do not have the meaning of a violation of a prohibition, but simply a way of referring to what can or cannot be done according to the rules defining the activity of playing chess. It can also happen, as in the example of Feis and Scofienza, that someone executes an invalid move with the intention of cheating, that is, not involuntarily, but deliberately with the intention of obtaining an undue gain. In this case, again, the play will not count as valid according to the rules of chess, but here we would reproach the cheater precisely because of this, not for executing an invalid move, and with that, for 'violating' the rules of chess, but for trying to obtain an undue gain from a breach of the rules establishing how to play chess. In other words, the rebuke

100 Cfr. (Searle 1969, 34).
101 Cfr. (Feis and Sconfienza 2012).

stems from the violation of *another* rule, of a moral and regulative nature, that prohibits cheating in a game.[102]

Nevertheless, the suggestion that it is possible to violate the rules of chess without playing a different game than chess is very relevant. The possibility that, however, Feis and Scofienza do not consider is that, from the point of view of those playing the game, it is possible to say that players who cheat violate the rules of chess, only seen not as constitutive rules, but as regulative rules.

If we examine von Wright's observations more carefully, it is not difficult to notice that the distinction between 'the point of view of the game of chess' and 'the point of view of the activity of playing the game of chess' parallelly corresponds with the distinction between 'not playing the game of chess' and 'playing the game of chess incorrectly'.[103] According to von Wright, of a person who does not play according to the rules of chess, we would say that: (i) he does not play chess if, for example, he does not care about following the rules or if he consciously and consistently plays according to different rules: and (ii) he plays chess incorrectly if, for example, he wants to follow the rules, but does not know or understand what they demand of him, or if he is trying to cheat his opponent.[104]

These observations allow us to suggest that, from the point of view of the activity of playing chess (or of the players), violating the rules of the game by cheating does not entail playing a different game, but playing chess incorrectly because, from that point of view, the rules of chess are seen as regulative rules.

To cheat is, as Feis and Scofienza suggest, to perform a prohibited conduct, but only to the extent that the players see the rules of the game as regulative rules. Analogously, from the point of view of those partaking in the legal practice of performing normative actions, it is prohibited to perform actions that violate norms of competence, the latter being seen as regulative rules. In other words, from this point of view, it is mandatory to do what the rules of competence say.

As we have seen, from the point of view of those partaking in the legal practice of performing normative actions, norms of competence are but autonomous prescriptions and, therefore, conclusions of first person practical silogisms. Thus, those who partake in that practice can decide to perform a normative action by following norms of competence starting from the following premises: (i) the want of the objective of performing those actions validly and, thus, the corresponding normative result, and (ii) the belief/knowledge/

102 Roversi seems to be in this same line when, in a second approach, he argues that the duty to play following the rules of the game may be appreciated not from a teleological perspective, but from an axiological perspective (Roversi 2018, 143–148).

103 (Bustos Fuentes 2024)

104 (von Wright 1963a, 5).

understanding that abiding by the rules of competence is a necessary condition to the fulfilment of that want.

From this perspective, norms of competence regulate in the same sense as regulative rules as they mandate, prohibit, or permit. The difference does not reside in the normative solution. It resides in that the generic case correlated with the normative solution or, to say the same, the condition of application of norms of competence, as they are seen by their addressees (as regulative norms), includes the circumstance that they want to obtain the objective of performing a valid normative action and, thus, the corresponding normative result.

Thus, and again from the point of view of those partaking in the legal practice of performing normative actions, the first norm of this practice, as a rule of closure and, therefore, second level rule, would have to be expressed, not in terms of powers and disabilities or in terms of liabilities and immunities but by asserting that every normative action of an authority that has not been explicitly permitted by a superior authority is prohibited. Given that the condition of application of that second level rule is but the verification of a case not solved by the first level norms of competence, its aptitude to close up the system of competences depends on it being of the same type as that of first level norms.

We have examined the thesis that systems of norms of competence require for their closure a rule of the kind 'Everything that is not permitted is prohibited', and the asymmetry that supposes with regard to the rule of closure of a system of first order. The explanation that seems to follow from this point is that while first order systems are systems of prescriptive or regulative rules, second order ones are systems of constitutive or determinative norms. In the first case, for an action to be prohibited is a prescriptive norm so establishing is required. Thus, if there is no norm prohibiting action *A*, that action is permitted in a negative sense. Instead, in the second case, for a subject to have the power to execute a normative action *NA*, there needs to be a constitutive norm attributing said power and failing the existence of that constitutive norm, the subject would be disabled in a negative sense. Now, while regulative rules refer to actions whose performance or omission is independent of said rules, such that both the performance and the omission of said actions can be qualified as mandatory, prohibited, or permitted, the power and disability of a subject can only refer to the performance of a (normative) action. This difference is so since normative actions are constituted by rules establishing the necessary and sufficient conditions for their valid or possible performance. Of course, a certain agent who has been given power to execute a normative action may perform it or not, and there may be regulative norms normatively qualifying the exercise of said powers. However, constitutive rules attribute power to perform normative actions. They do not refer to the omission of said actions, which connects with the idea, as we have tried to justify, that competence systems cannot be incomplete.

In fact, von Wright refers to this point: when he analyzes the principle *nullum crimen nulla poena sine lege*, he wonders if it would be possible to close up a normative order through the principle according to which 'every action whose performance is not permitted is prohibited'. His answer is that, by virtue of the laws of deontic logic, a similar principle follows that, if in the normative system there is no norm permitting the execution of an action nor one permitting its abstention, both things would be prohibited, which would be contradictory. The difficulty of admitting the reverse principle to that of *nullum crimen* would then be that while it is not possible to prohibit to perform and abstain from executing one and the same action without contradiction, it is possible to permit without contradiction the execution and the abstention of one and the same action.[105]

In contrast, with regard to the rules relative to normative actions it would be natural to conceive a principle such as 'that which is not permitted is prohibited' since, if we understand 'that which' as referring only to the performance of normative actions and not to their abstention, there would be no contradiction,[106] beyond the fact that the adequate reading of the principle, from the perspective of the system of norms of competence and, therefore, understanding them as constitutive rules should be something like 'The constituted normative authorities are disabled to perform normative actions that have not been explicitly assigned to their power by a superior authority'.

When von Wright refers to the closure of the systems of second order and contrasts it with the principle *nullun crimen*, it seems clear that he is assuming that norms of competence are constitutive rules. However, and considering that the point of view of the individuals to whom these rules are addressed and applied reconstructs them as regulative rules, it does not make explicit the conclusion that the closed nature of the power of delegated authorities is not grounded in a rule of closure but in conceptual reasons.

References

Alchourrón, Carlos, and Eugenio Bulygin. 1971. *Normative Systems*. Wein-New York: Springer Verlag.

Alchourrón, Carlos, and Eugenio Bulygin. 1983. "Definiciones y normas". In *El lenguaje del derecho. Homenaje a Genaro Carrió*, coordinated by Eugenio Bulygin et al., 11–42. Buenos Aires: Abeledo Perrot. Cited by the publication *Análisis lógico y derecho*, by Carlos Alchourrón and Eugenio Bulygin, 1991, 439–463. Madrid: Centro de Estudios Políticos y Constitucionales.

Alchourrón, Carlos, and Eugenio Bulygin. 1984. "Permission and Permissive Norms". In *Theorie der Normen*, edited by Werner Krawietz et al., 349–372. Berlin: Dunker & Humboldt.

Arriagada, María Beatriz. 2015a. "La imposibilidad de equiparar derechos sociales y liberales". *Revista Chilena de Derecho* 42 (3): 819–842. http://dx.doi.org/10.4067/S0718-34372015000300004.

105 (von Wright 1963a, 87–88).
106 (von Wright 1963a, 194).

Arriagada, María Beatriz. 2015b. "Las cortes constitucionales frente a los 'derechos civiles y políticos'. Una mirada desde la teoría analítica del derecho". *Revista española de derecho constitucional* 105: 105–136. http://dx.doi.org/10.18042/cepc/redc.105.04.

Arriagada, María Beatriz. 2015c. "¿Protege derechos fundamentales el tribunal constitucional chileno?" *Revista de Derecho (Universidad Austral de Chile)* 28 (1): 145–169. https://doi.org/10.4067/S0718-09502015000100007.

Arriagada, María Beatriz. 2020. "Inmunidades fuertes y débiles. El imperio contraataca". *Revista de Derecho (Universidad Austral de Chile)* 33 (1): 9–29. https://doi.org/10.4067/S0718-09502020000100009.

Arriagada, María Beatriz. 2021a. "The Closure of the Systems of Competence Legal Norms. Episode I: The Normative Powers of Public Authorities". *Revista Revus. Journal for Constitutional Theory and Philosophy of Law* 43: 59–84. https://doi.org/10.4000/revus.7374.

Arriagada, María Beatriz. 2021b. "Las dos caras del precedente vinculante". In *Teoría y práctica del precedente*, coordinated by Álvaro Núñez, María Beatriz Arriagada and Iván Hunter, 365–400. Madrid: Tirant Lo Blanch.

Arriagada, María Beatriz. 2022a. "Las 'piezas' de Alchourrón y Bulygin". In *Eugenio Bulygin en la teoría del derecho contemporánea*, 1, coordinated by Jordi Ferrer, Juan José Moreso, Pablo Navarro and Jorge Rodríguez, 263–285. Madrid: Marcial Pons.

Arriagada, María Beatriz. 2022b. "Los derechos y los deberes bajo la lupa de Alf Ross. La defensa de una teoría analítica de las normas jurídicas". In *Materiales para una teoría de los derechos. Ensayos de filosofía analítica*, edited by Miguel Fernández, 95–144. Madrid: Marcial Pons.

Atianza, Manuel, and Juan Ruiz Manero. 2004. *Las piezas del derecho*. Barcelona: Ariel.

Atria, Fernando. 2005. "El derecho y la contingencia de lo político". *Derecho y Humanidades* 11: 19–39. https://derechoyhumanidades.uchile.cl/index.php/RDH/article/view/17049.

Atria, Fernando. 2016. *La forma del derecho*. Madrid: Marcial Pons.

Bertea, Stefano. 2013. "Constitutivism and Normativity: A Qualified Defence". *Philosophical Explorations* 16 (1): 81–95. Cited by the publication in *University of Leicester School of Law*, 2014, Research paper No. 14-13. https://ssrn.com/abstract=2396551.

Biasetti, Pierfrancesco. 2015. "Hohfeldian Normative Systems". *Philosophia* 43: 951–959.

Bermúdez, Jorge. 2014. *Derecho Administrativo General*. Santiago: Thomson Reuters.

Bustos Fuentes, Mirko. 2024. "Sentidos del punto de vista del jugador en Norma y Acción de G.H. von Wright". Forthcoming.

Bulygin, Eugenio. 1976. "Sobre la regla de reconocimiento". In *Derecho. Filosofía y lenguaje. Homenaje a Ambrosio L. Gioja*, edited by Jorge Bacqué. Buenos Aires: Astrea. Cited by the publication *Análisis lógico y derecho*, by Carlos Alchourrón and Eugenio Bulygin, 1991, 383–391. Madrid: Centro de Estudios Políticos y Constitucionales.

Bulygin, Eugenio. 1992. "On Norms of Competence". *Law and Philosophy* 11 (3): 201–216. Cited by the publication *Essays in Legal Philosophy*, edited by Carlos Bernal, Carla Huerta, Tecla Mazzarese, José Juan Moreso, Pablo Navarro and Stanley Paulson, 1995, 272–283. New York: Oxford University Press.

Bulygin, Eugenio. 2010. "Sobre la equivalencia pragmática entre permiso y no prohibición". *Doxa. Cuadernos De Filosofía Del Derecho* 33: 283–296. https://doi.org/10.14198/DOXA2010.33.14.

Carré de Malberg, Raymond. 1922. *Contribution à la théorie générale de l'état, spécialement d'après les données fournies par le Droit constitutionel français.* Paris: Societé du Recueil Sirey. Cited in the Spanish translation *Teoría general del Estado*, translated by José Deperte, 1988. Mexico D.F: Fondo de Cultura Económica.

Carré de Malberg, Raymond. 1931. *La loi, expresión de la volonté gérérale.* París: Sirey. Cited in the Spanish translation *La ley, expresión de la voluntad general. Estudio sobre el concepto de la ley en la Constitución de 1975*, translated by Ignacio Massot Puey, 2011. Madrid: Marcial Pons.

Carrió, Genaro. 1991. "Nota preliminar". In *Conceptos jurídicos fundamentales*, by Wesley Hohfeld, 7–21. Mexico D.F: Fontamara: 7–21. Translation into Spanish of "Fundamental legal conceptions as applied in judicial reasoning". *The Yale Law Journal* 23 (1): 19–59.

Cordero Quinzacara, Eduardo. 2009. "El sentido actual del dominio legal y la potestad reglamentaria". *Revista de Derecho (Pontificia Universidad Católica de Valparaíso)* 42: 409–440. http://dx.doi.org/10.4067/S0718-68512009000100012.

Cruz Parcero, Juan. 2007. *El lenguaje de los* dere*chos. Ensayo para una teoría estructural de los derechos.* Madrid: Trotta.

Ezquiaga, Javier. 2001. "Sobre inconstitucionalidad y derogación". *Discusiones* 2: 65–78. https://www.cervantesvirtual.com/nd/ark:/59851/bmcz03m9.

Feis, Guglielmo, and Umberto Sconfienza. 2012. "Challenging the Constitutive Rules Inviolability Dogma". *Phenomenology and Mind* 3: 102–110. https://doi.org/10.13128/Phe_Mi-19612.

Ferrer, Jordi. 2000. *Las normas de competencia. Un aspecto de la dinámica jurídica.* Madrid: Centro de Estudios Políticos y Constitucionales.

García, Gonzalo, and Pablo Contreras. 2014. "Diccionario constitucional chileno". *Cuadernos del Tribunal Constitucional* 55: 752–753.

García de Enterría, Eduardo. 1994. *La lengua de los derechos. La formación del derecho público europeo tras la revolución francesa.* Madrid: Alianza. Cited by the edition in "Ensayo" of 1999.

González Lagier, Daniel. 1995. *Acción y norma, en G.H. Von Wright.* Madrid: Centro de Estudios Políticos y Constitucionales.

Guastini Riccardo. 2001. *Estudios de teoría constitucional.* Mexico D.F: Fontamara.

Guastini Riccardo. 2014. *La sintassi del diritto.* Torino: Giappichelli Editore.

Guastini Riccardo. 2016. "Legalità". In *Rule of law. L'idealle della legalità*, edited by Giorgio Pino and Vittorio Villa, 137–152. Bologna: Il Mulino.

Guastini Riccardo. 2017. *Filosofia del diritto positivo.* Lezioni. Torino: Giappicheli Editore.

Hart, Herbert. 1953. "Definition and Theory in Jurisprudence". *The Law Quarterly Review.* Cited by the publication *Essays in Jurisprudence and Philosophy*, 1983, 21–48. Oxford: Clarendom Press.

Hart, Herbert. 1961. *The Concept of Law.* Oxford: Oxford University Press.

Hohfeld, Wesley. 1913. "Fundamental Legal Conceptions as Applied in Judicial Reasoning". *The Yale Law Journal* 23 (1): 19–59. Cited by the Publication *Fundamental Legal Conceptions as Applied in Judicial Reasoning*, edited by Walter Wheeler Cook, 2010, 23–64. New Heaven/London: Yale University Press.

Hohfeld, Wesley. 1917. "Fundamental Legal Conceptions as Applied in Judicial Reasoning". *Faculty Scholarship Series* paper 4378. Cited by the publication *Fundamental Legal Conceptions as Applied in Judicial Reasoning*, edited by Walter Wheeler Cook, 2010, 65–114. New Heaven/London: Yale University Press.

Kazor, Kamel. 2013. "Problemas teóricos en torno a las potestades normativas y a la necesaria redefinición de la reserva legal en el Estado constitucional chileno". *Ius et praxis* 19 (1): 35–76. https://dx.doi.org/10.4067/S0718-00122013000100003.

Kazor, Kamel. 2016. "La esfera de la función legislativa del Congreso Nacional a la luz de la relación ley-reglamento en la Constitución chilena". *Revista de derecho público* 65: 14–27. https://doi.org/10.5354/rdpu.v0i65.42447.

Kelsen, Hans. 1960. Reine Rechtslehre. Wien: Frans Deuticke. Cited in the English translation *Pure Theory of Law*, translated by Max Knight, 1967. Berkeley and Los Angeles: University of California Press.

Kramer, Matthew. 2000. "Rights without Trimmings". In A *Debate Over Rights*, by Matthew Kramer, N.E. Simmonds and Hillel Steiner, 7–111. New York: Oxford University Press.

Kurki, Visa. 2017. "Hohfeldian Infinities: Why Not to Worry". *Res Publica* 23: 137–146. http://dx.doi.org/10.2139/ssrn.2497999.

Lindahl, Lars. 1977. *Position and Change. A Study in Law and Logic*. Dordrecht-Boston: Reidel.

MacCormick, Neil. 1977. "Rights in Legislation". In *Law, Morality and Society*, edited by P.M.S. Hacker and Joseph Raz, 189–209. Oxford: Clarendom Press.

MacCormick, Neil. 2007. *Institutions of Law. An Essay in Legal Theory*. New York: Oxford University Press.

Mañalich, Juan Pablo. 2021. "La clausura de los sistemas de normas de sanción penal como sistemas de reglas constitutivas". *Revus. Journal for Constitutional Theory and Philosophy of Law* 44. https://doi.org/10.4000/revus.7473.

Mazzarese, Tecla. 2000. "Permesso forte e permesso debole: note a margine". In *Análisis e diritto*, edited by Pablo Comanducci and Riccardo Guastini. Torino: Giappichelli. Cited in the Spanish translation "Permisión fuerte y permisión débil. Notas al margen". In *Lógica, derecho, derechos*, translated by María Cristina Redondo, 2012, 39–64. Mexico D.F: Fontamara.

Merkl, Adolf. 1927. *Allgemeines Verwaltungsrecht*. Viena/Berlín: J. Springer. Cited in the Spanish translation *Teoría general del derecho administrativo*, 2018. Buenos Aires: Olejnik

Moraga Klenner, Claudio. 2008: "Derecho público chileno y los principios de legalidad administrativa y de juridicidad". In *Derecho administrativo, 120 años de cátedra*, coordinated by Rolando Pantoja Bauzá, 277–323. Santiago: Editorial Jurídica de Chile.

Moreso, José Juan, and Josep Vilajosana. 2004: *Introducción a la teoría del derecho*. Madrid: Marcial Pons.

Navarro, Loreto. 2024. "Otras cuestiones sobre las reglas técnicas. En torno a su vínculo con los silogismos prácticos". Forthcoming.

Núñez, Álvaro. 2018. "Precedente en materia de hechos". *Revista de derecho (Universidad Austral de Chile)* 31 (1): 51–78. https://doi.org/10.4067/S0718-09502018000100051.

Núñez, Álvaro. 2021. "¿Son obligatorios los precedentes? La regla del precedente como norma(s) constitutiva(s)" In *Teoría y práctica del precedente*, coordinated by

Álvaro Núñez, María Beatriz Arriagada and Iván Hunter, 333–364. Madrid: Tirant Lo Blanch.

Orunesu, Claudia, and Jorge Rodríguez. 2022. "Reglas constitutivas y mundos constitucionalmente posibles". In *Reglas constitutivas y derecho*, edited by Lorena Ramírez and Josep Vilajosana, 187–222. Madrid: Marcial Pons.

Prieto Sanchís, Luis. 2009. *Apuntes de teoría del derecho.* Madrid: Trotta.

Rainbolt, George. 1993. "Rights as Normative Constraints on Others". *Philosophy and Phenomenological Research* 53 (1): 93–111.

Rainbolt, George. 2010. *The Concept of Rights.* Dordrecht: Springer.

Raz, Joseph. 1975. *Practical Reason and Norms.* London: Hutchinson. Cited by the second edition of 1990. Princeton: Princeton University Press.

Redondo, María Cristina. 2006. "Sobre la completitud de los sistemas jurídicos". *Análisis filosófico* 26 (2): 294–324.

Ribera, Teodoro. 2001. "Reserva legal, potestad reglamentaria y Constitución de 1980". *Revista de derecho público* 63: 471–488. https://doi.org/10.5354/rdpu.v0i63.36306.

Rodríguez, Jorge. 2002. *Lógica de los sistemas jurídicos.* Madrid: Centro de Estudios Políticos y Constitucionales.

Rodríguez, Jorge. 2021. *Teoría analítica del derecho.* Madrid-Barcelona-Buenos Aires: Marcial Pons.

Ross, Alf. 1958. *On Law and Justice.* London: Stevens & Sons Ltd. Cited for publication in Berkeley & Los Angeles: University of California Press, 1959.

Ross, Alf. 1961. "On the Concepts 'State' and 'State Organs' in Constitutional Law". *Scandinavian Studies in Law* 5: 111–129.

Ross. Alf. 1968. *Directives and Norms.* London: Routledge and Kegan Paul. Cited for publication in New York: Humanities Press.

Ross, Alf. 1969. "On the On Self-Reference and a Puzzle in Constitutional Law". *Mind* 78 (309): 1–24.

Ross, Alf. 1972. "The Rise and Fall of the Doctrine of Performatives". In *Contemporary Philosophy in Scandinavia*, edited by Raymond Olson, 197–212. Baltimore-London: John Hopkins Press.

Roversi, Corrado. 2010. "Constitutive Rules in Context". *Archiv für Rechts- und Sozialphilosophie/Archives for Philosophy of Law and Social Philosophy* 96 (2): 223–238.

Roversi, Corrado. 2018. "Constitutive Rules and the Internal Point of View". *Argumenta* 4 (1): 139–156.

Ruiz Manero, Juan. 2007. "Una tipología de las normas constitucionales". In *Fragmentos para una teoría de la constitución*, edited by Josep Aguiló, Manuel Atienza, and Juan Ruiz Manero, 63–112. Madrid: Iustel.

Schauer, Frederick. 1991. *Playing by the Rules.* Oxford: Oxford University Press.

Schauer, Frederick. 2015. *The Force of Law.* Cambridge, MA and London: Harvard University Press.

Searle, John. 1964. "How to Derive 'Ought' from 'Is'". *The Phlosophical Review* 73 (1): 43–58.

Searle, John. 1969. *Speech Acts: An Essay in the Philosophy of Language.* New York: Cambridge University Press.

Searle, John. 1995. *The Construction of Social Reality.* London: Simon and Schuster.

Searle, John. 2018. "Constitutive Rules". *Argumenta* 4 (1): 51–54.

Soto Kloss, Eduardo. 2012. *Derecho Administrativo. Temas fundamentales.* Santiago: Abeledo Perrot.

Troper, Michel. 1994. *Pour une théorie juridique de l'État.* Paris: Presses Universitarires de France. Cited in the Spanish translation *Por una teoría jurídica del Estado,* 2001. Madrid: Dykinson.

Varas, Guillermo. 1940. *Derecho administrativo. Nociones generales.* Santiago: Nascimento.

Verdugo, Mario, Emilio Pfeffer, and Humberto Nogueira. 1994. *Derecho constitucional. Tomo I.* Santiago: Editorial Jurídica de Chile.

Vilajosana, Josep. 2010. *El derecho en acción. La dimensión social de las normas jurídicas.* Madrid: Marcial Pons.

von Wright, Georg. 1963a. *Norm and Action. A Logical Inquiry.* London: Routledge & Kegan Paul.

von Wright. Georg. 1963b. *The Varieties of Goodness.* London: Routledge & Kegan Paul.

von Wright, Georg. 1963c. "Practical Inference". *The Philosophical Review* 72: 159–179. Cited by the publication *Practical Reason. Philosophical Papers,* 1983, 1: 1–34. New York: Cornell University Press.

von Wright, Georg. 1971. *Explanation and Understanding.* London: Routledge & Kegan Paul.

Wellman, Carl. 1978. "Legal Rights". *Uppsalaskolam-och efferat,* 213–221. Stockholm: Almqvist.

Williams, Glanville. 1956. "The Concept of Legal Liberty". *Columbia Law Review* 56 (8): 1129–1150.

7 Constitutivism about practical reasons and the idea of legal norms

A tale of two constitutivisms

Stefano Bertea[1]

7.1 Introduction

In this chapter, I will explore the theoretical implications that endorsing a given meta-normative approach—constitutivism about practical reasons—has on the way in which legal norms should be conceptualized. This work is then intended as a contribution to a general theory of legal norms, which is traditionally regarded as a central dimension of any comprehensive philosophy of law, in turn defined as the theoretical study of law and its fundamental notions, characteristic properties, and distinctive traits. As a result, the proposed argument will engage with a long-standing issue in legal philosophy and so with a topic that has attracted the attention of researchers with different theoretical orientations and diverse philosophical backgrounds.[2] What specifically characterizes my study of legal norms and contributes to securing its originality is the fact that it approaches such an issue from a meta-normative perspective. Accordingly, the starting point of my engagement with legal norms will not be some stance internal to the philosophy of law. Rather, I will look into the idea of the legal norm through the lens of a broader discipline—metaethics—, which is directly connected with, and yet is conceptually distinguishable from, the philosophical study of law.

Before I proceed with the exploration, I should (a) introduce an important terminological clarification and (b) make the main theoretical assumption underlying my argument explicit. (a) To begin with, regarding the vocabulary in use in this chapter, what is meant by 'legal norm' is any kind of standard, be it a rule, a principle, a policy, or what-not, engendered by a system of

1 This research was supported by a Maria Zambrano Fellowship at the University of Barcelona. I would like to thank the participants in the 2022 Lisbon Meeting on Legal Theory held at the University of Lisbon for insightful comments on an earlier version of this work. I am especially grateful to Bartosz Brozek, Ruth Chang, Cecile Degiovanni, David Duarte, Jaap Hage, and Jorge Sampaio for their feedback and constructive criticisms. Needless to say, the responsibility for the views expressed herein, as well as for any error of form or content, rests solely with me

2 Just to refer to the post Second World War debate, see Bobbio (1958), Ross (1958), Kelsen (1945, 1967), Hart (1994), Raz (1970 and 1975), and Alexy (2002), among many others.

DOI: 10.4324/9781032670553-8

laws. This is a broad meaning of a 'legal norm': under this capacious umbrella they find their place standards of law that significantly differ in form, kind, and function as well as general, particular, and individual standards, including those that are non-directive in quality (such as classificatory standards). (b) To continue, the key assumption structuring the argument that follows is the claim, shared within a theoretical tradition, particularly influential in contemporary legal philosophy that a legal norm is to be conceived as a justificatory reason for action (of a specific kind).[3] The view conceptualizing the norms of law as justificatory practical reasons is in turn justified by two closely connected general theses.[4] On the one hand, there is the assertion that norms are complex entities. As such, they are best understood and analyzed in terms of more basic, elemental, or fundamental notions. On the other hand, we have the claim that the most basic, elemental, or fundamental concept structuring the normative dimension of human experience is the notion of a justificatory reason.[5] On this view, then, reasons are claimed to be essential to normativity in a constitutive sense, since they fundamentally establish what it means for some-

3 This view of legal norms is pioneered in Raz (1975) and widely accepted (as well as discussed, fine-tuned, qualified, and elaborated on) in analytical legal philosophy since then.

4 One may doubt that standards can be justificatory reasons, in consideration of the fact that by their nature standards are intersubjective in quality, whereas reasons may well be (or, in some views, even necessarily are) particular and agent-relative. To this objection, I would reply that reasons too are inherently intersubjective, public, and so general justificatory principles, as opposed to particular and agent-relative requirements, by virtue of their intrinsic connection with the idea of justification, which in its turn is an essentially intersubjective and public practice. To briefly elaborate on this statement, conceptually justificatory reasons are not concerns that only a particular agent should take as grounded, while other individuals may legitimately fail to recognize them. For, insofar as one has a reason for action, as a matter of concept, that action is supported by a statement that others cannot refrain from treating as a sound basis for action without misunderstanding the predicament at stake. In other terms, justificatory practical reasons are essentially public considerations, so they are necessarily recognized as valuable justifications for action not only by the agent they directly apply to but also by anyone else thinking clearly, including those who may have different, or even conflicting, interests. Related to that, particular and agent-relative considerations, such as idiosyncratic preferences, private motives, and personal interests, cannot be understood as justificatory practical reasons, since no consideration can be qualified as a practical reason unless it is intersubjectively acknowledgeable as a meaningful ground of action and so it makes normative claims that a generality of subjects, as opposed to just the relevant agent, will have to regard as (at least presumptively) valid. For a more extended discussion of this dimension of justificatory reasons, see Bertea (2017). I would like to thank Jaap Hage for bringing this point to my attention.

5 Sophisticated arguments for this thesis can be found in Raz (1999, 67–89). In that work, Raz (1999, 67) claims that 'the normativity of all that is normative consists in the way it is, or provides, or is otherwise related to reasons. The normativity of rules, or of authority, or of morality, for example, consists in the fact that rules are reasons of a special kind, the fact that directives issued by legitimate authorities are reasons, and in the fact that moral considerations are valid reasons. So ultimately the explanation of normativity is the explanation of what it is to be a reason, and of related puzzles about reasons'. In another work, Raz (2008, 5) states that 'normative phenomena are normative in as much as, and because, they provide reasons or are partly constituted by reasons. This makes the concept of a reason key to an understanding of

thing to be normative, to the effect that there cannot be normativity without reasons. As Thomas Scanlon (1998, 17) puts it, a reason is *the* fundamental notion structuring the normative domain, since 'any attempt to explain what it is to be a reason for something seems ... to lead back to the same idea: a consideration that counts in favour of it. "Counts in favour how?" one might ask. "By providing a reason for it" seems to be the only answer'.[6] In this theoretical framework, thus, the notion of a reason is normatively primitive and provides the basic building block of the normative realm at large. Correspondingly, any normative notion can be constructed in terms of the idea of a reason, namely, as a reason of some specific type or as a combination of reasons (possibly of different kinds).

Now, it is the acceptance of the thesis that *legal norms* are *practical reasons* (of a specific kind) that ultimately justifies the decision to rely on the conceptual resources made available by a *general account of reasons for action*—constitutivism about practical reasons—to investigate the idea of the legal norm. Indeed, from the perspective of those accepting the theoretical assumption just introduced, the relevance of constitutivism for the study of legal norms is hardly deniable. For, on the one hand, legal norms are conceived as practical reasons (of some kind); on the other hand, constitutivism is a comprehensive account of practical reasons (in general). Arguably, as a general theory of practical reasons, constitutivism is in a privileged position to explain the idea of the legal norm, when the latter is understood as a (specific kind of a) practical reason. That is, insofar as constitutivism takes the shape of an all-embracing approach to reasons for action and legal norms are conceived as (a subclass of) practical reasons, the significance of constitutivism for the conceptualization of legal norms arguably is obvious and straightforward.

These introductory remarks should suffice to indicate that the key terms of the discussion carried out in what follows are (i) constitutivism, (ii) reasons (in their practical instantiation), (iii) action, and (iv) (the idea of) legal norms. More specifically, (i) constitutivism is the philosophical framework that will be used to conceptualize legal norms. As a result, it figures as the theoretical tool for one to arrive at a better understanding of a given subject matter—(iv) the idea of the legal norm. For their part, (ii) reasons and (iii) action, in their combination, secure the connection between the proposed approach (constitutivism) and object (legal norm): it is because legal norms are explainable in terms of reasons for action that we are justified in relying on a given account of reasons for action—constitutivism—to conceptualize legal norms.

---

normativity'. See also Scanlon (1998, 17–77 and 2014, 1–15), Dancy (2004, 15–37 and 2009, 93–112), Parfit (2011, 31–38), and Raz (2011).

6 This stance is challenged in Hage (2022), where an attempt is made to analyze the idea of a reason, which nonetheless is taken to be a fundamental normative notion, in terms of a combination of facts and rules.

In fact, the conceptual connection holding between the four key terms of the proposed discussion is twofold and, then, quite deep. First, as just indicated, on the one hand, constitutivism is a theory of reasons for action; and, on the other hand, a conceptualization of legal norms consists in a theoretical account of something—legal norms—that is analyzable in terms of reasons and action (for, as per the theoretical assumption introduced above, legal norms are reasons for action of a given kind). This means that constitutivism, qua a philosophical account of reasons for action in general, should be expected to have the resources to conceptualize all forms of reasons for action, inclusive of the reasons for action generated by the law, and thus to conceptualize legal norms. This is why there is an at least prima facie justification for taking constitutivism seriously when theorizing about legal norms. Secondly, constitutivism is a meta-normative approach that distinctively puts action front and centre in its explanation of practical reasons. For, in a nutshell, constitutivism claims that the normative authority of practical reasons (that is, the capacity reasons can be argued to have to guide action and justify the performance of a certain course of conduct) is grounded in the essential properties of agency, namely, in our status of action-performers. Likewise, central is the place of the practical domain—the domain of action—in the study of legal norms, since legal norms are generally understood as standards governing the courses of action that are carried out in a given setting—the legal world. This is why our conception of action can be expected to bear on our conceptualization of legal norms. That is to say, there is an apparent substance-related overlap between constitutivism, qua a philosophical stance intrinsically linked to a theory of action, and the conceptualization of legal norms, which are standards of action, as action is carried out in the legal setting. Ultimately, this overlap is granted by the fact that action lies at the centre of both constitutivist accounts of practical reasons and conceptual explorations of legal norms. Hence the theoretically significant continuity of constitutivism and theories of legal norms, which both are aimed at (among other things) providing us with conceptual frameworks for the study of the practical domain—the sphere of action. In exploring the implications of embracing constitutivism for our understanding of legal norms, I take this continuity and overlap seriously, by thus making the most of the fact that action and its standards are the object, or subject matter, of both constitutivism and theories of legal norms.

7.2 Constitutivism, reasons, and action

In this work, I will rely on a given meta-normative approach—constitutivism about practical reasons—to elucidate the idea of the legal norm. Because constitutivism plays a key role in my argumentative strategy, an introduction to the main claims underpinning that stance is in order here.

Once it is understood as a meta-normative thesis,[7] constitutivism about practical reasons is a strategy purporting to ground our practical reasons in essential dimensions of action and agency.[8] Action and agency are in turn understood by the proponents of constitutivism as twin notions—action being construed as what an agent paradigmatically does, and agency as one's capacity to engage in action. The main question the proponents of constitutivism address—call it the 'authority question'—is, what grants the normative authority of reasons for action over us? Otherwise stated, the key question constitutivists set out to answer is, why ought we to undertake the courses of conduct that are supported by practical reasons? The answer constitutivists of all stripes give to this question proceeds roughly along the following lines: the normative claims practical reasons make on us are sourced in the features defining our action and agency. Accordingly, constitutivists are committed to the proposition that 'certain normative claims apply to us merely by virtue of the fact that we are agents', or action-performers, and that some normative reasons are grounded 'in facts about the nature of agency', qua capacity to undertake action (Katsafanas 2018, 367). Conversely, normative reasons for action arise simply from the fact that we have the capacity to act and so we constitutively are agents. Constitutivism, in other terms, can be introduced as the view that there are certain traits of action and agency that engender normative reasons and, related, acting in accordance with the relevant normative reasons defines at least in part what it is to carry out action and so what it is to be an agent. From this theoretical perspective, it is by clarifying the relationship between reasons, action, and agency that one finds the answer to the question as to what gives practical reasons normative authority over us and so why we ought to act as they indicate. For, if practical reasons define who we are as action-performers, by thus also establishing what features are essential to us as agents, we cannot possibly disregard them in the practical realm without thereby refraining from undertaking the type of conduct that is paradigmatically ours, by thus denying who we essentially are in the relevant realm—the practical one. Therefore, for a constitutivist the question, why ought we to engage with practical reasons? finds a straightforward answer: we ought to do so because doing otherwise is to fail to engage in action proper, thereby ceasing to qualify as agents (or at least as paradigmatic, or core, agents) and doing away with who we practically are at a general and fundamental level. In sum,

7 In fact, constitutivism about practical reasons can take the shape of both an ethical theory and a meta-normative account. In this work, I am concerned exclusively with the latter.

8 Proponents of (different versions of) constitutivism include Gewirth (1978, 21–42), Korsgaard (1996a, 1996b, 2008, 2009), Schapiro (1999, 2001), Velleman (2000, 2009), Street (2012), Walden (2012, 2018), Katsafanas (2013), and Smith (2013, 2015). Recent discussions of constitutivism about practical reasons can also be found in Ferrero (2009), Silverstein (2012, 2015), Bertea (2013, 2023), O'Hagan (2014), Baiasu (2016), Lindeman (2017), Ferrero (2018, 2019), Katsafanas (2018), Paakkunainen (2018), and Mayr (2019), among other places.

the normative force of practical reasons ultimately derives from our essential practical identity itself.

Constitutivism about practical reasons, as it is defended in the contemporary meta-normative literature, comes in several versions that vary significantly in their details.[9] Among the many distinctions internal to constitutivism, one is of special significance in the context of an exploration of legal norms, since it sets apart two variants of constitutivism that, in offering different accounts of practical reasons and action, also present us with distinct and mutually irreducible conceptualizations of legal norms. This is the distinction between (what I will call) function-constitutivism and (what I will refer to as) capacity-constitutivism. In this section, I will focus on those varieties of constitutivism in turn.

The first version of constitutivism that is of interest in this context is structured around the thesis that the authority of practical reasons is best accounted for in terms of facts about the constitutive function of ideal agency. To generalize, on this view, the foundational normative role is played by the function the idealized counterpart of a given kind is constitutively associated to. Relatedly, the notion of *constitutive function* is acknowledged to possess the resources not only for discriminating between sound and defective instances of the kind of items it constitutes but also for establishing reasons that non-defective instantiations of the relevant kind should regard as authoritative. Once this constitutivist approach is used to specifically determine whence the normative authority of practical reasons comes from—this is the authority question central to any version of meta-normative constitutivism—it amounts to the thesis that such an authority is owed to the constitutive function played by the ideal counterpart of our agency. Henceforth, I will use the phrase of '*function-constitutivism*' to refer to the thesis grounding the authority of practical reasons in the function constitutively, or essentially, performed by idealized agency. Function-constitutivism, then, claims that practical reasons have a normative bite on us by virtue of the fact that they track the function of our ideal selves in the practical sphere.

Function-constitutivism is theorized in Michael Smith's (2013, 2015) recent work, for instance.[10] Smith builds on Judith Jarvis Thomson's (2008) sophisticated study of normativity, which he critically revisits. Thomson claims that, at least for certain kinds of items—these are the so-called 'functional kinds'—the truth of normative judgements is settled by reference to facts constitutive of the class the judgement-maker belongs to. In order to ground the authority of *practical reasons*, Smith relies on this remark, which he integrates with original considerations about the function essentially served by idealized agency. So, after criticising meta-normative realists for being unable to elu-

9 A recent introduction to the varieties of constitutivism is offered in Smith (2017).

10 Another advocate of function-constitutivism, who pays specific attention to the implications that this variant of constitutivism has for legal theory is Kathryn Lindeman. See Lindeman (2017, 2019a, 2019b).

cidate the grounds of the normative authority of practical reasons,[11] Smith (2013, 9–17) defends the claim that agency should be conceived as a functional kind in Thomson's sense of the phrase. Agency is a functional kind because agents have a distinctive, or constitutive, function: that of realizing their desires. Noticeably, this necessary function gives agents access to non-contingent desires: the desires indexed (not to an actual agent but) to an agent's idealized, or non-contingent, counterparts, namely, the desires that an agent performing their essential function optimally has. For, while different agents have distinct function-based reasons to realize their contingent desires, every agent has a (non-hypothetical) reason to realize the desires that the function constitutive of agency generates. On Smith's view, then, there is a non-hypothetical reason for agent A to do something S just in case that agent's idealized counterpart constitutively desires to do that something. By an agent's idealized counterpart Smith means the agent 'himself in the nearest possible world in which he has and exercises a maximal capacity to know the world in which he lives and realize his intrinsic desires in it'.[12]

In sum, in Smith's philosophical construction, the desires that are constitutive of being an ideal agent establish which sorts of conduct actual agents have reasons to perform or to abstain from performing. Facts about what we have reasons to do are, thus, fixed by the function-related desires of our idealized practical counterpart, namely, by our ideal agency.[13] In other terms, the function constitutive of ideal agency—this is the function to realize one's non-contingent desires—is what grounds the authority of the reasons for action that we have. Relatedly, practical reasons are to be explained in terms of the responses to the specific circumstances in which someone finds themselves that an idealized agent would give.[14]

The claims about practical reasons made by the champions of function-constitutivism have important implications for the theory of *action*. From the perspective of function-constitutivism action too is constrained by the function of idealized agency. In this framework, 'action' is a term of art standing for what an agent *distinctively* does. On this view, not everything that one

11 Smith (2013, 14–15) argues that meta-normative realists simply *appeal* to the idea that something can be intrinsically normative, by thus falling short of *explaining* why and how something is intrinsically normative.

12 Smith (2013, 18). As Smith (2015, 187) also puts it, ideal agents are 'we ourselves in the nearest possible worlds in which we are fully informed and our desires are maximally coherent and unified'.

13 These desires, Smith (2015, 192) claims, are two in number: (a) the desire not to interfere with anyone's current or future exercise of their rational capacities—this is the desire not to interfere, in Smith's jargon—and (b) the desire of helping others, namely, the desire to see to it that those lacking basic agential capacities acquire and maintain those capacities—this is the desire to help, in Smith's vocabulary.

14 Recent critical discussions of Smith's function-constitutivism can be found in Bukoski (2016) and Enoch (2020). By contrast, Lindeman (2019a) sets out to defend the core claims underpinning function-constitutivism.

does can be catalogued as action proper. For action proper is irreducible to conduct in a generic sense and thus it does not stand for anything that is just done (namely, it is not coextensive with behaviour, once the latter is naturalistically understood to mean any movement that is causally guided by the agent's mental states).[15] By contrast, the paradigmatic kind of action essentially ***intentional conduct*** and is, thus, inherently associated with an agent's processes of practical thought, of which it is the outcome, or end-point. On this view, practical thinking—the set of deliberative processes having one's undertaking as its object—typically results in a change in the world. It is such a change—the change produced by one's practical thinking—that takes the specific name of action.[16]

This means that function-constitutivism conceptualizes action as intended, purposive, and consequence-direct behaviour, namely, as the outcome of someone's decision aimed at realizing a goal they recognize to be good and, thus, are determined to pursue. Apparently, this conception of action as intentional behaviour contains both a consequentialist element and a teleological element. For it defines action in terms of both what it produces—its consequences—and the goals and purposes absent which it cannot be said to make sense—its telos or overarching aim. That is to say, action is inherently oriented towards realizing a result, or consequence, deemed to be good, or valuable, by the agent, who sets such a result as their practical end, or telos. Moreover, insofar as acting means to engaging in a form of conduct that is oriented to an end, action should be conceived as constitutively stepwise: each specific course of conduct we embark on as a part of an end-oriented action is geared to—it is a step towards—a termination point. As a result, from this theoretical perspective, action (necessarily and sufficiently) involves the exercise of one's capacity to form reliable beliefs about the world and one's capacity to comply with the means-ends principle. In that respect, the notion of action associated with function-constitutivism is conceptually continuous with the so-called 'calculative view' of action.[17]

In sum, in the function-constitutivist approach the inherent structure of action consists in bringing something about, or producing, something. That is, acting is a form of 'doing-an-act-in-pursuance-of-a-goal-the-agent-recognize s-to-be-valuable'. This conception, as one can appreciate, should be qualified as a rather thin account of action. Here, action stands for any goal-directed

15 Apparently, here action denotes a conceptual entity, as distinct of a brute, or sheer performance. A quasi-naturalistic conception of action is, instead, very influential in contemporary philosophy of action, as it is theorized in Davidson (1980) and Bratman (1988, 1999, 2007), among others.

16 As Paul (2013, 289) notices, on this view, practical reasoning is 'a unified process that begins in thought and terminates in action'. In this process, one starts with a question about either what to do or what ought to be done, and ends with the performance of some act.

17 This view, which is introduced in Schapiro (2001, 94–95) and Millgram (2020, section 1), finds a systematic theorization in Vogler (2002) and Thompson (2008).

movement that is responsive to, or even caused by, both the volitional states of the agent—typically, desires—and their cognitive states—their representations of, or beliefs about, the external environment—as those volitional and cognitive states are processed in practical reasoning.

This thin account of action is mirrored by a likewise parsimonious understanding of agency. From the function-constitutivist perspective, agency is conceived as the exercise of causal power and, hence, as the 'effect' of a power we qua agents have. Agency, in other terms, is conceptualized as purposive efficient causality: in acting one is ultimately concerned with the effects one produces in the world. That is, an agent is someone who makes use of causal connections in the world in order to achieve a goal.[18] Hence, from the perspective of function-constitutivism, agency is associated with an empiricist moral psychology. That is, agents are claimed to take into account their desires and beliefs when determining how they should act. Accordingly, they are the inclinations of our minds (especially in the form of desires and beliefs) what ultimately determines action—they are our volitional and cognitive pressures that conclusively establish the way in which we go about, or even ought to go about, in the world.

An alternative variant of constitutivism claims that the authority of practical reasons can be accounted for in terms of facts about the *capacities* that are constitutive of agency. On this view, agency is essentially connected with certain enabling properties—the dispositional traits that a subject necessarily possesses in order to be able to carry out action. They are those fundamental enabling properties that provide us with reasons for acting in this or that way, by thus distinguishing what we have reasons to do and what we have reasons not to do. This means that the ground of the authority of practical reasons lies in the essential features enabling our undertaking action and exercising agency. Namely, practical reasons have normative authority over us by virtue of the fact that they respond to the basic capacities shaping our agency—the capacities that supply the very preconditions of undertaking action. From now on I will refer to the variety of constitutivism anchoring the authority of practical reasons to the agential fundamental capacities as '*capacity-constitutivism*'.

In a nutshell, capacity-constitutivism claims that the normative authority of practical reasons is rooted in the necessary identity we have as inhabitants of the practical territory, whose identity is in turn defined in terms of certain capacities. It is by virtue of their internal relationship with the dispositional features defining what we paradigmatically do and who we essentially are within the practical sphere that certain reasons for action are compelling for individuals like us. The reasons that we regard as normative in the practical sphere are, hence, requirements set by properties that are essential to us as acting creatures, namely, traits without which we cannot possibly exist or

18 On this point, see Darwall (1995, 285), who links this conception of action to an instrumental idea of agency.

operate in the practical territory.[19] Once it is so understood, capacity-constitutivism is influentially championed by Christine Korsgaard. A reconstruction of Korsgaard's position has, thus, the potential to further clarify the basic claims underpinning capacity-constitutivism.[20]

In order to explain the normative authority of *practical reasons*, Korsgaard offers an original treatment of action and agency. In this context, she (2009, 1) claims that for creatures like us action is a 'plight': we 'are *condemned* to choice and action' and so have no option but to act. Because action is necessary for us—it is an 'inexorable fact' of us, something that deeply and necessarily characterizes our condition (Korsgaard 2009, 2)—we are inevitably agents. Hence, an account of action and agency is a contribution to an understanding of what we distinctively do and who we of necessity are. Importantly, for Korsgaard agency, as it applies to creatures like us, has a peculiar and distinctive structure. We are self-conscious creatures in a sense of being both conscious and in control of the grounds on which we act.[21] This form of self-consciousness means that we do not act simply because we have a desire or feel some internal pressure. Being aware of desires and feeling internal pressures—call desires and other internal pressures 'incentives' for short—we can discipline them by means of rational deliberation. As a result, action requires (creatures like) us to choose the basis on which it proceeds. That is, such a basis is not given to us in the same way as incentives are presented to us, but is rather something we have the task to work out by ourselves through rational deliberation about the incentives we experience. The introduction of rational considerations into the picture means that (for creatures like us) action is inherently and essentially guided by reasons. In turn, this means that rationality decisively contributes to establish the way in which we act, or go about in the world.

These considerations have a direct impact on the study of the normative authority of *practical reasons*. For the combination of (a) the thesis that action and reasons are necessarily related with (b) the statement that we are condemned to perform actions justifies (c) the conclusion that the authority of practical reasons is rooted in our essential agential constitution, which is the rational structure we, qua performers of action, are necessarily endowed with. The conclusion that can be drawn from Korsgaard's argument, thus, is that for creatures like us it is one's practical and rational constitution that supplies the source of the normative authority of practical reasons. Or, to put it the other

19 This statement also makes it clear that, for an advocate of capacity-constitutivism, the requirements ensuing from agency are non-optional, or non-hypothetical, namely, their authority does not depend on an individual subject's specific inclinations, contingent desires, or particular affections.

20 Korsgaard's capacity-constitutivism takes shape in Korsgaard (1996a and 1996b), which also sets the direction of her successive work in practical philosophy. That work culminates in Korsgaard (2009). This is the reason why in my introduction to Korsgaard's thought I will refer to the latter.

21 See Korsgaard (2009, 18–26).

way around, the authority of practical reasons is grounded in our essential form, namely, in our agency, in turn understood as the capacity to undertake action.

Likewise important, this construction frames *action* as necessarily directed by someone understood as a whole unit distinct from the specific incentives one happens to feel. As such, action is the product of a unified whole, not just of particular components running through an agent and only loosely, or contingently, related one to another.[22] It is only insofar as one is unified that one's movements can be regarded as one's own and so produced by principles expressive of oneself rather than by the pressures one happens to experience at a particular moment of time. Action, in other terms, requires personal integration. For, in the absence of personal integration, we would not be agents but rather bunches of disparate forces operating in a largely passive subject that provides little more than a mere location for those forces to unfold; accordingly, no undertaking could be attributed to the whole of us and so, by virtue of the connection existing between wholeness and action, no action at all would take place. That is to say, in this framework of thought, by its very structure action is authored and owned by the agent as a unified whole.[23]

This philosophical framework implies that normativity too, being conceptually connected to our agency, can be associated to us only insofar as we preserve the personal integration, or unity, that makes us agents in the first instance. Relatedly, the lack of personal integration casts us away from our own agency. Accordingly, our very existence as normative animals—beings that are sensitive to normative concepts and indeed partake of the normative dimension—gets lost or, at least, turns into something less than necessary. The normative dimension of our experience is, thus, conditioned to our preserving some kind of wholeness. This statement, in turn, reinforces the claim that the normative status of practical reasons resides in their relation with our unity as agents. A reason for action can be regarded as valuable, and so invested with normative force, insofar as it demands courses of conduct that are functional to preserving our unity and so to securing our agency; by contrast, any ground of action that threatens our unity, or weakens our personal integration, will have to be regarded as unsupported by practical reasons.[24]

22 This argument is the focus of Korsgaard (2009, 109–132).

23 As Korsgaard (2009, 19; original emphasis) puts it, 'for a movement to be my action, for it to be expressive of *myself* in the way that an action must be, it must result from my entire nature working as an integrated whole'.

24 Importantly, the relation between a practical principle and personal integration may be more nuanced and so be a matter of degree. For, practical principles are not simply either conducive to one's unity or adverse to it; some of them may well be more or less functional to promoting one's agency than other principles. Accordingly, the normative force of the reasons for action can be distinguished by degree too. In other words, in Korsgaard's account, since some reasons for action succeed in unifying us better than others, they have greater authority, or normative force, on us than other reasons. Building on this idea, Korsgaard (2009, especially

This statement indicates that capacity-constitutivism is associated with a robust and discriminatory account of *action*.[25] This is the account singling out *authorship*, or *ownership*, as the distinctive quality of action. On this view, there is no action without an agent fully owning, or endorsing, it. In a slogan, there is no action without an author, or an owner, of it. In turn, authorship, or ownership, as it applies to action is a demanding idea. For it is not sufficient that a deed is brought about by someone for action to come to existence.[26] It is rather necessary that an individual (constituted) as a unified whole, vis-à-vis certain components, or subparts, of such an individual, undertakes a course of conduct. A direct implication of this conception is that action is to be conceived not just as a means to an end—a phenomenon that can be exhaustively described in light of its output or consequences. For we cannot fully appreciate what action is until we look at the *reasons* for which agents do what they do.[27] Which reasons, in turn, are irreducible to either the end of action or the consequences that agents (intend to) bring about through their conduct. Reasons for action, instead, provide the rationale of one's behaviour, or what justifies it, by thus giving it meaning and value.[28] Practical reasons can, in this sense, be understood as the indispensable basis of action—they are what provides the structure of action—such that no (fully-fledged) action, as distinct from mere conduct, can be said to take place unless what is done is not only intended—this is intentional behaviour—but rather it is intended for a reason that justifies the relevant piece of conduct either to ourselves or to others or, ideally, to both—call it *principled* conduct. This is why, on this account, instrumentalist and consequentialist approaches result in incomplete conceptualizations of action. Action is an inherently reflexive and (self-)conscious undertaking that not only incorporates the (causally determined) end it is meant to achieve as a consequence to be produced—hence, it is not just accountable in terms of that end and consequence, as instrumentalism and consequentialism would suggest—but it is also organized around, and struc-

45–58) argues that the principles of practical rationality—in particular, the moral principle, or autonomy, and the instrumental principle, or efficiency—should be regarded as the fundamental norms governing action since they are the principles most functional to unifying our will.

25 I elaborate on this point in Bertea (2023, …).

26 Such an account of action is known by the name of the 'authorship view'. The authorship view is introduced in some detail in Millgram (2020, section 2), and paradigmatically theorized in Korsgaard (2009, esp. 8–26). Accounts of action that, in my understanding, are similar to the one associated with capacity-constitutivism are defended in Buss (1999) and Schapiro (2001).

27 The connection between action and reasons is systematically explored not only in Korsgaard (2009) but also in Velleman (2000, 2009).

28 Related to this, no aim, or endpoint, can be considered worthwhile until we know the reasons justifying that aim being pursued. This also means that the worth of an action cannot be measured simply by the value of its outcome, since we cannot fully appreciate the worth of an undertaking until we know what the rationale is that stands behind it, or what the justificatory reasons are for which it is sought.

tured by, a principle, or rationale, on the basis of which the end is achieved and the consequence is produced.

To conclude, the capacity-constitutivist conception of action merges three components into the single idea of action. Action combines (a) the thing done—the act that is carried out—with (b) the end for which the act is performed and (c) the reason for, or rationale underlying, the act. None of those components can do without the other. For, on the one hand, a reason for doing something is not action until something is actually done in pursuance of the relevant end. On the other hand, the thing done for the relevant end cannot qualify as action unless it is done for a reason that justifies the action carried out in pursuance of the end. This means, in sum, that, on this view, action is an enterprise essentially shaped by reasons and, thus, inherently has the following structure, or form: doing-something-for-a-reason-and-in-pursuance-of-an-end.

7.3 Two constitutivist conceptualizations of legal norms

So far, I have claimed that two distinct families of constitutivism about practical reasons—function-constitutivism and capacity-constitutivism—are associated to significantly different and mutually irreducible accounts of practical reasons (as well as their authority) and action. Now, at a conceptual level practical reasons and action are directly connected to legal norms. For, at least in an influential tradition of legal philosophy, *legal norms* are law-engendered *reasons* making courses of *action* permissible, prohibited, or compulsory. This means that the idea of a legal norm can be explained in terms of the notion of a reason (for a reason figures as the essential element in the definition of a legal norm) and in terms of the concept of action (for action provides the scope of a legal norm). Insofar as this is the case, the way in which one characterizes the notions in terms of which idea of the legal norm is explainable—reasons and action—should be expected to have direct implications on the way in which the legal norm itself is conceptualized. For any concept resulting from a combination of other notions closely depends in its definition and structure on one's understanding of its compound notions. Otherwise stated, the idea of the legal norm closely depends on both the way in which its defining element—a practical reason—and its subject matter—action—are conceptualized.

Now, the fact that legal norms are essentially and directly linked to practical reasons and action makes it relevant the question, how do the function-constitutivist and capacity-constitutivist conceptions of practical reasons—what legal norms are—and action—what legal norms are about—bear on the idea of the legal norm? This is the question that I intend to address in this section, where I specifically consider the implications that accepting the conceptions of practical reasons and action defended by the champions of function-constitutivism and those theorized by the advocates of capacity-constitutivism have for the idea of the legal norm. Accordingly, in what follows I intend to elucidate which idea of the legal norm can be associated with the acceptance of function-constitutivism (and its accounts of practical reasons and action) and which idea of the legal norm can be extracted from the endorsement of capacity-constitutivism (and its conceptions of practical reasons and action).

The specific working hypothesis that will be explored in what follows can then be summarized so. The function-constitutivist conceptualization of a legal norm, based as it is on the understanding of practical reasons as rational considerations grounded in the constitutive function of idealized agency and the view of action as intentional conduct, significantly differs from the capacity-constitutivist conception of a legal norm, based as it is on the understanding of practical reasons as rational standards sourced in agency qua ownership of what one does and the view of action as principled conduct. This working hypothesis sets a question for us, namely, what are the implications of accepting function-constitutivism and capacity-constitutivism for our understanding of legal norms? Otherwise stated, the question to be addressed in this section is, how are legal norms best conceived from the perspective of function-constitutivism and how are legal norms to be conceptualized from the standpoint of capacity-constitutivism?

A caveat should be added before proceeding with the exploration. The main claim that will be made in this section is not that certain conceptions of practical reasons and action *logically* compel us to conceptualize a legal norm this or that way. In this section, I will not look into the logical relations between function-constitutivism and capacity-constitutivism—their accounts of practical reasons and action—on the one hand, and certain conceptions of legal norms, on the other. The proposition I am going to defend, then, is not that the acceptance of function-constitutivism *necessarily* leads one to conceptualize the legal norm in a given way (here the necessity at stake being logical necessity). Nor is my thesis that capacity-constitutivism logically forces one to accept an idea of the legal norm that is different and arguably alternative to the one I associate to function-constitutivism. By contrast, the thesis I am committed to is that different concepts of legal norms are highly *coherent with*, as distinct from logically derivable from, the theorization of function-constitutivism and capacity-constitutivism. In other terms, those advocating function-constitutivism can be *reasonably* expected to, and most obviously driven towards, an understanding of legal norms that is significantly different from, or even alternative to, the understanding of legal norms that the champions of capacity-constitutivism would find sensible. In a nutshell, in what follows I will be exploring a relation of congruence, not a logical derivation: it makes sense to characterize legal norms in a certain fashion, I will argue, if one endorses function-constitutivism; likewise, those who embrace capacity-constitutivism should be expected, as opposed to being compelled by the force of logic, to conceptualize legal norms differently. Hence, in this section, I will introduce the possible (by which I mean non-analytically-necessary and so merely potential) implications that accepting two distinct varieties of constitutivism has on the idea of the legal norm.

With this caveat in place let us consider the implications that accepting the basic claims underpinning function-constitutivism has for the idea of the legal norm. Function-constitutivism conceptualizes action as intentional conduct. This is quite a broad understanding of action as in this construction action stands for any outcome of one's practical deliberation, or any performance intended by an agent. Insofar as legal norms are primarily concerned with action—or a subset of it, namely, legally relevant action—in this theoretical perspective legal norms are best conceptualized as standards primarily regulating courses of intentional conduct, namely, as directives about the end-results of a legal subject's practical reasoning. Apparently, this is an all-encompassing definition of the legal norm. For, on the view conceptualizing a legal norm as a distinctive, law-sourced, species of reasons for or against certain courses of intentional conduct, any standard of intentional conduct can potentially become a norm of law. This statement is revealing of the fact that function-constitutivism comes with a comprehensive, thin, and non-discriminatory conception of legal norms. True, legal norms are claimed to single out a specific kind of practical reasons, since certain forms and procedures need to be followed for a practical reason to be considered legally valid and so for it to specifically exist as a legal standard of action. However, from the conceptual point of view, there is no obstacle to the fact that legal norms take the most diverse contents. In principle, any standard of action, be it reasonable or not, can be incorporated into a legal system. In this theoretical framework, then, there are no conceptual limitations to the contents that legal norms may take up. It is entirely up to the law-making institutions of a given jurisdiction to determine the substance of the legal norms of their system. Insofar as those institutions deem it fit to make a reason for or against certain courses of intentional conduct legal, such a reason will be turned into a legal norm. In other terms, conceptually legal norms can have any content whatsoever, since on this view the substance of a legal norm is independently established by those in charge with making the law and so it exclusively depends on what those in authority consider it appropriate to be part of the law, qua distinctive system of regulation of action.[29] This is why, to put it bluntly, in the function-constitutivist conceptualization, a norm is legally valid insofar as those in authority say so. Otherwise stated, the will of those in authority is the final determinant of which practical norms are legal and which practical norms cannot be so characterized.

Let me rephrase and expand on these points. In the conceptual framework associated with function-constitutivism, legal norms are practical reasons and practical reasons are considerations dealing in action. Action, in turn, is generically understood as the intentional production of some effect in the world. This means that a legal norm should be expected to be conceptualized broadly

29 This point echoes an influential stance in legal philosophy, which is well exemplified in Kelsen (1967, 198).

as a law-sourced reason that deals in intentional conduct. A legal norm is, in other terms, a *device* serving the purpose of realizing authoritatively set ends and channelling the courses of conduct undertaken by a legal community towards the achievement of practical goals, as those goals are established by legal officials and authorities in general.

This conception of legal norms is both wide-encompassing in scope and instrumentalist in quality. It is a wide-encompassing view, since in this conceptualization there is no pre-established content that, for conceptual reasons, legal norms need to incorporate. Conceptually, legal norms can take the widest possible spectrum of contents, since they are shaped by the most variable and contingent goals that the group of people living under the jurisdiction of the law set for themselves.[30] The function-constitutivist account is also an instrumentalist conception of legal norms for, on this approach, legal norms have no special value in themselves. Legal norms are far from intrinsically worthwhile, because independently of the practical goals, purposes, and objectives they are introduced to achieve, legal norms are of little value. Any worth legal norms may have, thus, is borrowed from something external to them (namely, from the possible value of the collective goals, purposes, and objectives they are functional to pursue). Hence, legal norms are best conceptualized (not as values, but rather) as tools.[31] The broad, undemanding, and tolerant conception of legal norms associated with function-constitutivism, thus, means that legal norms are best conceived as means, or instruments, to achieve certain collective goals: they are standards functional to reaching the objectives set by the law-making institutions recognized within a given legal community. This is a merely instrumentalist understanding of legal norms, which in the legal-philosophical literature finds a parallel in the positivist tradition of legal thought. That is, the all-embracing and instrumentalist conception of legal norms associated with function-constitutivism fits well within the conceptualization of legal norms theorized within the tradition in the philosophy of law that is 'realist and unromantic in outlook', embarks on 'the enterprise of demythologizing the law', and resists any 'moralizing myths' (Raz 1999, 194).

30 This is not to say that legal norms are under no substantive constraint at all. Indeed, one may argue that any practical directive that may systematically jeopardize the legal enterprise itself would have to be considered unintelligible, or at least unpractical, as a specifically legal norm. For such a norm would frustrate the very normative system it belongs to. However, apparently this substantive constraint is merely internal to the law itself. Conversely, insofar as the content of a directive does not make that norm *legally* inconsistent, it has the potential to become the substance of a legal norm. Which is why, from the perspective of function-constitutivism, the only limitations to the contents of legal norms are not conceptual but rather merely legal, or internal to the legal enterprise itself.

31 One place where this view is upheld in legal philosophy is Raz (1979, 226), where it is stated that law 'is a tool in the hands of men differing from many others in being versatile and capable of being used for a large variety of proper purposes'.

In sum, the conception of the legal norm most coherent with the views of practical reasons and action theorized by the advocates of function-constitutivism is broad, generic, less-than-discriminatory, and instrumentalist in quality. Legal norms refer to any standard, issued by an appropriate authority in accordance with certain procedures, that is instrumental to directing the courses of conduct of a social group towards certain collective objectives, ends, or goals.

The conception of legal norms that best coheres with the capacity-constitutivist approach to practical reasons and action could hardly be more different. Capacity-constitutivism conceives of practical reasons as rational considerations sourced in agency and defines action as principled conduct, namely, behaviour essentially shaped by rational considerations. This combination establishes an essential connection between action and rationality in the practical domain: action necessarily accounts for practical reasons so that the former is conceived as a reasoned exercise of one's agency. Insofar as action is conceptualized as inherently rationally defensible conduct, severing the link between what is done and what practical rationality demands one to do means denying the conceptual specificity of action. Or, to put it radically, it means (just) behaving, as distinct of (specifically) acting. Now, as long as legal norms primarily deal in action and action intrinsically is principled, or rationally justifiable, conduct, a conceptual link connects legal norms and the principles of practical rationality. Those principles provide the bridge between norms of law and their subject matter—action, qua principled, and so reason-driven, conduct. This is to say that the principles of practical rationality shape (not only action, as action is understood from the perspective of capacity-constitutivism, but also) legal norms. Legal norms, as a result, are to be conceived as law-sourced rational directives and, thus, as rationally defensible considerations for or against certain courses of collective conduct. This statement has two important conceptual implications.

First, from the perspective of capacity-constitutivism, legal norms are conceptually constrained by considerations that are external to the legal sphere: the principles of practical rationality. That is, for conceptual reasons the contents of legal norms end up being partly established by rational considerations. This proposition does not deny that the substance of legal norms is dependent on the will of those in power to a significant extent. For, at least in the view of the influential Kantian strand of capacity-constitutivism, the principles of practical rationality that essentially shape legal norms and their contents are constitutively abstract, partly indeterminate, and incomplete. As a result, they are claimed to only introduce general and unspecific requirements of action. In other terms, the principles of practical rationality set out general goals and objectives, by thus failing to be necessarily informative about the rightness and wrongness of specific courses of action. Those principles, then, do not typically single out the detailed courses of conduct that are to be regarded as correct, or rationally required. They introduce, instead, comprehensive ideals that can be realized by means of different courses of conduct sensitive to the specific contexts, situations, traditions, and cultures within which they are performed.[32] This means that the recognition of the existence of certain principles of practical rationality is compatible with the fact of evaluative pluralism. Indeed, on this view, the principles of practical rationality operate like a compass purporting to guide us through a world populated of a plurality of ends, creeds, and interests that are not necessarily coherent one with another.[33] For this reason, the will of those in power does play an important and often decisive role in filling the gaps left open by the principles of practical rationality, by thus determining which norms are specifically in force in a given legal system. However, such a will can hardly be described as the sole determinant of legal norms and their contents, as an advocate of function-constitutivism would describe them. For the principles of practical rationality too are constitutive of the norms governing action in law. As a result, legal norms can incorporate a wide variety of contents, most of which are fixed by the will of those in power. Yet, they cannot be said to have any content whatsoever, as instead a champion of function-constitutivism would argue. Indeed, there are contents—the contents that, even if they were willed by those in power, prove to be incompatible with the principles of practical rationality—that are not legally possible. In the capacity-constitutivist construction, those contents are not only rationally flawed but also (and, in fact, by virtue of their rational flaws) legally defective. Namely, from this philosophical perspective, legal norms can be legally faulty just because their contents are rationally questionable, qua incompatible with the principles of practical rationality.

Importantly, in consideration of the fact that the principles of practical rationality are, as mentioned, inherently abstract, partly indeterminate, and incomplete, capacity-constitutivism is not committed to the conclusion that

32 For a structured theorization of this view of practical rationality, see O'Neil (2001), for instance.

33 In sum, practical rationality enables us to move through ends in a non-arbitrary way and to direct our choice as to which ends ought to orient our action. It is against the background of the recognition of the multiplicity and conflictive quality of ends, therefore, that the conception of practical rationality sketched here makes sense. This means that practical rationality cannot necessarily provide the one right answer to each and every practical question. Practical rationality offers us non-instrumental rational deliberative procedures to approach sensitive questions. But appealing to practical rationality is no guarantee that we can cope with all the practical questions. Especially, insofar as we travel in lands distant from those inhabited by practical necessities, to the effect that the relevant ends are merely contingent (and yet rationally defensible), the assistance provided by practical rationality is less than conclusive. Which, additionally, means that not all the practically rational ends have to be—and typically are—acknowledged as rationally necessary. Some practical ends can be recognized as rational qua necessary, to the effect that no agent could do without them. Yet, our practical world also makes allowance for ends that are deemed to be contingent—they depend on circumstances about the agent herself—and are still of relevance in rational deliberation about what one ought to do. Practical rationality, thus, does not solely determine the ends that are practically necessary but also enables agents to rank ends that are contingent and justify our preferring some contingent ends over others.

legal norms coincide with the standards of rationality. By contrast, the claim made by the advocates of capacity-constitutivism is more modest. It states that legal norms cease to be what they are—they cease to be conceptualizable as law-engendered reasons governing action qua principled conduct—as long as their contents can be proved to be incompatible with the principles of practical rationality. In that context, legal norms can well permit, prohibit, and make compulsory courses of conduct that are less than rationally necessary. For instance, they can well, and typically do, cover issues that are rationally indifferent, indeterminate, or even uncertain. Hence, legal norms hardly lose their legal quality whenever they go beyond the directives one can extract by means of the exercise of one's rational faculties. The recognition of the rational quality of legal norms, then, only commits one to the statement that a legal norm cannot be fundamentally irrational without dissolving as a reason for action. That is, there are certain contents—those inconsistent with the principles of practical rationality—that no legal norm can incorporate without by thus ceasing to be a legal norm. This is due to the fact that, from the perspective of capacity-constitutivism, legal norms essentially are rational considerations for or against courses of principled conduct. Hence, a standard losing its rational status—a standard conflicting with the demands of practical rationality—will ipso facto stop being conceivable as a legal norm.

This thesis, modest and qualified as it certainly is, is far from theoretically insignificant. For, and this is the second point that I would like to make here, it supports the conclusion that legal norms are not mere devices for guiding action. By contrast, from the perspective of capacity-constitutivism, legal norms are best conceived as *valuable* standards of action. More specifically, they are standards inherently valuable from the rational perspective, because they constitutively are rationally defensible standards. Namely, legal norms are directives that essentially are not incompatible with the principles of practical rationality. Therefore, insofar as we agree that practical rationality is a value—not necessarily the only value informing the practical domain, nor the overarching one; but a value nonetheless—legal norms, qua rationally defensible standards—standards that constitutively cohere with the principles of practical rationality—are intrinsically valuable. In other terms, the value inherent in practical rationality is transmitted to the standards, such as legal norms, that are constitutively informed to rational ideals and principles. This frames legal norms as entities that are conceptually continuous with values and ends, rather than means. Hence, insofar as (a) we acknowledge that what is practically rational has a value in itself—this value not being merely instrumental, or derivative on the goals it enables one to pursue—and (b) we accept the capacity-constitutivist proposition that legal norms are rationality-bound standards, (c) we are in the position to conclude that legal norms belong to the realm of ends and values, as opposed to being conceptualizable as mere means.

Let me briefly restate the main implications of capacity-constitutivism for the conceptualization of legal norms. The starting point of my reflection on those implications is the idea that legal norms primarily deal in action. Insofar as action is understood as a rationally justified move—this is the conception of action as owned conduct that is theorized by the advocates of capacity-constitutivism—it is reasonable to conceive of legal norms as rationally defensible social standards, namely, as directives oriented to, and constrained by, rationally justifiable considerations. This account of legal norms is encompassing, since the principles of practical rationality are acknowledged to be unable to offer sufficiently detailed and conclusive practical guidance in all circumstances. Yet, the resulting account of legal norms is more discriminatory and demanding in its scope when compared to the conception of legal norms associated with function-constitutivism.

The capacity-constitutivist account of legal norms should be qualified as discriminatory and demanding, since it states that the principles of practical rationality contribute to establishing the contents legal norms are conceptually allowed to fit in. Far from being amenable to incorporating anything those in authority deem fit—that is, far from being exclusively determined by the will of those in power—legal norms are, thus, claimed to be essentially constrained by the principles of practical rationality. This statement does not mean that legal norms make no difference in our practical reasoning. For, on the one hand, there are circumstances where legal norms legitimately direct us to do something that the principles of practical rationality do not demand from us; and, on the other hand, far from being *subordinated* to the principles of practical rationality, on this view, legal norms are only conceptually *connected* with them. Accordingly, an advocate of capacity-constitutivism is in the position to recognize that the contents of legal norms may not coincide with the principles of practical rationality, to the effect that legal norms can make a difference in our practical deliberation. Relatedly, the outcome of one's practical reasoning, as it is carried out in compliance with legal standards, does not need to coincide with the outcome of one's reasoning, as it is shaped directly by practically rational principles.

From this it follows that capacity-constitutivism does not overestimate the resources of practical rationality. Practical rationality is acknowledged to perform an essential guidance function in the domain of action by setting out fundamental action-guiding principles. However, if practical rationality is taken in isolation from other practices and institutions programmatically meant to govern our conduct, such as legal norms and systems, it will turn out to lack the resources needed to offer comprehensive, specific, and far-reaching guidance in all circumstances. In fact, the principles of practical rationality are inherently abstract, partly indeterminate, and incomplete. Hence, they are typically inconclusive. The claims that practical rationality makes on us, thus, call for, and need to be fleshed out by, directives associated with other action-guiding enterprises, among which law (and its norms) figures prominently. Far from providing exhaustive direction, the principles of practical rationality do leave a significant number of issues open. And when we face issues that we cannot work out in any definite way on the sole basis of the principles of practical rationality, we can legitimately turn to the guidance of institutional practices and norms—inclusive of legal norms—that accordingly may go beyond the dictates of the bounds of practical rationality. Precisely for this reason, these other practices and norms, in carrying out their practical function, may issue recommendations and demands the contents of which do not map exactly onto the contents that one would extract from the principles of practical rationality.

In sum, the capacity-constitutivist view of practical reasons and action fits well with a discriminatory and non-instrumentalist conceptualization of legal norms, which are claimed to be fundamentally constrained by the principles of practical rationality and, thus, intrinsically valuable from a rational perspective.

References

Alexy, R. 2002. *A Theory of Constitutional Rights*. Oxford: Oxford University Press.

Baiasu, S. 2016. "Constitutivism and Transcendental Practical Philosophy: How to Pull the Rabbit Out of the Hat". *Philosophia* 44: 1185–1208.

Bertea, S. 2013. "Constitutivism and Normativity: A Qualified Defence". *Philosophical Explorations* 16: 81–95.

Bertea, S. 2017. "Why Practical Reasons Are Not Just One's Own Private Affair". *Philosophical Inquiry* 41: 63–85.

Bertea, S. 2023. "Is the Autonomy of the Will a Paradoxical idea?". *Synthese*, 201: 133–15.

Bobbio, N. 1958. *Teoria della norma giuridica*. Torino: Giappichelli.

Bratman, M. 1988. *Intentions, Plans and Practical Reason*. Cambridge, MA: Harvard University Press.

Bratman, M. 1999. *Faces of Intention*. Cambridge: Cambridge University Press.

Bratman, M. 2007. *Structures of Agency*. Oxford: Oxford University Press.

Bukoski, M. 2016. "A Critique of Smith's Constitutivism". *Ethics* 127: 116–146.

Buss, S. 1999. "What Practical Reasoning Must Be If We Act for Our Own Reasons". *Australasian Journal of Philosophy* 77: 399–421.

Dancy, J. 2004. *Ethics without Principles*. Oxford: Oxford University Press.

Dancy, J. 2009. "Reasons and Rationality". In *Spheres of Reasons*, edited by S. Robertson, 93–112. Oxford: Oxford University Press.

Darwall, S. 1995. *The British Moralists and the Internal Ought*. Cambridge: Cambridge University Press.

Davidson, D. 1980. *Essays on Actions and Events*. Oxford: Oxford University Press.

Enoch, D. 2020. "Constitutivism: On Rabbits, Hats, and Holy Grails". In *The Routledge Handbook of Practical Reason*, edited by R. Chang and K. Sylvan. London: Routledge.

Ferrero, L. 2009. 'Constitutivism and the Inescapability of Agency'. *Oxford Studies in Metaethics* 2: 303–333.

Ferrero, L. 2018. "Inescapability Revisited". *Manuscripto* 41: 113–158.

Ferrero, L. 2019. "The Simple Constitutivist Move". *Philosophical Explorations,* 22, 146-162

Gewirth, A. 1978. *Reason and Morality*. Chicago: University of Chicago Press.

Hage, J. 2022. "Rules and the Social World". *L'Ircocervo* 21: 16–35.

Hart, H. 1994. *The Concept of Law*. 2nd ed., with a Postscript. Oxford: Clarendon Press.

Katsafanas, P. 2013. *Agency and the Foundation of Ethics: Nietzschean Constitutivism.* Oxford: Oxford University Press.

Katsafanas, P. 2018. "Constitutivism about Practical Reason". In *Reasons and Normativity*, edited by D. Star, 367–391. Oxford: Oxford University Press.

Kelsen, H. 1945. *General Theory of Law and State.* Cambridge, MA: Harvard University Press.

Kelsen, H. 1967. *Pure Theory of Law.* Berkeley: University of California Press.

Korsgaard, C. 1996a. *Creating the Kingdom of Ends.* Cambridge: Cambridge University Press.

Korsgaard, C. 1996b. *The Sources of Normativity.* Cambridge: Cambridge University Press.

Korsgaard, C. 2008. *The Constitution of Agency.* Oxford: Oxford University Press.

Korsgaard, C. 2009. *Self-Constitution.* Oxford: Oxford University Press.

Lindeman, M. 2017. "Constitutivism without Normative Thresholds". *Journal of Ethics and Social Philosophy* 12: 231–258.

Lindeman, M. 2019a. "Functional Constitutivism's Misunderstood Resources: A Limited Defense of Smith's Constitutivism". *Ethics* 130: 79–91.

Lindeman, K. 2019b. "Legal Metanormativity". In *Dimensions of Normativity*, edited by D. Plunkett, S. Shapiro, and K. Toh, 87–104. Oxford: Oxford University Press.

Mayr, E. 2019. "Blame for Constitutivists: Kantian Constitutivism and the Victim's Special Standing to Complain". *Philosophical Explorations* 22: 117–129.

Millgram, E. 2020. "Practical Reason and the Structure of Actions". In The Stanford Encyclopedia of Philosophy, edited by Edward N. Zalta. 2020 Edition. http://plato.stanford.edu/archives/sum2009/entries/practical-reason-action/.

O'Hagan, E. 2014. "Shmagents, Realism and Constitutivism about Rational Norms". *The Journal of Value Inquiry* 48: 17–31.

O'Neil, O. 2001. "Consistency in Action". In *Varieties of Practical Reasoning*, edited by E. Millgram, 301–329. Cambridge, MA: MIT Press.

Paakkunainen, H. 2018. "Doing Away with the 'Shmagency' Objection to Constitutivism". *Manuscrito* 41: 431–480.

Parfit, D. 2011. *On What Matters.* Vol. 1. Oxford: Oxford University Press.

Paul, S. 2013. "The Conclusion of Practical Reasoning: The Shadow Between Idea and Act". *Canadian Journal od Philosophy* 43: 287–302.

Raz, J. 1970. *The Concept of a Legal System.* Oxford: Oxford University Press.

Raz, J. 1975. *Practical Reason and Norms.* London: Hutchinson.

Raz J. 1979. *The Authority of Law.* Oxford: Oxford University Press.

Raz, J. 1999. *Engaging Reason.* Oxford: Oxford University Press.

Raz, J. 2008. "Reasons: Explanatory and Normative". In *New Essays on the Explanation of Action*, edited by C. Sandis, 184–202. Houndmills: Palgrave.

Raz, J. 2011. *From Normativity to Responsibility.* Oxford: Oxford University Press.

Ross, A. 1958. *Directives and Norms.* London: Routledge.

Scanlon, T. 1998. *What We Owe to Each Other.* Cambridge: Harvard University Press.

Scanlon, T. 2014. *Being Realistic About Reasons.* Oxford: Oxford University Press.

Schapiro, T. 1999. "What Is a Child". *Ethics* 109: 715–738.

Schapiro, T. 2001. "Three Conceptions of Action in Moral Theory". *Nous* 35: 93–117.

Silverstein, M. 2012. "Inescapability and Normativity". *Journal of Ethics and Social Philosophy* 6: 1–26.

Silverstein, M. 2015. "The Shmagency Question". *Philosophical Studies* 172: 1127–1142.

Smith, M. 2013. "A Constitutivist Theory of Reasons: Its Promises and Parts". *Law, Ethics and Philosophy* 1: 9–30.

Smith, M. 2015. "The Magic of Constitutivism". *American Philosophy Quarterly* 52: 187–200.

Smith, M. 2017. "Constitutivism". In The Routledge Handbook of Metaethics, edited by Tristram McPherson and David Plunkett, 201–213. London: Routledge.

Street, S. 2012. "Coming to Terms with Contingency: Human Constructivism about Practical Reason". In *Constructivism in Practical Philosophy*, edited by J. Lenman and Y. Shemmer, 40–59. Oxford: Oxford University Press.

Thompson, M. 2008. *Life and Action*. Cambridge, MA: Harvard University Press.

Thomson, J. 2008. *Normativity*. Chicago: Open Court.

Velleman, D. 2000. *The Possibility of Practical Reason*. Oxford: Oxford University Press.

Velleman, D. 2009. *How We Get Along*. Cambridge: Cambridge University Press.

Vogler, C. 2002. *Reasonably Vicious*. Cambridge, MA: Harvard University Press.

Walden, K. 2012. "Laws of Nature, Laws of Freedom, and the Social Construction of Normativity". *Oxford Studies in Metaethics* 7: 37–79.

Walden, K. 2018. "Morality, Agency, and Other People". *Ergo* 5: 69–101.

8 The sanctioner's dilemma

The disruptive impact of a Kantian constitutivist approach

Carla Bagnoli

8.1. Introduction

Although Kant's philosophy has undoubtedly been a source of inspiration in international law and democratic peace theory, it is generally deemed too metaphysically burdensome and morally demanding to be of practical use in the theory and practice of international relations. In this chapter, I argue that the main reservations against the political significance of the Kantian approach can be set aside by focusing on a Kantian argument in support of moral obligations. This argument grounds moral obligations on the norms of rationality, which are taken to be binding insofar as they are constitutive of rational agency.[1] As opposed to other varieties of constitutivism, Kant's constitutivism relies on the capacity of reason to generate new incentives for action and, most importantly, to elicit a moral feeling of 'reverence for the law-making capacity of humanity'.[2] The role of reverence is crucial in explaining how human agents can act on principle even when it goes against their inclination or interest.[3] According to this perspective, while the norms of rationality define human rational agency, they can guide human action only if they hold normative sway over subjects. Thus, a particular type of moral sensibility explains the subjective normativity, that is, the bindingness of these norms in the exercise of rational agency.

To show the promise of the Kantian constitutivist approach to international relations, I consider its relevance in the case of the 'sanctioner's dilemma'. This dilemma arises when the costs of sanctioning a state for the violation of international law seem prohibitive, for instance when a state is strategically important and its absence would significantly undermine global cooperation, or when the proposed sanctions would have humanitarian consequences. This

1 These norms allow individuals to act with others and give rise to shared, organized, and institutional forms of rational agency; they also give us the framework for reciprocal justification and accountability. For a survey, see Katsfanas 2018. For Korsgaard, constitutivism is the only possible justificatory strategy in ethics; see Korsgaard 2009, 32.

2 See Bagnoli 2022 §1.

3 Kant C2 5:75.

DOI: 10.4324/9781032670553-9

case is generally analyzed in terms of cost–benefit and discussed against the background of strategic rationality. My contention is that the instrumentalist view fails to fully capture the nature of the dilemma. Instead, the constitutivist argument offers a deeper understanding of the dynamics of power and authority inherent in the sanctioner's dilemma and highlights some morally perplexing aspects of sanctions. The discussion brings to the fore the potentially disruptive impact of a Kantian constructivist approach in the field of international relations.

8.2 A Kantian approach to international relations?

International relations are largely understood in terms of strategic interactions, modelled on a Hobbesian rather than a Kantian framework.[4] According to this model, states are the primary political actors in international relations, and their decision-making shapes the landscape of international affairs. States are typically motivated by self-interest, which also sustains internal cohesion and grounds domestic justice. Consequently, they cooperate if and when it is in their interest to do so. Cooperation is rationally justified to the extent that self-interested states converge on a shared end to be pursued collectively (e.g., peace and security). This model entails minimal presuppositions about the rational powers of political actors and their willingness to cooperate and, therefore, it is economical in terms of both ontology and psychology. This is widely regarded as an advantage over the Kantian model, inasmuch as the latter relies on transcendental idealism, which is associated with questionable metaphysical assumptions.[5] Second, it is often objected that the Kantian model is question-begging because it tacitly relies on ethical or psychological altruism, which represents the power of reason as irresistible.[6] Such criticisms are not entirely unfounded. But they fail to consider the significance and implications of the constitutivist strategy, as it is reformulated in contemporary metaethics. Interestingly, this shortcoming also undermines recent commendable efforts to defend the Kantian approach to international relations.

Matthew Lindauer attributes the limited influence of Kantian thought to a disconnect between moral and political philosophy within the Kantian tradition in the field of international relations. In the attempt to provide a remedy, he appeals to Christine M. Korsgaard's moral constructivism. In his view, a renewed attention to Kant's moral writings and to Korsgaard's constructivism serves two purposes. First, it shows that the main features of a Kantian

4 See also Hurrell 1990, and Schlereth 1977, 124–125. On the influence of Kant's ideas on contemporary international relations and law, see Doyle 1983a, 1983b.

5 On the vulnerability of Kant's philosophy to the queerness objection, see Mackie 1977, cf. Bagnoli 2022.

6 See Sterba 2013, cf. Bagnoli 2014. On Kant's view, psychologically, humans are capable of altruism, but this is not a value, nor is it the driving element of morality, which is justified and structured by shared norms of rationality.

ethical theory can be preserved without any cumbersome metaphysics, thereby unseating the main assumptions underlying a general skepticism regarding the Kantian approach. Second, and more importantly for present purposes, attention to Kant's practical philosophy brings to the fore considerations that challenge the appeal of realism in international relations. Kant remarks that the stability of domestic societies depends on there being a solution to the problem of anarchy on the world stage, and that the only way to satisfactorily address this problem is to develop a law-governed relationship between states.[7] Domestic justice depends on international order. For without the latter, states would inexorably face international war, devastation, and upheaval until the 'complete exhaustion of their inner powers'.[8] By reclaiming Kant's moral and political philosophy, Lindauer allows us to reconstruct a strong argument in support of the subordination of domestic to international justice, which proves useful as a contrast and a challenge to dominant varieties of realism.

The appeal to Korsgaard's constructivism is crucial in addressing the objection that the Kantian approach is incompatible with a naturalistic ontology. However, Lindauer avails himself of the theoretical resources afforded by metaethical constructivism to only a very limited extent. In fact, his defence does not rely at all on the constitutivist argument outlined above. Rather, on his reconstruction, 'the self-interested motives of human beings progressively give way to moral motivations and expanding, just political institutions'.[9] This appeal to the progress of moral sentiments renders the Kantian approach vulnerable to the second objection, namely that it assumes, without argument or empirical support, that we have the capacity to develop a benign nature out of our unsociable sociability. The suspicion of question-begging is a decisive ground for seeking an alternative route. The constitutivist argument is a promising alternative. In the next sections, I argue that once the constitutivist argument is established, the alleged comparative advantages of realism are not obvious, and in the end, may be only apparent.

8.3 The appeal to Kantian constitutivism

There are two reasons for refocusing on a Kantian constitutivist strategy. The first is that the constitutivist argument is an indispensable element in a constructivist account of the efficacy and subjective authority of practical reasoning, as argued elsewhere.[10] The second is that the constitutivist argument may

7 'The problem of establishing a perfect civil constitution depends on the problem of law-governed external relations among nations and cannot be solved unless the latter is', Kant, AK 8:22–23; see also the claim that perpetual peace is 'the supreme political good', Kant, AK 6:355.

8 Kant, AK 8:22–23.

9 Lindauer 2018, 15–16.

10 Bagnoli 2021, 2022, §2.

have a far-reaching and disruptive impact in international relations. I cannot develop a comprehensive argument here, but I hope to show its potential.[11]

As opposed to the argument from the progress of moral sentiments, the constitutivist argument holds that norm compliance depends on the autonomy of practical reason rather than on any empirical considerations. To be autonomous, that is, self-governing, and self-authenticating,[12] reason must be governed by constitutive norms that explain its normativity from inside. Kant's distinctive conception of 'practical reason' requires humans to be able to act morally in the absence of incentives extraneous to morality. The authority of moral obligation does not rest on the psychological premise that rational agents are naturally altruistic or cooperative by default. The moral feeling of respect for the law-making capacity of humanity is the subjective condition of authority, representing morality as an incentive. This moral feeling is the mark of our capacity to act on moral principle.

Second, and consequently, the possibility of a basic agreement on what counts as a reason descends from the claim that rational agency is constituted by the exercise of rational norms. Thus, rational norms are not efficacious on the condition that they serve preestablished moral concerns fixed by nature, or the interests of individual subjects on particular occasions but rather because they are constitutive of their agency. If this is correct, then rational agents can be motivated to act cooperatively, to the extent that cooperation is prescribed by rational norms, even when compliance with such norms seems counter to self-interest. Ultimately, however, genuine self-interest must align with the prescriptions of the constitutive rational norms. That is because such norms set the framework for cooperative interactions as solutions to the individual problem of sustaining a struggle with others to have everybody's rights respected and enforced. This justification differs from the ones represented by altruism and egoism.

In the domain of individual rational agency, the purported merit of this argument is that it explains the normativity of moral obligations by showing that they are requirements of rationality that hold first-personal authority rather than via appeal to external sanctions and rewards.[13] Its intended result is to show that moral obligations are compelling rational requirements only to the extent that they rely on the moral incentive of respect.[14] The extension of this argument to international relations brings to the fore considerations that

11 This extension builds on the 'constitutional model', which draws an analogy between the constitution of the self and that of a polis (Korsgaard 2009, 134). However, I contend that the constitutivist argument fundamentally differs in both kind and scope from Korsgaard's method (1996), see Bagnoli 2022, §2, see O'Neill 2018.

12 O'Neill 1992, cf. Bagnoli 2022, §1.

13 On the advantages of the constructivist conception of normativity vis à vis accounts based on sanctions, see Bagnoli 2011; on Kant's argument regarding moral incentives, see Bagnoli 2021.

14 See, e.g., Bagnoli 2014.

have previously not been taken into account. The keystone is that reason has the power of producing new motives for action through a ranking of incentives.[15] Like the variety of constructivism rehearsed by Lindauer, its ontological commitments are minimal.[16] In contrast to Lindauer's argument, however, the constitutivist argument we are considering here does not invoke the progress of moral sentiments: in fact, the argument undercuts the very dichotomy between altruism/self-interest that drives the debate between realism and idealism in international relations. Thus, the constitutivist argument makes room for a Kantian approach that emphasizes the compelling role of international norms, interdependence, and cooperation among states.[17] The resulting view is morally constrained but pragmatic, and thus represents a viable alternative to both realist and social constructivist views of international relations.[18]

8.4 Further objections: agency, power, and authority

While constitutivism seems a promising step forward in the debate on the plausibility of the Kantian approach to international relations, it is itself a controversial theory. David Enoch has recently argued that the constitutivist argument fails to explain the normativity of reason because it presupposes an interest in being an agent, but it is not inconceivable to be content with being a 'shmagent'. The 'shmagency objection' has large currency in the domain of individual agency and retains some force against the more ambitious versions of Kantian constitutivism, despite a plethora of replies.[19] Interestingly, however, when transferred to the domain of international relations, the shmagency objection is moot: constituting themselves as self-governing agents is the primary interest of any state or putative political actor.[20] The problem is not whether political actors *want* to be self-governing agents; the question is how to contain this motivation so as to allow for a peaceful coexistence and cooperation with all others political actors. Therefore, the constitutivist argument may be especially rewarding when brought to the international arena.

However, the constitutivist argument is vulnerable to a further objection, which concerns not the presumptive normative powers of reasoning in

15 On self-constitution, see Korsgaard 2009, 188–206; for an alternative construal, see Bagnoli 2021. For a non-constructivist account of this claim, see Nagel 2005.

16 See Bagnoli 2022.

17 These features are generally associated with 'idealism' in international relations; see Wilson 2011.

18 On social constructivism, see Onuf 1989, Wendt 1992.

19 Enoch 2006; on the ensuing debate, see Bagnoli 2022, §2. This problem is directly related to the possibility of bad action in a constitutivist account; see Fitzpatrick 2013 and Prezas 2022.

20 The key feature in this case is the artificiality of agency. Modern and contemporary states seek stability over time. However, there might be kinds of states that aim at their own dissolution, e.g., when their constitutive purpose is achieved.

governing and constituting agency but rather the conditions in which practical reasoning is engaged. It is arguable that in non-ideal conditions, where power relations do not match relations of rational authority, the greatest normative influence on political actors' decisions comes from outside reason itself. If so, then considerations rooted in power relations count as genuine reasons, rather than being disruptions of reasoning to be dismissed. The sanctioner's dilemma is a case in point.

This is a common case in international relations and arises when the costs of sanctioning a state for a serious violation of international norms (e.g., for violating human rights) are too high. This case is generally analyzed in terms of strategic rationality. In fact, it can be considered the paradigmatic case in which the 'moral reasons' for sanctioning a state for transgressing an international standard (e.g., violating human rights) are outweighed by 'strategic' or 'prudential' reasons (the sanctioner's self-interest).

The task of the following sections is to show the theoretical and practical advantages of adopting a Kantian constitutivist analysis of the sanctioner's dilemma, which encompasses the moral dimension of the predicament and illuminates the broader issue of international law enforcement. Before embarking on this analysis, it is necessary to conduct a preliminary discussion of sanctions.

8.5 Sanctions as a normative practice

Sanctions may take various forms and apply to a state when and if it violates international norms of conduct.[21] Typically, sanctions are either economic (e.g., trade restrictions, asset freezes, or financial penalties) or diplomatic (e.g., the expulsion of diplomats or suspension of diplomatic relations), or they impose other forms of political isolation and exclusion from specific political roles, activities, networks, or organizations.[22] In some cases, sanctions are intended to restrict access to benefits earned by full participation in cooperative schemes.[23] For instance, in the case of the United Nations (UN), the

21 I define sanctions as normative responses applied in cases of a violation of a shared norm within a coalition. The Global Human Rights Sanctions Regimes, also known as 'Magnitsky sanctions', are designed to target perpetrators of severe human rights violations committed abroad. The United States was the first country to establish such a legal framework with the Global Magnitsky Human Rights Accountability Act in 2016. This framework has since been adopted by 35 countries worldwide, including the EU through decision (CFSP) 2020/1999 and regulation (EU) 2020/1998, and the UK through the Global Human Rights Sanctions Regulations in 2020. These acts encompass various restrictive measures targeting both natural and legal persons. It is arguable that the Magnitsky sanctions framework can contribute to the formation of customary international law on third-party countermeasures, see Jia 2023.

22 Hathaway and Shapiro (2011) introduce 'outcasting' as a novel form of international sanction. Like ostracism, this is an ancient practice of boundary negotiation, which often weaponizes moral attitudes, such as blame and shame; see Bagnoli 2021b.

23 I emphasize the centrality of the cooperative scheme, which I take to be implicit in, if not a constitutive rationale of, the sanction regime.

sanctions regime is meant for the promotion of international peace and security, but it is arguable that the cooperative scheme is more generally intended for the sake of the stability the UN, whose existence depends on peace and security.[24]

The pressure that sanctions exert depends on the specific roles, activities, networks, or organizations that are targeted. In some cases, the effects are largely reputational, calling attention to the unreliability of the target states in cooperative interactions. More generally, however, the expulsion or suspension of membership rights from an international organization has substantial consequences, far beyond a reputational cost: it changes the normative status of a member, its normative powers, and its authority within the coalition (see, e.g., Russia's expulsion from the Council of Europe).

Sanctions are largely understood to be non-violent, and as such, to be a tool of foreign policy to induce compliance.[25] They can be applied unilaterally or multilaterally.[26] The latter carry greater weight and have more impact than the former. By involving multiple countries or international bodies, multilateral sanctions signal a unified stance against the target and can exert more significant economic, political, and diplomatic pressure. Furthermore, multilateral sanctions are often perceived not only as more effective but also as more legitimate insofar as they reflect a consensus among a broader coalition of nations. This is the case when sanctions are decided or authorized by the Security Council under the Charter of the UN. The coordination required to sustain multilateral sanctions can be a challenging task, given that states differ in their interests, priorities, and policies. Consequently, a workable convergence may result from local compromises rather than being the expression of a 'rational agreement', that is, an agreement on shared reasons. In Section 8.8, I cast some doubts on the non-violent nature of sanctions, even when they are preferable to military interventions.[27]

24 See Ruys 2017, cf. Van Rooij and Daniel 2021.

25 Opinions vary regarding the classification of sanctions as 'diplomatic' interventions, depending on the specific types of sanctions involved. This categorization may extend to military sanctions, as argued by Charron (2011) and noted by Shapiro and Hathaway (2017) and Subedi (2021). I find it valuable to differentiate sanctions from military intervention, although both aim to address violations of norms enforced by international agreements. It is important to note that the mere threat of military intervention can act as a deterrent.

26 The distinction lies between sanctions imposed or authorized by the UN (which are multilateral by definition) and autonomous sanctions. Autonomous sanctions can be unilateral or multilateral when imposed by states belonging to the same region (e.g., the EU) or by states that share a similar worldview (e.g., Western states).

27 The argument concerns further normative characterizations of sanctions in relation to the purpose of the sanctioner and allows for the distinction between reactive and proactive sanctions, protective and aggressive sanctions, and other forms of sanctions. This normative taxonomy may be useful, even though the actual effects of sanctions may differ from those anticipated or designed by the sanctioner, and for strategic or non-strategic reasons that could not have been anticipated.

8.6 Justification, legitimacy, and effectiveness

In the context of international relations, the application of sanctions poses several philosophical issues, beginning with their *justification*. Questions arise about the *legitimacy* of using coercive measures to influence the behaviour of other states and the tension between state sovereignty and international intervention.[28] The imposition of sanctions on sovereign states potentially infringes upon the rights and autonomy of targeted populations. The fundamental postulate of liberal international theory holds that states have the right to be free from foreign intervention, and hence from external sanctions. In relation to the principle of state sovereignty, the primary concern is that transnational legal regimes may disrupt the existing international legal order. It seems to follow that sanctions may apply with *legitimacy* only when a state intentionally violates an agreement, which violation was known to be enforced by the imposition of sanctions. By consenting to the agreement, a state thereby commits to accepting sanctions in the event of any future violation, unless exceptional circumstances or cases of necessity arise. Arguably, then, when political actors fail their international obligations, for instance by violating a shared norm or by disregarding a shared timeline, sanctions appropriately apply.[29]

A second philosophical issue arises in consideration of constraints on the ways in which sanctions are applied. There are procedural requirements of warning (i.e., the state should be warned before being subjected to sanctions), proportionality (in relation to the violation performed, or the general purpose pursued), and compliance with non-derogable norms (e.g., prohibition of force, and torture). These constraints are legal, but they may rest on moral and political grounds. Although sanctions are morally permissible as a means of addressing perceived wrongdoings by states, they are subordinate to independent grounds of moral permissibility. Their moral permissibility depends on their consistency with principles of justice, fairness, and respect for human dignity. For instance, when striving for safety, there may be valuable information that can be obtained through coercion, but ethical considerations limit the methods by which truth can be acquired, and such limitations prevent truth from being extracted through force or violence. This is a specific instance of the kind of moral dilemmas that arise when the only means to achieve a

28 I define the wrongness of such coercive relations in Bagnoli 2023. I am not suggesting that all coercive measures are wrongful; in this case, the point of sanctions is to coercively enforce legitimate norms.

29 This claim may indicate a line of response to those who are skeptical regarding the normativity of international law in the absence of a central authority with the power to enforce its dictates. Insofar as the latter condition lacks, international law is merely a system of norms without true legal force. The possibility of sanctions agreed within an international coalition—but unilaterally or multilaterally administered, rather than collectively by a unified body—may be taken to show that international law can indeed be enforced, with legitimate authority, as Hathaway and Shapiro (2011) have argued. My worry regarding this interpretation is that it renders the normativity of law dependent on its efficacious enforcement.

seemingly positive outcome are morally reprehensible. Analogously, the use of sanctions that cause economic hardship or limit access to essential goods and services may affect vulnerable or marginalized groups within the targeted country in ways that legitimately raise humanitarian concerns. These moral considerations suggest that there should be moral constraints on the application of sanctions, independently of whether they are appropriate responses to violations. This argument gives priority to morality over politics in international relations.

This leads us to a separate but related issue concerning the effectiveness of norms and the efficacy of sanctions as modes of social, legal, and moral enforcement in foreign policy. The effectiveness of a norm is determined by the extent to which it is complied with. It can be argued that different types of sanctions may be expected to be effective to varying degrees in achieving their intended goals, namely, improving norm compliance. The question is whether, and to what extent, political actors represent themselves as bound by norms and agreements, for reasons independent of the shmagency objection regarding their nature as agents, and relative to the scope of the agreement or the external conditions of its enforcement. Precisely because political actors are supremely interested in and care about their status as self-constituting agents, on some occasions, they may decide that it is prudent to withdraw from or occasionally to violate an agreement.

8.7 The relational features of sanctions' efficacy

The efficacy of sanctions in improving norm compliance is circumstantial and depends on various relational factors, including (i) the capacity and power of the targeted state to bear the specific costs imposed by sanctions and to withstand or mitigate the effects of isolation; (ii) the power of the targeted state in the international community, which is often also perceived as a power of retaliation; (iii) the willingness of the states in the coalition to cooperate in imposing sanctions, which may reflect their respective standing in the community and/or different perceptions or assessments of the risk involved; (iv) the evaluation of the effectiveness of other complementary diplomatic strategies—such as positive incentives, third-party mediation, nudging, and coercive pressure—to address the relevant international disputes and to promote adherence to international law and norms; (v) the assessment of the legitimacy of the norms being enforced, which may depend only partially on well-grounded reasons regarding the compliance of actual policy-making with international law norms and procedures; (vi) e willingness and capacity of the state to impose the costs of sanctions (or let the costs fall) on some subset of its population; and (vii) the availability of other, alternative partners.

8.8 The aims and rationales of sanctions

The acknowledged aim of sanctions is twofold: (1) to impose costs on offending states for their behaviour, and (2) to pressure them into conforming to international standards of conduct shared by the coalition in which they belong. Presumably, conformity is functional to cooperative interactions, which are the core drivers of the international community, if not its constitutive aim. However, different rationales may exist behind the application of sanctions.

First, sanctions may be imposed as a *punishment* for violation, which reacts to the breach of an agreement or custom. In such cases, sanctions are backward-looking and address the transgressor; their meaning is punitive and retaliatory. Punishment meaningfully applies to partners in cooperative interactions and typically carries a symbolic significance, beyond its tangible effects.[30] That is, in addition to the material costs, sanctions *express and signal disapproval* of the government of the target state, with domestic political effects (Grauvogel, Licht, & von Soest 2017). This is also a *communicative* act, which translates into a reputational cost that alters cooperative schemes. In most cases, the sanctions have *normative effects* equivalent to losing privileges and entitlements associated with membership of an institution or a position of power (e.g., the case of Russia's exclusion from the EU Council). The delegitimating effects of the normative change that sanctions impose are broad and may extend beyond the loss in status. Being subjected to sanctions may determine dramatic changes in the economy of credibility, inflicting a drastic loss of bargaining power within the coalition. Internally, this may translate into a corresponding fear of being excluded from cooperative interactions as an unreliable partner. Punishment highlights the breach of trust that has occurred, while also reminding participants in the relevant cooperative interactions of their mutual dependence and reliance.[31]

Relatedly, sanctions aim at a broader audience beyond the targeted violator when they operate as *deterrents*. They can be adopted as a means to

30 Empirical research shows that cases in which punishment is applied even though it is costly for the punisher and yields no material gains are common. This phenomenon is known as 'altruistic punishment' and is considered a key mechanism in cooperative interactions, where it targets defection. Fehr and Gachter (2002) argue for a strict correlation: cooperation flourishes if altruistic punishment is possible and breaks down if it is ruled out. This research considers negative emotions towards defectors as the proximate mechanism behind altruistic punishment. It may be useful to compare this research programme on negative emotions in altruistic punishment with the philosophical discussion concerning the category of 'reactive attitudes' defined by Strawson (1962). On the punitive and offensive functions of reactive attitudes as elements of larger mechanisms of boundaries negotiation, see Bagnoli 2021b.

31 It is often the case that international sanctions are intended to exert pressure on the targeted government by signalling support for the opposition. Based on qualitative evidence, Grauvogel, Licht, and von Soest (2017) argue that sanctions work as international certifications of approval for the opposition internal to targeted regimes and encourage collective action against them.

discourage further future deviations from all other partners in the coalition by singling out the violator as a negative exemplar and underscoring the costs imposed by the sanctions. In this way, sanctions may be adopted as a *proactive* practice to encourage compliance with established norms and to reinforce the sense of international community. On this construal, they are instrumental to the deterrence of non-compliance, to the prevention of conflict, to improving diplomatic relations, and to the consolidation of a sense of global community. The effectiveness of sanctions under this rationale is less obvious and more difficult to prove retrospectively, given the complexity of the factors involved. Nonetheless, the forward-looking or proactive intended effect of sanctions remains a crucial rationale in their justification. In general, sanctions are identified as a means of enforcing the norms that underpin the international coalition.

8.9 The sanctioner's dilemma: four scenarios

In a typical scenario, the international coalition faces a hard choice regarding whether to impose sanctions against another state for a serious breach, such as the violation of human rights. This presents a moral dilemma, because it involves morally grounded considerations. To provide a clearer illustration, a more specific example may be helpful. In one scenario, the offending state is strategically important in terms of its standing and credibility in the coalition, its natural resources, economic influence, or geopolitical position. The prospect of imposing sanctions or isolating the offending state could have negative repercussions for the individual sanctioner (A), or more generally for global cooperation, trade, or security arrangements (B). Importantly, these dilemmas arise because political agents do not have the same normative powers, and this is because they do not have equal standing in the coalition.

In another scenario, the sanctions that would be most effective against the offending state would have heavy humanitarian consequences for its population, potentially leading to famine (C), or exacerbating domestic tensions that may also have repercussions beyond the borders of the offending state (D). In the former case, the coalition faces a dilemma whereby it must weigh the moral imperative to address human rights abuses against the potential costs and risks of taking a punitive action that undermines the coalition itself and may trigger retaliatory effects. In the latter case, the conflict arises because the alternative options fall under the same humanitarian moral principle, but their implementation is mutually exclusive. The morally perplexing feature of both these cases is that the effectiveness and the normative significance of the sanctions are compromised by the high profile of the offending state.

It may happen that political actors decide to apply sanctions despite their negative effects, in cases such as A and B. Empirical social psychology mentions the phenomenon of 'altruistic punishment', which names cases in which the sanctioner applies sanctions even though the effects of the application would be negative for the sanctioner. Fehr and Gachter (2002) argue that cooperation flourishes if 'altruistic' punishment is possible and breaks down if it is ruled out. However, this hypothesis does not have any predictive power in international relations, where altruistic punishment is not the norm. Some varieties of the dilemma can be mitigated by constraints that restrict the scope of sanctions (e.g., by recognizing the priority of the protection of humanitarian interests in the context of sanctions regimes). For instance, Resolution No. 2664 (2022) of The United Nations Security Council introduces a humanitarian carve-out to almost all asset-freezing sanctions, exempting humanitarian operations from the scope of application of UN resolutions, which represents a crucial development in the UN's effort to protect human rights.[32] However, the implementation of targeted sanctions is problematic because the activities of targeted individuals or groups and legitimate humanitarian actors often overlap from a financial standpoint. The effectiveness and legitimacy of the carve-out largely depend on the specifics of its implementation.

8.10 The standard approach

The standard description of this case borrows the language of cost–benefit analysis: it is a dilemma that arises when the potential costs of sanctioning the offending country are deemed too high in comparison with its expected benefits. All varieties of the sanctioner's dilemma seem to underscore the complex trade-offs and tensions involved in international relations, where states must navigate between moral principles and pragmatic considerations. The pervasiveness of such dilemmas by itself discourages the adoption of rigorist policy and suggests that coalition leaders should engage in a careful cost–benefit analysis, and perhaps search for reasonable compromises.[33]

It is possible, if the analysis is sufficiently careful, that dilemmas can be explained away. The resolution should be the option that causes less global disruption in the former case and less domestic damage in the latter case. The moral characterization of such disruption requires the adoption of a normative theory. For instance, utilitarian theory would recommend a choice that maximizes utility or at least minimizes the disutility, based on the assessment of outcomes. The realist approach may easily appropriate the utilitarian calculation or the cost–benefit analysis to assess the potential costs and benefits in terms of geopolitical dynamics, strategic alliances, and national security interests. This combination often presents itself as the only viable course of action. However, there are difficulties regarding this methodology that should discourage anyone from taking it as a solution.

32 The issue of the adverse effects of sanctions was addressed at meeting number 8962 of the Security Council, 7 February 2022; see Seatzu and Vargiu 2023.

33 As I explain later, this is a difficulty also for some varieties of constitutivism; see, e.g., Korsgaard 2009, and cf. Fitzpatrick 2013.

8.11 Two reasons for rejecting the cost–benefit analysis

There are two major problems with the cost–benefit analogy. First, it is difficult to measure the impact of sanctions and thus to determine exactly its costs and benefits. The problem is partly generated by substantial disagreements regarding the kind of measurement, but also regarding the very objects of measuring.[34] For instance, scholars tend to interpret the absence of observable change in target behavior as a lack of efficacy, but there are kinds of normative changes that cannot be tracked from the outside and that thus require a different kind of qualitative exploration. Some of these normative changes emerge slowly in time and would require a dynamic analysis. Thus, the prevalent use of static data from existing sanctions databases reduces the ability of researchers to study various time-specific factors affecting the probability of success in the application of sanctions. These methodological habits greatly undermine our understanding of the phenomena of enforcement and compliance.

Second, cost–benefit analysis underappreciates the moral significance of the sanctioner's predicament and explains away its dilemmatic appearance. This is particularly important in cases A and B, which originate in power asymmetries. The objection is twofold. On the one hand, a method that fails to capture the moral significance of choice is phenomenologically inapt: it fails an important descriptive goal of any plausible scientific explanation. On the other hand, the objection is normative: a method that eludes the moral dimension of rational choice obscures the normative effects of sanctions. It suggests that sanctions should be considered morally legitimate only if the costs are not expected to be too high. In Section 8.5, I noted that the effectiveness of sanctions is contextual and heavily dependent on the profiles of the states that form the coalition, the profile of the targeted state, and other circumstantial factors. If the moral legitimacy of sanctions is understood to be a function of their efficacy or effectiveness, then the very existence of this dilemma proves that the application of sanctions is illegitimate in such cases. But is there any reason to take the sanctioner's moral perplexity seriously? The cost–benefit analysis misdescribes the very nature of the sanctioner's dilemma.

8.12 Sanction under coercive threat

The moral predicament of the sanctioner's choice in A and B can be elucidated by noticing that its structure is analogous to dilemmas under conditional threats. In such dilemmas, an agent is asked to condone something

34 See Peksen 2019, for further details. As noted by Peksen (2019), studying sanctions in isolation from other instruments offers only a partial understanding of their specific role in shaping the foreign policy landscape. Aaken and Simsek (2021) emphasize the concept of rewarding as an under-theorized mechanism for encouraging compliance, providing an alternative to sanctions. However, measuring and assessing the impact of rewards faces similar difficulties to those encountered when evaluating sanctions.

immoral under threat of a worse scenario that his refusal to submit to the coercer will produce. These scenarios are triggered by complex dynamics in which the coercive power of conditional threat opposes legitimate authority. The cost–benefit approach fails to consider that the agent is making his decision under a conditional threat of coercion, which undermines the normative status and whose normative significance does not easily translate in terms of performative outcomes. Coercion is impactful but the nature and complexity of its impact is such that it eludes the reductive language of costs and benefits unless the coercive challenge to the sanctioner's normative standing results in an outward performance.

The focus on performance coheres with the instrumentalist bent of the cost–benefit analysis but leads to the following paradoxical result. If the retaliatory conduct of the targeted offending state is expected to be sufficiently strong to outbalance the positive effects of the application of sanctions, then, on the instrumentalist account, the coalition has compelling instrumental *and* moral reasons not to impose sanctions on the offender. This is to say that the coalition is both instrumentally and morally obligated to comply with the conditional threats of the offending state. The utilitarian calculation thus fails to recognize that the proposed solution to the dilemma is a submissive action under a conditional threat of coercion, by which the coalition renounces its normative and agential authority, as it acts on reasons that are imposed by the offending state. The unacknowledged normative element of this scenario is that when the coalition is overpowered via conditional coercive threats, its decisions no longer fully represent or express the free exercise of its normative agency. On this construal, the dilemma does not originate in a trade-off between costs and benefits, but it presents a threat to the colation's agential, ethical and political authority.

The constitutivist strategy enables us to acknowledge that if a state bypasses or blatantly violates the constitutional procedures in the pursuit of its own (non genuine) interest, it coerces all others into acquiescence. It is that state that rules, and not the coalition, and it rules by violence. This characterization of the sanctioner's moral predicament in deliberating under coercive threat is more perceptive and perspicuous than the instrumentalist. In fact, combined with the instrumentalist approach to practical reasoning, the cost–benefit analysis leads to a dangerous conflation of brute power with the normative authority of the parties involved. The moral significance of rational choice under conditional threat cannot be fully understood in terms of strategic and instrumental principles. Arguably, the constitutivist account of the sanctioner's dilemma also fits better with the moral phenomenology of deliberating over sanctions under coercive threat, but its advantages are not restricted to the phenomenology of hard choice. The main lesson is that to fully understand and capture the impact of international sanctions, we must refocus on the moral significance of the sanctioner's choice.

In this perspective, the moral reasons why coercion by conditional threat is wrong in interpersonal relations extend *mutatis mutandis* to international relations. This statement concurs with Lindauer's general argument in favor of the Kantian approach and adds pressure to the realist approach to international relations but does not rely on altruism.[35] The Kantian approach to the sanctioner's dilemma shows identifies a variety of coercion that does not simply block or bypass the agent's deliberative powers but rather exploits them.

8.13 Moral concerns and instrumental considerations

It may seem that the sanctioner's dilemma exposes a tension internal to practical rationality itself: the import of non-strategic moral concerns, such as the duty to defend human rights, is pitted against the import of strategic and pragmatic considerations, which are routinely set aside. In the first variety of the predicament, strategic considerations are intuitively and pragmatically compelling. In the second variety of the dilemma, the sanctioner is in a bind because moral concerns are non-negotiable;[36] thus, the dilemma is not solvable through rational means. Cost–benefit analyses may seem to be the only remedy, because they treat such dilemmas as spurious and resolvable by calculation—at least in principle. In Section 8.8, I have presented two reasons to think that this may not be a decisive advantage. In this section, I shall explain how the Kantian approach compares on this issue.

A current argument in the constructivist literature is that the principle of instrumental rationality does not stand by itself.[37] Its normativity—that is, its normative and subjective authority on rational agency—depends on the non-instrumental principle of rationality, which is warranted by the fundamental norm of the categorical imperative. The categorical imperative is fundamental in the distinctive sense that it articulates the stance of rational agency. The principle of instrumental reason is also a constitutive principle of agency, but its normative authority depends on the more basic authority of the non-instrumental principle of rationality.[38] The categorical imperative commits itself to its realization in practical action and thus includes prescriptions about the means to achieve the end. Therefore, the principle of instrumental reason cannot be separated from the categorical imperative. It is best understood as an aspect of the categorical imperative that warrants its efficacy. Ultimately, there is only one principle of practical reason: the categorical imperative. If this argument is correct, then the constitutivist variety of Kantian constructivism sidesteps the shortcomings of the deontologist and rigorist interpretations of Kant's ethics.

35 See also Rudall 2020.

36 Correspondingly, juridical obligations to protect fundamental rights and human dignity are 'absolute': non-negotiable, inalienable, and irrevocable.

37 I take Kantian constructivism to rely on the constitutivist argument; see Bagnoli 2022. On the dependence of the principle of instrumental rationality on the principle of non-instrumental rationality see O'Neill 1989, 73–74; and Korsgaard 2009, xii, chapter 3; Bagnoli 2022, 29ff.

38 For a crisp formulation of this principle, see Korsgaard 2009, 67–68, 92.

Applying this approach to the moral dilemma faced by the sanctioner brings into sharp relief that the pragmatic considerations, which clash with the moral considerations, should be justified by the same principles of rational agency. These considerations do not track independent and separate sources of reasons. By appealing to the constitutive norm of rational agency, the decision-maker can reconcile both horns of the dilemma and formulate a proper maxim of action. This action will be ultimately justified by the categorical imperative, which makes sense of both strategic and non-instrumental grounds.

8.14 Too quick?

The solution presented in the previous section may seem hasty, seriously downplaying the sanctioner's predicament, albeit for reasons different from those discussed in regard to the cost–benefit analysis in Section 8.11.[39] The appeal to compelling constitutive norms of rationality makes the appeal to sanctions unnecessary. If moral obligations are rational requirements, and ultimately justified by norms that exert normative authority over humans as agents, why do they need to be implemented by sanctions at all? This question is relevant for two reasons. First, it calls into play the distinction between rational agents as such, and human rational agents, who are 'animals endowed with reason'. Kantian constitutivism is frequently defended in the abstract, thereby obscuring the complications presented by human embodiment and finitude, social embeddedness, and interdependence, all of which are constitutive aspects of the human condition. Second, it calls for a clarification regarding the role of enforcement. Kant argues that duties of right are enforceable by an omnilateral will but their normativity is not derived from their enforceability by sanctions. The discussion of these two points provides an opportunity to highlight further aspects of its relevance for—and its potentially disruptive impact on—international relations.

Regarding the first point, I have argued that Kant's theory of practical reasoning should be interpreted as a variety of embodied and embedded constitutivism.[40] This interpretation highlights its distinctive merits as a theory of meta-normativity, which acknowledges norms of rationality as constitutive

39 See note 6 for some alleged difficulties of the constitutivist model. Some of these difficulties may stem from an ambiguity that requires resolution: is this model individualist, extended to the political dimension? Or is it a political model extended to the individual? The differences between accepting and inflicting sanctions can be seen as morally significant within a constitutivist account, given the various ways of exercising rational agency. Acquiescing under coercive threat may hold symbolic significance and emotional resonance beyond observable material consequences, making them difficult to calculate, especially over time. However, a significant division among Kantian constitutivists concerns whether it is possible to be a rational agent without being autonomous: some argue that it is possible, whereas others argue that it is not. The former view is associated with Kant, and the latter with Korsgaard (2003, 2009).

40 Bagnoli 2022, cf. Rodriguez-Blanco 2011, and Bagnoli forthcoming.

aspects of human agency. They represent the bare structure of rational agency, which is practised in context by embodied, interdependent, and mutually vulnerable agents. This exercise involves practical reasoning and typically begins by considering the 'circumstances of justice' in which human agents operate. These circumstances should include the fact that agents are finite, interdependent, and mutually vulnerable rational beings with equal moral standing who must deal with scarce resources. According to this perspective, justice is not a tool for remedying the inevitable power struggles that arise in the face of scarcity. More importantly, the point of the concept of justice is to regulate the relationships between rational agents who have equal normative standing and authority.

This brings us to the second point. In respectful relationships between agents of equal normative standing, each agent can unilaterally act in a way that binds everyone else. However, the bond is genuine only when the authorization is public. With some simplification, we can affirm that the categorical imperative gives the form of such public authorization.[41] Such a structure allows agents engaged in such reasoning to respect each other as having equal normative standing. This is a moral obligation, but it is also a rational requirement. The constitutivist argument demonstrates that these obligations are *direct*—they apply to all rational agents simply by virtue of their rational capacity and address each of them for the same reason. They are authoritative prior to and independently of any intermediary institution, although their enforcement can be institutionalized. This claim represents a challenge to many positions held in international relations. Typically, sanctions are understood to address governments. In contrast, the constitutivist argument reminds us that

41 In this case, it is appropriate to understand the form as a 'procedure' (Rawls 1980, Bagnoli 2022). Ripstein refers to 'omnilateral' authorization (Ripstein 2009, 157). I prefer the term 'public' authorization over 'omnilateral' because it implies a richer condition that the law aims to establish: the creation of a commonwealth of shared ends (Bagnoli 2021). 'Omnilateral' authorization suggests a more modest equitable and enforceable agreement, possibly based on self-interest—for example, where all count as one and no more than one. Cooperative interactions can be strategically justified as a form of coordination with individual payoffs distributed over time and can be the focus of an agreement based on everyone's interest, rather than solely driven by concern for collective interest or coalition stability. Ripstein remarks that the categorical imperative plays a role analogous to L.H.A. Hart's norm of recognition (Ripstein 2009, 157). Although there may be some overlap between legal positivism and certain forms of constitutivism, Hart's conception of law primarily emphasizes the social and institutional dimensions of legal systems, rather than grounding legal authority in constitutive moral or rational principles. Unlike the rule of recognition, however, the norm constitutive of rationality is not itself socially constructed and cannot be evaded or avoided by humans, insofar as they are rational. This is the specific sense in which the normativity of rational agency is inescapable, although its norms can be violated. This is a contestable claim (Enoch 2006; Bagnoli 2022). See also the debate on the constitutive role of the concept of rule as 'practice', which attributes functional statuses, as identified by Rawls (1955). An analogous issue concerns the source of normativity of law, which I cannot discuss in this chapter, but see Plunkett and Schapiro 2017.

the actual target of sanctions are their citizens—human beings—who posit constraints that one cannot trespass while preserving one's moral legitimacy.

8.15 Enforcement by mutual constraints

A widespread approach in international relations relates the need for sanctions to the possibility and unfortunate pervasiveness of violations.[42] Kant provides a perspective on the moral and political significance of sanctions that differs radically from the dominant understanding, presenting an argument that is entirely a priori. Insofar as obligations towards humanity are moral and thus (based on the constitutive argument) rational requirements, then their normative authority does not reside in sanctions but rather in their constitutive relations to agency. This does not imply that they can function without enforcement. On the contrary, enforceability is their defining feature as juridical obligations. However, according to Kant's view, enforceability of obligations to humanity is distinct from the application of sanctions. Enforcement is a constitutive element of the concept of right, although its modes may vary, especially in consideration of the international contex.[43]

The dialectic of private attitudes towards public rules refers to the dynamic of power and authority. Individual rational agents have the agential normative power to press claims (unilaterally), but such claims gain normative authority only through public authorization (i.e., by bringing them under a law). Mutual constraints are not reducible to sanctions because their significance does not reduce to a corrective or backward-looking remedial function that applies in the aftermath of moral transgression. Rather, sanctions belong to the conceptual elucidation of the meaning of right, understood as a system of mutual constraints that protect freedom. This argument points to a broader justification of international law in terms of cooperative interactions under universal law, which protects the freedom of each and all by mutual constraints. For agents thus constituted, violating mutual constraints imposed by right is possible but self-defeating: violation defeats the constitutive purpose of interdependent and mutually vulnerable agents. The result also depends on the self in question, but in the case of traditional states, the result of violation is disaggregating.

Because of its underlying a priori argument, the Kantian account of enforcement thus sketched sharply departs from tradition and from current practice in international relations. It concerns the very concept of right, rather than any empirical considerations. In contrast to the Hobbesian view, the argument is

42 Arguably, this is an approach that extends an argument that is current in criminal law to international law.

43 Kant, *Perpetual Peace: A Philosophical Sketch* (1795): 'Second Definitive Article for Perpetual Peace' or 'Second Definitive Article: The Federation of Free States'. This passage seems also to refer to an empirical argument, but it should be interpreted in light of Kant's pragmatic anthropology.

not strategic. Rather, it shows right to be essential to the constitution of interdependent, embodied, and socially embedded rational agents. The Kantian argument, which is based on the protection of individual freedom, provides us with strong grounds for condemning violations of human rights, including those caused by the application of sanctions. More importantly, it does not rely on sanctions to demonstrate that international law is normative and authoritative. Rather, it encourages us to search ways to enforce international law without appealing to external sanctions.

8.16 Sanctions as a political exercise of power

The preceding section may be subject to criticism from various perspectives within the broader debate. It stands in contrast to the prevailing norms of international relations, as the imposition of sanctions represents a shared approach to influencing the course of global events and is regarded as a non-violent diplomatic instrument, in contrast to military intervention. Applying sanctions is often thought to be the primary means of enforcing international law. This tendency reflects a traditional critique of international law, which has been described as ineffective and therefore not 'real law'. One prominent response has it that international laws are enforced through the implementation of economic measures and the practice of outcasting, which exclude violators from the cooperative benefits derived from participation in a coalition. Such sanctions modify the equilibrium of cooperative interactions. In certain instances, these sanctions may also indirectly affect the party imposing them. In such cases, Hathaway and Shapiro posit the necessity for the provision of incentives to sanctioners to encourage the application of sanctions. Do sanctioners need additional reasons to apply sanctions when required? Make sanctions mandatory, Hathaway and Shapiro advise.[44]

The literature on the effects of sanctions indicates that the moral predicament of the sanctioners may not be rooted in the worry to run a risk that undermines their own interest. A serious worry is the stability of the coalition, and more deeply, the humanitarian effects of the application of sanctions. On the one hand, sanctions can indirectly affect the political landscape by mobilizing collective action against governments in favour of human rights enforcement,[45] although they do not fully explain nor warrant compliance.[46] On the other hand, sanctions may have a detrimental impact and cause severe humanitarian predicaments.[47] In the latter case, making sanctions with multilateral requirements aggravates, rather than helps, the situation.[48]

44 Hathaway and Shapiro 2011, 320ff, cf. 311.
45 Grauvogel, Licht, and von Soest 2017.
46 Van Aaken and Simsek 2021.
47 Peksen 2019; Kwaku Afesorgbor and Renuka Mahadevan 2016; Choi and Luo 2013.
48 For a critical review of the literature of the effectiveness of sanctions, see Peksen 2019.

This empirical evidence calls for a reconsideration of the political meaning of sanctions, including the various forms of exclusion and outcasting. First, their status as a diplomatic means can be called into question. Although sanctions apply without the use of military force, they are themselves modes of exercising power and can be considered violent, given their effects. This is true both of economic sanctions and of practices of outcasting, both of which aim at excluding the target countries from cooperative benefits earned through participation in a given coalition. The threat of exclusion may have domestic humanitarian consequences as heavy as direct economic sanctions. In the face of a documented negative impact on the population, this categorization is highly questionable.

Second, the application of sanctions can be used offensively, not just defensively, with the sole intention of responding to an ascertained violation. In fact, sanctions are often employed as a violent instrument of domination. One method of monitoring this is by paying attention to the temporal scope of their application. The temporality of sanctions affects both their effectiveness and their legitimacy. Their effectiveness is largely dependent on their timing: the application of sanctions on a multilateral basis over an extended period of time increases their effectiveness. However, the legitimacy of sanctions is also strictly related to their temporality and does not co-vary with their effectiveness. For instance, sanctions may be justified as an immediate defensive reaction against a terrorist attack. However, prolonging sanctions disproportionately becomes a powerful mode of aggression. It is therefore clear that the temporal extension of sanctions should be regarded as a criterion for assessing them as a proportionate response to a violation.[49]

In addition to the issue of proportionality, other considerations suggest that the temporality of the application of sanctions is a matter of significant legal and political sensitivity. A state imposing sanctions may be willing to do so more promptly if it is individually advantageous for it to do so. It may be reluctant to abide by a collective decision to apply multilateral sanctions depending on a calculation of risks that an application would produce a negative impact on its economy or politics. Consequently, sanctions can be readily transformed from a means of enforcement into a means of exerting political power by force. It is therefore evident that the aforementioned sanctions are not, in fact, non-violent modes of exerting political authority. Sanctions can be harsh methods of exerting power over the target country and of altering the dynamics within the coalition, which may not be perceived as legitimate.

49 The criterion can be finessed further. Grauvogel and von Soest (2020) argue that sanctions' termination can be disaggregated by means of the target's compliance and the sanctioner's capitulation, with the determinants of both outcomes significantly diverging. This study shows that poor economic health and high political volatility in the target country make it significantly more likely to comply, whereas political alignment between the sanctioner and target, as well as leadership changes in the sanctioner's country, lead to a higher probability of the sanctioner's capitulation.

8.17 The empowering approach

When transposed to the international domain, the Kantian constitutivist argument acknowledges the deeper role of the constitutive norms of rationality.[50] These norms play a crucial role in the justification of a conception of justice, rather than merely in its implementation. This is evidenced by the key role of their constitution of institutions and practices. This claim also challenges a general assumption underlying contemporary theories of rational choice regarding the incentivizing effects of rewards and penalties. The primary advantage of this approach is that it preserves the independence of the dimension of normative legitimacy from the dimension of effectiveness. This is achieved by making enforcement internal and constitutive to a broader moral and political project, namely the protection of individual freedom. Nevertheless, this particular feature may give rise to concerns regarding its implementation.

In conclusion, I present a few practical considerations. The Kantian argument is characterized by a forward-looking orientation and a focus on future deliberation. From the standpoint of a policymaker, the effectiveness of this approach is primarily evident in the context of envisioning new political relations. In contrast, from the perspective of a sanctioner, the efficacy of this approach is more evident in the context of determining whether and how to respond to a violation. The use of sanctions is justified when the impairment of international relations is beyond remedy. The fundamental Kantian recommendation is that the sanctioner should conceptualize themselves as a policymaker dedicated to a shared cooperative plan of safeguarding and advancing freedom. From this perspective, the focus is on fostering renewed diplomatic engagement and strengthening social and political networks, rather than on isolating the defector. The objective of these activities is to foster awareness of interdependence and shared responsibility towards one another and towards those who suffer the consequences of human decisions. Within such a large cooperative scheme, violations not only carry unbearable reputational costs but are also destabilizing and ultimately self-defeating.

8.18 Conclusion: beyond mutual constraints

The constitutivist argument is key to Kant's account of the kind of enforcement distinctive of obligations to humanity, which are moral and yet enforceable. Kant's argument for their enforceability is entirely a priori and does

50 The constitutivist argument can be integrated with the so-called 'institutionalist' view; see, e.g., Rawls 1993: 262, 1980: 305–306 and 322–330; Beitz 1999; Wenar 2001; Nagel 2005: 119–122. A practice, in Rawls's sense is 'any form of activity specified by a system of rules which defines offices, roles, moves, penalties, defenses, and so on, and which gives the activity its structure'; see Rawls 1955/1999, 20. Insofar as its structure is provided by the norms of rationality, the institutionalist view may appropriate the Kantian constitutivist argument. On the definition of the 'institutionalist' in contrast to 'culturalist' views, see Sangiovanni 2008.

not rest on the fear of defection, nor on the urge of punishing an infraction. Obligations to respect human rights are moral insofar as they are grounded on the value of humanity and are thus absolute. As duties of right, they *are* enforceable, but they are not authoritative *because* they are enforceable. Their normative (juridical and moral) authority rests on practical reason. They are compelling on grounds prior to and independent of their external enforcement. The latter conclusion follows from Kant's constitutivist argument. I have argued that renouncing it would diminish the significance and feasibility of a Kantian approach to international relations.

These considerations should counter concerns regarding Kant's claim that the enforceability of juridical duties is the distinguishing feature of a legal system, which appears to be overly restrictive and insufficient in explaining the normativity of duties owed to humanity. Paradoxically, the emphasis on the enforceability of moral obligations is often seen to discount the possibility that moral principles can guide human agency in the absence of legal enforcement, thereby exposing a lack of genuine authority. Critics object that Kant's account of the system of equal freedom in terms of reciprocal constraints is insufficient to address positive obligations to promote justice, equality, and the common good.[51] In response to this concern, constitutivism should acknowledge the dimension of embodiment and embeddedness that characterizes the human condition. This is the key to recognizing that the notion of duty of right does not only help to negotiate boundaries but rather evidences the mutual interdependence of political actors and identifies fair modes of shared interactions that expand individual agency and are mutually enhancing.[52]

51 For all of these critiques and a thorough explanation and sustained defence of Kant's system of rights, see Ripstein 2009.

52 See Bagnoli 2022, 2023. In conversation, Zylberman objected that the distinction between duties of right and duties of virtue is lost. However, duties of right are also (in my view, indubitably), moral duties, although they admit of external enforcement. The possibility of external enforcement does not entail that they are not also moral; it entails only that they can be fulfilled by mere external compliance, in which case the right action does not have moral worth. To explain the double nature of the duties of right, juridical and ethical, we should look at their grounding and thus at the relation between the Categorical Imperative and the Principle of Right. This relation is underappreciated by taking the line pursued by Ripstein (2009) whose driving idea is that the domain of right is modelled on a spatial understanding of embodiment. It seems to me that it is limiting and reductive to take embodiment and finitude solely in terms of spatial incompatibility. There are other features that Kant seems to acknowledge as specifications of embodiment, although not reducible to it, such as interdependence, for instance. Interdependence—with its root in animality and its expansion through humanity—seems to me the key to uncovering specific vulnerabilities and, thus identify specific wrongs. At the same time, interdependence can be transformed by reasoning into a strength, that is, the capacity for rational shared agency. The constitutivist argument vindicates the relation between the principle of right and the categorical imperative, understood as the constitutive norm of reason; the embodied variety of constitutivism is best suited to highlighting the faceted significance of interdependence; see Bagnoli forthcoming.

Acknowledgements

An abridged version of this chapter was presented at the international conference 'What kind of constitutivism' at the University of Erlangen, and at the Department of Philosophy at the University of Amsterdam, in 2024. I would like to thank these audiences and Stefano Bertea, Luca Ferrero, Jeremy Fix, Matthias Haase, Erasmus Meyr, Vincenzo Pacillo, Paolo Vargiu, Garrath Williams and Ariel Zylberman for comments on a previous draft. This work was supported by the Fund for Interdisciplinary Research FAR 2023 of the University of Modena and Reggio Emilia (Project: Conflict Resolution by Ethical and Religious Authority—CUP E83C23002460001).

References

Afesorgbor, Sylvanus Kwaku and Mahadevan, Renuka. 2016. "The Impact of Economic Sanctions on Income Inequality of Target States," *World Development*, edited by Elsevier, 83 (C): 1–1.

Bagnoli, Carla. 2011. "Emotions and the Categorical Authority of Moral Reasons", in *Morality and the Emotions*, edited by C. Bagnoli, 62–8, Oxford: Oxford University Press.

Bagnoli, Carla. 2014. "Morality as Compromise vs. Morality as a Constraint". *International Journal of Applied Philosophy* 28: 159–169.

Bagnoli, Carla. 2021a. "Respect and the Dynamics of Finitude". In *Respect*, edited by R. Dean and O. Sensen, 121–139, Oxford: Oxford University Press.

Bagnoli, Carla. 2021b. "The objective stance and the boundary problem". *European Journal of Philosophy*, 29 (3): 646–663

Bagnoli, Carla. 2022. *Ethical Constructivism.* Cambridge: Cambridge University Press.

Bagnoli, Carla. 2023. "Responsibility and Coercion". In *Routledge Handbook of the Philosophy of Responsibility,* edited by Maximilian Kiener, 261–273, London: Routledge.

Bagnoli, Carla. forthcoming. "Embodied Constitutivism: Hope and the Efficacy of Practical Reason". In *Reason, Agency, and Ethics: Kantian Themes in Contemporary Debates*, edited by C. Bagnoli & S. Bacin, Oxford: Oxford University Press.

Beitz, Charles R. 1999. *Political Theory and International Relations.* Princeton, NJ: Princeton University Press.

Charron, A. 2011. *UN Sanctions and Conflict: Responding to Peace and Security Threats.* Abingdon: Routledge, 8–16.

Choi, S. W., and Luo, S. 2013. "Economic Sanctions, Poverty, and International Terrorism: An Empirical Analysis". *International Interactions*, 39 (2): 217–245.

Doyle, Michael W. 1983a. "Kant, Liberal Legacies, and Foreign Affairs". *Philosophy and Public Affairs* 12 (3): 205–235.

Doyle, Michael W. 1983b. "Kant, Liberal Legacies, and Foreign Affairs". *Philosophy and Public Affairs* 12 (4): 323–353.

Enoch, D. 2006. "Agency, shmagency: Why normativity won't come from what is constitutive of action". *Philosophical Review*, 115 (2): 169–19.

Fehr, Ernest, and Simon Gachter. 2002. "Altruistic Punishment in Humans". *Nature* 415: 137–140.

Feldman, Yuval. 2018. *The Law of Good People: Challenging States' Ability to Regulate Human Behavior.* Cambridge: Cambridge University Press.

Fitzpatrick, William. 2013. "How Not to Be an Ethical Constructivist: A Critique of Korsgaard's Neo-Kantian Constitutivism". In Constructivism in Ethics, edited by Carla Bagnoli, 41–62. Cambridge: Cambridge University Press.

Friedrich, Carl J. 1947. "The Ideology of the United Nations Charter and the Philosophy of Peace of Immanuel Kant 1795–1945". *The Journal of Politics* 9 (1): 10–30.

Grauvogel, Julia, and Christian von Soest. 2020. "The Termination of International Sanctions: Explaining Target Compliance and Sender Capitulation". *European Economic Review* 129: 103565.

Grauvogel, Julia, Amanda A. Licht, and Christian von Soest. 2017. "Sanctions and Signals: How International Sanction Threats Trigger Domestic Protest in Targeted Regimes". *International Studies Quarterly* 61 (1): 86–97.

Hathaway, Oona A., and Scott J. Shapiro. 2011. "Outcasting: Enforcement in Domestic and International Law". *Yale Law Journal* 121 (2): 252–349.

Hathaway, Oona A., and Scott J. Shapiro. 2017. *The Internationalists: How a Radical Plan to Outlaw War Remade the World.* Cambridge: Cambridge University Press.

Hurrell, Andrew. 1990. "Kant and the Kantian Paradigm in International Relations". *Review of International Studies* 16(3): 183–205.

Jia, Y. 2023. "Global Human Rights Sanctions and State Sovereignty: Does the New Tool Challenge the Old Order?" *Athena – Critical Inquiries in Law, Philosophy and Globalization* 3 (2): 1–36.

Kant, I. 1907. Critique of Pure Reason, *in* Kants gesammelte Schriften. Vol. 4. Berlin: Preussische Akademie der Wissenschaften.

Kant, I. 1907. *Kants gesammelte Schriften.* Berlin: Preussische Akademie der Wissenschaften.

Katsafanas, Paul. 2018. "Constitutivism about Practical Reasons". In *The Oxford Handbook of Reasons and Normativity*, edited by Daniel Star, 367–394. Oxford: Oxford University Press.

Korsgaard, Christine M. 1996. *The Sources of Normativity.* Cambridge University Press.

Korsgaard, Christine M. 2003. "Realism and Constructivism in Twentieth Century Moral Philosophy". *Journal of Philosophical Research*, APA Centennial Supplement: Philosophy in America at the Turn of the Century: 99–122.

Korsgaard, Christine M. 2009. *Self-Constitution: Agency, Identity, and Integrity.* Oxford: Oxford University Press.

Lindauer, Matthew. 2018. "Kantian Themes in Ethics and International Relations". In *The Routledge Handbook of Ethics and International Relations*, edited by B. Steele, and E. Heinze, 30–42. New York: Routledge.

Mackie, J. L. 1977. "Ethics". *Inventing Right and Wrong.* London: Penguin.

Nagel, Thomas. 2005. "The Problem of Global Justice". *Philosophy & Public Affairs* 33: 113–147.

O'Neill, Onora. 1989. "Constructions of Reason: Explorations of Kant's Practical Philosophy". New York: Cambridge University Press.

O'Neill, Onora. 1992. "Vindicating reason. In Paul Guyer" (ed.), *The Cambridge companion to Kant.* New York: Cambridge University Press, 280–30.

O'Neill, Onora. 2000. *Bounds of Justice.* Cambridge: Cambridge University Press.

O'Neill, Onora. 2018. *From Principles to Practice: Normativity and Judgement in Ethics and Politics.* Cambridge: Cambridge University Press.

Onuf, Nicholas Greenwood. 1989. *World of Our Making: Rules and Rule in Social Theory and International Relations.* Columbia, SC: University of South Carolina Press.

Peksen, D. 2019. "When Do Imposed Economic Sanctions Work? A Critical Review of the Sanctions Effectiveness Literature". *Defence and Peace Economics* 30 (6): 635–647.

Prezas Ioannis. 2022. "Democratic Sanctions and International Law". In *Democracy and Sovereignty: Rethinking the Legitimacy of Public International Law*, edited by Daniel Erasmus Khan, Evelyne Lagrange, Stefan Oeter and Christian Walter, 235–268. Leiden: Brill.

Rawls, John. 1955. "Two Concepts of Rules". *The Philosophical Review* 64 (1): 3–32.

Rawls, John. 1980. "Kantian Constructivism in Moral Theory". *Journal of Philosophy* 77 (9): 515–572.

Rawls, John. 1993. *Political Liberalism.* New York: Columbia University Press.

Rawls, John. 1999. *Collected Papers.* Edited by S. R. Freeman. Cambridge, MA: Harvard University Press.

Ripstein, Arthur. 2009. "Force and freedom: Kant's legal and political philosophy". Cambridge: Harvard University Press.

Rodriguez-Blanco, V. 2011. "The Moral Puzzle of Legal Authority". In *Normativity in Morality and Law*, edited by G. Pavlakos and S. Bertea, Oxford: Hart Publishing.

Rousseau, Jean Jacques. 1755. *Discourse on the Origin and Basis of Inequality Among Men.* Indianapolis, Indiana: Hackett Publishing Co.

Rudall, Jason. 2021. *Altruism in International Law.* Cambridge: Cambridge University Press.

Ruys, T. 2017. "Sanctions, Retortions and Countermeasures: Concepts and International Legal Framework". In *Research Handbook on UN Sanctions and International Law*, edited by L. Van Den Herik, 19–51. Cheltenham: Edward Elgar.

Sangiovanni, Andrea. 2008. "Justice and the Priority of Politics to Morality". *Journal of Political Philosophy* 16 (2): 137–164.

Schlereth, Thomas. 1977. *The Cosmopolitan Ideal in Enlightenment Thought.* Notre Dame, IN: Notre Dame University Press.

Seatzu, Francesco, and Paolo Vargiu. 2023. "Peace & Security – Paix et Securité Internationales". *Euromediterranean Journal of International Law and International Relations)* 11: 73–94.

Strawson P.F. 1962. "Freedom and Resentment", *Proceedings of the British Academy*, 48: 1–2.

Sterba, James. 2013 *From Rationality to Equality.* New York: Oxford University Press.

Subedi, Surya P., ed. 2021. *Unilateral Sanctions in International Law.* London: Bloomsbury.

van Aaken, Anne, and Betül Simsek. 2021. "Rewarding in International Law". *American Journal of International Law* 115 (2), 195–241.

Wenar, L. 2001. "Contractualism and Global Economic Justice". *Metaphilosophy*, 32 (1–2): 79–9.

Van Rooij, Benjamin, and D. Daniel Sokol, eds. 2021. *Cambridge Handbook of Compliance.* Cambridge: Cambridge University Press.

Wendt, Alexander. 1992. "Anarchy is what States Make of it: the Social Construction of Power Politics". *International Organization* 46 (2): 391–425.
Wilson, P. 2011. "Idealism in International Relations." In *Encyclopedia of Power*, edited by Keith Dowding, 332–33. Thousand Oaks: Sage Publications.

9 Towards a neo-Hartian account of the 'natural' relation between law and coercion

Distinct, rational, necessary, quasi-constitutivist

Pablo A. Rapetti[1]

9.1 Introduction

It is not uncommon to attribute to Hart the final blow to the idea that there is some kind of 'essential' relation between law and the threat and imposition of sanctions.[2] But what does 'essential' stand for? In the absence of said clarification, such an attribution seems intuitively inadequate, since Hart did emphasize that there is an important relation between the two. Moreover, he stressed that there is more than one important form of relation. Furthermore, to the extent that his work implies some kind of relaxation of the way the relations between law and coercion are to be understood, compared to comprehensions established before his time, it is possible that Hart's work is indeed a genuine step ahead on this issue, as there are reasons to think that the relation between law and coercion may be less intense than some, both in the past and now, have believed.[3]

1 I presented this work in seminars at the University of Costa Rica and the University of Murcia (Spain). Many thanks to the attendees in both events for their helpful feedback. Special thanks are due to those who provided me with written comments to earlier versions of this chapter: Andrés Bouzat, Jorge Cerdio, Diego Dei Vecchi, Loreto Navarro, Natalia Scavuzzo, and Guilherme Vasconcelos. I would also like to thank my research assistant, Emiliano Miranda, for his great contribution in the final composition of this text.

2 As is known, the most *explicit* proponent of the idea that there is no 'essential' connection between law and coercion is, rather, Joseph Raz (see Raz 1999, 154–162), through the well-known *argument of the angelic society*, of a Kantian vein. However, it is easy to find at least implicit attributions to Hart that coercion is not part of the 'nature' of law. See, e.g., Green 1996, 1702–1703; Coleman 2001, 70–71; Gardner 2008, 273; and, *perhaps*, Shapiro 2011, 92. Apart from some brief specificities I will bring to the table below, in this chapter I will not try to offer a polished notion of *coercion*. Suffice it to say that its core lies in a kind of serious pressure for compliance, as many have remarked. See, e.g., Lamond 2001, 43–44; Yankah 2008, 1216–1217; Miotto 2021, 235. This, by the way, is compatible with a distinction between that which is *coercive* and that which is *coactive* (the latter broadly understood as the effective realization of what was previously threatened).

3 Indeed, if we move away from legal-philosophical texts and approach those of comparativists, legal anthropologists, and legal historians, the picture might even be reversed. See, for instance, the commentary by Sucar 2017, xix–xx.

DOI: 10.4324/9781032670553-10

My aim in the following lines is to elaborate on the Hartian ideas about the relation between law and coercion. I will argue that, against established opinion, Hart contends that there is a *necessary* connection between law and coercion. Indeed, he argues that there are *three* forms of necessary connection between them. These three forms of necessary connection vary from one to another. The three connections are empirical, conceptual, and 'natural'. The latter is the most mysterious, the one that Hart develops the least out of the three. In this sense, I will especially attempt to elaborate on it further.[4] My goal is to present it as a sensible and distinct necessary connection between law and coercion, but I will not try here to fully endorse or defend the view, since that would require at least another chapter. Finally, I will highlight some of the important affinities that this conception has with the view known as *constitutivism* in metaethics and the philosophy of action. This parallelism reflects an interesting convergence in thinking and paves a way for further discussing the topic.

9.2 Methodological cautions

In *The Concept of Law*, Hart explicitly states that his object of study encompasses the bulk of contemporary Western legal systems. He also clarifies that he does not intend to elucidate the meaning of the *word* 'law' but rather to explore *legal phenomena* in terms of their most general and salient characteristics. In doing so, he also explicitly leaves open the possibility that in certain contexts it may be linguistically correct to speak of 'law' to refer to forms of social organization that do not possess the distinctive characteristics that Hart himself stresses throughout his work as inherent of *our current* legal systems (Hart 2012, 1–17).[5]

These preliminary cautions offered by Hart must be taken into consideration in order to comprehend his reflections on the relation between law and coercion. Hart addresses the role that coercion plays in contemporary Western legal systems (those which, due to their stage of development—at least in the simple historical-chronological sense—can be referred to as 'paradigmatic cases or examples of law'), rather than in any forms of social organization that might be called 'law' in contexts different from the one established by him as the framework for his own inquiry.

4 There is an additional reason why this point will be my focal centre and I should also mention it as a sort of disclaimer. The exegetical literature on Hart's position regarding the relation between law and coercion is extensive and, in my opinion, there is a rather definitive work in that line, to which I emphatically refer: Pintore 2014. See also Schauer 2015 and its bibliographic references. Hence, I do not intend to add to the exegesis of Hart's work but to further advance, in a substantial sense, one of the aspects of his conception.

5 These considerations are then revisited by Hart, with particular mention of the question of the relation between law and coercion, in the tenth and final chapter of his book.

As is well known, Hart was a proponent of legal positivism. Positivism is distinguished from its opposing antipositivist approaches by a specific conceptual thesis regarding law. Or, if preferred, by a specific thesis about the (content of the) concept of law: antipositivism claims that there is a certain conceptual relation between law and morality that positivism denies. The dispute between legal positivists and antipositivists is fundamentally a matter at the conceptual level. Now, our concern here is with the relation between law and coercion; if I draw attention to legal positivism and Hart's endorsement of it, it is because the comparison is relevant when it comes to understanding what Hart holds with regard to the relation between law and coercion in particular: are Hart's theses about this relation of a conceptual nature, akin to those that characterize and express his positivist stance on the relation between law and morality?

The short answer to the preceding question is the following: *yes, but not solely.*[6]

9.3 Three kinds of necessities and relations

In the section of *The Concept of Law* where he examines what he calls the 'minimum content of natural law' (Hart 2012, 193–200), Hart distinguishes between three kinds of necessities and relations. In analyzing whether there are specific contents that the law (qua legal system) must have, he distinguishes between *empirical* necessities on the one hand, *logical* or *conceptual* necessities[7] on the other, and—in a sort of intermediate space—*natural* necessities (Hart 2012, 199). With regard to the content of the law, this implies the following. In one respect, there are normative contents that legal systems 'must necessarily have', in an empirical sense. This means that their absence would gravely (and probably) compromise the empirical viability of the respective legal systems, and it can be understood in terms of *efficacy*. Thus, e.g., a

6 Mention of legal positivism and Hart's endorsement of it is also important for the following disclaimer: inasmuch as one conceives of legal positivism as fundamentally a *conceptual* view, the *rational* necessary connection between law and coercion that I will try to develop in this chapter is not (and cannot be) a *part* of a positivistic view of law. It neither is nor implies a rejection of positivism. It is simply an account that may or may not be held as a complement or addendum to other positivistic accounts of the law and legal features and institutions.

7 There are those who would seek to distinguish between logical and conceptual considerations. Furthermore, it is increasingly common in jurisprudence to differentiate both logical and conceptual considerations from *metaphysical* ones. Indeed, many now prefer to cast the above-mentioned divide between positivism and antipositivism in metaphysical, rather than conceptual terms. See, e.g., Chilovi and Pavlakos 2019 (I find this trend rather unfortunate for several reasons I am unable to delve into here, but see Patterson and Tripkovic 2023 for some related concerns). This is also true of the treatment of the relation between law and coercion: see Miotto 2020, and Gkouvas 2023. Whether this partition is useful or not depends on the purposes one has in mind. For the purposes of this chapter, I think we can rest content with Hart's tripartite classification.

legal system that does not include norms that punish murder is likely to be inefficacious.

At the other end of the spectrum is the realm of conceptual or logical requirements, which is of primary interest to Hart throughout the rest of his book and, more broadly, to jurisprudence in general. A normative system that does not satisfy the conceptual necessities for the existence of law will not count as a legal system. Thus, for instance, a normative system that contains only primary norms of obligation, without any secondary norms (especially a rule of recognition), cannot, conceptually, be taken as a (paradigmatic case of a) legal system.

However, in between there are the 'natural' necessities that Hart speaks of, which may be understood in terms of *rationality*. Hart (2012, 191–192) refers to the contents that constitute what he terms the 'minimum content of natural law' as those we have a *reason* to include in our legal systems by virtue of our nature and condition as human beings, and that provide a *reason* to voluntarily obey the law. Hart claims that there is a 'distinctively rational connection' between our nature and such minimal contents, that must be distinguished from the empirical-causal connections ultimately reflected in the efficacy conditions of legal systems—which disciplines such as psychology or sociology may identify. The rational connection, instead, 'relate[s] the existence of certain rules to the conscious aims or purpose of those whose rules they are' (Hart 2012, 194)—a relation that need not always be traced when establishing causal bonds.[8]

Certainly, this first approach to what the 'natural necessities' are may seem insufficient. I will attempt to further elaborate it. But before that, let me say a bit more about the empirical and conceptual connections between law and coercion.

9.4 The empirical connection

Many of Hart's commentators seem to have mistakenly understood that he saw the relation between law and coercion as limited to the empirical dimension.[9] As noted above, in this empirical sense the relation between law and coercion is to be understood in terms of efficacy. This means that a legal system that does not impose sanctions for the violation of its requirements is likely to prove ineffective and is therefore destined to disappear eventually.

In his considerations at this level, Hart maintains an *intuitive* discourse: it is intuitively plausible that a system that does not impose sanctions will

8 Hart is less explicit in distinguishing between rational and conceptual connections. Hence, some authors seem to interpret him as equating them (see, e.g., the note by Leslie Green—*The 'minimum content' thesis*—in Hart 2012, 322–323). Below I will try to show that equating them is a mistake.

9 See, e.g., Bix 2004, 93–94; Chiassoni 2013, 478; Dereboylular 2020, 127–128; Drury 1981, 541–543; Summers 1963, 652; Yankah 2008, 1235.

eventually disappear. In other contexts, a more serious empirical support, including experiments, historical examples, and statistical information would be required to substantiate this intuition. However, beyond the fact that the intuition seems reasonable, it is clear that his work does not intend to fully embrace this empirical form of analysis. His concerns were philosophical and so are ours here, hence we need not dwell much further on this type of relation between law and coercion. Suffice it to emphasize that for Hart it is empirically 'necessary' (with the quotation marks that the expression requires when in this context) for the law to include coercion, and in the peculiar way of providing institutionalized sanctions in cases of non-compliance with what is established by legal norms.

9.5 The conceptual connection

According to Hart's conception of law, there is a necessary connection between law and coercion at the conceptual level. It is worth noting that not every legal norm must necessarily provide for sanctions in the event of non-compliance. Nor is it the case that there must be a general norm that provides for sanctions in the face of non-observance. This is incompatible with much of what Hart claims, such as, e.g., that legal norms cannot be well understood by likening them to orders backed by threats, or that nullity cannot be identified with sanctions (Hart 2012, 18–49). The conceptual connection, which is *necessary* in a strong sense, lies in the rule of recognition.

The rule of recognition (Hart 2012, 100–123) is the product of a certain collective endeavour. In particular, it is the product of the practice of identifying the law by its primary appliers, i.e., the judges. The rule consists of the criteria that judges (and perhaps other officials) develop in their work of identifying the law for its subsequent application to specific cases. This is one of its defining and distinguishing features. This feature should be emphasized, insofar as it implies an important peculiarity for us here: the rule of recognition is, by virtue of its special type of origin, a social (or, rather, socio-legal) rule. Indeed, if Hart first discusses the nature of social rules, characterizing their defining elements, and only *later* focuses on legal rules in particular, it is because in his conception there is an unavoidable bridge between social and legal rules: whereas not every legal rule must have the typical characteristics of social rules, there is at least one legal rule that does, and this is none other than the rule of recognition, which is ultimately the source of the legal validity of every other rule belonging to a legal system. The conformation and subsistence of the rule of recognition require that (at least) most judges in a community converge in the use of the same criteria of validity, and that this convergence does not occur merely by chance but by virtue of the development of the internal point of view among that majority of judges towards the criteria in question.

Hart further clarifies that the internal point of view with respect to rules is provided by the attitude he calls 'acceptance': one has the internal point of view with respect to a rule if and when one 'accepts' it. To be an acceptor of a rule is to have the disposition to use it in situations in which, according to its content, the rule applies. In particular, an acceptor is able to use the norm to evaluate both her own behaviour and that of others, to criticize deviations from what the norm prescribes, and to commend the correspondence between the norm and the behaviour being evaluated. In this sense, the attitude of acceptance is not fundamentally theoretical or cognitive, but practical, conative, normative. The crucial point to note is that acceptance involves a readiness for criticism or praise. That is to say, acceptance has a *reactive* dimension, which, in turn, implies a coercive dimension with the potential for sanction-imposing.

Now, the pressure for conformity ingrained in acceptance as its reactive dimension is a matter of degree. But I find it most plausible to assume that the degree of pressure involved (even if unconsciously) in the forming and persistence of rules of recognition is always comparatively high, since it relates to the ultimate criteria of validity and thus to the very foundations of legal systems. It is a serious and thus *coercive* pressure.[10]

Having assembled the various elements of the Hartian conception, we can now spell out the argument for a conceptual connection between law and coercion:

(1) The existence of a rule of recognition is a conceptually necessary condition for the existence of a (paradigmatic case of a) legal system;
(2) The existence of a rule of recognition depends on a convergent practice of certain individuals to identify and apply certain norms *as* specifically *legal* norms to instant cases;
(3) These individuals must be acceptors of the rule of recognition, which is thus a socio-legal rule;
(4) The attitude of accepting legal norms is a practical, normative attitude that involves the disposition to use accepted norms to assess, in terms of those norms, the actions and states of affairs to which they refer, and, consequently, to deem right (praiseworthy) or wrong (blameworthy) the conformity or non-conformity, respectively, with what is established by those norms;
(5) This reactive aspect revealed by the acceptance of norms constitutes a form of coercion, at least when it comes to the acceptance of the very rule of recognition;

(C) Therefore, at the foundations of every legal system lies a form of coercion. Coercion is, thus, a conceptually necessary condition for the existence of legal systems.

10 This also helps explain why many commentators have taken the rule of recognition to be a duty-imposing (perhaps even 'obligation-imposing') rule. I think this is only partially correct, for the rule of recognition is a conceptual or constitutive rule *as well*. See Dei Vecchi and Rapetti 2022; and Bertea 2013.

Here are two glosses about this argument. First, the coercion referred to concerns 'official' behaviour (at a minimum, judges), but not necessarily the behaviour of citizens and other legal subjects. Second, according to this argument coercion is not necessarily a *part* of legal systems, but a condition of their existence. As Kenneth Himma (2020, 14) points out, the coercive sanctions that somehow 'back' the rule of recognition are *informal* in the sense that they are not authorized by the rule of recognition itself or any other legal rule. In the terminology I prefer: this is a form of *non-institutionalized* coercion in contrast to sanctions provided by specific legal norms (other than the rule of recognition), which would therefore be forms of *institutionalized* coercion.[11]

The foregoing implies some form of conceptual connection, albeit a less pronounced one than some might expect. The case of Himma himself provides an example, as he has devoted an entire book to argue for a conceptual connection between law and coercion in a formal, institutionalized sense. Elsewhere (Rapetti 2021),[12] I have attempted to show that his most ambitious claim is fraught with difficulties that render it untenable; I cannot reiterate them now. Nor can I provide an argument (as I do not have one) to establish definitively that a conceptually necessary connection between law and *institutionalized coercion* is impossible, although I am at present unaware of any that achieves as much.

9.6 The 'natural' connection I: rationality and distinctiveness

Now, what about the more mysterious 'natural' connection between law and coercion? As I said above, Hart suggests that coercion is 'naturally' necessary for the law. The sense in which this is a necessity lies somehow between the weak sense in which the law empirically 'necessitates' coercion, and the strong sense in which the law conceptually necessitates coercion. These 'natural' necessities are to be understood in terms of *rationality*. Hart (2012, 191–192) refers to the contents that constitute the 'minimum content of natural law'—and provision for institutionalized coercion makes for one of those minimum contents—as those we have a *reason* to include in our legal systems by virtue of our nature and predicament as human beings, and that provide a *reason* to voluntarily obey the law. Hart claims that there is a 'distinctively rational connection' between our nature and such minimal contents. The rational connection 'relate[s] the existence of certain rules to the conscious aims or purpose of

11 This argument, duly developed and detailed, is the core of Vázquez Álvarez 2024. It is from this work that I have adopted the *institutionalized/non-institutionalized* distinction, and I refer to it—in particular for a thorough elaboration of premise (5).

12 In fact, I believe Himma's proposal is better construed as an attempt in line with mine in this chapter. That means his approach concerns less the conceptual connection between law and coercion than their rational connection. However, (i) that is not how he views his own project, and (ii) he tackles rather scarcely what rationality is and what it involves regarding a possible *distinct* link between law and coercion.

those whose rules they are' (Hart 2012, 194)—a relation that need not always be traced when establishing causal bonds.[13]

In a nutshell—soon to be unpacked—the way in which to understand these contents that Hart considers 'naturally necessary' in legal systems is the following: *they are contents the absence of which in a given legal system would make living under the aegis of that legal system irrational.* Thus, returning to the example of rules punishing murder, it can be said that it would be irrational to live in a community whose legal order did not include them. This, as Hart points out, can be explained by various elements that comprise human nature and predicament as we can grasp it—elements that he elucidates.[14] These factors are not logically or metaphysically necessary but potentially mutable, albeit in a laborious way that resists equating them, on the other end, with mere factual contingency (Hart, 2012, 190–192).

Natural necessity is also different from the other two because in a certain sense it does not require either of them. The existence of a legal system does not seem to demand logically or conceptually the institutionalization of an explicit mechanism providing for the punishment of murder: a system which does not include it is conceivable. Conversely, it does seem to require it at least as an *intuitive* empirical matter of efficacy. But these 'empirical necessities' are only so in the quote-unquote sense precisely because they are mere matters of fact, as such always contingent and subject to probability. Although intuitively unlikely, it is (logically) possible for a legal system which does not establish the punishment of murder to flourish and endure over time.[15] 'Natural' necessities are different because they are due to the peculiar factors that make up the human predicament and because they do not have the relativity of empirical 'necessities' while also not reaching the absoluteness of conceptual or logical necessities.[16] Therefore, although the institutionalized prohibition of murder

13 Some would perhaps want to say that, when dealing with the causes of actions by rational beings such as we humans, fully grasping said causes involves taking also into account their ends, desires and beliefs, interests, and social institutions (see, e.g., Margain 1978, 39; Mele 2009, 144). I take this to be just terminologically different from what is stated in the main text.

14 Hart alludes (2012, 194–198) to (i) human vulnerability, (ii) the approximate equality of conditions among persons, (iii) our limited altruism and egoism, (iv) the constraint of our available life resources, and (v) our also limited understanding and strength of will. For an analysis in an intriguingly similar line, see Warnock 1971, 12–26, and (for an interesting addition) 80–85.

15 Factors such as the force of social morality, respect and affection, tradition, widespread fear, or many others could well give rise to a community where people generally do not kill each other simply because it is not legally prohibited for them to do so.

16 Discussing Kant's categorical imperative, Pereda 1994, 245–246, suggests another way of distinguishing between the rational and the conceptual domains in terms of incoherence, that is, by distinguishing between *conceptual incoherence* and *rational incoherence*. It would be conceptually incoherent for an agent to intend—say—the universalization, as a law, of promise-breaching. For that would render the whole notion and practice of promising as void and meaningless. Rational incoherence, on the other hand, has to do with the self-denying

is not conceptually necessary to correctly assert the existence of a legal system in a certain community, it might still be appropriate to say that it is irrational to live under a regime configured by a legal system which does not include such a prohibition. This is even the case in an imaginary context in which people do not generally kill each other even though they are not legally barred from doing so. Such a judgement of irrationality could be based, for instance, on the fact that the value of life is generally considered to be so significant in such context that the mere *risk*—however small—of it being threatened at any moment is so concerning as to require prohibition and the threat of punishment, even in the face of the present fact (statistically proven, under this hypothesis) of its respect. This is the key to the 'rationalist' reading of the 'natural necessities' to which Hart refers.

9.7 The 'natural' connection II: rationality, risk, emotion

The notion of *rationality* implied in this framework deserves a much more extensive analysis than I can provide here.[17] Still, I find the just-mentioned connection between this notion and that of *risk* intriguing enough. Let us explore it further.

Initially, part of what it means to behave 'rationally'[18] is to deal with various aspects of our lives and relations with the world in a certain (precisely:

as a rational agent. Think of an agent willing to universalize, as a law, the absolute lack of benevolence. A world of only non-benevolent people is conceivable, but a minimally rational agent would not want such a world: if an agent refuses to help others when they are in need, she must be willing to want that nobody help her when she is in need; however, a rational agent would always want to have in hand all the means that could help her achieve her goals, and would therefore want to be helped whenever her goals so require it. Thus, the non-benevolence universalizing agent is someone who makes an attempt on her own rationality.

17 As held in Olivé 1988, 272, the notion of rationality is one of the 'most difficult to elucidate in philosophy, for it will always have to be presupposed in any attempt of elucidation'. (My translation.) I readily admit (i) that I will not attempt to provide a novel, thorough, and detailed conception of rationality and (ii) that some of the considerations formulated below will turn out to be incompatible with certain extant conceptions. This latter point is especially true of some conceptions belonging to the *rational choice* literature in economics (see, e.g., Becker 1976; Green and Fox 2007). Of course, I think there are good reasons for rejecting such conceptions: for an interesting cue coming from experimental psychiatry see Jeung, Schwieren and Herpetz 2016.

18 I will speak indifferently of *being rational* and *behaving rationally*. Of course, one could draw a plausible distinction for other purposes. The distinction is indeed ingrained in our linguistic practices. As Pereda 1994, 23–24 notes, there is a difference between a statement like 'Humans are rational, but cats and toads are not' and one like 'Peter acted hardly rationally yesterday'. In the first case we use what Pereda calls a 'substantive concept' of rationality, whereas in the second we use an 'adjective concept'. The former seems to set a category, a natural kind; the latter seems to set a normative kind. The latter presupposes usages of the former, and it admits of degrees (one may act more or less rationally), while the former does not. The former alludes to certain capacities, the latter alludes to their functioning. However, Pereda himself notes as well that 'the best way of knowing a capacity is investigating its func-

rational) way. Assume, for now, that we can at least intuitively describe some of those aspects as 'non-rational' or 'extra-rational'. Think of human *emotions*. If we grant that our emotions are somehow manifestations of non-rational aspects of our personality (see Whiting 2011; Ortiz-Millán 2019),[19] then the question arises regarding the nature of the actions and activities we undertake to express, enhance, contain, modify, abandon (etc.) our emotions. It seems plausible that among the various actions and activities we can undertake for these purposes, many deserve the label of 'rational'. That is to say: even if our emotions are inherently non-rational (even irrational), we can—at least on occasion—engage in a *rational management* of them. For instance, going to therapy, working out as a deliberate way of not getting into a fight, playing board games to unwind after long sessions of existentialist readings, etc., are various ways in which we can attempt to contain and mitigate certain negative emotions. And these are attempts that are rational in the simple but important sense that they respond to reasons.[20] If I choose to play a game that amuses me when I find myself at the outset of an uncomfortable and potentially escalating argument, I thereby make it less likely that the escalation will occur, thus avoiding a potential larger problem. The fact that the game relaxes me in relation to the impending conflict[21] gives me a reason to go and play it, abandoning the context of said conflict (to the extent that I indeed *prefer* to avoid it).[22]

That the management of our emotions is rationally possible on occasion implies that, to some extent, we can exert forms of control over the emotions we experience. Under the assumption that our emotions, as such, are a manifestation of the non-rational within us, it can then be said that some emotions, nonetheless, have a 'rational origin'. This comes as no surprise. Nor is it surprising that, however, some of our emotions are, in turn, of inherently

---

tioning' (my translation), so the distinction should not be overstated. I may add that there is a third linguistic usage that connects these two we have seen. Think of 'Leandro is a very rational man', a statement with which we say that Leandro behaves rationally most of the time.

19 Below I will show that the account I advance of the necessary rational connection between law and coercion is also compatible with assuming the potential rationality of emotions.

20 As stressed in Jones 2003, 190, to be able to *respond* to reasons (which is more than merely *tracking* reasons) agents require (i) critical reflective ability, (ii) dispositions to bring that ability to bear when needed, and (iii) dispositions to have the results of such reflection control their behaviour. Anyhow, I am far from even trying to offer an integral conception of the notion of rationality, so this should not be understood as a commitment to the idea that rationality *specifically consists* (in one way or another) in the appropriate response to reasons. The expression I use in the main text only seeks, more modestly, to allude to the obvious fact that there is some kind of relation between rationality and reasons. For a conception of rationality effectively articulated in terms of the appropriate response to reasons, see Kolodny 2008; for a response to such a conception, see Broome 2013.

21 It may also be necessary for me to believe that the game will provide relaxation, but there is no need to dwell on this here.

22 I am setting aside the enormous question of *determinism* and its connected debates (compatibilism, etc.), the consideration of which would severely complicate the argument—though, in my view, not necessarily decide its plausibility.

irrational and/or non-rational origins. In the latter cases, rational management is not impossible, though it is, by definition, subsequent to the gestation and development of the emotion in question.

9.8 The 'natural' connection III: *our* (ir)rationality

Let us now revisit the connection between rationality and risk as a means of understanding Hart's notion of 'natural' necessities. I earlier submitted that it is conceivable that, in a certain community, people do not generally kill each other without justification, even if it is not legally prohibited to do so. I also held that such a situation is conceivable even if there is serious empirical evidence to suggest that people in said community are very unlikely to act otherwise in the future. Still, I claimed that in this case it can even be rational for members of the community to advocate for coercive prohibition in the face of the mere risk, however minimal, that at some point the status quo will change, at least if they hold life in very high regard. Under this hypothesis, it is indeed highly improbable that the situation will change, making the risk consequently minimal. Nevertheless, what we are dealing with is a *sense* of risk—an emotion. Perhaps it might be necessary to acknowledge that this is an emotion stemming from something inherently irrational, as paying attention to the evidence suggesting a highly improbable change in the scenario could lead to abandoning the sense of risk. However, we can infer the following: since rationality may imply a rational management of our emotions, it does not necessarily imply—conversely—the complete absence of emotions, that is, the non-rational and irrational. Postulating something different would completely void the notions of rationality and irrationality, as it would consequentially lead to the conclusion that hardly anyone is ever rational (or acts rationally). For no person is devoid of emotions.[23] A conclusion that is evidently absurd and scarcely reflects the manner in which we ordinarily behave and employ these notions.

Furthermore, it is plausible that rationality is gradable, which means that one can act in more or less rational ways. While it makes sense to consider a (blurry) dividing line between rationality and irrationality, both domains allow for gradation within themselves. Thus, by analyzing the imaginary example we have been working with, one might argue that if the individuals in the community were perfectly rational they would not be concerned, in the face of evidence suggesting little likelihood of change, of the risk getting actualized. However, since we are not necessarily perfectly rational, and/or we are not always so, there is no reason to dwell too much on this.

Therefore, even in the imaginary community of our reflection, where people indeed refrain from killing each other despite the absence of prohibition

23 Except, perhaps, for certain clinical cases that nonetheless make for the exception rather than the rule.

and although it is unlikely that they will do so regardless, it remains rational for them to maintain a sufficiently low tolerance for the risk of that situation changing—given the high value they place on life—so as to actively seek[24] the institution of coercive prohibition. Aversion to this risk may be an indication of suboptimal rationality, but it is not sufficient proof of irrationality; whereas the intention to establish the coercive prohibition seems to be indicative of a disposition to rationally manage such aversion to that risk. Moreover, even if it were conceded that aversion to this risk is fairly indicative of irrationality, that alone would not make it consequently irrational to seek coercive prohibition: as I mentioned above, it seems plausible that emotions of an irrational origin can be rationally managed and, in this supposition, the irrational aspect would be the aversion to risk rather than the proposed means for dealing with it.

Let us imagine, however, a critic still inclined to insist. Our critic proposes a new hypothetical scenario. In a Razian vein, she argues that we could conceive of an angelic society perfectly disposed to comply with what is mandated by the law: if we know that no one will fail to comply with what is legally prescribed, then there would be no reason to be guarded against the possibility of non-compliance. Faced with this insistence, we may wonder what sort of postulate this perfect disposition to compliance amounts to.

If the postulate is of an empirical nature, this would mean that the proposed mental experiment requires us to assume that the imagined population has ample evidence that the status quo will not change. The response I have already put forward seems sufficient to meet the objection so understood: perhaps perfect rationality would entail that establishing a coercive apparatus is unnecessary, but suboptimal forms of rationality—still far from the realm of irrationality—might make it sufficiently advisable.

Alternatively, the objector might insist that the postulate must be pondered not in an empirical sense, but rather in a metaphysical or conceptual one. This would imply that it should be assumed *by definition* that it is impossible for the situation to change. Thus, the reply in terms of suboptimal rationality would be unfeasible, and one would have to conclude that the intention of the imagined community to fortify itself under a coercive system would be irrational. The response to this stronger alternative lies in pointing at its *denial of rationality as a factor*, a denial that thereby does not truly lead to a conclusion of irrationality, but instead to excluding any consideration of the matter in terms of (ir)rationality. This is so because *our* rationality presupposes the human condition, which includes elements that the thought experiment thus understood *asks us to deny*: limited altruism, a particular concern for self-interest, lack of omniscience, etc.[25]

24 Which presupposes the possibility of *choosing*, certainly a platitude about rationality. Hart would agree: see, e.g., Hart 2008, 44–46. See also Warnock 1971, 13 and 144.

25 This is an alternative formulation of an argument previously expounded in Rapetti 2015, regarding the discussion of Raz's angelic society argument. There, additional theoretical and

In this way, I believe we can reject our critic's insistence in any of its versions.

9.9 The 'natural' connection IV: subjectivism vs. objectivism and the rationality of our emotions

However, we can still complicate the discussion a bit more. Suppose our critic presses her point by drawing the distinction between *objective* and *subjective* rationality. Objective rationality relates to the attitude that we have most reason to have (or form) in certain kinds of situations, whereas subjective rationality relates to the link between two or more of our own attitudes viewed in abstraction from the reasons for them (see Kolodny 2005, 509–510; Caracciolo 2009, 71–73).[26] Suppose that I say to Julene that I want to smoke and then ask her whether I should open the pack of cigarettes I hold in my hand. She could reply something like, 'You shouldn't, it is irrational of you to smoke (for it is unhealthy, etc.)' or she could reply something like, 'Well, since you want to smoke, it would be irrational of you not to open the pack'. The first reply illustrates a claim to objective rationality, while the second illustrates a claim to subjective rationality. The latter applies fundamentally to means-ends relations and its core lies in the notion of coherence, while the former applies both to means-ends relations and to ends themselves.[27]

Now, our critic goes back to the Razian scenario to restate her last objection. 'I'm not claiming', she says, 'that you should think—in the way of a conceptual (or metaphysical) postulate—of the angels as having solid evidence indicating that the status quo won't change. Nor as an empirical assumption, for that matter. I'm arguing in your own terms: I'm arguing about what is *rational* for the angels to believe—and therefore to do on the basis of the correct beliefs'. With this, our critic is implying two things:

---

metatheoretical arguments were provided to supplement the discussion. One of the latter kind of arguments, that appears relevant here, is, in a nutshell, as follows: Raz states that the aim of the philosophy of law is, fundamentally, to elucidate the nature of law, for which it is necessary to clarify our concept of law, presupposing a distinction between *the* concept of law (in itself) and *our* concept of law. If we are to elucidate our concept of law, then it is to be expected that it is the concept due to *us* and that *we* employ. This 'us' is of crucial importance. However, positing in a metaphysical or conceptual sense the quality of an unwavering disposition to comply with the law radically alters our condition, thereby substituting the relevant 'us' for a different one. This makes it impossible to claim that Raz's mental experiment has the effect of informing us something about *our* concept of law. For Raz's methodological premises, see Ruiz Manero 1991, and Raz 2007a and 2013, chaps. 2 and 4.

26 Both objective and subjective rationality merit a further distinction between the theoretical or epistemic domain and the practical domain. Thus, the attitudes they demand of us will respectively be doxastic attitudes such as a belief, on the one hand, and practical intentionality, on the other.

27 And perhaps on occasion may even be better served by incoherence. For instance, it *might* be the case that it is more objectively rational for one to hold two incompatible beliefs, one of which is justified and true whereas the other is none, than to hold two coherent beliefs both of which are unjustified and untrue.

(i) that my reply involves the notion of subjective rationality: since the angels fear the change of the status quo, it is subjectively rational for them to adopt a coercive prohibition; but
(ii) her objection relies on objective rationality: my reply should dismiss their fear because that fear is irrational, and it is irrational because it is unjustified in factual terms—it is a fact (given the assumed premises of the scenario) that the status quo will highly likely persist.

Indeed, she would even be further implying—because (ii) does—that

(iii) attitudes are not to be taken as a given when discussing rationality: not even an emotion such as fear is outside the scope of rationality; in fact, assuming that emotions are non-rational manifestations of our personality is a mistake—some emotions are rational (or it is rational to have them), whereas others are not (or it is irrational to have them). Since the proposed scenario involves the fact that the status quo's change is highly unlikely, objectively rational angels would not come to fear such a change.[28]

There are many ways to deal with the objection so formulated. To begin with, I should say I am rather sympathetic to the idea behind (iii). Whereas it is true that emotions have been and still are to a large extent considered as non-rational (or even irrational) both in the history and present of philosophy, the view that they are within the scope of rationality seems quite plausible. Take Daniel González-Lagier's conception as an example (González-Lagier 2009, 110).[29] He holds that emotions may be either rational or irrational as a function of four criteria—which he also does not take to be exhaustive—, so that an emotion *E* is rational if:

(a) *E* is based on justified beliefs or value judgements;
(b) *E* is coherent with the kind of belief that causes it;
(c) *E* is proportionate: neither too exaggerated nor too 'cold'; *or*
(d) the actions prompted by *E* comprise an adequate strategy for pursuing one's life-plans, preferences, etc.

This seems appealing. But it is important to note two things here. First, that this framework on emotions makes room for the above-mentioned *gradability* of rationality. Particular emotions may be rational according to one or more of

28 Or, perhaps, they would *know* that the status quo will probably remain the same and *thus* would not come to fear the change.
29 See also Pereda 1994, 35–37, 60–91; Tappolet 2018, 893–897; and Moya 2000. For a neuroscientific approach, see Garcés and Finkel 2019.

these criteria but fail to be so in light of other(s).[30] Second, that the framework is offered in connection to subjective rationality, and not objective rationality. That much is shown clearly by criterion (a), which is formulated regarding the justification of base beliefs or value judgements, and not regarding their truth or correctness.[31] In this respect, therefore, my original reply to the critic remains in place: the angels of our scenario are not all-knowing, and perhaps they even lack (for non-unjustified motives) serious evidence showing the very low probability of change, so their fear may be rational according to each of these criteria. Even if we modify criterion (a) so as to read

(a') *E* is based on *true/correct* beliefs or value judgements,

the suboptimality claim in my original reply stays in hand, and even showing more clearly its force: while the angels' fear may not be rational according to (a'), it may still be so according to (b), (c), and (d). Indeed, even if we sticked to the original (a) criterion and granted that the angels have all the relevant evidence at their disposal, their fear could perhaps be irrational according to (a) but still perfectly rational according to (b), (c), and (d). Even more so: emotions may be based on complex combinations of beliefs and value judgements, so González-Lagier's formulation of (a) could plausibly be amended to become

(a'') *E* is based on justified beliefs *and/or* value judgements.

Again, in a worst-case scenario we can grant that our angels are not rational according to (a), (a'), and (a''), but they would still be rational regarding (b), (c), and (d). But (a'') opens up a new possibility: that our angels are rational regarding (b), (c), and (d) and even regarding their base *value judgements* as pertaining to (a'')—the relevant value judgement being their high praise of life—although maybe not regarding their base *beliefs* as pertaining to (a'')—the relevant belief being the estimation of the likelihood of change of the status quo.

Notice also that there is an important link between criterion (c) and (d). This allows us to deepen the analysis of the angelic scenario. An element with which to assess the (subjective) rationality of the proposal by the angels of having a system of coercive prohibition has to do with the *specific way* in which

30 Indeed, despite appearances, my original formulation of this issue was not that far from where we are now, because I distinguished between the possible *origins* of our emotions as rational or otherwise.

31 I take this to be a proper presentation of what objective rationality would require. I assume we could alternatively speak of *justification from an objective point of view*, as opposed to *justification from the agent's point of view*. The choice is merely verbal. If anything, talk of *truth/correctness* seems suitably more straightforward.

they intend to configure and implement such a system. The relevant details would enable us to better evaluate whether their fear of change is proportionate (c), while they also *amount to* their strategy for pursuing what they want (d)—in this case, a *reinforced* status quo, one which they could expect to have even less chances of changing than what they already had. Thus, the relevant question now becomes: how costly would their system be?[32] Too costly a system could be taken as a sign—indeed as a reason—that their fear is irrational. But if the system they intend to implement does not come at a high cost, then there is more reason to think that the angels do satisfy criterion (c) and (d), and thus not only that their fear is rational, but that the way in which they intend to manage their fear is rational as well.[33]

What else is there to say about this new form of the objection? Well, we could grant that the analysis of this modified Razian scenario shows that there is no necessary objectively-rational connection between law and coercion, yet insist that there is such a connection in subjectively-rational terms. This is an important result anyway. Think again of the conceptual connection by way of analogy: the Hartian conception entails that there is a conceptual connection between law and coercion, though perhaps not as stringent as many would have it. Something similar obtains, at the very least, regarding the rational connection.

9.10 Final remarks on the 'natural' connection as a *rational* connection

If willing to offer a more thorough defence of this neo-Hartian conception, one could try a somewhat more engaged reply. Given that I aim only to reasonably sketch the conception, but not to fully defend it now, I will confine myself here to three basic, interrelated remarks.

32 'Costly' is to be understood here in a broad sense, not restricted to material inputs. I mean to take into account issues as the following: will the angels establish new officials solely working for/as the coercive system, or will they simply add new functions to the offices they already had? Will they invest in building new facilities for the imposition of sanctions to non-compliers? Will they set complex, multi-layered procedures to identify and punish non-compliance, or will they be simple, fast procedures? The answer to questions like these makes for the degree of 'cost' their system will amount to. Even if the extent to which their fear is rationally justifiable is in the abstract rather sparse, how sparse it *actually* is stands partially as a function of what the management of their fear—as they intend and propose such management—requires of them. Hart himself has reflected on how a system of (criminal) sanctions can be more or less rational depending on other considerations: see Hart 2008, 170–171.

33 The angels' devising of a coercive system may be understood as a *precommitment* in Jon Elster's terms. See Elster 1979 and 2000.

(1) Objective rationality *is*, or at any rate *works for us*[34] as a regulative ideal: it is (or it works for us) more of (as) a normative goal than (as) an existing state of affairs or something alike. So the discussion the critic offers relates actually not to whether there is a rational connection between law and coercion—which is what we are trying to ascertain—but rather to whether there should be such a connection.[35] And this is shown by the substitution of (a) by (a') rehearsed—to little effect—just above. If we are to distinguish between objective and subjective rationality, it is plausible that, while the latter traffics in the justification of beliefs (evidence) and value judgements, the former deals rather with their truth or correctness. But *we humans* may not know what is true or correct. Even more so, we may be ignorant in a justified way.[36] We may be rightly justified in thinking that *p* when in fact *p* is not the case. An objectively rational agent would be fully informed, i.e., would know all that is epistemically relevant for any given situation (Kolodny 2005, 510).[37] However, such a quality is far from the human predicament. And if we postulate said quality into the (already 'angelic') angelic scenario we thus end up by making it meaningless *to us*,[38] as I claimed above;

(2) In the previous remark I said that we may not know what is true or correct in/of certain situations and that, even more so, we may be ignorant in a justified way. But our critic may want to insist that I mean a *subjectively justified* way, which is off the point since her objection regards objective rationality. This is all true. But does it not show how the strategy of questioning the recourse to one type of rationality 'from' the other can be used both ways? Why—we may ask—should we even care to face an objection of objective irrationality when we are trying to show a connection between law and coercion in terms of subjective rationality? This takes us back to the not very costly concession made three paragraphs above;

(3) The critic may respond by saying that objective rationality is 'more important' than subjective rationality. Or that it is 'ultimately' the 'only' or 'real' rationality. So, if on any occasion the requirements of objective rationality pull in a different direction from that in which the requirements of subjective rationality pull, then the former prevail. Leaving aside the epistemic problem that no one seems especially entitled to know the requirements

34 While the difference between how things are and how things work for/are taken by us is very important in many other contexts, it is immaterial in the present discussion.

35 I admit this is too blunt. In Section 9.11 below I will qualify this point, beginning by the recognition that both subjective and objective rationality may be cashed out as sets of *demands* upon us.

36 As elegantly put in Warnock 1971, 162–163. See also Raz 2007b, 33.

37 Alternatively, we may say that objectively rational agents are 'fully rational', yet '"[f]ully rational" agents are *hypothetical* agents purged of all irrationalities' (Paakkunainen 2018, 403. My emphasis).

38 And *our* understanding of *our* law, etc.

> of objective rationality (as opposed to what she just thinks they are)—so that in turn no one has a special claim to be able to tell when there is an actual conflict between the requirements of both types of rationality—there is also the problem of justifying the prevalence of one type over the other. As (2) above illustrates, each type of rationality claims for itself an absolute prevalence in its own realm. Should we adjudicate a conflict between the objective and subjective points of view, we could only do so, in a non-question-begging fashion, from a third standpoint which does not collapse into any of those. Now, if there were such a standpoint (and if we found it), the temptation of making it *the* standpoint of (ultimate, real, etc.) rationality would be hard to avoid. But what if a conflict arises between the rational requirements of this third standpoint and those of either objective or subjective rationality? Since these would still entail a claim to absolute prevalence in their own terms, such a conflict would have to be adjudicated from a new, higher, fourth standpoint. This leads to an infinite regress.[39] If this argument is sound, then our critic cannot force upon us anything regarding the requirements of objective rationality.[40]

With any luck, all the foregoing makes for a feasible conception of 'natural necessities' qua 'subjective rational necessities' and points to a necessary connection between law and coercion which is rational in kind. A kind of connection that is distinct, meaning different from both empirical and conceptual connections. While Hart is perhaps overly brief in his characterization of 'natural necessities', he is explicit about the connection between them and the demands of rationality. In his own words:

> except in very small closely-knit societies, submission to the system of restraints [configured by the set of norms on how one should behave] would be folly if there were no organization for the coercion of those who would then try to obtain the advantages of the system without submitting to its obligations. 'Sanctions' are therefore required not as the normal motive for obedience, but as a *guarantee* that those who would voluntarily obey shall not be sacrificed to those who would not. To obey, without this, would be to risk going to the wall. Given this standing danger, what reason demands is *voluntary* co-operation in a *coercive* system. (Hart 2012, 198)

39 I have built this argument by an analogy with the one David Copp offers considering potential conflicts between moral and prudential reasons. Such an argument favours the view that practical reason is *fragmentary*, against the more widespread view that it is *unitary*. See Copp 2007, chap. 9. See also Caracciolo 2009, chap. 13 for related discussion.

40 Of course, the same goes the other way round. Perhaps, the objective and the subjective amount to two different points of view which are, in their own ways, 'natural and necessary' (Nagel 1991, 210). And, as I have hinted at, the potential conflicts among them are, in a sense, irresolvable.

9.11 The quasi-constitutivist aspect

The account I have given of the distinct necessary rational connection between law and coercion has some interesting affinities with constitutivism in metaethics and the philosophy of action. We could say I have offered a *quasi-constitutivist* account of the connection between law and coercion.

Constitutivism is a view that relates reasons and agency. According to this view, some features constitutive of our being agents entail normative standards—and therefore reasons—bearing on our attitudes and actions. Typically, constitutivism is somehow restricted to the practical realm of intention and action, perhaps even to only some reasons pertaining to such realm (though this is to be taken with a grain of salt, given the many obvious ways in which belief and other doxastic attitudes are connected to action—ways that constitutivists try to account for). Also typically, constitutivists focus on what they argue to be *aims* that are defining of action-types, and so eventually of agency itself. Actions pursue ends, and so these aims work as success conditions for token-actions.[41]

It is uncontroversial that being at least minimally rational is closely linked to agency, so that being an agent equates to being an at least minimally rational agent (Paakkunainen 2018, 40). As we will see below, this element is crucial for the '*quasi*-constitutivist' adjective of my account.

Now, we can cast rationality in terms of *demands* or *requirements* on our attitudes and actions. I have been doing so occasionally hitherto. This in turn shows affinities between my discussion and constitutivism. Being rational implies abiding to certain normative standards. Or, put differently, to act rationally is to act in a way that conforms to certain standards. More generally, to have rational attitudes is to form them or get to them in a way which conforms to certain standards. For example, we saw that advocating for some manner of institutionalized coercive prohibition of murder is rational, since it may be a successful way of safeguarding life. This means that there are reasons in favour of such prohibition, in favour of proceeding to establish it (which requires acting). We also saw that the angels of the well-known thought experiment may rationally fear a change of their status quo. This means that they would do fine in coming to get that emotion, which would correspond to their holding life in high regard and that could also prompt them to do things that might further safeguard their treasured lives. This can all be translated into more thoroughly normative terms: in order to be rational, you should fear risk of damage to things you hold dear, and you should act accordingly trying to safeguard those things (even more so if it were the case that you should

41 Smith 2018 begins with a wider characterization of constitutivism, though he goes on to focus on agential constitutivism anyway. For other general overviews on constitutivism see Katsafanas 2018; Nye 2018; Southwood 2018. For specific constitutivist proposals see, e.g., Korsgaard 2009; Velleman 2009; Street 2012; Katsafanas 2013; Smith 2013.

hold dear those things you actually hold dear). And perhaps you should be rational in order to be an agent.[42]

The affinities between my account of the necessary rational connection between law and coercion, on the one hand, and constitutivism on the other, show that, in a certain sense, there is such a necessary connection between law and coercion because that is how it should be. It is how it rationally should be. Interestingly, the parallelism with constitutivism might also help see why the connection between law and coercion backed by my account can be aptly put in two ways that, while different in principle, merge together in a manner distinctive of constitutivist approaches: between law and coercion there is a *necessary rational* connection and(or) a *rationally necessary* connection.

Now, I would only want to take the parallelism so far, and that is why I have labelled my account as '*quasi*-constitutivist'. This is due to two main concerns.[43]

First, different constitutivist proposals vary regarding both the kind and source of the normative standards they claim to be derived from agency. This has to do, in part, with the distinction between subjective and objective rationality. Some authors seem to think that there are normative standards which flow from an idealized conception of agency, which is idealized to the extent that it assumes the model of an objectively (fully) rational agent. Other authors seem to offer constitutivist accounts stemming from a conception of agency linked to demands of subjective rationality—or at any rate a not completely idealized model or rational agent.[44] Indeed, the distinction between objective and subjective rationality is not too often drawn in constitutivist literature, and for a reason that leads us to the next point. Before that, though, I should finish stating the present qualm: as discussed above, my account of the 'natural' relation between law and coercion makes use of a subjective conception of rationality, precisely because it takes rationality in the way in which it is constitutive of *our* agency—and, therefore, of *us*, in the way our predicament actually *is*.

The second and most important qualm is related to the first as regards the reason why the distinction between objective and subjective rationality is not too often drawn in constitutivist literature: rationality is not normally taken to be a *feature* of agency, but rather as a sort of *prerequisite* of it. As said above, the typical feature of agency pointed at in constitutivist proposals relates to the defining *aims* of actions. Different proposals vary in what they argue are the defining aims of agency, and thus may also vary in the specific normative standards that, according to them, follow from such defining aims.[45] Rationality (at

42 Though see the *second qualm* below.

43 Constitutivism faces many challenges (see, e.g., Enoch 2006; Tiffany 2011; Tubert 2011). For the purposes of this chapter, I can remain neutral about them.

44 Smith exemplifies the former camp, Katsafanas the latter, whereas Korsgaard is perhaps somewhere in-between.

45 For example, Katsafanas 2013 argues for a Nietzschean kind of constitutivism according to which there are two constitutive aims of action: *activity as equilibrium* and *power* (chaps. 5–6).

least minimal) is presupposed in all of this, and the aims constitutive of action and agency go beyond mere rationality. Since my account is committed only to the rationality of linking law and coercion—a link that is necessary given the human condition, *our* human condition, and thus called for in subjective terms—its likeness to constitutivism turns out to be much more structural than substantial.[46]

9.12 Conclusion

In this chapter, I have argued for a neo-Hartian conception of the relation between law and coercion. According to such a view, law and coercion are connected at the empirical, the conceptual, and the 'natural' levels. The three connections are necessary, though in their own ways.

Empirically, coercion seems (intuitively) 'necessary' for the efficacy—and therefore existence and persistence—of legal systems. This is admittedly a weak form of necessary connection, but implies coercion in a strong, institutionalized sense. Conversely, at the conceptual level there is a strong necessary connection, since for a Hartian view there is no (paradigmatic) legal system without a rule of recognition and there is no rule of recognition without coercion. But the coercion thus necessitated is rather weak, in the sense that it is not institutionalized.

My central efforts have been devoted to the idea that there is a 'natural' relation between law and coercion. A relation that, as Hart hinted at, is to be understood in terms of rationality. I have tried to further develop this idea. In particular, I have tried to show how this kind of connection is indeed a third, *distinct* form of relation which does not collapse into either the empirical or conceptual realms. Moreover, I have sketched the basics of an understanding of *rationality* that fits such third and distinctive way and allows us to see why the connection between law and coercion (in a strong, institutionalized sense) is *necessary* at this rational level so conceived. Finally, I have stressed the interesting affinities that the resulting account has with constitutivism in metaethics and the philosophy of action—affinities that, however, seem largely structural rather than substantial, thus granting the *quasi-constitutivist* label for the account.

From these two aims follow some normative standards such as that the idea that all values are universally applicable ought to be rejected, that some extreme versions of egalitarianism ought to be rejected as well, and that we should seek a life of continuous attainment (chap. 8).

46 To continue with Katsafanas's proposal as an example, we may say that I have argued that intending to establish a legal coercive system is required by (subjective) rationality—a rationality that is a prerequisite to aiming to activity as equilibrium and to power—, but that I have not argued that said intending is necessarily conducive to either activity as equilibrium or power.

References

Becker, Gary. 1976. *The Economic Approach to Human Behavior*. Chicago: University of Chicago Press.

Bertea, Stefano. 2013. "Constitutivism and Normativity: A Qualified Defence." *Philosophical Explorations: An International Journal for the Philosophy of Mind and Action* 16 (1): 81–95.

Bix, Brian. 2004. "Natural Law: The Modern Tradition." In *The Oxford Handbook of Jurisprudence and Philosophy of Law*, edited by Jules Coleman and Scott Shapiro. Oxford: Oxford University Press.

Broome, John. 2013. *Rationality Through Reasoning*. Chichester: Wiley-Blackwell.

Caracciolo, Ricardo. 2009. *El derecho desde la filosofía. Ensayos*. Madrid: Centro de Estudios Políticos y Constitucionales.

Chiassoni, Pierluigi. 2013. "The Model of Ordinary Analysis." In *Reading H. L. A. Hart's The Concept of Law*, edited by Luís Duarte d'Almeida, James Edwards, and Andrea Dolcetti. Oxford: Hart Publishing.

Chilovi, Samuele, and George Pavlakos. 2019. "Law-Determination as Grounding: A Common Grounding Framework for Jurisprudence." *Legal Theory* 25 (1): 53–76.

Coleman, Jules. 2001. *The Practice of Principle. In Defence of a Pragmatist Approach to Legal Theory*. New York: Oxford University Press.

Copp, David. 2007. *Morality in a Natural World. Selected Essays in Metaethics*. New York: Cambridge University Press.

Dei Vecchi, Diego, and Pablo Rapetti. 2022. "Un *reconocimiento* a lo Eugenio Bulygin: identificación del derecho y descripción de deberes jurídicos." In *Eugenio Bulygin en la teoría del derecho contemporánea*, vol. II edited by Giovanni Ratti, Julieta Rábanos, and María Cristina Redondo. Madrid: Marcial Pons.

Dereboylular, Özde. 2020. "H. L. A. Hart's 'Minimum Content of Natural Law'." *Istambul Medipol Üniversitesi Hukuk Fakültesi Dergisi* 7 (2): 119–130.

Drury, Shadia. 1981. "H. L. A. Hart's Minimum Content Theory of Natural Law." *Political Theory* 9 (4): 533–546.

Elster, Jon. 1979. *Ulysses and the Sirens: Studies in Rationality and Irrationality*. Cambridge: Cambridge University Press.

Elster, Jon. 2000. *Ulysses Unbound: Studies in Rationality, Precommitment, and Constraints*. Cambridge: Cambridge University Press.

Enoch, David. 2006. "Agency, Shmagency: Why Normativity Won't Come from What Is Constitutive of Action." *Philosophical Review* 115 (2): 169–198.

Garcés, Mario, and Lucila Finkel. 2019. "Emotional Theory of Rationality." *Frontiers in Integrative Neuroscience* 13: 1–24.

Gardner, John. 2008. *Law as a Leap of Faith*. Oxford: Oxford University Press.

Gkouvas, Triantafyllos. 2023. *The Place of Coercion in Law*. Cambridge: Cambridge University Press.

González-Lagier, Daniel. 2009. *Emociones, responsabilidad y derecho*. Madrid: Marcial Pons.

Green, Donald, and Justin Fox. 2007. "Rational Choice Theory." In *The SAGE Handbook of Social Science Methodology*, edited by William Outhwaite and Stephen Turner. London: Sage.

Green, Leslie. 1996. "The Concept of Law Revisited." *Michigan Law Review* 94 (6): 1687–1717.

Hart, Herbert. 2012. *The Concept of Law*. 3rd ed. Oxford: Oxford University Press.
Hart, Herbert. 2008. *Punishment and Responsibility*. 2nd ed. Oxford: Oxford University Press.
Himma, Kenneth. 2020. *Coercion and the Nature of Law*. Oxford: Oxford University Press.
Jeung, Haang, Christiane Schwieren, and Sabine Herpetz. 2016. "Rationality and Self-Interest as Economic-Exchange Strategy in Borderline Personality Disorder: Game Theory, Social Preferences, and Interpersonal Behavior." *Neuroscience & Biobehavioral Reviews* 71: 849–864.
Jones, Karen. 2003. "Emotion, Weakness of Will, and the Normative Conception of Agency." In *Philosophy and the Emotions*, edited by Anthony Hatzimoysis. Cambridge: Cambridge University Press.
Katsafanas, Paul. 2013. *Agency and the Foundations of Ethics: Nietzschean Constitutivism*. Oxford: Oxford University Press.
Katsafanas, Paul. 2018. "Constitutivism about Practical Reasons." In *The Oxford Handbook of Reasons and Normativity*, edited by Daniel Star. Oxford: Oxford University Press.
Kolodny, Niko. 2005. "Why Be Rational?" *Mind* 114 (455): 509–563.
Kolodny, Niko. 2008. "Why Be Disposed to Be Coherent?" *Ethics* 118 (3): 437–463.
Korsgaard, Christine. 2009. *Self-Constitution: Agency, Identity, and Integrity*. Oxford: Oxford University Press.
Lamond, Grant. 2001. "Coercion and the Nature of Law." *Legal Theory* 7 (1): 35–57.
Margain, Hugo. 1978. *Racionalidad, lenguaje y filosofía*. Ciudad de México: Fondo de Cultura Económica.
Mele, Alfred. 2009. *Effective Intentions: The Power of Conscious Will*. Oxford: Oxford University Press.
Miotto, Lucas. 2020. "From Angels to Humans: Law, Coercion, and the Society of Angels Thought Experiment." *Law and Philosophy* 40: 277–303.
Miotto, Lucas. 2021. "What Makes Law Coercive When It Is Coercive?" *Archiv für Rechts- und Sozialphilosophie* 107 (2): 235–250.
Moya, Carlos. 2000. "Emociones y libertad." *Thémata* 25: 67–79.
Nagel, Thomas. 1991. *Mortal Questions*. 2nd ed. New York: Cambridge University Press.
Nye, Howard. 2018. "The Wrong Kind of Reasons." In *The Routledge Handbook of Metaethics*, edited by Tristram McPherson and David Plunkett. New York: Routledge.
Olivé, León. 1988. "Racionalidad y relativismo: relativismo moderadamente radical." In *Racionalidad. Ensayos sobre la racionalidad en ética y política, ciencia y tecnología*, edited by León Olivé. Ciudad de México: Siglo XXI.
Ortiz-Millán, Gustavo. 2019. "Nussbaum, las emociones y los muchos sentidos de 'cognitivo'." In *Emociones y racionalidad. Cuatro ensayos*, edited by Francisco Serrano and Rocío Cázares Blanco. Ciudad de México: Ediciones Coyoacán.
Paakkunainen, Hille. 2018. "Normativity and Agency." In *The Routledge Handbook of Metaethics*, edited by Tristram McPherson and David Plunkett. London: Routledge.
Patterson, Dennis, and Bosko Tripkovic. 2023. "The Promise and Limits of Grounding in Law." *Legal Theory* 29 (3): 202–228.
Pereda, Carlos. 1994. *Razón e incertidumbre*. Ciudad de México: Siglo XXI.

Pintore, Anna. 2014. "'*A Rule-Governed Gunman Writ Large*'? El puesto de la coerción en *The Concept of Law*." *Doxa. Cuadernos de Filosofía del Derecho* 37: 125–142.

Rapetti, Pablo. 2015. "*Estudio preliminar*: Ángeles a punta de pistola." In *Fuerza de ley*, by Frederick Schauer. Translated (into Spanish) by Pablo Rapetti. Lima: Palestra.

Rapetti, Pablo. 2021. "Law's Function, Descriptive Conceptual Analysis, and Legal Positivism: Some Methodological Qualms." *Revus. Journal for Constitutional Theory and Philosophy of Law* 45: 93–105.

Raz, Joseph. 1999. *Practical Reason and Norms*. 2nd ed. Oxford: Oxford University Press.

Raz, Joseph. 2007a. "Teoría y conceptos: réplica a Alexy y Bulygin." In *Una discusión sobre teoría del derecho: Joseph Raz, Robert Alexy, Eugenio Bulygin*, edited by Hernán Bouvier, Paula Gaido, and Rodrigo Sánchez Brígido. Translated by Rodrigo Sánchez Brígido. Madrid: Marcial Pons.

Raz, Joseph. 2007b. "The Argument from Justice, of How Not to Reply to Legal Positivism." In *Law, Rights and Discourse: The Legal Philosophy of Robert Alexy*, edited by George Pavlakos. Portland: Hart Publishing.

Raz, Joseph. 2013. *Between Authority and Interpretation. On the Theory of Law and Practical Reason*. Oxford: Oxford University Press.

Ruiz Manero, Juan. 1991. "Entrevista con Joseph Raz." *Doxa. Cuadernos de Filosofía del Derecho* 9: 321–344.

Schauer, Frederick. 2015. *The Force of Law*. Cambridge, Massachusetts: Harvard University Press.

Shapiro, Scott. 2011. *Legality*. Cambridge, MA: Harvard Belknap Press.

Smith, Michael. 2013. "A Constitutivist Theory of Reasons: Its Promise and Parts." *Law, Ethics, and Philosophy* 1: 9–30.

Smith, Michael. 2018. "Constitutivism." In *The Routledge Handbook of Metaethics*, edited by Tristram McPherson and David Plunkett. New York: Routledge.

Southwood, Nicholas. 2018. "Constructivism about Practical Reasons." In *The Oxford Handbook of Reasons and Normativity*, edited by Daniel Star. New York: Oxford University Press.

Street, Sharon. 2012. "Coming to Terms with Contingency: Humean Constructivism about Practical Reason." In *Constructivism in Practical Philosophy*, edited by James Lenman and Yonatan Shemmer. Oxford: Oxford University Press.

Sucar, Germán. 2017. "*Presentación:* Sacro judicial y filosofía del derecho." In *La gracia de los jueces. La institución judicial y lo sagrado en Occidente*, by Robert Jacob. Translated (into Spanish) by José Gutiérrez Privat. Valencia: Tirant lo Blanch.

Summers, Robert. 1963. "Professor H. L. A. Hart's 'Concept of Law'." *Duke Law Journal* 4: 629–670.

Tappolet, Christine. 2018. "Reasons and Emotions." In *The Oxford Handbook of Reasons and Normativity*, edited by Daniel Star. Oxford: Oxford University Press.

Tiffany, Evan. 2011. "Why Be an Agent?" *Australasian Journal of Philosophy* 90 (2): 223–233.

Tubert, Ariela. 2011. "Korsgaard's Constitutive Arguments and the Principles of Practical Reason." *Philosophical Quarterly* 61 (243): 343–362.

Vázquez Álvarez, Rafael. 2024. *¿Es la coerción una propiedad necesaria del concepto de derecho?* PhD thesis presented at UNAM. Supervised by Pau Luque Sánchez, Diego Dei Vecchi and Pablo Rapetti.

Velleman, David. 2009. *How We Get Along*. Cambridge: Cambridge University Press.

Warnock, Geoffrey. 1971. *The Object of Morality*. London: Methuen & Co.
Whiting, Demian. 2011. "The Feeling Theory of Emotion and the Object-Directed Emotions." *European Journal of Philosophy* 19 (2): 281–303.
Yankah, Ekow. 2008. "The Force of Law: The Role of Coercion in Legal Norms." *University of Richmond Law Review* 42 (5): 1195–1255.

10 Robert Alexy's legal constitutivism

Torben Spaak[1]

10.1 Introduction

Constitutivism about practical reason is the view that human action has a constitutive aim or else involves some sort of constitutive principle, and that this aim, or principle, is what turns an event into an action and yields normative standards of assessment for action. Such constitutivism is interesting inter alia because if it works out, it will help us make progress in the debate between internalists and externalists about reasons for action by entailing that all agents have at least one necessary aim, namely, one that is constitutive of human action. The theory of constitutivism is not without its problems, however. One may, in particular, doubt whether it is possible to identify an aim or a principle of human action that applies to all different types of human actions while also yielding normative standards of assessment for all these types of actions. Hence it may be worth a legal philosopher's while to try to figure out whether there might be room for a more limited type of constitutivism, namely, a *legal* constitutivism according to which specifically legal actions have such a constitutive aim or involve a constitutive principle that turns a non-legal event or action into a legal action while also yielding standards of assessment for such action. But instead of discussing the possibility of legal constitutivism in the abstract, I shall focus on an extant version of legal constitutivism, namely, the dual-nature theory of law defended by distinguished legal philosopher Robert Alexy. Although to my knowledge Alexy has never said that he is a legal constitutivist, I believe it is fair to say that his dual-nature theory of law is, or can be seen as, a version of legal constitutivism. The reason is that he argues (i) that legal acts necessarily raise a claim to correctness (the correctness

1 I would like to thank Stefano Bertea, Åke Frändberg, and Victor Moberger as well as the participants in the advanced seminar in practical philosophy at the Department of Philosophy, Uppsala University, for helpful comments on the text. Of course, the responsibility for any remaining errors and imperfections lies solely with the author. In addition, I would like to thank Robert Carroll for checking my English. Note, finally, that my discussion of Alexy's theory in sections 4-6 builds on and develops ideas I have put forward in Spaak (2020). A few paragraphs can be found, more or less verbatim, in the publication just mentioned.

DOI: 10.4324/9781032670553-11

thesis), which is to say that they constitutively aim at correctness; (ii) that it follows from law's raising a claim to correctness that law has a dual nature (the dual nature thesis); (iii) that the dual nature of law yields normative standards of assessment for legal actions by implying that legal acts that do not raise a claim to correctness, or raise one but fail to satisfy it, will lack legal character or else will be legally defective; (iv) that the dual nature of law is incompatible with the separation thesis of legal positivism; and (v) that it follows from law's dual nature that legal argumentation is a special case of general practical argumentation (the special case thesis).[2] In addition, he maintains (vi) that if we were to reject the idea that legal acts necessarily raise a claim to correctness, that is, that they constitutively aim at correctness, we would thereby completely change the theory and practice of law and, indeed, ourselves. For, he reasons, we would then be unable to distinguish between what is true and what is false, between substantiation and persuasion, between what is objective and what is subjective, and so on.

I am, however, going to argue (A) that even if in some sense legal acts necessarily raise a claim to correctness, it does not follow that law has a dual nature; (B) that even if it did follow that law has a dual nature, while it would follow from law's dual nature in turn that legal acts that do not raise a claim to correctness, or raise one but fail to satisfy it, lacked legal character or else were legally defective, it would not follow (i) that the separation thesis of legal positivism was false, or (ii) that legal argumentation was a special case of general practical argumentation; and that this means that interesting and well-argued as it is, Alexy's legal constitutivism fails; and (C) that this in turn suggests that constitutivists about practical reason are fighting an uphill battle, since it must reasonably be even more difficult to identify an aim or a principle that is constitutive of, and yields normative standards for, human action in general, than to do this in the case of legal action.

I begin by introducing the central ideas of constitutivism about practical reason (Section 10.2) and proceed to illustrate these ideas by briefly considering Christine Korsgaard's Kantian version of constitutivism (Section 10.3). I then introduce Alexy's legal constitutivism (Sections 10.4 and 10.5) and raise certain objections to Alexy's claims that the correctness thesis implies the dual-nature thesis (Section 10.6), that the dual-nature thesis contradicts the separation thesis of legal positivism (Section 10.7), and that the dual-nature thesis implies the special case thesis (Section 10.8). The chapter concludes with a brief consideration of a possible way to allay Alexy's worries about the broader consequences of rejecting the idea that law necessarily raises a claim to correctness (Section 10.9).

2 I discuss these claims in more detail in Sections 10.4–10.8, especially Section 10.5.

10.2 Constitutivism about practical reason: a short introduction

As I have said, constitutivism about practical reason is the view that action in general has a constitutive aim, or else involves some sort of constitutive principle, and that this aim, or principle, (i) turns an attitude or event into an action and (ii) yields normative standards for the assessment of action. If we are concerned with constitutivism focusing on the constitutive *aim* of action, we might say, following Paul Katsafanas (2018, 369–370), that if *A* is a type of attitude or event and *G* is a goal, then *A* constitutively aims at *G* if, and only if, (i) each token of *A* aims at *G*, and (ii) aiming at *G* is part of what constitutes an attitude or event as a token of *A*.[3] If instead we are concerned with constitutivism that focuses on action in accordance with a constitutive *principle*, we might say that if *A* is a type of attitude or event and *P* is a principle, then *A* constitutively involves action in keeping with *P* if, and only if, (i) each token of *A* involves action in keeping with *P*, and (ii) action in keeping with *P* is part of what constitutes an attitude or event as a token of *A*. As we shall see (in Section 10.4), Alexy's legal constitutivism is of the former type, that is, it focuses on the constitutive aim of legal action and not on a constitutive principle. And if action does have a constitutive aim, or involves a constitutive principle, we might say that this aim, or this principle, functions as a standard of success in such a way that it generates normative standards of assessment for action. For example, if chess-playing has a constitutive aim of checkmating the opponent, we can assess the actions of chess players by looking and seeing whether they are conducive to the goal of achieving checkmate (ibid., 369).

While there may be several reasons to take an interest in constitutivism in law and elsewhere, one good reason is that if it works out, it will help us make progress in the debate between internalists and externalists about reasons for action. While *internalism* is the view that a consideration can be a normative reason for an agent only if it is grounded in what Bernard Williams (1981, 102) refers to as the agent's subjective motivational set, which includes the agent's aims, desires, values, etc., *externalism* is the view that a consideration can be a normative reason for an agent even if it is not grounded in this way. Both theories have their problems, however: whereas internalists have found it difficult to generate universal normative claims, such as 'you ought not to murder', since not everyone has the relevant aims, externalists have found it difficult to explain the motivating force of external reasons: if the relevant consideration is not included in the agent's subjective motivational set, how can it motivate the agent to act on it? As Williams points out (ibid., 107–111), if the externalist holds that the agent needs to *believe* that there is a specific external reason to act in the relevant way in order to be motivated, it seems that either externalism will collapse into internalism or all external reasons statements will

3 Although it seems to me that (i) is redundant since (ii) seems to entail (i), I shall follow Katsafanas here.

be false. The appeal of constitutivism, then, at least from the point of view of an internalist, is that it promises to show that there is indeed something that is included in each and every agent's subjective motivational set, namely, the aim or principle that is constitutive of human action.

10.3 Constitutivism about practical reason: Christine Korsgaard

In her article 'Self-constitution in the ethics of Plato and Kant' (1999), Christine Korsgaard defends (what she calls) the Constitutional Model of action, according to which the function of action is self-constitution.[4] She argues, more specifically (ibid., 3), (P1) that an agent can be said to be performing a certain type of action, say, voting or making a promise, if, and only if, the purported action can be attributed to the agent conceived as a unified whole; (P2) that the action can be attributed to the agent conceived as a unified whole if, and only if, the principle of the agent's action fully unifies the agent; and (P3) that the one principle of action that fully unifies the agent is the categorical imperative. The conclusion, then, is that the agent is performing the relevant type of action if, and only if, the principle of his action is the categorical imperative.

Korsgaard points out that both Plato and Kant are committed to something like the Constitutional Model of action. For example, she explains (ibid., 5–7) that Plato likens the soul of a person to a *city* and maintains that just as the three classes in the city—the rulers, the auxiliaries (roughly, policemen and soldiers), and the citizens—must work together and avoid interfering with the tasks of the other classes if the city is to be able to act as an agent, the three parts of the soul—reason, spirit, and appetites—must work together and avoid interfering with the tasks of the other parts if the soul is to be able to function as an agent.

As Korsgaard also points out, both Plato and Kant first identify a *metaphysical* property of action—constitutionality in Plato's and autonomy in Kant's case—and then identify this property with a *normative* property, justice in Plato's and universalizability in Kant's case. Hence if action has the metaphysical property, *M*, it must have the normative property, *N*, too, say that of being good, or being such that it ought to be performed: necessarily, if *M* then *N*. But, she points out (ibid., 14), this appears to entail that bad actions are not actions. For if the action has *M*, it must have *N*, too. But since a bad action does not have *N*, it cannot have *M* either, and, on Plato's and Kant's analyses, if it does not have *M*, it cannot be an action.

Korsgaard attempts to handle this problem by introducing a distinction between internal and external standards, where an *internal* standard is one

4 Korsgaard offers a more comprehensive and systematic discussion of the Constitutional Model of action in Korsgaard (2009), especially Chapters 7 and 8. For our purposes, however, the discussion in Korsgaard (1999) is sufficient.

that 'arises from the nature of the object to which it applies, that is, from the functional or teleological norms which make the object the object that it is', and an external standard is a standard that is not internal (ibid., 14). She then argues that the *moral* standards that we apply to action are precisely internal standards, that is, they arise from the functional or teleological norms which make the action the action that it is, and that this is important because unlike external standards, internal standards can easily meet challenges to their normativity:

> An agent cannot simply set aside the question whether his action is universalizable or just, for if he falls too far short of the internal standards for actions, what he produces will simply not be an action. In effect this means that even the most venal and shoddy agent must try to perform a good action, for the simple reason that there is no other way to try to perform an action. Performing a good action and performing an action are not different activities: for both are activities in which we must be guided by the functional or teleological norms implicit in the idea of an action. Obviously, it doesn't follow that every action is a good action. It does, however, follow that performing bad actions is not a different activity from performing good ones. *It is the same activity, badly done.* (Ibid., 15)

So, as Korsgaard sees it, although an action that does not fully meet its internal standards is indeed an action, it is *defective* as an action (ibid., 14). And, she continues, (ibid., 16), if this is so we can explain why our actions must meet moral standards, namely, that '[u]njust or nonuniversalizable actions would be *defective*: they would be bad *as actions*'. Having discussed some sample cases, she then points out (ibid., 20) that in the case of both Plato and Kant bad action is action that is governed by a principle that is not reason's own principle, that is, justice (in the case of Plato) or universalizability (in the case of Kant), but is, say, a principle of honour, prudence, or wantonness. The idea appears to be that if the agent follows the wrong principle, say, a principle of honour, or a principle of prudence, he will not be fully unified, and if he is not fully unified, his action will be defective; and the reason why the agent will not be fully unified is that the unity achieved by following the wrong principle will be contingent and thus unstable in the sense that the circumstances that will, so to speak, create civil war in the agent's soul may or may not occur, as the case may be, and the agent can only hope that they won't occur.

10.4 Alexy's legal constitutivism

I shall argue in this section that Robert Alexy can be fairly classified as a legal constitutivist, because, although he speaks of a necessary claim to correctness and the dual nature of law, he can also be understood to maintain (a) that legal acts constitutively aim at correctness, namely, by necessarily raising a claim to correctness (the correctness thesis); (b) that it follows from law's constitutive aim at correctness that law has a dual nature (the dual nature thesis); (c) that the dual nature of law yields normative standards of assessment for legal actions by implying that legal acts that do not raise a claim to correctness, or raise one but fail to satisfy it, will lack legal character or else will be legally defective; (d) that the dual nature of law is incompatible with the separation thesis of legal positivism; and (e) that it follows from law's dual nature that legal argumentation is a special case of general practical argumentation (the special case thesis).

I shall not, however, be primarily concerned in what follows with logical implication (entailment), or analytical implication (which holds in virtue of *meaning*, not logical form), between the above-mentioned theses (a), (b), and (e), but with a metaphysical relation called *grounding* which concerns states of affairs.[5] While Alexy does *not* speak of 'grounding', but appears to view himself as being primarily concerned with conceptual analysis and thus with analytical entailment, I believe he is ultimately concerned with the metaphysics of law—after all, he is focusing on the *concept* of law in order to clarify the *nature* of law (Alexy 2008, 291–292; 2007, 41–42); and I also believe the idea of a grounding relation between states of affairs, although not without its problems, is an idea that fits not only Alexy's discussion, but most contemporary discussions of the nature of law. If we thus allow ourselves to change our focus from the conceptual to the metaphysical level of thinking, and to focus on the grounding relation, we may say that Alexy holds that the circumstance (the state of affairs) that law's constitutive aim, that is, law's necessary raising of a claim to correctness, (a*) grounds the dual nature of law (b*), that the dual nature of law (b*) grounds the practical character of legal argumentation (e*), and that therefore law's constitutive aim (a*) grounds the practical character of legal argumentation (e*).

Whereas the entailment relation is truth-functional, in the sense that its truth-value is a function of the truth-values of its component statements, we see that the truth-value of the statement '*X* grounds *Y*' does not depend solely on the truth-values of the corresponding statements, '*X* is the case', and '*Y* is the case', but also presupposes precisely that *X grounds Y*; and while causal relations and grounding relations share the property of being non-truth-functional, they are clearly different. Thus, whereas the falling rain causes the streets to be wet and the stone causes the window to break, the shape of the clay grounds, but does not cause, the clay's property of being a statue of Napoleon, and the action's property of being a life-saving action grounds, but does not cause, the action's status as a morally right action.

The grounding relation thus conceived is irreflexive, asymmetric, and transitive. That is to say, *X* does not ground *X*; if *X* grounds *Y*, then *Y* does not

5 On grounding in the field of law, see, e.g., Gizbert-Studnicki 2016, 132–141; Patterson and Tripkovic 2023.

ground *X*; and if *X* grounds *Y* and *Y* grounds *Z*, then *X* grounds *Z*. Thus, in our case, the raising of the claim to correctness does not ground itself; if the raising of the claim to correctness grounds the dual nature of law, the dual nature of law does not ground the raising of the claim to correctness; and if the raising of the claim to correctness grounds the dual nature of law and the dual nature of law grounds the practical character of legal argumentation, the raising of the claim to correctness grounds the practical character of legal argumentation.

In light of this, we may say, on a grounding interpretation of Alexy's analysis, that law's necessary raising of a claim to correctness, or law's constitutive aim, grounds law's dual nature, that law's dual nature in turn grounds the practical character of legal argumentation, and that therefore law's necessary raising of a claim to correctness, or law's constitutive aim, grounds the practical character of legal argumentation. Figure 1 illustrates this.

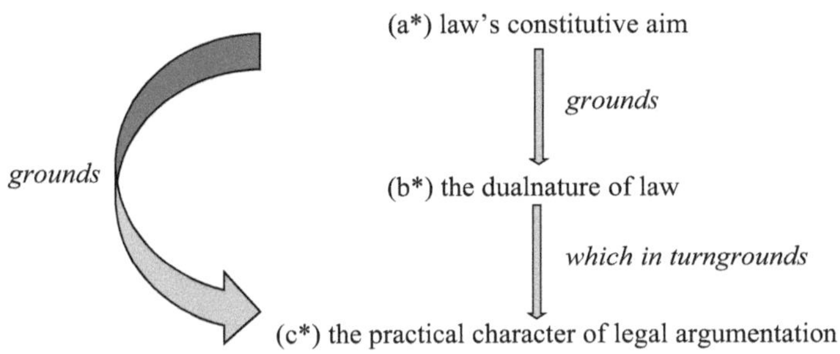

Figure 10.1 Grounding interpretation of Alexy's analysis.

Let us now in turn consider the relations between (a*) and (b*) and between (b*) and (c*). As regards the relation between (a*) and (b*), Alexy reasons that whereas the elements of authoritative issuance and social efficacy constitute the real dimension of law, the necessary raising of the claim to correctness constitutes the ideal dimension. And, he points out, this means that the dual-nature thesis implies non-positivism (2010, 167): '[i]f one claims that social facts alone can determine what is and what is not required by law, that amounts to the endorsement of a positivistic concept of law. Once moral correctness is added as a necessary third element, the picture changes fundamentally. A non-positivistic concept of law emerges'. As I understand him,[6] he reasons (i) that all positivist theories accept the separation thesis, which has it that the concept of law is to be defined such that no moral elements are included, whereas all non-positivistic theories accept the connection thesis, which says that the concept of law is to be defined such that moral elements are included (2002, 3–4); (ii) that law's necessary raising of a claim to

6 As I have said, Alexy does not speak of 'grounding', and even if he did, he might well prefer to simplify the argument, perhaps by eliminating step (iii) and reformulating step (ii).

correctness, or law's constitutive aim, grounds a necessary connection between law and morality; (iii) that the necessary connection between law and morality grounds, or is identical with, law's dual nature; (iv) that law's dual nature grounds the connection thesis, and (v) that the connection thesis contradicts the separation thesis.

Note, however, that Alexy's separation thesis is not identical to the separation thesis of legal positivism (on the latter see, e.g., Hart 1958; Kelsen 1992, 56; Coleman 2001, 104), which has it that there is no necessary connection between the content of law and true morality. One might think that the two theses are equivalent, or at least that the former thesis entails the latter (Alexy 2002, 3), or vice versa, but this might not be so.[7] I am, however, convinced that in any case Alexy meant to discuss precisely the separation thesis of legal positivism, and I shall therefore focus in what follows precisely on this thesis, not Alexy's version of the thesis.

Note also that the separation thesis of legal positivism can be understood in two different ways, namely, (i) as a thesis about the content of (first-order) legal statements, according to which such legal statements do not entail corresponding (first-order) moral statements (see, e.g., Kelsen 1959–1960, 273; Hart 1982, 159–161, 266–267),[8] or (ii) as a thesis about legal status, according to which a legal norm does not lose its legal status on account of being immoral (see, e.g., Kelsen 1992, 56).[9] And, as we are about to see, Alexy is concerned only with the separation thesis conceived as a thesis about legal status.

Alexy clearly believes that law's dual nature yields normative standards of assessment for legal action. Invoking a distinction between classifying and qualifying connections between law and true morality, he explains (2002, 35–36) (i) that a normative system that does not even raise a claim to correctness lacks legal character (he dubs this a *classifying* connection between law and morality), (ii) that a legal system that does raise a claim to correctness, but fails to satisfy it, is a legally defective system (he dubs this a *qualifying* connection), and (iii) that individual legal norms and decisions that either do not

7 One might argue that there can be a necessary connection between the content of law and true morality, even if the concept of law is so defined that no moral elements are included, say, if (a) the content of law is for some reason necessarily such that it includes all and only those norms that maximize utility and (b) utilitarianism is the true moral theory. For (a) is in keeping with Alexy's separation thesis since utility-maximization is a factual property, while the combination of (a) and (b) violates the separation thesis of legal positivism by establishing a necessary connection between the content of law and true morality. An example of this general type was suggested to me by Jens Johansson.

8 I believe methodological positivism, which has it that legal science is value-neutral, takes aim at this version of the separation thesis. On this type of legal positivism, see Spaak and Mindus (2021, 13–14) with references.

9 For more on the two versions of the separation thesis, see Spaak and Mindus (2021, 9–10).

raise a claim to correctness at all, or do raise one but fail to satisfy it, are legally defective norms or decisions (a *qualifying* connection, too).

Alexy does not explain precisely what it means to say that an act is legally defective, or why some faults lead to loss of legal character whereas other faults lead only to legal defectiveness. If, however, we invoke Korsgaard's discussion of internal standards (in Section 10.3 above), we might say that an act 'lacks legal character' if, and only if, it *completely* fails to meet the relevant internal standards, and that it is 'legally defective' if, and only if, it does not *fully* meet the internal standards. Here 'internal standards' refers to the functional or teleological standards that make the relevant act the act that it is; in the present case, the central internal standard is that the act constitutively aims at correctness. On this analysis, then, the relevant difference appears to be that in the former cases the agent is not acting in accordance with any aim, whereas in the latter cases he is acting in accordance with the wrong aim, and that the unity he achieves by acting in accordance with the wrong aim will be contingent and unstable.

Of course, this does not explain why, on Alexy's analysis, a normative system that does *not* raise a claim to correctness lacks legal character, while individual norms and decisions that do *not* raise a claim to correctness are only legally defective. For in both cases there is, as far as I can see, a *complete* failure to meet the constitutive aim of law. I shall not, however, pursue this objection, but shall proceed in what follows on the assumption that the distinction between loss of legal character and legal defectiveness can be defended in Alexy's theory and that law's dual nature thus yields normative standards of assessment for legal action in the sense just explained.

As regards the relation between (b*), the dual nature of law, and (c*), the practical character of legal argumentation,[10] I am guessing that Alexy reasons (P1) that general practical discourse *must* proceed in accordance with certain norms of discourse, because proceeding in accordance with such norms is 'a condition of the possibility of linguistic communication' or else because such rules are constitutive of certain speech acts that we cannot do without, except by, in a sense, giving up on aspects of our humanity (1989, 185–186); (P2) that these norms of discourse are practically correct, or can be treated as such on the grounds that their necessity renders the question of correctness moot; (P3) that these practically correct norms of discourse satisfy law's constitutive aim, or the claim to correctness; and that therefore (C) they become part of the ideal dimension of law (2018, 254–256).[11]

10 According to Alexy (1989, 20), the special case thesis is the thesis that 'specifically legal and general practical arguments should be combined at all levels and applied jointly'.

11 Strictly speaking, Alexy (1989, 180–187) says as regards (P1) that he can see at least four possible ways to justify the norms of discourse, one of which is the universal-pragmatic mode of justification, described above. He is quite clear, however, that this mode of justification has its problems, and that the same can be said about the other possible modes of justification. I pre-

I have doubts about the cogency of Alexy's argument, however. I doubt not only that the norms of discourse are necessary in the sense explained (P1), but also that such necessity would imply practical correctness, or that we would be justified in treating them as if they were practically correct, on the grounds that their necessity renders the question of correctness moot (P2); and if either of these objections hold, the norms of discourse cannot become part of the ideal dimension of law on the grounds that they satisfy law's constitutive aim. And if this is so, the dual nature of law does not ground the practical character of legal argumentation.

10.5 The correctness thesis: meaning and justification

As we have seen, the correctness thesis—that law necessarily raises a claim to correctness—is the keystone in Alexy's legal philosophy; most, or at least much, of what Alexy says about the nature of law and legal argumentation depends in one way or another on the truth and meaning of the correctness thesis. But what, exactly, is the meaning of the correctness thesis? And is the thesis really true?

To raise a claim to correctness, Alexy explains (1998, 208), involves (i) asserting that the relevant legal act is substantially and procedurally correct, (ii) guaranteeing that it can be justified, and (iii) expressing the expectation that the addressees of the act will accept the act as correct. These three elements, he continues (ibid., 208–209), are connected not only to institutional legal acts, such as the acts of enacting a law or handing down a court judgement, but also to legal acts performed by other participants in the legal system, such as the act of a citizen claiming that a certain behaviour is legally permitted. He adds (ibid., 209) that the criteria of correctness in the claim to correctness are characteristically open and may vary from one field of law to another and from one legal system to another. He does not, however, elaborate on this claim.

Observing that in the final analysis only *persons* can make claims, Alexy (ibid., 206) explains that law can raise a claim to correctness in the sense that those who 'act for and in law by creating, interpreting, using, and enforcing it' raise a claim to correctness. To clarify the sense in which the spokesmen of the law raise a claim to correctness, he introduces a distinction between a subjective and an objective raising of a claim and explains that he has in mind the latter (ibid., 206): whereas a person raises a claim subjectively if he wishes to raise it (and does raise it), he raises a claim objectively if the claim is necessarily connected to his role as a participant in the legal system. The idea, then, is that if law-makers, judges, and others who participate in the legal system didn't

sent his argument formulated in stronger terms, however, because it needs to be this strong to establish that the dual nature of law grounds the practical character of legal argumentation.

raise a claim to correctness in performing their legal tasks, they would not be acting as participants at all, or else would be acting as defective participants.

To substantiate the correctness thesis, Alexy considers a hypothetical constitutional article (CA) and a hypothetical court judgement (CJ) (2002, 35–39). His strategy is to identify an *absurdity* in the very idea of a legal act—such as an act of legislation, a court judgement, or an act-in-the-law, or the more informal act of defending a certain interpretation of a statute—that does not involve a claim to correctness, and to argue that such an absurdity can only be explained by reference to the occurrence of (what he calls) a *performative contradiction*. The constitutional article reads as follows:

> (CA) X is a sovereign, federal, and unjust republic.

And the court judgement reads as follows:

> (CJ) The accused is sentenced to life imprisonment, which is an incorrect interpretation of prevailing law.

Beginning with (CA), Alexy points out that the absurdity is not due to a technical, moral, or conventional fault, but to a performative contradiction. What he means is that the reason why (CA) is absurd is that the act of legislation necessarily involves precisely the raising of a claim to correctness, and that this claim is contradicted by the *content* of (CA). For the declaration that *X* is an *unjust* republic contradicts the claim to correctness, which, as we have seen, involves the subsidiary claim that the act is substantially and procedurally correct. Turning to (CJ), he employs the same type of reasoning. That is to say, he argues that the reason why (CJ) is absurd is that rendering a judgement necessarily involves the raising of a claim to correctness, and that this claim is contradicted by the *content* of (CJ) (ibid., 39). For the declaration that the judgement *incorrectly interprets* the prevailing law clearly contradicts the subsidiary claim that the act is substantially and procedurally correct. And since this is so, we have in this case, too, a performative contradiction. Note that whereas the absurdity in (CJ) appears to be strictly legal in the sense of having no moral component, the absurdity in (CA) appears to be of a moral nature. Hence if the claim to correctness is to explain the absurdity in the case of (CA), it must have moral content (on this topic, see also Alexy's open texture argument in 1998, 214–215).

As I understand it, on Alexy's analysis, a performative contradiction is a contradiction that arises because the agent *misuses a concept* that is involved in his claim (2002, 37, 39). For example, to maintain 'I know the cat is on the mat, but I don't believe it' is to fail to appreciate that knowledge (I *know* the cat is on the mat) implies belief (I *believe* the cat is on the mat); and to maintain '*X* is a sovereign, federal, and unjust republic' or 'the accused is sentenced to life imprisonment, which is an incorrect interpretation of prevailing law' is to fail to appreciate that the concepts of a legislative act and of a court decision both include the concept of a claim to correctness, which contradicts the content of the relevant statement. However, elsewhere Alexy points out that performative contradictions also include violations of rules that are constitutive of, or are presupposed by, speech acts (Alexy 1998, 210).[12] This means, I take it, that one who attempts to make an assertion, say, without raising a claim to correctness, is either not making an assertion at all or else is making a defective assertion.

We see, then, that Alexy reasons that the best explanation of the existence of performative contradictions in the cases of (CA) and (CJ) is (1) that legal acts necessarily raise a claim to correctness that involves (a) asserting that the relevant legal act is substantially and procedurally correct, (b) guaranteeing that it can be justified, and (c) expressing the expectation that the addressees of the act will accept the act as correct; and (2) that the claim to correctness thus conceived has moral content. We may express the same idea in constitutivist terms by saying that Alexy reasons that the best explanation of the existence of performative contradictions in the cases of (CA) and (CJ) is (1*) that legal acts constitutively aim at correctness in the sense of (1a-c), and (2*) that the constitutive aim is at least partly a moral aim.

Let us now turn to consider the important question of whether the best explanation of the existence of a performative contradiction in the cases of (CA) and (CJ) really is that legal acts necessarily raise a claim to correctness in Alexy's sense or, if you prefer, that legal acts constitutively aim at correctness. As we shall see, this may not be the case.

10.6 The correctness thesis and the dual-nature thesis

Is Alexy right? Does law raise a claim to correctness, and if so, does it follow that law has a dual nature? Joseph Raz (2008) objects to Alexy's analysis, that Alexy misunderstands the nature of the claim to correctness. He maintains, more specifically, (i) that the correctness thesis—the thesis that legal acts necessarily raise a claim to correctness—is really a special case of a general and formal thesis about *intentional action*, according to which every intentional action commits its agent to its own appropriateness in the following sense (ibid., 26): 'if [the] agent acts intentionally and is proven to have acted inappropriately or unwisely ... he must, once convinced of his mistake, believe that he should not have acted as he did, on pain of irrationality'; (ii) that the standards that determine whether a given type of action is appropriate vary with the type of intentional act under consideration; and (iii) that this means that Alexy cannot use the correctness thesis to clarify the nature of law, but must instead use independently available insights into the nature of law to clarify the correctness thesis. In particular, if the claim to correctness has moral content, as

12 This is in keeping with what Alexy says above (in Section 10.4) about the two senses in which the norms of discourse are necessary to general practical discourse.

Alexy holds, then this is so, Raz points out, because it follows from the nature of law, not from the nature of intentional action. Hence Alexy cannot use the correctness thesis to throw light on the nature of law. Here is Raz:

> The thesis [Raz's general thesis about intentional action] is formal in that it does not determine what standards apply. Obviously, since it is so general, applying to all purposeful conduct, it cannot do that. Different standards apply to different activities and pursuits. It is the nature of various activities, and of the circumstances in which they are undertaken, which determines which standards apply to them. If the law is committed to standards of justice this follows from the nature of law, not from the nature of purposeful activity. It follows that nothing can be learnt from the correctness thesis about the nature of law. Rather, once we have established, in light of other arguments, what is the nature of law, and only then, will we be able to conclude which commitments the law makes, or what claims it makes. The correctness thesis, being a formal thesis, while true, offers no specific help in elucidating the nature of law. (Ibid., 28)

We see here that Raz points out that the general claim to appropriateness is *formal* in the sense that it does not and cannot itself determine which acts are appropriate, but depends on the available standards in the relevant fields of activity to do so: without those standards, the claim to correctness, conceived as an instance of a general claim to appropriateness, will have almost no content. As he says (in the quotation above), '[o]bviously, since it [the claim to appropriateness] is so general, applying to all purposeful conduct, it cannot [determine the content of appropriateness]'. But this is precisely to reject constitutivism about practical reason, of which Alexy's legal constitutivism is an instance, for it is to reject precisely the idea that human action, including legal action, has a constitutive aim that generates normative standards of assessment for action. So, on this analysis, even if there are normative standards of assessment for action, including legal action, those standards do *not* come from the constitutive aim of human action, including legal action, but from the nature of the relevant activities or pursuits. And what this means, of course, is that the necessary claim to correctness, or the constitutive aim of legal action, does not ground the dual nature of law—if anything, the dual nature of law grounds the necessary claim to correctness.

Now if the necessary claim to correctness, or the constitutive aim of legal action, does not ground the dual nature of law, then it does not ground, by transitivity, the further claims (1a-b)–(3) (to be discussed below) either; and this is to say that it fails to generate normative standards for the assessment of legal action. That is to say, the necessary claim to correctness, or the constitutive aim of legal action, does not ground, by transitivity, the theses (or claims) (1a) that a whole normative system that does not even raise a claim to correctness will lack legal character; (1b) that a whole normative system that raises but fails to satisfy the claim to correctness, as well as individual legal norms and decisions that either do not raise a claim to correctness or else raise one but fail to satisfy it, will be legally defective; (2) the connection thesis, which contradicts the separation thesis of legal positivism; or (3) the practical nature of legal argumentation. For if Raz is right, then even if Alexy is right that law has a dual nature and that the dual nature grounds claims (1)–(3), the dual nature of law itself is *not* grounded by the necessary claim to correctness, or the constitutive aim of legal action. The central problem, as we have seen, is that if Raz is right the claim to correctness is not a free-standing legal claim, as Alexy believes, but only an instance of a formal and general claim to appropriateness of intentional actions, as Raz holds; then whatever content the claim to correctness has it gets from the nature of law, and not the other way around. The inescapable conclusions are, first, that interesting and stimulating as it is, Alexy's legal constitutivism fails, and, secondly, that constitutivists about practical reason are fighting an uphill battle, since it must reasonably be even more difficult to identify an aim or a principle that is constitutive of, and yields normative standards of assessment for, human action in general than to do this in the case of legal action.

There is a difficulty in Raz's line of argument, however, namely, that the appropriateness thesis is presented as a general thesis about intentional action, that is, a thesis not only about assertions, but also about actions such as commands and orders. The reason why the presence of commands and orders in the general category of intentional actions is problematic in this context is that commands and orders must reasonably receive a *noncognitivist* analysis, and that it is difficult to see what the *content* (or meaning) of a claim to correctness could be on a noncognitivist analysis.[13] For if an agent who issues a command or an order is doing nothing more than expressing his emotions, attitudes, or preferences, what could the content of a claim to correctness raised by that agent be? As we shall see in the last section, Alexy shares this worry about noncognitivism and correctness, insisting as he does that assertions, and only assertions, necessarily raise a claim to correctness. It seems to me, however, that Raz could elude this difficulty by modifying his claim about the appropriateness of intentional action in general, making it instead a more limited thesis about those types of intentional actions that could reasonably receive a cognitivist analysis—provided, of course, that legal acts were included in this category. If he did, his idea that the claim to correctness is an instance of a

13 A defender of Raz might be tempted to seize on the fact that Raz's thesis concerns the *appropriateness* of intentional actions, whereas Alexy's thesis concerns the *correctness* of legal (and moral) actions, and argue that being appropriate is less demanding than being correct and therefore less problematic from the point of view of a noncognitivist analysis. The problem with this move, however, is that it risks undermining Raz's central idea, that the claim to correctness is an *instance* of the more general claim about appropriateness of intentional actions. For if appropriateness is something importantly different from correctness, how could the claim to correctness be an instance of the claim to appropriateness?

more general thesis about the appropriateness of intentional action would, I believe, still be persuasive.

10.7 The dual-nature thesis and the separation thesis

What I have been arguing (in Section 10.6) is that Alexy's legal constitutivism fails as regards the tasks it has set itself, that is, to ground the states of affairs indicated in claims (1)–(3). What I have *not* been arguing is that Alexy's line of argument taken as a whole, including the discussion of (CA) and (CJ), fails. For I would not rule out that Alexy has been able to show, by means of these arguments, and in keeping with Raz's claim (in Section 10.6) that one cannot use the correctness thesis to clarify the nature of law, but must use independently available insights into the nature of law to clarify the correctness thesis, that law has a dual nature in the sense explained; and if this is so, the question arises whether the dual nature of law grounds non-positivism, or, if you will, whether the dual-nature thesis contradicts the separation thesis.

My view is that the dual-nature thesis does not contradict the separation thesis, however, because it does not follow from the dual-nature thesis that there is a necessary connection between the *content* of law and true morality, which is what the separation thesis denies, but only that there is a necessary connection between law's constitutive *aim* (or necessary claim to correctness) and true morality. One might, of course, think that if legal acts have a constitutive aim that is moral, then there is a necessary connection between the content of law and true morality. To think so would in my view be a mistake, however, because a legal act that does have a moral aim may nevertheless have a non-moral or even an immoral content.[14] For example, when Alexy contemplates a situation in which a legal act raises a claim to correctness without satisfying it, in which case the act will be legally defective, he is contemplating precisely a situation in which the aim of the relevant act is moral, even though the content of the act is not. Hence it appears that even if Alexy is right that law has a dual nature in the sense explained, the separation thesis still stands.

10.8 The correctness thesis, the dual-nature thesis, and the special case thesis

We have seen that Alexy maintains that the correctness thesis implies the dual-nature thesis, and that the dual-nature thesis implies the special case thesis, or, as I have preferred to put it, that the necessary claim to correctness, or the constitutive aim of law, grounds the dual nature of law, and that the dual nature of law grounds the practical character of legal argumentation. But I have just been arguing (in Section 10.6), following Raz, that the necessary claim to correctness, or the constitutive aim of law, does *not* ground the dual

14 Soper (1996, 230) appears to take the same view.

nature of law, and this means that even if it turns out that the dual nature of law grounds the practical character of legal argumentation, it does not follow that the necessary claim to correctness, or the constitutive aim of law, grounds, by transitivity, the practical character of legal argumentation. Actually, as I indicated above (at the end of Section 10.4), my own view is that the dual nature of law does *not* ground the practical character of legal argumentation. But from the viewpoint of one who is concerned with Alexy's legal constitutivism, the question of whether the dual nature of law grounds the practical character of legal argumentation is, strictly speaking, neither here nor there, as long as the necessary claim to correctness, or the constitutive aim of law, does not ground the dual nature of law.

10.9 Noncognitivism and the claim to correctness

As I have said (in Section 10.1), Alexy considers the idea that legal acts necessarily raise a claim to correctness to be of the first importance. As he sees it, if we were to give up the idea that assertions in general, including legal and moral statements, involve a claim to truth or correctness, we would also be giving up the difference between substantiation and persuasion, between subjectivity and objectivity, between manipulation, on the one hand, and correctness and truth, on the other. We would, indeed, be giving up on what makes us human:

> To renounce the claim to correctness would change our language, together with the way we understand ourselves, and thus our lives completely. Instead of judgements and assertions there would only be emotions and opinions; substantiation would become persuasion; and successful manipulation and deeply rooted beliefs would take the place of correctness and truth. Everything would be subjective, nothing objective. (1998, 214. Footnote omitted.)

I am inclined to agree with Alexy that legal statements (and statements in general) necessarily raise a claim to correctness in some sense or other; that if we were to give up this idea, our situation would be very different from what it is now; and that noncognitivist theories are, or at least seem to be, unable to account for the content of a claim to correctness. Since I also find noncognitivism in the moral domain attractive, as Alexy does not,[15] I would like to

15 Alexy (1998, 214) writes: 'Moral statements that do not raise this claim [the claim to correctness] are … at most "utterances of an emotional reaction". The interpretation of moral statements as reports on individual attitudes and emotions, or as an appeal to feel like the speaker—formerly common in analytical philosophy—is also failing "the real meaning of moral judgements". Moral value and obligation judgements are "real assertions", and assertions are speech acts which raise a claim to truth or correctness'. (Footnotes omitted.)

briefly consider the question of whether, and if so how, a noncognitivist could account for the idea of a claim to correctness.

It seems to me that the most promising avenue for a noncognitivist would be to consider a quasi-realist account of moral and legal judgements, such as the ones proposed by Simon Blackburn (1984, 181–223; 1993) and Alan Gibbard (1990). The quasi-realist idea, Blackburn explains, is that noncognitivists can in good conscience mimic the talk and reasoning of moral realists and other cognitivists and speak and reason as if there were moral and legal truths and facts, as if legal and moral questions had correct answers, and so on, even though there really are no such facts and truths (call this modest quasi-realism). Doing this turns out to be a rather complicated affair, however, which involves working out the implications of the agent's set of attitudes, emotions, preferences, and the like, in a way that makes the set free of conflicts, so that the set can guide behaviour. Discussing a type of inference which features moral statements in both asserted and unasserted contexts—(P1) it is wrong to lie; (P2) *if* it is wrong to lie, it is wrong to get little brother to lie; (C) it is wrong to get little brother to lie—Blackburn proposes that, on a quasi-realist analysis, one who accepts (P1) and (P2) *must*, if he wishes to reason logically, accept (C) as well.[16] For if a person accepts (P1) and (P2) but *not* (C), his set of attitudes will be *fractured* in the sense that it will fail to include a combination of attitudes that he approves of;[17] and such a fractured set of attitudes cannot function as a means to the end of evaluating behaviour and so cannot guide behaviour; and this means that one cannot have a positive attitude to it (1984, 195).

Blackburn then proposes (ibid., 197–202) that having come this far, the quasi-realist take a further step and constructs a notion of moral (or legal) *truth*, given only a notion of improvement and of possible fault in a set of attitudes (call this ambitious quasi-realism). If he does, the quasi-realist may

16 This example is meant to illustrate a problem for noncognitivists, namely, that despite appearances the premises in the argument do not entail the conclusion. The reason is that, on a noncognitivist analysis, 'wrong' does not have the same meaning in (P1) and the conclusion, in which it is asserted, and in (P2), in which it is not asserted. On a noncognitivist analysis, one who reasons in this way would thus be committing a fallacy of equivocation, which does not seem right. On this, see, Blackburn (1984, 189–196).

17 The idea, as I understand it, is that the combination of attitudes that the agent approves of consists of a pro-attitude to (P1), a pro-attitude to (P2), and a pro-attitude to (C). Yet since the agent does not accept (C), he does not have a pro-attitude to (C), and this means that the set of attitudes that he has a pro-attitude to, that is, the set consisting of (P1), (P2), and (C), fails to include an attitude that he has a pro-attitude to, namely, (C). The reason why the agent is supposed to have a pro-attitude to a set of attitudes that includes not only (P1) and (P2), but also (C) is that, on Blackburn's analysis, a pro-attitude to (P2) is *defined* as a pro-attitude to the combination of a pro-attitude to the antecedent, 'lying is wrong', and a pro-attitude to the consequent, 'it is wrong to get little brother to lie'. (1984, 192–193) Alternatively, as regards (P2), one could say that the agent has a negative attitude to having a negative attitude to lying without having a negative attitude to getting little brother to lie.

say that a given normative statement or value-statement is true if, and only if, the attitude it expresses is a member of, or is implied by, the best possible set of attitudes. On this analysis, then, the agent is no longer speaking *as if* there were moral and legal truths and facts, *as if* legal and moral questions had correct answers, but is really making true or false statements, as the case may be, because there *are* actually moral and legal truths and facts, and legal and moral questions do have correct answers.

My own tentative view, however, is that it is going to be difficult to construct a logic of attitudes along the lines indicated above. One difficulty is that it is not clear that clashing attitudes are really *inconsistent* (contradictory), and if they are not inconsistent, the existence of clashing attitudes will not be a *logical* fault, though it might be a *moral* fault. That is to say, an agent who has a fractured set of attitudes seems to be guilty of a moral rather than a logical mistake.[18] And the ambitious version of quasi-realism strikes me as even more problematic, depending as it does on the questionable assumption that we may plausibly speak of a best possible set of attitudes on an expressivist analysis (see ibid., 197–202). Blackburn's view appears to be that we can ground such a set in our human nature,[19] but it is not easy to see how our human nature could yield one and only one reasonably determinate set of attitudes rather than several competing sets of attitudes. My preliminary conclusion, then, is that if the idea of a claim to correctness is problematic on a noncognitivist analysis, it is almost as problematic on a quasi-realist analysis.

What to do? This is, of course, a very big question, but I myself would try instead a *relativist* account of legal norms and statements, according to which they do have representational content and can be true or false relative to the relevant legal system, and then modify the content of the claim to correctness accordingly. Needless to say, this would be a topic for another occasion.

References

Alexy, Robert. 1989. *A Theory of Legal Argumentation. The Theory of Rational Discourse as Theory of Legal Justification.* Translated into English by Ruth Adler and Neil MacCormick. Originally published 1978 as *Theorie der juristischen Argumentation.* Oxford: Oxford University Press.

Alexy, Robert. 1998. "Law and Correctness". In *Current Legal Problems*, edited by M. D. A. Freeman, vol. 51, 205–221. Oxford: Oxford University Press.

18 Blackburn has attempted to handle this difficulty in later writings and some believe he has been successful in doing so. See Blackburn (1993, 182–197) and Miller (2003, 64–68). I discuss his attempt in Spaak (2019, 127–131).

19 Blackburn (1984, 197) writes: 'Just as the senses constrain what we can believe about the empirical world, so our natures and desires, needs and pleasures, constrain much of what we can admire and commend, tolerate and work for. There are not so many livable, unfragmented, developed, consistent, and coherent systems of attitude'.

Alexy, Robert. 2002. *The Argument from Injustice. A Reply to Legal Positivism*. Oxford: Oxford University Press.

Alexy, Robert. 2007. An Answer to Joseph Raz. In *Law, Rights and Discourse. The Legal Philosophy of Robert Alexy*, edited by George Pavlakos, 37–55. Oxford and Portland, Oregon: Hart Publishing.

Alexy, Robert. 2008. "On the Concept and Nature of Law". *Ratio Juris* 21 (3): 281–299.

Alexy, Robert. 2010. "The Dual Nature of Law". *Ratio Juris* 23: 167–182.

Alexy, Robert. 2018. "The Special Case Thesis and the Dual Nature of Law". *Ratio Juris* 31: 254–259.

Blackburn, Simon. 1984. *Spreading the Word. Groundings in the Philosophy of Language*. Oxford: Clarendon Press.

Blackburn, Simon. 1993. *Essays in Quasirealism*. Oxford: Oxford University Press.

Coleman, Jules. 2001. *The Practice of Principle*. Oxford: Oxford University Press.

Gibbard, Alan. 1990. *Wise Choices, Apt Feelings. A Theory of Normative Judgment*. Cambridge, MA: Harvard University Press.

Gizbert-Studnicki, Tomasz. 2016. "The Social Sources Thesis, Metaphysics and Metaphilosophy". In *Metaphilosophy of Law*, edited by Pawel Banas, Adam Dyrda, and Tomasz Gizbert-Studnicki, 121–146. Oxford: Bloomsbury.

Hart. H. L. A. 1958. "Positivism and the Separation of Law and Morals". *Harvard Law Review* 71: 593–629.

Hart, H. L. A. 1982. *Essays on Bentham. Jurisprudence and Political Theory*. Oxford: Oxford University Press.

Katsafanas, Paul. 2018. Constitutivism about Practical Reasons. In *The Oxford Handbook of Reasons and Normativity*, edited by Daniel Star, 367–391. Oxford: Oxford University Press.

Kelsen, Hans. 1959–60. "What Is the Pure Theory of Law?" *Tulane Law Review* 34: 269–276.

Kelsen Hans. 1992. *Introduction to the Problems of Legal Theory*. Translated by Bonnie Litschewski Paulson and Stanley L. Paulson. Oxford: Oxford University Press. (Originally published 1934 in German under the title *Reine Rechtslehre* by Österreichische Staatsdruckerei, Vienna.)

Korsgaard, Christine M. 1999. "Self-Constitution in the Ethics of Plato and Kant". *The Journal of Ethics* 3: 1-29.

Korsgaard, Christine M. 2009. *Self-Constitution. Agency, Identity, and Integrity*. Oxford: Oxford University Press.

Miller, Alexander. 2003. *An Introduction to Contemporary Metaethics*. Cambridge: Polity Press.

Raz, Joseph. 2008. "The Argument from Injustice, or How Not to Reply to Legal Positivism". In *Law, Rights and Discourse. The Legal Philosophy of Robert Alexy*, edited by George Pavlakos, 17–35. Oxford and Portland, Oregon: Hart Publishing.

Patterson, Dennis, and Bosko Tripkovic, The Promise and Limits of Grounding in Law (draft). Soper, Philip. 1996. "Law's Normative Claims". In *The Autonomy of Law. Essays on Legal Positivism*, edited by Robert P. George, 215–247. Oxford: Clarendon Press.

Spaak, Torben. 2019. "Legal Realism and Legal Reasoning: A Quasi-Realist Approach". In *Vienna Lectures on Legal Philosophy. Volume 2: Normativism and Anti-Normativism*, edited by Christoph Bezemek, Michael Potacs, and Alexander Somek, 113–139. Oxford: Hart.

Spaak, Torben. 2020. "Robert Alexy and the Dual Nature of Law". *Ratio Juris* 33: 150–168.

Spaak, Torben, and Patricia Mindus. 2021. "Introduction". In *The Cambridge Companion to Legal Positivism*, edited by Torben Spaak and Patricia Mindus, 1–36. Cambridge: Cambridge University Press.

Williams, Bernard. 1981. "Internal and External Reasons". In *Moral Luck*, edited by Bernard Williams, 101–113. Cambridge: Cambridge University Press.

Index

Kolibri 360 GmbH
Ferdinand-Jühlke-Straße 7
99095 Erfurt, Deutschland
produktsicherheit@kolibri360.de